Daniel

Twelve Principles of Leadership, Success, and Achievement

Daniel

Principles of Leadership, Success, and Achievement

Jerry Johnston

First Family Inspirations

Overland Park, Kansas

Library of Congress Card Number 2007922012

ISBN-13 978-1-934438-00-8
ISBN-10 1-934438-00-6

All inquiries should be addressed to:
First Family Inspirations
7700 W. 143rd Street
Overland Park, Kansas 66223

Printed in USA

*To my beautiful mother, Joyce,
who is one of God's greatest trophies of grace.
Thank you for your untiring love and support
of the vision God has given to me.*

Contents

Preface

As a pastor I often think about the day when I stand before Jesus Christ and He reviews the quality of my ministry. It is a sobering thought! In that day, He will ask me, "Jerry, did you teach my Word faithfully to the people?" Were your sermons shallow or did you 'cut the Word straight' to the hungry hearts I stewarded to you? More than anything I want to be faithful to teach God's Word. Fads come and go. God's Word is eternal. In my opinion you can listen to a minister and discern in the first five minutes of his message how much confidence he has in the Word of God. We have a famine in our pulpits today of God's Word. Repeatedly I have been drawn to Paul's strategy of establishing a church in the hedonist Las Vegas of his day, Corinth. How did he do it? Such a difficult, immoral place. Luke gives us the clue in Acts 18:11, "And he continued there a year and six months, teaching the word of God among them." The Word of God builds, gives life, and produces spiritual maturity. In 1996 God called me to pioneer a local church in my hometown, one of the most affluent counties in the nation, and something of a graveyard for churches. No less than five evangelical churches started and died before the launch of First Family Church in this same geography. Early on I decided my style of ministry would be the Word. And we have watched the Word of God build First Family Church into a congregation of thousands. In Daniel we see again a deep well of immense biblical truth. Get ready to have your mind filled with the wonder of prophetic truth and the fascinating calendar of end time events so exquisitely presented in Daniel. The illustrious city of Babylon is in ruins and yet the challenging life of Daniel continues to motivate believers even to this day. Be sure to obtain my book on Zechariah which correlates with the rich prophetic elements of DANIEL. Let's turn many to righteousness so someday we can "shine like the brightness of the firmament ... like the stars forever and ever" (Daniel 12:3).

Jerry Johnston
Kansas City

Using This Book

As the messages contained within this volume have developed from pulpit to page, they have been adapted with three different audiences in mind.

The simplest use of this book will be as straight-forward reading. Such a use requires little if any explanation from the author. You might be tempted to jump ahead to a chapter title that seems especially compelling. Who can resist the lure of Daniel's Seventy Weeks? Regardless of what order you might visit these chapters, the first chapter will give you a rationale for the others that follow. Similarly, the final chapter provides a good summary of the lessons mentioned in the title..

It is also hoped that these pages will provide a strong curriculum for small-group studies. If you choose to use it in that fashion, let me suggest that you avail yourself of the extra information to be found in the Sermonars pages beginning on page 265. These Sermonars began as sermon outlines, provided to our church members. Teachers will find them useful as teaching guides and class plans. Also, notice that each chapter ends with a set of "Discussion Questions." Most of these questions are open questions without set, limited answers. In active classes, they should provide a great deal of discussion fodder. However you use these resources, be sure to approach such a group teaching situation with considerable prayer and Bibles at the ready.

The final way in which we envision this book being employed is as ready-made sermons for a pastor hoping to cover this same material. God has blessed the author with a very supportive and well resourced church. It is his prayer that some of those blessings might then bless others if they provide other pastors with materials, usable as they are or adapted to fit your particular needs. The Sermonars were the original

Chapter One

Why Daniel? End Times, Soon or Later?

"Therefore when you see the 'abomination of desolation' spoken of by Daniel the prophet, standing in the holy place" (whoever reads, let him understand).

Matthew 24:15

We have a tendency when we think about the Old Testament book of Daniel to envision images of Daniel in the lions' den and all the familiar stories we have heard. While these stories certainly make for exciting Sunday School fare, they do not contain the dynamic truth that lies at the heart of the incredible message of Daniel. This message is absolutely crucial to the life of the church and to every one who is attempting to discover a life of leadership, achievement, and success.

As we begin our study of Daniel, let's look at the words of Jesus Christ in Matthew 24, a fine example of the New Testament correlating with the Old Testament. Jesus said in Matthew 24:14–21:

> And this gospel of the kingdom will be preached in all the world as a witness to all the nations, and then the end will come. Therefore when you see the "abomination of desolation," spoken of by Dan-

1

iel the prophet, standing in the holy place (whoever reads, let him understand), then let those who are in Judea flee to the mountains. Let him who is on the housetop not go down to take anything out of his house. And let him who is in the field not go back to get his clothes. But woe to those who are pregnant and to those who are nursing babies in those days! And pray that your flight may not be in winter or on the Sabbath. For then there will be great tribulation, such as has not been since the beginning of the world until this time, no, nor ever shall be.

Now, look at what Daniel wrote in Daniel 1:1-7:

In the third year of the reign of Jehoiakim king of Judah, Nebuchadnezzar king of Babylon came to Jerusalem and besieged it. And the Lord gave Jehoiakim king of Judah into his hand, with some of the articles of the house of God, which he carried into the land of Shinar to the house of his god; and he brought the articles into the treasure house of his god. Then the king instructed Ashpenaz, the master of his eunuchs, to bring some of the children of Israel and some of the king's descendants and some of the nobles, young men in whom there was no blemish, but good-looking, gifted in all wisdom, possessing knowledge and quick to understand, who had ability to serve in the king's palace, and whom they might teach the language and literature of the Chaldeans. And the king appointed for them a daily provision of the king's delicacies and of the wine which he drank, and three years of training for them, so that at the end of that time they might serve before the king. Now from among those of the sons of Judah were Daniel, Hananiah, Mishael, and Azariah. To them the chief of the eunuchs gave names: he gave Daniel the name Belteshazzar; to Hananiah, Shadrach; to Mishael, Meshach; and to Azariah, Abed-Nego.

Notice what Jesus said in Matthew 24, "this gospel of the kingdom will be preached in all the world and then the end will come." Look closely at the last phrase: "and then the end will come." I do not want us to miss this lesson, because it was Jesus, not any denomination or religious fanatic, who said that time itself would come to an end. There was a time in the world when everything seemed rather pleasant, and this idea of the end of the world coming seemed quite remote. However, those days are over. We are living in a time, interestingly, much like Daniel's. We are literally seeing biblical prophecy being fulfilled every week and every month. This is a rare opportunity to be alive when so much biblical prophecy is unfolding before our eyes.

Newsweek magazine once ran an article that I would have never thought I would read in those pages. In the article, the author described a government plan under consideration that would assign every American a national identification card and number. Due to fears of terrorism, we are headed for a world where very soon our fingerprints and the retinas of our eyes will be scanned for safer, more accurate identification. Perhaps someday our national identification number could be conveniently tattooed invisibly on our body. This would be done, of course, for our own protection.

Jesus told us that there will be a time when the end will come. There are two curious books which address in detail this concept of the apocalypse, the end of the world, and the coming of the Lord: Daniel in the Old Testament and Revelation in the New Testament. Much attention has been paid to Revelation, but we could not understand Revelation without Daniel. The key that opens the door to the book of Revelation is the book of Daniel. Since most of us have spent so little time studying Daniel and have never absorbed its deep truths, Revelation remains mystifying to us. How long has it been since you read Daniel, the book that Jesus encouraged us to read and to understand?

Jesus affirmed the prophecy of Daniel by calling him a prophet and telling us how important he was. Within Daniel's twelve chapters, there is literally an arsenal of wisdom and an incredible perspective on the future. When you understand the timetable of Daniel, it gives you absolute confidence in God's Word. Although Daniel is highly prophetic, it is also an extremely practical book. The twelve chapters of this book teach us how to live a life of Christian distinction in a world that is absolutely against us. For instance, God has given us a model in Daniel of how we are to live as we attend public schools or public universities or work in typical jobs surrounded by co-workers who have no concept of faith. We are not alone—God sent someone ahead of us to model and typify the way that we are supposed to live: Daniel.

Every year, when I attend camps, I see many kids who make decisions for Christ. This is wonderful, but then, when I attend youth events later in the year, I can see just by the way some of the kids look at me that some of them are growing distant from God. This lack of longevity concerns me. Why is there such a high mortality rate among young people and others who make sincere decisions but have no long haul value? Why is it that when they get back to their universities or high school, back circulating around their friends, they absolutely collapse in their Christian walk? Why is this? Daniel is going to give us the key.

Critics of the Bible and liberal theologians absolutely despise this book. Ministers who do not believe in the inspiration of Scripture ignore Daniel just like they ignore Revelation. They do not want to have anything to do with these books. Just as with the book of Revelation, they have an interpretation of Daniel that is incorrect. One of the current ideas advanced by higher criticism is that all of Daniel is about Antiochus Epiphanies and the Maccabean revolt in 165 BC. However, this is a distortion and an absolutely wrong interpretation. Why do the liberal scholars and higher critics dislike Daniel so much? Daniel reinforces the authority and inspiration of the Bible. If Daniel's prophecies are accurate, then all of God's Word is accurate and must be taken seriously.

Jesus affirmed the prophecy of Daniel by calling him "the prophet." Don't miss that. He didn't call him a prophet; he called him "the prophet." We place a great deal of emphasis on Solomon as the wisest man that ever lived. However, at the end of Solomon's life, he lived in spiritual defeat. One scholar says that Solomon died of venereal disease. Solomon had sexual relationships with at least a thousand different women. Not Daniel. When the book begins, Daniel is fourteen to sixteen years of age. And when it ends, he is nearly 100, having been faithful to God for over seventy years!

Background

Before we look at the text of Daniel, let's begin by exploring its background. Because we do not live in Daniel's era, we cannot really appreciate the Assyrian empire as the dominant world superpower that controlled all of the area of the Middle East and beyond (including what is present day Iraq). Assyria reigned supreme until suddenly, in 626 BC, Babylon rose to power and attacked the capital city of Assyria, Nineveh (the city we identify with Jonah). In an incredible conquest in 612 BC, Babylon finally defeated Nineveh. History books, religious and secular alike, record Babylon's victory over the Egyptian army at Karkamesh in 605 BC. Nebuchadnezzar, Babylon's powerful and young king then moved south and decimated the Holy Land, Palestine, and Jerusalem.

Daniel 1:21 is a key in understanding the background and historical setting of Daniel: "Then Daniel continued until the first year of King Cyrus." In Daniel 1:1, we read about King Nebuchadnezzar in Babylon. However, at the end of chapter 1, Cyrus is king. This is significant because by comparing 1:1 with 1:21, Dr. J. Vernon McGee points out, "we can learn Daniel's lifespan. Coming to Babylon at about age seventeen, he died when he was approximately ninety years of age. He bridged the entire seventy years of captivity. He did not return to Israel but apparently died before the people left Babylon."[1] Daniel, a Jewish man with faith in God, was in the city of Babylon over seventy years. He not only outlasted Nebuchadnezzar but also the three subsequent kings after him.

Why Daniel?

Why did God choose Daniel? Why should we study his life and his prophecy? Let's look at the eight reasons below.

1. The Perfect Plan of God

We see in the Book of Daniel an absolutely perfect plan of God's sovereignty. Sovereignty means that God is in absolute control. Daniel is an excellent reminder that God is in total control of our lives. Have you ever experienced a disappointment and said, "Why in the world did that happen?" Have you ever lost your job, gone through a personal crisis or emotional difficulty, and felt like your life was completely out of control? Whenever you feel that your life is spinning out of control, all you need to do is to study Daniel. You will come away from the book understanding that God, and God alone, is in absolute control. Additionally, God is not only in control of the people who love him; he is in absolute control of all people, whether they know it or not.

For example, consider Daniel 1:1-2b, "In the third year of the reign of Jehoiakim king of Judah, Nebuchadnezzar king of Babylon came to Jerusalem and besieged it. And the Lord gave Jehoiakim king of Judah into his hand..." The word translated "Lord" in this verse is the Hebrew word adonai, a very interesting word that means "master" or "owner."

The ultimate ruler, God, gave the King of Judah into the hands of a pagan king. When we disobey or allow compromise in our spiritual life, God sometimes uses the Enemy or those aligned with him in a remedial way to correct us. Jehoiakim was not listening to God, and he thought he was going to get away with it. However, Adonai, the Lord, the Master, took Jehoiakim and gave him into the hands of King Nebuchadnezzar. Throughout Daniel we learn that whether a nation honors God or not, He is in absolute control.

Nebuchadnezzar has a series of dreams in the book. Daniel, whom Nebuchadnezzar understood was full of wisdom, was called on to interpret the dreams. For example, in Daniel 4:25 Nebuchadnezzar explains a dream to Daniel. Daniel then proceeds to interpret the king's dream. He stands in front of the king and says, "They shall drive you from men. Your dwelling shall be with the beast of the field, and they shall make you eat grass like oxen. They shall wet you with the dew of heaven and seven times they shall pass over you until you know that the Most High rules in the kingdom of men, and gives it to whomsoever he will." How would you like to be Daniel giving that message to a powerful king who had killed people on the spot for displeasing him?

Additionally, we read in Daniel 2:37 of the first dream Daniel interpreted for Nebuchadnezzar: "You King Nebuchadnezzar, our king of kings, for the God of heaven has given you a kingdom, power, strength, and glory." What did Daniel, this little twenty-year-old kid, tell the most powerful king of his day? Daniel told Nebuchadnezzar that he would not have been on that throne without God putting him there. During the presidential elections in the year 2000, we waited late into the night to hear the results of the election. That night, thousands of Christians around the country were praying. Do you think it is a coincidence that President Bush is where he is right now? Do you think he is in the White House by random chance? No. God put him there to lead the United Sates through all of the incredible challenges that are happening in our world today.

2. Perfect Timetable

We see in Daniel that God is not only in control but that He also has a perfect timetable. This reminds us that God has a perfect timetable in the life of the believer too. Our disappointments can be His appointments. Sometimes the dead-end roads we face are God's way of tilling the soil of our hearts in order to shape us into the men and women He desires us to be. We see many examples of this perfect timetable in Scripture and in our lives. For instance, Daniel 9:1 reads, "In the first year of Darius, the son of Ahasuerus, of the lineage of the Medes, who is made king over the realm of the Chaldeans—in the first year of his reign, I, Daniel, understood by the books the number of years specified by the word of the Lord through Jeremiah the prophet that he would accomplish seventy years in the desolation of Jerusalem."

What is so significant about this verse? Daniel is in Babylon, 900 miles away from Judah, God's Promised Land. While he was there, he wanted to know how long the captivity was supposed to last, so he sifts through writings of the prophet Jeremiah. Jeremiah had told the Jewish nation, as God's prophet, that because they had ignored God, they would be sent into captivity for seventy years.

Why seventy years? Several centuries earlier, when the Jews were about to enter the Promised Land, God instructed them to devote every seventh year to Him. This year was called the sabbatical year. However, the Jews did not do what they were supposed to do. They resisted God. They ignored him. They cheated God out of seventy of those seventh years. Every seventh year for 490 years, they ignored Jehovah. God did not forget that His people had ignored His command. As a result, God punished Israel by sending them into captivity for 70 years: one year for every Sabbath year they had ignored. The timetable is exact.

Daniel was sent to Babylon in the first deportation (606 BC). Later, Nebuchadnezzar went back a second time and deported 10,000 more Jews. The prophet Ezekiel was in this second group. Finally, Nebuchadnezzar went back a third time and destroyed and burned the temple in 586 BC.

3. Peculiar Place and People

Look closely at Daniel 1:1 again, "Nebuchadnezzar, King of Babylon, came to Jerusalem and he besieged it." Following the siege, Nebuchadnezzar took Daniel back to the city of Babylon which had been constructed by Nebuchadnezzar. Herodotus said the city was a square—each side was 14 miles long. The city was enclosed by strong walls that were 311 feet high and 87 feet thick. Actually, there were two sets of walls. In between the two walls, there was a deep ravine (much like a moat). If invaders scaled the first wall, they would end up in deep water. Along the walls were towers manned by armed soldiers ready to kill any invading forces. Babylon was an absolute fortress.

Inside the city, there were scores of temples and public buildings. The Temple of Zeus was there. At this temple, worshipers of Zeus took newborn Babylonian babies and offered them as human sacrifices. All over the walls, Nebuchadnezzar had painted incredible murals and laid intricate mosaics of many different animals and women. It was not uncommon for the Babylonians to start drinking, get in a party, and have a virtual orgy as the women would undress. We see this in Daniel 5, when Belshazzar invited a thousand of the aristocrats to a special banquet.

This is the cultural environment into which Daniel is thrust. He was from the land of the Bible, the land of the Law of God. However, as a fourteen-year-old boy, he woke up one day in a city that makes Las Vegas look like a Sunday School picnic. Babylon was definitely a peculiar place with an array of peculiar people. If you were a teenager living in this city 900 miles away from mom and dad, were given enough money to buy anything you wanted, were given permission to enjoy any pleasure you wanted, what would you have done?

Although we seldom mention it, Daniel was immediately made a eunuch when he was brought to Babylon. J. Vernon McGee says, "Most conservative scholars agree that Daniel was taken captive when he was about seventeen years of age. He was made a eunuch and so you can understand why Daniel never married or had children."[2] Clarence Larkin notes, "We see from this scripture that the four Hebrew captives, Daniel, Hananiah, Mishael and Azariah, were of royal blood and descendants of the good King Hezekiah and that they were made eunuchs. This is confirmed by the fact that they were turned over to the prince of eunuchs, who changed their names, and who had supervision over them for three years."[3] Yet, Daniel and his friends had no anger or animosity toward God. They were trained in the literature and language of the Chaldeans, which had no reference to deity in it. For three years, they were in an incredible brainwashing program that would make any of our secular universities today seem tame. Nevertheless, they stayed true to God.

In Daniel 2, we meet Arioch, the captain of the guard who was commanded to kill every wise man in Babylon because they could not understand Nebuchadnezzar's dream. In Daniel 5:9, we meet Belshazzar, who was greatly troubled, but whose countenance was changed when he took part in an orgy. It was during this drunken orgy that the mysterious hand wrote on the wall. The hand wrote these words: "mene mene tekel uparsin." The foundation of that wall was recently discovered through archaeological digs. (It is located fifty miles south of Baghdad in the remains of Babylon.) This once again validates the historicity of the Old Testament.

Additionally, we also read about angels in this book. In fact, we read about two leading angels. Our understanding of angels is dramatically increased in this dynamic book. In chapter ten, we read about the touch of angels on physical bodies. They touched Daniel several times. Billy Graham has said that he has felt the touch of angels at certain times to strengthen him when he was doing God's work.[4] In Daniel 8:16, we read about Gabriel. In Daniel 10, we learn about Michael.

4. Paradigm of Daniel's Life as our Example

Daniel's life reminds us that every one of us can live a life of Christian distinction, no matter what culture we are fighting against, no matter what environment we are in. So when a teenager comes up to me and says, "You just don't understand my family. I can't do this." When they say, "You don't understand my friends at school. You don't understand how rough it is," I say to them, "Wait a minute. If Daniel could do it, I know you can. Don't tell me you can't." Daniel 1:8 reads, "But Daniel purposed in his heart that he would not defile himself." Frankly, this is the problem with many of us. We want to live the Christian life, but we do not purpose in our hearts to live it consistently, day in and day out.

Evil men attempted to destroy Daniel. They tried to find some impropriety in his life. However, Daniel 6:4 says, "They could find no charge or fault because he was faithful. There was no error, no fault found in him." In chapter nine, Daniel prayed to God for help. God answered by sending to Daniel an angel who said to him, "I have come to tell you for you are greatly beloved" (Daniel 9:23). Because Daniel's life was so righteous, God gave him the prophecy of the seventy weeks and the coming of the Messiah. This should give us hope that God will reward us if we will be willing to live a life of Christian consistency. It tells us that if there is no compromise in our life, God will bless us.

5. Prayer's Secrets and Power

Daniel gives us the secrets of prayer and reminds us of the dynamic power we have in prayer. Daniel 6:10 says, "Now when Daniel knew that the writing was signed, he went home. And in his upper room, with his windows open toward Jerusalem, he knelt down on his knees three times that day, and prayed and gave thanks before his God, as was his custom since early days." In chapter six, a new king ruled long after Nebuchadnezzar, Darius. Some of righteous Daniel's old enemies remembered him as the pet of Nebuchadnezzar. They went to King Darius and convinced him to quickly make a decree that no one could pray to any other god. Darius signed the decree with his signet ring.

Daniel's enemies thought they had sealed his fate because they knew that Daniel would continue to pray in spite of the decree. When Daniel knew that the writing was signed, Daniel 6:10 states, "he went home. And in his upper room, with his windows open toward Jerusalem, he knelt down on his knees three times that day." Even though praying made Daniel an outlaw, he continued to pray. At this point in the book, Daniel was nearly ninety years old. He had been praying three times a day toward Jerusalem for seventy years.

When Daniel's enemies discovered he had broken the decree, they took this ninety-year-old man and threw him in the lions' den. How would that raise your anxiety level at ninety years of age? In the lions' den Daniel prayed and God shut the lions' mouths. The next morning, Darius ran to that hole to discover Daniel's fate. When Darius called to Daniel, Daniel responded, "My God sent His angel and shut the lions' mouths, so that they have not hurt me, because I was found innocent before Him." We can have that same peace in our lives when we face the various storms that come our way if we have a deep confidence in God.

Daniel 10:13 tells us that the prince of Persia interfered with Daniel's prayers. This tells us that there are times when we pray that we actually encounter demonic interference. Sometimes when we are seeking God, demons are literally trying to stop our prayers from getting to God. I do not want to be over dramatic, but I can honestly tell you there are certain days in my life when I have felt incredible satanic opposition to what God wants me to do. There are times in our lives when we can almost feel the evil trying to keep us from really being what God wants us to be in our private life before Him. Daniel went through that, he also tells us how to overcome it.

6. The Precision of the Prophecy

Daniel reminds us all throughout the book, that God is working out His preset plan in the world. This plan will culminate with the Second Coming of Jesus Christ. Daniel 12:8-9 says, "Then I said, 'My Lord what shall be the end of these things?' And he said, 'Go your way, Daniel, for the words are closed up and sealed till the time of the end.'" When will Jesus return? At the end of time. Whose words are sealed until the end? Jesus' words. Of Daniel's 357 verses, 162 are prophetic in nature.

In Daniel 2:28, on the heels of Nebuchadnezzar's vision, Daniel says, "But there is a God in heaven who reveals secrets, and he has made known to King Nebuchadnezzar what will be in the latter days." Daniel gives us an accurate timetable of the coming of the Messiah to the month. It also gives us the timetable of the Tribulation and the sequence of the Second Coming of Jesus Christ. When Daniel is writing in Daniel 2, the times of the Gentiles had begun. The "times of the Gentiles" meant that Israel was under the control of Gentiles. When Daniel interprets Nebuchadnezzar's dream, he delineates the four Gentile world powers, initiated by Babylon and Nebuchadnezzar, which would control Jerusalem until the times of the Gentiles were fulfilled.

Chapters two and seven give us a sweeping panorama of these four world kingdoms. The first was Babylon, followed by the Medo-Persian Empire. The third is Greece, under the command of Alexander the Great. After Alexander's death, Rome ruled for several centuries.

7. Panic Caused by the Antichrist

In addition to telling us the timetable of these world governments that now have been corroborated by history, Daniel also tells us of the panic that will be caused by the Antichrist at the appointed hour when he enters the world. Daniel also reminds us that the Tribulation will happen, an era we will want to avoid. Daniel prophesies about the Antichrist in Daniel 7:24-25:

> The ten horns are ten kings who shall arise from this kingdom. And another shall rise after them; he shall be different from the first ones, and shall subdue three kings. He shall speak pompous words against the Most High, shall persecute the saints of the Most High, and shall intend to change times and law. Then the saints shall be given into his hand for a time and times and half a time.

11

The phrase "a time and times and half a time" is an Aramaic expression meaning "three and a half years." Notice what the Antichrist will do. First, just as he is revealed, he will subdue three kings. Could one of those be America? What nations are those? A big question everybody asks about prophecy is where is the United States in it? Second, the Antichrist will be different than any other king. He will persecute the saints, and he will change the times and law. I believe, along with others, that the Antichrist will probably change the calendar system because the foundation of our calendar system is the life of Jesus Christ. Thus, when the Antichrist comes on the scene, he will change the times. Additionally, because he will change the law, our world will fall into deeper moral decline.

Look at how the Antichrist is described in Daniel 8:23-25:

> And in the latter time of their kingdom, when the transgressors have reached their fullness, a king shall arise, having fierce features, who understands sinister schemes. His power shall be mighty, but not by his own power; he shall destroy fearfully, and shall prosper and thrive; he shall destroy the mighty, and also the holy people. Through his cunning he shall cause deceit to prosper under his rule; and he shall exalt himself in his heart. He shall destroy many in their prosperity. He shall even rise against the Prince of princes; but he shall be broken without human means.

The Antichrist has "fierce features." What does this expression mean? It means he is particularly handsome. Fierce to us means abhorrent. The Hebrew vernacular, on the other hand, conveys the idea that this guy is going to walk on the stage, and everybody's going to say, "Wow, is he hot." He is going to understand sinister schemes. He is going to destroy fearfully, and he is going to prosper and thrive. Can you imagine Daniel seeing this? What impact did it have on him? Daniel 8:27 says, "And I, Daniel, fainted and was sick for days; and afterward, I arose and went about the king's business. I was astonished by the vision."

8. Peace and Fulfillment of the Covenant by Messiah

The Book of Daniel, in addition to all that we just discussed, reveals God's plan for peace and the fulfillment of the covenant that will come by the Messiah. What does that say to us? It says that God will keep His promise to His people. One of the greatest proofs of the validity of Scripture is God's preservation of the Jewish people throughout history. Although many have tried to decimate and exterminate this people, no one has ever succeeded. That fact alone proves to me the validity of Scripture. God always keeps His promises to His people.

Daniel 9:24 says:

> Seventy weeks are determined for your people and for your holy city, to finish the transgression, to make an end of sins, to make reconciliation for iniquity, to bring in everlasting righteousness, to seal up vision and prophecy, and to anoint the Most Holy. Know therefore and understand, that from the going forth of the command to restore and build Jerusalem until Messiah the Prince, there shall be seven weeks and sixty-two weeks; the street shall be built again, and the wall, even in troublesome times.

These final seventy weeks are the culmination of the prophecy. In that beautiful prophecy, God said to Daniel, "Daniel, when my people in Babylon hear me, and when I raise up a king who is going to actually allow some to leave and go back to Jerusalem, and when they start rebuilding that wall and that city, at that exact moment, the sixty-nine weeks will begin." In Hebrew, a week can refer to seven years as well as seven days. The context makes it clear that years are in view rather than days. When they start rebuilding the wall of Jerusalem, the timetable will start. One scholar notes:

> Daniel's prophecy of the Seventy Weeks (9:24-27) provides the chronological frame for the coming of Jesus, the Messiah, from the time of Daniel to the establishment of His kingdom on earth. It is clear that the first 69 weeks were fulfilled at Christ's first coming. The vision of the 69 weeks (9:25-26) pinpoints the coming of the Messiah. The decree (9:25) took place on March 4, 444 BC (see Neh 2:1-8). The 69 weeks of the seven years, or 173,880 days (using 360-day prophetic years). This leads to March 29, AD 33, the date of Christ's Triumphal Entry in Jerusalem.[6]

What a prophetic timetable, accurate to the day. In our study of Daniel, we will see that God has the prophetic plan for the whole world in the palm of His hand. He is in control. If He is in control of world governments, don't you think He is in control of your life? Do you think God can handle your headaches this week? We are also going to extrapolate twelve principles of leadership, success, and achievement from the book because we all want to be successful. If we want to be faithful (and faithfulness is God's definition of success), then we must apply these principles we find in Daniel's life. As you prepare to read this study of the book of Daniel, take a moment to pray and ask God for His help in understanding and applying the truths contained in His Word.

Discussion Questions

1. Why is the book of Daniel crucial to the life of the church and our lives as individuals? Why do we have to understand Daniel in order to understand Revelation?

2. How do we balance analyzing current events and how they may fit into biblical prophecy and date setting or being too quick to identify individuals or nations as the Antichrist or participants in Armageddon?

3. List specific ways the study of biblical prophecy ought to affect our lives. How should prophecy affect our passion and compassion for those who do not know Jesus?

4. In this chapter we looked at eight answers to the question, "Why Daniel?" What are they? What does each one teach us about God's character, His Word, and Daniel's character?

5. When Daniel's enemies tried to find some impropriety in his life, they could not. Does your life reflect that level of integrity? List some practical ways you can develop an integral life.

6. If we truly believe in God's sovereignty in the life of Daniel and in the life of the nations of the world, why do we fear and worry?

That's Not All

You can find sermon outlines and other extras in the "Sermonars" section at the back of the book. These pages may be freely reproduced, either from the book or from the accompanying CD-ROM for any devotional or ministry use.

Chapter Two

The Amazing Journey to one of the Wonders of the World

A Quick Overview

When you think of the wonders of the world, your mind might go to the pyramids or the Grand Canyon, but today we'll look at a true wonder. We are studying one of the most awesome and intriguing books of the entire Bible: the book of Daniel. Let us begin this chapter by quickly reviewing chapter one, where we posed and answered the question "Why Daniel?" Why should we focus on this book, which is commonly despised by the critics of the Bible?

Those who do not take the Scriptures literally do not give any serious consideration to this book. They immediately try to discount it whenever they have the opportunity to do so. There are a number of reasons for this dismissal. First, Daniel's prophecy is probably the most comprehensive of all the prophetic books. It is the first prophecy to give a consecutive history of the world from the time of its writing until the end of the world. In 606 BC, the teenager Daniel was deported from Jerusalem (in Judah) to Babylon. Years later, Nebuchadnezzar had a dream that God used to communicate His message to the world. In the king's dream was hidden a comprehensive history of the world from Daniel's day until the millennial reign of Jesus Christ. This is simply astonishing!

Second, it is also important to note that the book of Daniel contains the first chronological prophecy about the coming of the Messiah. This book tells us when the Messiah's First Coming would take place. It is also interesting to realize that the times of the events predicted by Daniel are so precise that Jewish religious leaders have done everything in their power to prevent the Jewish people from following the date-setting of Daniel's book. After all, if Daniel is correct (and it is), Jesus, the promised Jewish Messiah, appeared at the exact time predicted by Daniel under the inspiration of the Holy Spirit.

There are, in the end, at least eight clear reasons why Daniel is worthy of our time and efforts:

1. Daniel is a book that presents the perfect plan of God's sovereignty. It shows us that God is in total control of the world. He is not just in control of the obedient, the just, and those who follow Him. God is in control of pagan worlds and pagan kings.

2. Daniel presents a perfect timetable of God's plan for human history, including key eschatological events (which we will cover in detail in the next chapters). This reminds us that God has a perfect timetable for us.

3. Daniel presents a peculiar place and a peculiar people, reminding us that our difficulties are not unique.

4. Daniel presents the paradigm of Daniel's life, an example to all of us and a reminder that we can be victorious in living a life of Christian distinction.

5. Daniel unveils the secrets and the power of prayer, challenging us to receive the riches God wants to give us through our communication with Him.

6. Daniel teaches us the precision of prophecy, reminding us that God is working His perfect plan in our world, a plan that will culminate with the return of Christ.

7. Daniel forewarns us of the panic and the destruction the Antichrist will cause, reminding us that the Tribulation will happen.

8. Daniel describes the peace the Messiah will bring along with the fulfillment of God's covenant, reminding us that God cannot lie; He will keep His promises to us! When we learn that, we will stop worrying and start trusting God for our needs.

These eight characteristics of Daniel remind us that studying this book is of great importance to those who really want to live godly in an ungodly and wicked society. Therefore, let us keep these reasons in mind as we begin our journey through this unique and marvelous prophetic book.

Taken to Babylon

With that overview in mind, we can now begin to look closely at this scriptural wonder of the world.

I find it interesting that the trouble spot of the world in our times is the very same area where our journey begins in Daniel 1. The remains of Babylon are about fifty-four miles south of modern day Baghdad in Iraq. Just as Iraq is a key area of our world today, Babylon was equally important in Daniel's days. Therefore, we cannot understand or appreciate the message of Daniel's book until we understand the ideas behind "Babylon," a term used in the Scriptures to convey multiple concepts (cf. Revelation 17-18).

The context behind Daniel 1 is as follows. Within Israel, civil war was tearing the nation apart. The twelve tribes had been divided into two groups: the ten northern tribes (Israel) and the two southern tribes (Judah). Outside of Israel, Babylon, under the leadership of Nebuchadnezzar, had defeated the Egyptian army

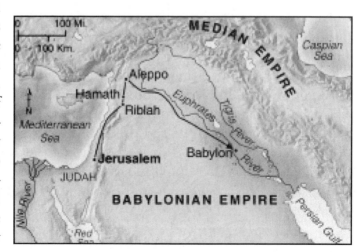

at Carchemish. The young king Nebuchadnezzar was so excited about his power that he quickly went north and devastated both Judah and Jerusalem, resulting in a series of three deportations of Jews to Babylon. The first deportation was in 606 BC, when Daniel and several others (part of the elite of the Jewish youth) were taken away to Babylon, 900 miles away from home.

Daniel and his friends entered Babylon through the Processional Way (the street used to enter Babylon through the Ishtar Gate). From then on, Daniel was totally separated from the influence of his parents, who either were killed or left behind in Jerusalem. The Jewish Temple and Judaism were things of the past as young Daniel and so many others entered a city famous for its promotion of polytheism. But against all environmental odds, Daniel stayed true to God.

Read carefully the first three verses of the book of Daniel:

> In the third year of the reign of Jehoiakim king of Judah, Nebuchadnezzar king of Babylon came to Jerusalem and besieged it. And the Lord gave Jehoiakim king of Judah into his hand, with some of the articles of the house of God, which he carried into the land of Shinar [another name for Babylon] to the house of his god; and he brought the articles into the treasure house of his god [Marduk or Baal, the prominent god among so many gods in the city of Babylon]. Then the king instructed Ashpenaz, the master of his eunuchs, to bring some of the children of Israel and some of the king's descendants and some of the nobles.

Did you notice that Daniel did not use the word "Babylon" a second time in verse two? Instead, he referred to Babylon as "the land of Shinar." Shinar was an ancient name for the district in which the cities of Babylon (Babel), Erech, and Accad were located. The use of "Shinar" in this passage has a historical connotation of a land of evil that was incredibly hostile to Jehovah. This was the country associated with Nimrod, the mighty hunter (Genesis 10:10) and also with the aggressively defiant men who built the Tower of Babel. In later biblical books, the area is called Chaldea. Therefore, Daniel wants to make it very clear that not only were they being deported, but they were being taken to a very horrible and despicable place.

Prophecy Fulfilled: Jerusalem's Destruction and Deportation: Isaiah 39:5-7; 2 Kings 21:10-13; Jeremiah 25:8-11

As we read these first three verses of Daniel, we must keep in mind that the destruction of Jerusalem and the deportation of these Jewish young men had been clearly prophesied by God years earlier. God had repeatedly warned Israel through His prophets, but His people did not listen. This lesson is applicable to so many of us today who try to ignore God when He is constantly trying to speak to our hearts. When we resist Him that way, God, because of His deep love for us, allows calamity to happen in our lives to show us that we are going down the wrong path.

In Israel's case, the prophecy foretold that the city of Jerusalem would be totally destroyed. Nearly 100 years before Daniel, the prophet Isaiah (740-681 BC) foretold Judah's destruction and the Jews' deportation to Babylon, which at Isaiah's time was not a superpower. (At that time, Babylon was subordinate to the Assyria.) Consider what Isaiah wrote in Isaiah 39:5-7 (cf. 2 Kings 20:16-19):

> Then Isaiah said to Hezekiah, "Hear the word of the LORD of hosts: 'Behold, the days are coming when all that is in your house, and what your fathers have accumulated until this day, shall be carried to Babylon; nothing shall be left,' says the LORD. 'And they shall take away some of your sons who will descend from you, whom you will beget; and they shall be eunuchs in the palace of the king of Babylon.'"

It is impossible not to notice how detailed Isaiah's prophecy was. First, the deportation was clearly foretold. Even though Judah was prosperous during Isaiah's lifetime, the prophet predicted that nothing would be left untouched after the arrival of the Babylonians (Isaiah 39:6). Second, Isaiah also predicted that the Jewish boys who would be taken captive would become eunuchs (meaning that Daniel and his friends were castrated almost immediately upon their entry in Babylon). This was done to them so they would be trustworthy before the king's women and also able to focus on the pagan, brainwashing education they were about to receive.

Besides the prophecy above, God had also warned Manasseh (697-642 BC), Hezekiah's evil son and Judah's king after his father, that he would be deported to Babylon (which at the time was a part of the Assyrian empire). Manasseh was the king who had rebuilt all the pagan shrines in Israel and sacrificed one of his own sons to idols. We find the prophecy of Manasseh's fate in 2 Kings 21:10-13, which reads:

> And the LORD spoke by His servants the prophets, saying, "Because Manasseh king of Judah has done these abominations (he has acted more wickedly than all the Amorites who were before him, and has also made Judah sin with his idols)," therefore thus says the LORD God of Israel: "Behold, I am bringing such calamity upon Jerusalem and Judah, that whoever hears of it, both his ears will tingle. And I will stretch over Jerusalem the measuring line of Samaria and the plummet of the house of Ahab; I will wipe Jerusalem as one wipes a dish, wiping it and turning it upside down.

God also used Jeremiah (627-586 BC) to warn the Israelites that Judah was going to fall to Babylon because of their sin. Jeremiah, unlike Daniel or Ezekiel, was not taken to Babylon. He wrote the following prophecy in Jeremiah 25:8-11:

> Therefore thus says the LORD of hosts: "Because you have not heard My words, behold, I will send and take all the families of the north," says the LORD, "and Nebuchadnezzar the king of Babylon, My servant, and will bring them against this land, against its inhabitants, and against these nations all around, and will utterly destroy them, and make them an astonishment, a hissing, and perpetual desolations. Moreover I will take from them the voice of mirth and the voice of gladness, the voice of the bridegroom and the voice of the bride, the sound of the millstones and the light of the lamp. And this whole land shall be a desolation and an astonishment, and these nations shall serve the king of Babylon seventy years.

Did you notice how Jeremiah described Nebuchadnezzar? He called him God's servant (Jeremiah 25:9). This gives us a glimpse into God's amazing sovereignty. The Lord does not use only the just to fulfill His purpose but also the unjust. Make sure you also note the prophesied length of the Babylonian Captivity: seventy years! In spite of all the ungodliness that was rampant in the Babylonian society, Daniel faithfully prayed facing Jerusalem for seventy years (cf. Daniel 9). But besides being a man of prayer, Daniel was also a diligent student of God's Word. Consider, for instance, Daniel 9:1-3, which reads:

> In the first year of Darius the son of Ahasuerus, of the lineage of the Medes, who was made king over the realm of the Chaldeans—in the first year of his reign I, Daniel, understood by the books the number of the years specified by the word of the LORD through Jeremiah the prophet, that He would accomplish seventy years in the desolations of Jerusalem. Then I set my face toward the Lord God to make request by prayer and supplications, with fasting, sackcloth, and ashes.

This clearly reveals that Daniel's mind and heart were focused on God as he studied the writings of the prophets and faithfully prayed to his God.

History of Prophecy Fulfilled: the Fall of the Northern and Southern Kingdoms

Read carefully what Bible scholar Phillip Newell has to say about Daniel and the fulfillment of prophecy:

> The book of Daniel opens with a historical statement which recounts the fulfillment of at least one definite prophecy (Jeremiah 25:8-11) in which God had plainly asserted that He would "send the king of Babylon, my servant... against the inhabitants thereof... and these nations shall serve the king of Babylon seventy years." As we read of the literal enactment of this prediction, in Daniel 1:1... we are struck immediately with a repetition of thought in the prophecy and in its fulfillment. In the prophecy, God plainly speaks of Nebuchadnezzar as "my servant," and in Daniel 1:2 we are told that "the Lord gave Jehoiakim king of Judah into his hands." This is surely indicative of that sovereign control of earthly matters, otherwise under the domination of Satan himself, exercised by God.[1]

Daniel lived at the close of the history of the divided kingdom of Israel. God brought punishment on those kingdoms because of their sins in the form of captivity to a strange land. Daniel and Ezekiel were among those taken. The division of Israel's united monarchy occurred in 931 BC. Rehoboam (931–914 BC) became king of the resulting southern kingdom of Judah, and Jeroboam (931–909 BC) became king of the northern kingdom of Israel. The northern kingdom continued on for a total of 209 years (931–722 BC) and then fell to the Assyrians. During this time, nineteen kings ruled, all of them described as evil in the sight of God. Unlike the northern kingdom, the southern kingdom (also called Judah) continued for 345 years (931–586 BC) and then fell to the Babylonians. It too had nineteen kings, which indicates that the average length of the southern kings' reigns was considerably longer than the northern kings'. Of the nineteen southern kings, God considered eight to be good (compared to all bad kings in the north). But sin still abounded, resulting in the captivity foretold by the prophets well in advance.

As foretold by the prophets, Jews were deported to Babylon (three times). Daniel and his friends were taken captive in the first deportation, which took place about 606 BC (2 Kings 24:1). The second deportation occurred in about 598 BC, eight years after Daniel went to Babylon. This is when Ezekiel (his Hebrew name means "God Strengthens") came to Babylon at age twenty-six. Ezekiel confirmed that Daniel, although young, was immensely blessed by God and promoted in the hierarchy of the Babylonian government. He wrote in Ezekiel 14:14, "'Even if these three men, Noah, Daniel, and Job, were in it, they would deliver only themselves by their righteousness,' says the Lord GOD." What a privilege for Daniel to be listed in the company of godly men such as Noah and Job.

The third and final deportation, together with the destruction of Jerusalem itself, took place in 588 BC, in the eleventh year of Kind Zedekiah (597–586 BC), who was the brother of Jehoiakim and the uncle of Jehoiachin (2 Kings 25:8–12; 2 Chronicles 36:20). God's prophecy was thus perfectly fulfilled!

The political and historical details we find in God's Word are simply astonishing. Every time we read references to kings in the Old Testament, the veracity of the Bible is put to the test. After all, if God's Word is accurate, history should confirm the existence of all the kings and empires we read about in the Bible. Conversely, if these references to kings are not absolutely accurate, then the Bible is in error. But this is never the case! Researchers are constantly confirming the trustworthiness of the Bible. In his book *Scientific Investigation of the Old Testament*, Dr. Robert Dick

Wilson reveals that all 184 cases where names of kings were translated into Hebrew were done accurately. This means that for 3,900 years the names of these kings have been faithfully transmitted. There were about forty of those kings living from 2,000 BC to 400 BC. Each appears in chronological order "with reference to the kings of the same country and with respect to the kings of other countries... No stronger evidence for the substantial accuracy of the Old Testament records could possibly be imagined, than this collection of kings."[2] Mathematically, there is one chance in 750,000,000,000,000,000,000,000 that this data would be correctly recorded.

The World's Largest City: Babylon

Babylon is mentioned 250 times in the Bible and is often referred to in the prophecies of Isaiah, Jeremiah, Daniel, and Habakkuk. It is estimated that the ancient city of Babylon was five times larger than present-day London and located on both sides of the Euphrates River. A stone bridge connected the two parts of the city. On the banks of the Tigris River, 225 miles north of Babylon, was another famous city: Nineveh, the capital of the Assyrian Empire that had obviously fallen to Nebuchadnezzar. It is estimated that Nineveh had a population of three quarters of a million people, while Nebuchadnezzar's Babylon had, at its peak, about 1.2 million people.

The Greatness of the City

Herodotus, the fifth-century Greek historian, called Babylon the world's most splendid city. In fact, Babylon was the first great city and the largest city of the world at one time, covering 2,500 acres. The city bore the proud name "Bab-Ilu," which meant "gate of the gods." The Hebrews translated the name into their language and called it Babel. In the Greek and the Latin languages, the name took the form of Babylon, and the plain on which the city stood was called Babylonia.

The palaces and the temples in Babylon were of vast dimensions. The beautiful Gate of Ishtar, the goddess of fertility, spanned the great seventy-five-foot-wide Processional Way (or street), which served as the main artery of city life and led to this temple of Marduk, chief God of Babylon (also known as Baal). It was to that pagan place that God sent Daniel so that he could, in due time, interpret the king's dream concerning the future of the world.

Near the temple stood a great terraced tower (ziggurat) built in seven receding stories with a sloping ramp spiraling around it to the top. This may have been the original Tower of Babel described in Genesis 11. Whatever the case, this was only one of the many artificial "holy mountains" in and around Babylon. Another famous feature of the city was the Hanging Gardens of Babylon, one of the Seven Wonders of the Ancient World.

The Processional Street, the great and royal and sacred road that led to the city, was paved with stone slabs that were three feet square in area. Near the entrance to the palace, the blocks are still in their place, just as they were when Daniel walked on them.

The Builder of the City

Nebuchadnezzar was celebrated as the builder who made Babylon the most famous city in the world. While he was best known for his military achievements, archaeological discoveries also depict him as an accomplished builder. Nebuchadnezzar's palace stood between the Processional Way and the Euphrates River. It was a huge complex of buildings protected by a massive double wall. The south walls of his throne room were twenty feet thick. The north side of his palace was protected by three walls. Just north of them were more walls that were fifty feet thick.

The Dimensions of the City

Let us also consider the amazing dimensions of Babylon. According to Herodotus, the city was a square, with each side being fourteen miles long, making it a circuit of nearly fifty-six miles and a total area of 196 square miles. Around this incredible city, there was a deep and broad moat full of water. The city was also surrounded by impressive walls that were 311 feet high and 87 feet thick! The walls also extended thirty-five feet below ground so that the enemies of the city could not tunnel underneath. There were also 250 towers on the wall, along with guard rooms for soldiers and 100 magnificent gates of brass.

One of the Seven Wonders of the World

Nebuchadnezzar built the Hanging Gardens of Babylon in the sixth century BC to please his wife. She had come from a hilly land and was tired of the plains of Babylon. This man-made hill was 400 feet long and 350 feet high. The queen was the only one who could use the staircase. Great terraces of masonry were built one on top of the other. On these were planted gardens of tropical flowers and trees and avenues of palms. These magnificent trees were irrigated by water pumped from the Euphrates River. Nebuchadnezzar and his queen could sit in the shade and look down upon the beauties of the city. Attached to the Hanging Gardens was Nebuchadnezzar's marvelous palace.

Temples

Daniel was definitely taken to a city that would greatly challenge his faith. In this city of 2,500 acres, there were at least fifty-three different temples to pagan gods and 180 altars to Ishtar—the fertility goddess—alone. The great temple of Baal adjoined the Tower of Babylon (Babel), and it was the most renowned sanctuary in all the Euphrates Valley. It contained a golden image of Baal and a gold table, which together weighed no less than 50,000 pounds. At the top, there were golden images of Baal and Ishtar, two golden lions, a golden table forty feet long and fifteen feet wide, and a human figure of solid gold that was eighteeen feet high. Truly, Babylon was the "city of gold." No wonder Daniel revealed Nebuchadnezzar to be the head of gold in the king's dream (Daniel 2:31–38) and Isaiah wrote in Isaiah 14:4, "That you will take up this proverb against the king of Babylon, and say: 'How the oppressor has ceased, *the golden city* ceased'" (emphasis added)!

Location

The location of Babylon was in present day Iraq, on the Euphrates River, fifty-four miles south of modern Baghdad (west of the present riverbed). Today, the nearest town is Al Hillah, five miles to the south. To put it in perspective, Iraq has about 170,000 square miles, being slightly larger than the state of California. If you look on a map, you will see the Tigris and the Euphrates rivers, which come together at the top. The valley of the Tigris and the Euphrates has been known through the centuries as "the cradle of civilization." Some scholars believe that the spot where the rivers come together was the location of the Garden of Eden. Many also believe that the descendants of Noah settled there after the Great

Flood. And it was in between those two dynamic rivers that the fabulous city of Babylon was built.

The Archaeological Remains

German archaeologists of the Deutsche Orient-Gesellschaft worked at the ancient ruins of Babylon from 1899 to 1940 in order to, among other things, thoroughly examine the ruins of the inner city. As a result, a vast system of fortifications, streets, canals, palaces, and temples was discovered. Furthermore, archeologists found in that same place more than 5,000 tablets inscribed with myths, epic tales, hymns, lamentations, and proverbs. On the site, archaeologists have also found documents that systematically describe the entire city. Several of these maps were preserved on clay tablets. One of such documents is the Cyrus Cylinder, one of the most famous documents ever recovered from Babylon. It is a baked clay cylinder about nine inches long and written in a very specific language (cuneiform).

Cyrus, the Persian king of Babylon from 538 to 529 BC, was responsible for setting the Jews free from their captivity under Nebuchadnezzar. Thus, once again, we have extra-Biblical literature that confirms the biblical record. This cylinder was prepared under Cyrus's direction and has on it a record called the "Nabonidus Chronicle," telling us of Cyrus' capture of Babylon without a battle, his return of prisoners to their own countries, and his restoration of treasures to the native temples. Therefore, it is clear that the external evidence supports the biblical record once again!

Another significant document that has been found is "The Babylonian Chronicle," which is now in a British museum. This ancient document narrates Nebuchadnezzar's successful battle at Carchemish and the capture of Jerusalem on March 16, 597 BC. Once again, this stunning archaeological evidence confirms the biblical account as recorded in 2 Kings 24:10–18 and 2 Chronicles 36:9–11.

Among the present day ruins of Babylon viewable today are the outer city wall, the inner city wall, a Greek theater (probably built in the fourth century by Alexander the Great), the Processional Street, the southern palace of Nebuchadnezzar, the Ishtar Gate, and the Ishtar Gate reconstruction, which stands at the modern entrance to the ancient Babylon. This reconstruction, built under Saddam Hussein, is half the size of the original, and it even contains bricks from the original gate built thousands of years ago.

In looking at the ruins today, it is hard to imagine that there once stood great Babylon, the city of extravagance and evil luxury beyond imagination. This magnificent city, still unsurpassed in the history of the world, is now the scene of utter desolation and ruins.

Education

Because of its political importance and its favorable geographical position, Babylon was the main center of education, commerce, and administration in Nebuchadnezzar's day. It was also the literary and religious center of all Babylonia. When Nebuchadnezzar took those fine young Jewish men to brainwash them, he knew exactly what he was doing. Needless to say, Babylon was highly polytheistic, promoting the worship of different gods. Among the great religious writings of the time when Daniel would have gone to school in Babylon was the "Enuma Elish," the Babylonian account of creation. The Babylonians believed that the world originated in chaos. From multiple deities, other deities were birthed, and eventually man appeared (How different is the Babylonian teaching from what evolution teaches today?). It is from these writings that Marduk (Baal), the god of Babylon, is venerated.

In mathematics, the Babylonians inherited the sexagesimal system from the ancient Sumerians. This unique system of numbering by sixties is still in use. We determine sixty seconds to the minute, and sixty minutes to the hour. The system is also used in the division of the circle into 360 degrees.

Closely related to Babylonian mathematics, and using it as an important tool, was the science of astronomy. By 800 BC, Babylonian astronomers had attained sufficient accuracy to assign positions to the stars and to make significant notations. The planets were named after the gods of Babylon. Ishtar, the Babylonian goddess of love, became Venus in the classical world. The days of the week were, in Babylonian thought, ruled by the heavenly bodies and, ultimately, each of the seven days was devoted to a specific god. The tribal name "Chaldean" came to be used as a specialized term for an astrologer or a magician by Greek and Roman writers.

It was in this pagan society that Daniel and other Jews found themselves. Everything in their new culture was based on multiple deities helping and interacting with man. But did all this affect Daniel? Did it cause him to abandon his devotion to God? The answer is a resounding "NO!"

Corrupt Morals

Babylon, as the center of a great kingdom, was the seat of boundless luxury, and its people were notorious for their addiction to self-indulgence. Historian Samuel Fallows writes,

> Nothing could be more corrupt than its morals, nothing more fitted to excite and allure to immoderate pleasures. The rites of hospitality were polluted by the grossest and most shameful lusts. Money dissolved every tie... The Babylonians were very greatly given to wine and enjoyments which accompany inebriety. Women were present at their convivialities, first with some degree of propriety, but, growing worse and worse by degrees, they ended by throwing off at once their modesty and their clothing.[3]

Once again, try to put yourself in Daniel's shoes: How would you have reacted had you been in his situation? How do you interact with the pagan society of our times? You see, in spite of thousands of years and much technological development, there is definitely much in common between our world and Daniel's.

The Destruction of Babylon Foretold

I find it very interesting that the same prophets who wrote that Jerusalem and Judah would be taken and that Daniel was going to end up in Babylon, also predicted that the city of Babylon would not last but be decimated under the judgment of God. Both Jeremiah and Isaiah predicted that Babylon would be brought to absolute ruin. Their prophecies included the fact that Babylon would never be inhabited again. Isn't that amazingly accurate? Take a look at the following examples:

> Isaiah 13:19-20, "And Babylon, the glory of kingdoms, the beauty of the Chaldeans' pride, will be as when God overthrew Sodom and Gomorrah. It will never be inhabited, nor will it be settled from

generation to generation; nor will the Arabian pitch tents there, nor will the shepherds make their sheepfolds there."

Isaiah 14:22-23, "'For I will rise up against them,' says the LORD of hosts, 'And cut off from Babylon the name and remnant, and offspring and posterity,' says the LORD. 'I will also make it a possession for the porcupine, and marshes of muddy water; I will sweep it with the broom of destruction,' says the LORD of hosts."

Jeremiah 51:37, "Babylon shall become a heap, a dwelling place for jackals, an astonishment and a hissing, without an inhabitant."

Jeremiah 51:43-44, "Her cities are a desolation, a dry land and a wilderness, a land where no one dwells, through which no son of man passes. I will punish Bel in Babylon, and I will bring out of his mouth what he has swallowed; and the nations shall not stream to him anymore. Yes, the wall of Babylon shall fall."

Have all these prophecies happened? Of course they have! Doesn't this give us confidence that Daniel's prophecies (which we will cover later on) will also be fulfilled? Absolutely!

What Babylon Represents in Scripture

God's Word uses the term "Babylon" to convey three different ideas:

First, "Babylon" refers to a literal city whose uninhabited remains are viewable in present day Iraq. Second Kings, 2 Chronicles, Daniel, and Jeremiah refer to the literal city discussed above.

Second, in the book of Revelation (chapter 17), Babylon represents apostate Christendom or ecclesiastical Babylon, the great harlot that will support the Antichrist. Simply stated, ecclesiastical Babylon is an amalgamation of all the religions that will come together to support and follow the Antichrist as he makes his announcement that he is God. At the beginning of the Tribulation, the Antichrist will come as a man of peace, as one who brings nations together. It is only in the middle of the Tribulation that he will announce that he is "God." He will enter the newly rebuilt Jewish temple, proclaim himself as God, and demand to be worshiped. (This is what Daniel called "the abomination of desolation.")

The Antichrist's false prophet will play a key role, since he will invite all the different religions of the world to unite under the leadership of the Antichrist. Does this sound similar to what we hear today in our world? Have you heard the plea of some religious and political leaders who strongly urge us to come together and to ignore the doctrines that divide us? This is the beginning of the cries of the Babylon we read about in Revelation 17.

Third, Dr. Franklin Logsdon and other scholars suggest that Revelation 18 typifies the United States during the Tribulation.[4] Take a look at Revelation 18:9-10, which says, "The kings of the earth who committed fornication and lived luxuriously with her will weep and lament for her, when they see the smoke of her burning, standing at a distance for fear of her torment, saying, 'Alas, alas, that great city Babylon, that mighty city! For in one hour your judgment has come.'" Consider these verses in the context of the Tribulation, when all Christians will be gone. How in the world could a city or an entire nation be decimated in one hour? What could be the only way? It would have to be a nuclear attack. Though this could refer to any ungodly nation, it could also easily fit the current situation of the United States. This is such a strong reminder that if we forget the God who made us and blessed us, we shall face His judgment. One of the biggest myths of modern Christianity is that God does not send judgment or discipline. That is not true! God never overlooks sin.

Daniel's Faithfulness

As we consider the incredible yet wicked city of Babylon, we read about Daniel's amazing attitude and resolution in Daniel 1:8, which says, "But Daniel purposed in his heart that he would not defile himself with the portion of the king's delicacies, nor with the wine which he drank; therefore he requested of the chief of the eunuchs that he might not defile himself." Daniel made up his mind not to sin against God. What an encouraging and challenging example he is. May we follow Daniel's lead and stand against our decadent and sinful culture.

Discussion Questions

1. Why do some scholars try to discredit the book of Daniel?

2. Why is the book of Daniel definitely worthy of our time and efforts?

3. Why did God allow the Jews to be taken captive?

3. What was Babylon like in the time of Daniel?

4. What were the sins and temptations of Babylon? How do we see these same tendencies today?

5. What are the three ideas that Babylon represents in the Scriptures?

6. Does God allow chastisement and punishment upon His people? When and why would He do so?

That's Not All

You can find sermon outlines in the "Sermonars" section at the back of the book. These pages may be freely reproduced, either from the book or from the accompanying CD-ROM for any devotional or ministry use.

Daniel

Chapter Three

P.O.W.s Who Wouldn't Break – Why?

Having learned a bit about the character of Daniel, we can discover even more by investigating his friends. We learn of them in Daniel 1:1–7:

> In the third year of the reign of Jehoiakim king of Judah, Nebuchadnezzar king of Babylon came to Jerusalem and besieged it. And the Lord gave Jehoiakim king of Judah into his hand, with some of the articles of the house of God, which he carried into the land of Shinar to the house of his god; and he brought the articles into the treasure house of his god. Then the king instructed Ashpenaz, the master of his eunuchs, to bring some of the children of Israel and some of the king's descendants and some of the nobles, young men in whom there was no blemish, but good-looking, gifted in all wisdom, possessing knowledge and quick to understand, who had ability to serve in the king's palace, and whom they might teach the language and literature of the Chaldeans. And the king appointed for them a daily provision of the king's delicacies and of the wine which he drank, and three years of training for them, so that at the end of that time they might serve before the king. Now from among those of the sons of Judah were Daniel, Hananiah, Mishael, and Azariah. To them the chief of the eunuchs gave names: he gave Daniel the name Belteshazzar; to Hananiah, Shadrach; to Mishael, Meshach; and to Azariah, Abed-Nego.

Before we proceed through the remainder of Daniel's opening chapter, we must keep the following observations in mind:

1. Nebuchadnezzar defiled the artifacts he took from the Jewish temple by presenting them to Baal, the pagan god of Babylon.

2. Daniel was among a group of Jewish teenagers in whom there was no blemish. They were good-looking, gifted in all wisdom, possessing knowledge, and quick to understand. These were very best among the Jewish youth.

3. Daniel and the others were selected to be taught the language and the literature (i.e., the worldview) of the Chaldeans. Following their "education," they would be able to serve before the king.

4. Notice also that their brainwashing included changing the names of Daniel and his friends.

Now, carefully read the rest of the first chapter of Daniel (1:8–21):

But Daniel purposed in his heart that he would not defile himself with the portion of the king's delicacies, nor with the wine which he drank; therefore he requested of the chief of the eunuchs that he might not defile himself. Now God had brought Daniel into the favor and goodwill of the chief of the eunuchs. And the chief of the eunuchs said to Daniel, "I fear my lord the king, who has appointed your food and drink. For why should he see your faces looking worse than the young men who are your age? Then you would endanger my head before the king." So Daniel said to the steward whom the chief of the eunuchs had set over Daniel, Hananiah, Mishael, and Azariah, "Please test your servants for ten days, and let them give us vegetables to eat and water to drink. Then let our appearance be examined before you, and the appearance of the young men who eat the portion of the king's delicacies; and as you see fit, so deal with your servants." So he consented with them in this matter, and tested them ten days. And at the end of ten days their features appeared better and fatter in flesh than all the young men who ate the portion of the king's delicacies. Thus the steward took away their portion of delicacies and the wine that they were to drink, and gave them vegetables. As for these four young men, God gave them knowledge and skill in all literature and wisdom;

and Daniel had understanding in all visions and dreams. Now at the end of the days, when the king had said that they should be brought in, the chief of the eunuchs brought them in before Nebuchadnezzar. Then the king interviewed them, and among them all none was found like Daniel, Hananiah, Mishael, and Azariah; therefore they served before the king. And in all matters of wisdom and understanding about which the king examined them, he found them ten times better than all the magicians and astrologers who were in all his realm. Thus Daniel continued until the first year of King Cyrus.

A Contemporary Comparison

I find it very interesting that many people believe that if we could assassinate Osama Bin Laden, then the terrorist scare would be over. Those who believe this must not be aware of the Islamic religious schools of Pakistan, where 1.75 million students are currently being trained to fight for Islam around the world. Ben Barber, a State Department Correspondent for the *Washington Times*, documents that the current members of the Taliban studied in these schools. There are seven thousand of these schools in Pakistan alone![1]

The major topic of study is Jihad, or Holy War. The students are expected to fight infidels once they complete their studies. It is chilling to think of 1.75 million young Osama Bin Ladens in training. When (and if) the U.S. assassinates Bin Laden, he will become a martyr to this nearly 2,000,000 strong army of eccentric Islamic trainees. Muslim leader Mohammed Ajmal Qadri recently told a reporter: "Eventually, all people must become Muslims, including every Christian and Jew living in the United States. The world has to go the way we want. It is our divine right to lead humanity."[2] Qadri has preached in hundreds of new mosques built by Muslim immigrants in the U.S. in the last decade. This is where he raises money for his school in Pakistan and where he teaches children to kill those who stand in the path of Islamic dominance in the world.[3]

One of those students, fourteen-year-old-student Anwer, stated, "Most kids here go for Jihad, and I will too, God-willing. Jihad is to fight for Islam and the pride of Islam." At age eighteen, Anwer will leave school behind and go to a military training camp along with several other young men his age.[4]

In Pakistan, those young students sleep on the floor of the school's mosque in sleeping bags, which they roll up each morning. They rise at 3:00 a.m. for study and prayers, breaking for play around 4:30 a.m. At 7:30 a.m., they have breakfast and then study the Koran until 11:00 a.m., when they sleep for two hours. They pray, study, have lunch, and then pray and study again until dinner at 9:30 p.m., after which they go to the mosque to sleep. They have no rooms or even a bed of their own. So goes life in Pakistan right now, where people are so indoctrinated that even the national airline begins its flights with a reading from the Koran or a prayer to Allah.

Meanwhile, in America, there are now over 3,000 mosques and schools where young Muslims are also indoctrinated. Mohammed Ajmal Qadri states, "These schools are a divine gift for Americans. The American civilization is a Monica Lewinsky civilization," he says with a hearty laugh. "It is empty and hollow from inside. Islam is the only cultural system that could bear the load of life the time to come."[5]

Do you see the connection between what Islam is doing and what Nebuchadnezzar tried to do to Daniel and his friends thousands of years ago? Like the Communists and even Hitler's Nazi Party, both Islam and Nebuchadnezzar resorted to brainwashing to mold the minds of those selected to carry on with their programs and traditions. Hitler, who employed this approach with the German youth, once wrote: "Effective propaganda is aimed at the masses; aimed at the emotions, not the intellect; set at the intellectual level of the most limited in the audience; designed so that the bigger the audience, the lower its intellectual level."[6]

Therefore, what Islamic extremists are doing and what Communists and the Nazis did is basically the same thing Nebuchadnezzar tried to do to his young Jewish slaves in the book of Daniel. Nebuchadnezzar went to Judah and captured a group of young minds who were both socially and intellectually privileged, bringing them back to Babylon so that he could mold them to his expectations. But to his surprise, events did not turn out as he had expected. Nebuchadnezzar made one important mistake: he left God out of the picture.

The Division of Daniel

Before we further analyze Daniel 1, it is important to understand where this first chapter fits within the entire book. Daniel is mainly divided into two sections. The first section (chapters 1-6) is primarily historical (with the exception of the king's dream in chapter 2), whereas the second section (chapters 7-12) is prophetic and includes four of Daniel's visions and a further interpretation of Nebuchadnezzar's dream (from chapter 2). Thus, chapters 7 and 2 go together. Furthermore, chapters 1-6 appear

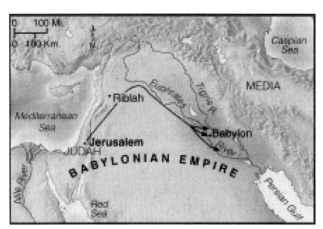

in chronological order, while chapter 7 suddenly goes back in time to a date shortly prior to the events of chapter 5. The four visions are then given in their own chronological order, beginning in chapter 7.

As we take a closer look into this amazing first chapter of Daniel, keep in mind that our goal is to learn as much as we can from this young man who succeeded to live for God in an ungodly culture. We want to do much more than just accumulate historical and religious facts about Babylon. Like Daniel, we live in a world that wants to do everything to destroy our faith in Christ and our commitment to our Lord. May the Lord use this magnificent book to work in our hearts, through His Holy Spirit, so that we will remain faithful to Him!

Let us then further investigate the subtlety of Nebuchadnezzar's techniques and marvel at how a young Hebrew remained faithful, receiving blessings from God because of his integrity.

Rabid Brainwashing of Prisoners of War— Daniel & Friends

How did Nebuchadnezzar attempt to brainwash his Jewish slaves and try to turn them into pagans? Consider the following techniques used by Daniel's captors:

1. Through the Vulnerability of Their Age

Remember that Daniel and his friends were very young. They were going through those foundational years in life when the simplicity of childhood is left behind and personal convictions are embraced and character is formed. Consider, once again, Daniel 1:3-4:

> Then the king instructed Ashpenaz, the master of his eunuchs, to bring some of the children of Israel and some of the king's descendants and some of the nobles, young men in whom there was no blemish, but good-looking, gifted in all wisdom, possessing knowledge and quick to understand, who had ability to serve in the king's palace, and whom they might teach the language and literature of the Chaldeans.

Daniel 1:3 describes Daniel and his friends as *children*. They were definitely young. The Hebrew word used in this verse is *yeled*, which means "borne one" and is used in reference to the infant Isaac in Genesis 21:8 and some young men in 2 Kings 12:8. Consider also how different Bible scholars have estimated Daniel's age to have been at the time of his arrival in Babylon:

- Jameson, Fausset, and Brown believe Daniel was between 15 and 20 years of age

- Dr. Arno Gaebelein: 14

years of age

• Sir Robert Anderson: 20 years of age

• Dr. J. Vernon McGee: 17 years of age

In spite of these small differences, all these scholars (and many others) agree that Daniel was basically a teenager when he faced the Babylonian pagan culture. This reminds us that it is never too early to teach our children the ways of the Lord. After all, if they are not being instructed in the Bible, they are learning from something or someone else. You see, learning is not an option. As we grow, we automatically learn new things about life. The question is: where will our learning come from? May Proverbs 22:6 always be true in the lives of our children: "Train up a child in the way he should go, and when he is old he will not depart from it."

2. The Change of Their Names

Besides choosing Daniel and his friends at a very young age, Nebuchadnezzar also tried to indoctrinate them by changing their names. Daniel's Hebrew name means "God is my judge," but his new name (Belteshazzar) meant "whom Bel favors" (Bel, or Baal, was the most prominent god in Babylon). Likewise, the names of his three friends also went from being focused on the God of the Bible to exalting pagan gods. Take a look:

• Hananiah ("Beloved of the Lord") vs. Shadrach ("inspired by the sun-god")

• Mishael ("who is God") vs. Meshach ("who is like Venus")

• Azariah ("the Lord is my help") vs. Abednego ("the servant of Nebo, the fire-god")

Consider also what Dr. Clarence Larkin and famous scholar Dr. Albert Barnes had to say about the significance of this change of names:

> The purpose in changing their names was to wean them away from their land and religion, and get them to adopt the religion and habits of the heathen nation where their future was to be spent.[7]

> This change of name, therefore, was designed to denote a consecration to the service of this idol-god, and the change was eminently adapted to make him to who it was given forget the true God, to

whom in earlier days, he had been devoted. It was only extraordinary grace which could have kept these youths in the paths of their
early training, and in the faithful service of that God to whom they
had been early consecrated, amidst the temptations by which they
were now surrounded in a foreign land, and the influences which
were employed to alienate them from the God of their fathers.[8]

Do you see the significance of this change in names? The very
calling of their names was to cause them to forget God and subtly lead
them to exalt false, pagan gods.

3. The Godless Babylonian Education–Change Their Thinking

Nebuchadnezzar also tried to brainwash the Jewish youth by giving
them a godless education that would radically alter their thinking. This
same strategy still happens today in the campuses of our colleges and
universities. Dr. James Dobson has stated that 80-85% of children that
are raised in Christian homes leave their faith at some point during their
college experience.[9] Another study shows that two-thirds of the children
who do not grow up going to church are not likely to start doing so after
they turn eighteen.

Sadly, I have witnessed many teens who grew up in Christian homes
be carelessly sent by their parents to secular schools that do all in their
power to undermine Christianity. Of course, this does not mean that it is
wrong for Christians to attend secular colleges. It only means that parents
need to be more active in ensuring that the minds of their children are
better protected when they go away for higher education.

John Leo, with *U.S. News and World Report*, once stated that "America
still does not understand what has happened to its campuses. A strong
culture has arisen around dangerous ideas."[10] The education given to our
children today is strongly influenced by alcohol, sex, drugs, liberal religious and political ideas, and many other dangerous influences (much
like Babylon and its multiple temples, plurality of gods, and rampant
sexual sins). Unfortunately, the church is often passive and fails to train
young Christian minds to persevere in their faith.

4. The Seduction of the City of Babylon

Nebuchadnezzar knew that the city of Babylon itself would be one of
his great assets in the process of converting the Jewish youth to paganism.
Like the permissive society we live in, Babylon was known for its almost

nonexistent standards of ethics and morality—one could do whatever one wished to do. Doesn't this sound similar to the America of the 21st century? Consider the following examples that clearly illustrate the type of culture we have to stand against as Christians:

- In 2003, the 30th annual American Music Awards was hosted by Ozzy and Sharon Osbourne and their kids, Jack and Kelly. The Osbournes gave network censors a real workout because of their constant use of vulgar language. They were bleeped so much because of their profanity during their opening introduction that it was hard for the TV viewers to understand what they were saying. That same night, Eminem, known for his bad language and sensual and even violent lyrics, won the favorite album in both pop rock & hip-hop categories.

- A young man once stated on the Oprah Winfrey show that Jesus Christ had transformed his life, that Jesus understood that the young man was a homosexual and was fine with that.

- Miss America Erica Harold was reprimanded by the organizers of the American pageant for supporting sexual abstinence, a cause that, according to them, should be avoided at all costs because of its unpopularity.

- According to *USA Today*, young people see two beer commercials for every tennis shoe commercial. In 2001 alone, $811 million were spent in alcohol advertising.

- New York's Museum of Sex had 15,000 visitors in its first six weeks open to the public.

- The Boy Scouts have been strongly criticized for their refusal to accept gay Scoutmasters.

- Prescription drugs for young people are soaring. Doctors have been increasingly prescribing drugs such as Prozac and Ritalin to children and teenagers.

Is it any surprise that Dr. Phil is a popular show? People are troubled and looking for answers in a society that, just like Babylon's, has completely lost its sense of right and wrong.

5. The Change of Their Diets

Daniel 1:8 states, "But Daniel purposed in his heart that he would not defile himself with the portion of the king's delicacies, nor with the wine which he drank; therefore he requested of the chief of the eunuchs that he might not defile himself." Dr. Albert Barnes comments on Nebuchadnezzar's attempt to entice Daniel and his friends through their new diet: "It may be presumed that this was the best kind of wine. From anything that appears, this was furnished to them in abundance; and with the leisure which they had, they could hardly be thrown into stronger temptation to excessive indulgence."[11] So young Daniel one day woke up to a new reality where self-imposed boundaries would be the only thing keeping him from indulgence and, ultimately, destruction. This sounds similar to some of today's youth who are given credit cards, cell phones, and cars without any parental supervision or guidelines. Unfortunately, not all of our teenagers are as resolute to do right as Daniel was.

Daniel never caved in; he stayed true to God! This is the faith we seek, a faith that helps us stay pure in an impure world. We seek a Savior who can so possess us with genuine spirituality that we rise above our environment, much like Paul did when he was imprisoned but continued to be filled with the joy of the Lord.

But what did Daniel have that helped him take such a strong stand for his God when practically everything around him was telling him to take the road of rebellion? What should we do to follow his example and be faithful to the Lord under pressure?

Reasons Nebuchadnezzar Failed to Brainwash Daniel

Consider the following seven reasons that explain Daniel's success:

1. Daniel grew up under a great spiritual leader.

From the time he was eleven until he turned sixteen, Daniel grew up under the godly king Josiah. Among all of Judah's kings, Josiah was the only one described as godly. Before Josiah, Judah had progressed in evil for fifty-four years under Manasseh (who reigned for fifty-two years) and his son, Amon (who reigned for two years). Amon was so evil that his own servants killed him. After that, Josiah became king at the age of eight and reigned for thirty-one years (640–609 BC).

When Josiah was twenty-six years old, something amazing happened.

As the Jews were working on repairing the temple and digging through all the rubble, they found a precious treasure they had lost years earlier. Second Kings 22:3 reads, "Then Hilkiah the high priest said to Shaphan the scribe, 'I have found the Book of the Law in the house of the LORD.' And Hilkiah gave the book to Shaphan, and he read it.'" They had found the Pentateuch with its five books written by Moses.

The High Priest then went to Josiah and read to him what he had just discovered. As he heard God's Word being read to him, young Josiah started to weep and tear his clothes. In his grief, the king called the people together, read the Word to them, and declared that they had collectively sinned against their God. As a result, he led one of the biggest revivals in the history of Judah.

Within God's providence, there was a young child called Daniel who was able to watch God move through King Josiah. The impact in Daniel's life was such that when he was taken to Babylon, Daniel did not cave in! May we learn this important lesson and place ourselves (and our children) under strong spiritual influence.

2. Daniel's parents had a love for God which they passed on to him.

We can assume that Daniel had godly parents because theirs was a royal family (Daniel 1:3), very likely close to King Josiah himself. Furthermore, the type of godly resolution we see in Daniel's life is frequently present in children who grow up under parents who live as commanded in Deuteronomy 6:4-8, which states:

> Hear, O Israel: The LORD our God, the LORD is one! You shall love the LORD your God with all your heart, with all your soul, and with all your strength. And these words which I command you today shall be in your heart. You shall teach them diligently to your children, and shall talk of them when you sit in your house, when you walk by the way, when you lie down, and when you rise up. You shall bind them as a sign on your hand, and they shall be as frontlets between your eyes.

3. Daniel, consequently, developed a heart for God.

Because of the godly influence of Josiah and his own family, Daniel developed a heart for God. Daniel 1:4 describes Daniel as follows: "Young men in whom there was no blemish, but good-looking, gifted in all wisdom, possessing knowledge and quick to understand, who had ability to serve in the king's palace, and whom they might teach the language and literature of the Chaldeans." But besides all these wonderful traits, Daniel also feared God to the extent of refusing to contaminate himself with the Babylonian way of life.

4. Daniel hid God's Word in his heart.

Do you remember what Josiah did when the Pentateuch was found? He read it before the entire people. Undoubtedly, that left a strong respect for God's Word in young Daniel's heart and mind. This is clearly seen in Daniel 9, where, years after he was taken to Babylon, Daniel was searching the writings of the prophet Jeremiah to find out the length of the captivity. Thus, from the time he was a young boy to when he was almost 90 years of age, Daniel had his heart focused on the Scriptures.

This reminds us that a strong commitment to God's Word is a trademark of strong Christians and strong churches. One of Satan's greatest joys comes when we fail to saturate our minds with the truth of God's Word. After all, the Bible is God's very sword, given to us as a precious weapon that helps us stand strong in God's grace (Ephesians 6:17). Consider also the following verses about the uniqueness and the importance of God's Word in our lives:

- Isaiah 40:8, "The grass withers, the flower fades, but the word of our God stands forever."

- Psalm 1:1-6, "Blessed is the man who walks not in the counsel of the ungodly, nor stands in the path of sinners, nor sits in the seat of the scornful; but his delight is in the law of the LORD, and in His law he meditates day and night. He shall be like a tree planted by the rivers of water, that brings forth its fruit in its season, whose leaf also shall not wither; and whatever he does shall prosper. The ungodly are not so, but are like the chaff which the wind drives away. Therefore the ungodly shall not stand in the judgment, nor sinners in the congregation of the righteous. For the LORD knows the way of the righteous, but the way of the ungodly shall perish."

5. Daniel selected godly friends.

Daniel was not alone in his spiritual journey. Hananiah, Mishael, and Azariah (known in Babylon as Shadrach, Meshach, and Abed-Nego) joined Daniel in his desire to pursue God's way above all else (cf. Daniel 1:11-17; 3:16-18). Godly friendships are essential to our spiritual health. I am reminded of this truth every time I look at the teens in our youth group: those who are serious about their relationship with Christ are those who surround themselves with peers who have the same heart for God. May we follow Daniel's example and pursue close relationships with people who love God with all their hearts!

6. Daniel was experienced and disciplined in prayer.

We see a strong emphasis on prayer all over Daniel's book. For instance, in chapter two Daniel pleads with God to reveal the meaning of Nebuchadnezzar's dream. In chapter six, we see Daniel faithfully praying even though there was a decree that forbid prayer to any god or man besides the king himself (Daniel 6:7). In chapter nine, we read one of Daniel's long and powerful prayers on behalf of his people.

The Hebrew Youth In Prayer
Both in emergencies and in normal times, Daniel sought his God in prayer, and the Lord never failed him.

Do you have the same commitment to prayer in your life? When problems arise, do you already have a habitual prayer life? How often do you kneel before the throne of God's grace? No matter the struggle, always remember that God is only one prayer away.

7. Daniel was resolute in his thinking.

Once again, consider Daniel 1:8, which states, "But Daniel purposed in his heart that he would not defile himself with the portion of the king's delicacies, nor with the wine which he drank; therefore he requested of the chief of the eunuchs that he might not defile himself." The New American Standard Version translated the beginning of this verse as "But Daniel *made up his mind*" (emphasis added). Isn't it amazing that a foreign teenager could be so resolute in his thinking to stand up against the most powerful man in his time? What excuses do we have?

Rewards of Spiritual Consistency

God always rewards those who are faithful to Him. You will always know the men and women around you who walk with God because their lives are filled with God's favor. Even when those godly people face hard times (because being blessed does not mean being immune to difficulties), God's blessings in their lives are still visible.

We can identify at least four benefits received by Daniel for his resolution to obey no matter the cost. Those same benefits will flow into our lives as we obey God:

1. God gives special insight.

Daniel 1:17 states, "As for these four young men, God gave them knowledge and skill in all literature and wisdom; and Daniel had understanding in all visions and dreams." God is more interested in the worker than in the work per se. God wants to work *in* the minister before working *through* him. But we tend to turn things completely around, don't we? We buy into the lie that what we do for God matters more than what God does in us. But God says, "Show me what you are and I will show you what your ministry is." God is more interested in what a man is than what he does. As we see in Daniel's life, God rewards us by molding our beings as we live for him (cf. Romans 12:1-2).

2. God bestows wisdom and favor.

God rewarded Daniel and his friends with two blessings we all wish we had: God's wisdom and God's favor. Take a look at Daniel 1:19, "Then the king interviewed them, and among them all none was found like Daniel, Hananiah, Mishael, and Azariah; therefore, they served before the king." One of the most amazing facets of this story is that God gave them favor before a heathen king who wanted nothing to do with God himself. God is so powerful that He rewarded Daniel and his friends with favor before the king so that they could serve him without compromising their spiritual walk.

3. God alone promotes and demotes.

I have had people ask me several times how to build a big church. My answer is simple: "I don't know. Just make sure that whatever you do, you walk with God!" Whatever successes we achieve in life, they are all given to us by God Himself. Read Daniel 1:20-21 carefully: "And in all matters of wisdom and understanding about which the king examined them, he found them ten times better than all the magicians and astrologers who were in all his realm. Thus Daniel continued until the first year of King Cyrus." As we continue to read through Daniel's book, we will see that his promotion lasted seventy years! God continued to lift Daniel up before the leadership of that ungodly nation as the prophet continued to walk faithfully with his God.

4. God makes us an influencer instead of a follower.

Follow God and he will put you in a position where others will follow you. This does not mean we should follow God for selfish reasons (which, after all, would not really mean following God but ourselves). We should follow God so that, as others follow us, they will be actually following Him (cf. Paul's admonition to the Corinthians in 1 Corinthians 11:1).

Freedom in Living God's Way

Shania Twain, one of the divas of country music, is quoted as having said, "I don't feel free." In spite of all her success, Shania has given up her freedom for the sake of following her husband and becoming a fellow devotee of Sant Mat, a strain of Sikh mysticism that advocates hours of daily meditation, abstinence from sex and alcohol, and copious journal keeping as the path to self-realization. Shania's brother, Darryl, described his sister to *Time* magazine as a robot.[12]

Like Shania, we, too, can get to the top. We can make for ourselves a name that will cause others to be envious of our success. But if we do not have Jesus Christ in our lives, we are ultimately empty! Christ wants to come into our lives and make us strong like Daniel and his friends. He wants us to follow Daniel's example and be light in a dark and corrupt society. He wants us to deny ourselves and find true freedom by standing up for him—just like Daniel did. Are you ready and willing to let God do this transforming work in your life?

Discussion Questions

1. Why did Nebuchadnezzar take Daniel and other Jewish youth to Babylon? What was he trying to do to them?

2. What was the significance of the names given to Daniel and his three friends? What did their Hebrew names signify?

3. What strategies did Nebuchadnezzar use to corrupt Daniel? What strategies does the world use to try to corrupt you? In what ways are they similar and different?

4. Why did Nebuchadnezzar fail to brainwash Daniel? What are some practical ways you can incorporate into your own life those things that enabled Daniel to resist Nebuchadnezzar's temptations?

6. Who are your closest friends? Consider your conversations with them and what you do when you spend time together. Are these close friendships leading you closer to God? Why or why Not?

7. What kind of friend are you? If you were one of Daniel's friends, would you have helped him to stand up for God? How so?

8. How does Daniel 1:8 relate to Romans 12:1-2? How can you apply these precious verses to your life? (Provide practical ways)

That's Not All

You can find sermon outlines in the "Sermonars" section at the back of the book. These pages may be freely reproduced, either from the book or from the accompanying CD-ROM for any devotional or ministry use.

Chapter Four

Daniel's Dream about the Future Which Came True!

Though Daniel 2:1-32 is a rather lengthy passage, let us take the time to read it before we analyze it in further detail:

Now in the second year of Nebuchadnezzar's reign, Nebuchadnezzar had dreams; and his spirit was so troubled that his sleep left him. Then the king gave the command to call the magicians, the astrologers, the sorcerers, and the Chaldeans to tell the king his dreams. So they came and stood before the king. and the king said to them, "I have had a dream, and my spirit is anxious to know the dream." Then the Chaldeans spoke to the king in Aramaic, "O king, live forever! Tell your servants the dream, and we will give the interpretation." The king answered and said to the Chaldeans, "My decision is firm: if you do not make known the dream to me, and its interpretation, you shall be cut in pieces, and your houses shall be made an ash heap. However, if you tell the dream and its interpretation, you shall receive from me gifts, rewards, and great honor. Therefore tell me the dream and its interpretation." They answered again and said, "Let the king tell his servants the dream, and we will give its interpretation." The king answered and said, "I know for certain that you would gain time, because you see that my decision is firm: if you do not make known the dream to me, there is only one decree for you! For you have agreed to speak lying and corrupt words before me till the time has changed. Therefore, tell me the

49

dream, and I shall know that you can give me its interpretation. The Chaldeans answered the king, and said, "There is not a man on earth who can tell the king's matter; therefore no king, lord, or ruler has ever asked such things of any magician, astrologer, or Chaldean. It is a difficult challenge that the king requests, and there is no other who can tell it to the king except the gods, whose dwelling is not with flesh." For this reason the king was angry and very furious, and gave a command to destroy all the wise men of Babylon. So the decree went out, and they began killing the wise men; and they sought Daniel and his companions, to kill them. Then with counsel and wisdom Daniel answered Arioch, the captain of the king's guard, who had gone out to kill the wise men of Babylon; he answered and said to Arioch the king's captain, "Why is the decree from the king so urgent?" Then Arioch made the decision known to Daniel. So Daniel went in and asked the king to give him time, that he might tell the king the interpretation. Then Daniel went to his house, and made the decision known to Hananiah, Mishael, and Azariah, his companions, that they might seek mercies from the God of heaven concerning this secret, so that Daniel and his companions might not perish with the rest of the wise men of Babylon. Then the secret was revealed to Daniel in a night vision. So Daniel blessed the God of heaven. Daniel answered and said: "Blessed be the name of God forever and ever, For wisdom and might are His. And He changes the times and the seasons; He removes kings and raises up kings; He gives wisdom to the wise and knowledge to those who have understanding. He reveals deep and secret things; He knows what is in the darkness, and light dwells with Him. I thank You and praise You, O God of my fathers; You have given me wisdom and might, and have now made known to me what we asked of You, For You have made known to us the king's demand." Therefore Daniel went to Arioch, whom the king had appointed to destroy the wise men of Babylon. He went and said thus to him: "Do not destroy the wise men of Babylon; take me before the king, and I will tell the king the interpretation." Then Arioch quickly brought Daniel before the king, and said thus to him, "I have found a man of the captives of Judah, who will make known to the king the interpretation." The king answered and said to Daniel, whose name was Belteshazzar, "Are you able to make known to me the dream which I have seen, and its interpretation?" Daniel answered in the presence of the king, and said, "The secret which the king has demanded, the wise men, the astrologers, the magicians, and the soothsayers cannot declare to the king. But there is a God in heaven who reveals secrets, and He has made known to King Nebuchadnezzar what will be in the latter days. Your dream, and the visions of your head upon your bed, were these: As for you, O king, thoughts came to your mind while on your bed, about what would come to pass after this; and He who reveals secrets has made known to you what will be. But as for me, this secret has not been revealed to me because I have more wisdom than anyone living, but for our sakes who make known the interpretation to the king, and that you may know the thoughts of your heart. You, O king, were watching; and behold, a great image! This great image, whose splendor was excellent, stood before you; and its form was awesome. This image's head was of fine gold, its chest and arms of silver, its belly and thighs of bronze.

Why Study Prophecy?

The front cover of the July 1, 2002, issue of *Time* magazine featured the following headline: "The Bible & the Apocalypse: Why More Americans Are Reading and Talking about the End of the World."[1] This interesting article highlights the apocalypse and also draws our attention to the following facts:

- Bestselling fiction books by Tim LaHaye and Jerry Jenkins, based on the book of Revelation, are selling as many copies as Tom Clancy and Stephen King novels (over fifty million copies sold!).

- Only about half of *Left Behind* readers are evangelical Christians. This shows that there is a large community outside of Christianity that is interested in the apocalypse.

- A *Time*/CNN poll revealed that more than one third of Americans say they are paying more attention now to how the current news might relate to the end of the world.

- Amazingly, 59% of Americans say they believe the events recorded in Revelation will come true.

As we study the book of Daniel, I am sure several might ask: Why does it matter? Why study a book filled with so many weird prophecies that are apparently so hard to understand? Can't we just stick with the familiar stories about brave Daniel and his faithful friends?

Unfortunately, this mindset reveals an important truth: the majority of our pulpits are silent about prophecy and, as a result, the average churchgoer knows very little about it. But prophecy is most definitely worthy of our time and our efforts. Why? Consider the following statistics about the Bible:

- One fifth of the Bible is prophetic, foretelling future events.

- One third of that one fifth focuses on the Second Coming of Jesus Christ.

- Of 660 general prophecies, 333 deal with the person of Jesus Christ. 109 of those were fulfilled in Christ's first coming. This means that 224 prophecies have yet to be fulfilled in Christ's Second Coming. These have to do with different nations, epochs, and cataclysmic events throughout history.

- Of the New Testament's 7,959 verses, 330 (1 in every 25) specifically point to the second coming of Jesus Christ.

- Jesus Himself referred to His second coming twenty-one times and commanded His disciples fifty times to watch and to be ready!

This is why it is so important for us to study the book of Daniel--because of the biblical mandate that commands us to do so! Every church should frequently focus its teaching on the Second Coming of Christ. So why focus specifically on Daniel? Daniel's prophetic portion is the key to understanding much of the prophecy found elsewhere in God's Word. Let us then, proceed with our study of Daniel's prophecy found in chapter two!

"The Times of the Gentiles"

Jesus stated in Luke 21:24, "And they will fall by the edge of the sword, and be led away captive into all nations. And Jerusalem will be trampled by Gentiles until the times of the Gentiles are fulfilled." What did Jesus mean by the expression "the times of the Gentiles?" To understand this expression, we need to notice four things. First, Jesus did not refer to the "fullness" of the Gentiles or to the "abomination of desolation" referred to by Daniel later on in his book. Second, Jesus clearly predicted that Jerusalem would be trampled by the Gentiles until their time is fulfilled. Third, we are living in the times of the Gentiles right now. Fourth, the times of the Gentiles have everything to do with Palestine and, more specifically, with Jerusalem.

"The times of the Gentiles" refers to the period of time in which God's holy city, Jerusalem, is under Gentile control. Daniel describes the beginning of this period of history in the first few verses of his book. King Nebuchadnezzar of Babylon was the most important pagan monarch in the entire Bible. More attention is devoted to him in the pages of Scripture than to any other Gentile king. It was Nebuchadnezzar who ultimately defeated the city of Jerusalem in 586 BC and burned the Jewish Temple to the ground! Thus, Nebuchadnezzar began "the times of the Gentiles."

Jerusalem, the city of God, and the Jewish temple have been under Gentile control ever since! As a result, today there are three major world religions that claim authority over Jerusalem and over its Temple: Judaism, Islam, and, of course, Christianity. But in spite of all the chaos we see in that area right now, Jesus promised this phase will one day come to an end. Jesus promised that when "the times of the Gentiles" are fulfilled (implying that they will come to an end), His earthly kingdom will begin!

Consider what Dr. J. Vernon McGee had to say about "the times of the Gentiles:"

> We will see in this section the history of the rule of this world by the Gentiles. Because of the failure of the house of David (Jews), God is now taking the scepter of this universe out from the hands of that line of David, and He is putting it in the hands of the Gentiles. It will be there until Jesus Christ comes again to this earth. Then Christ will take the scepter and rule on this earth as King of kings and Lord of lords. The "times of the Gentiles" is from the day of Nebuchadnezzar right down through our day until the Lord comes to reign.[2]

Therefore, there are three important facts we must keep in mind about "the times of the Gentiles:"

1. It began in 586 BC with Nebuchadnezzar's destruction of Jerusalem.

2. It will conclude with the Second Coming of Jesus Christ, which will initiate the millennial kingdom reign of Christ on this earth (Revelation 20:4–6).

3. God has allowed it to happen because of the Jews' sin and consistent disobedience to God.

Consider also what Dr. Arno Gaebelein commented about "the times of the Gentiles:"

> The expression "the times of the Gentiles" is not found in the Book of Daniel, but it is a New Testament phrase. Our Lord used it exclusively... The times of the Gentiles did not begin when Jerusalem rejected the Lord from heaven... The times of the Gentiles started with the Babylonian captivity by Nebuchadnezzar. The Glory of the Lord departed from Jerusalem... the dominion was then taken away from Jerusalem and transferred to the Gentiles.[3]

The Context

The first thing we should do when studying a passage is to make sure we understand its context. In this case, Daniel established the historical context of the events described in Daniel 2 in the first few verses of the chapter. Daniel wants us to know when these events took place. According to him, this happened in the second year of Nebuchadnezzar (Daniel 2:1). Because Daniel takes us back to the second year of Nebuchadnezzar's reign, we know the time of these events falls between April 603 and March 602 BC. The king's dream occurred during Daniel's three-year education under the king's instructions (1:5). Daniel was called upon as a "senior" in college, roughly at age 20, to give an accurate interpretation of the dream or to be killed!

But besides establishing the historical context of Daniel 2, it is equally important to determine where the passage fits within Daniel and within the Scripture as a whole. According to Dr. Arno Gabelein, Daniel 2 introduces us to the "first great prophetic unfolding. It may well be called one of the pivotal chapters of the Bible. It is the foundation of all the other visions which follow in Daniel."[4] Agreeing with Dr. Gabelein, Moody Church's former pastor, H. A. Ironside, once wrote: "This second chapter of Daniel has well been called 'the ABC of prophecy.' I suppose it contains the most complete, and yet, the most simple, prophetic picture that we have in all the Word of God."[5] With these remarks in mind, remember that the prophecy of Daniel 2 about future Gentile world governments was given 2,500 years ago! Its accuracy (as we will see in the next chapter) should take our breath away.

It was in Babylon, near modern day Baghdad, that Nebuchadnezzar had a dream. God used his dream, along with Daniel's accurate interpretation of it, to clearly convey four future Gentile world powers which would not only control Jerusalem, fulfilling the "the times of the Gentiles," but also lead up to the second coming of Christ. Psalm 137:1-4 gives us a glimpse into the hearts of the Jews who were taken captive and who were alive when "the times of the Gentiles" began. This Psalm reads:

> By the rivers of Babylon, there we sat down, yea, we wept when we remembered Zion. We hung our harps upon the willows in the midst of it. For there those who carried us away captive asked of us a song, and those who plundered us requested mirth, saying, "Sing us one of the songs of Zion!" How shall we sing the LORD's song in a foreign land?

It was in that context of much grief and pain that God revealed, through dreams and prophecies, His plans--filled with hope--for the world in general and for the Jews in particular.

Disturbing Dreams

The first three verses of the second chapter of Daniel read as follows:

> Now in the second year of Nebuchadnezzar's reign, Nebuchadnezzar had dreams; and his spirit was so troubled that his sleep left him. Then the king gave the command to call the magicians, the astrologers, the sorcerers, and the Chaldeans to tell the king his dreams. So they came and stood before the king. And the king said

to them, "I have had a dream, and my spirit is anxious to know the dream."

Do not miss the irony of these verses: Nebuchadnezzar was the most powerful man of his time, a man who had built a heavily fortified city and a magnificent palace. But in spite of all his luxury, he could not sleep. Something was disturbing him. His dreams were keeping him awake and his spirit was troubled. The Hebrew word for "dream" is in the plural, thus indicating that the king had more than one dream that bothered him. These dreams caused him to be "troubled," which refers to a deep disturbance. Thus, in our vernacular these dreams could be called nightmares. Sitting at the very top of the world, Nebuchadnezzar wondered about the future. He really wanted to find out the meaning of his dreams, and until he did so, his spirit could find no peace. Unfortunately, it is hard for us to understand what these dreams meant to Nebuchadnezzar in his polytheistic society. Dr. Fred M. Wood states:

> In almost every generation people have attached some significance to dreams. In ancient Babylon, however, they were considered to play an important role in the life of people—especially those in positions of a nation's leadership. Rulers did not disregard them because they believed the dream often conveyed the will of the gods. This is one of the reasons kings surrounded themselves with astrologers and diviners whose chief business was the interpretation of dreams and other omens.[6]

A Different Language

Another aspect of this passage that people usually fail to take into consideration is the two different languages Daniel used. Notice Daniel 2:4, "Then the Chaldeans spoke to the king in Aramaic, 'O king, live forever! Tell your servants the dream, and we will give the interpretation.'" Unlike the previous verses, Daniel 2:4 was written in Aramaic, not Hebrew. The entire Old Testament, outside of a couple of other passages, was written in Hebrew, the language of the Jews. But we find something quite peculiar between Daniel 2:4 and Daniel 7:28—this entire narrative was written in Aramaic, the Gentile language. Why was this entire portion, including chapter 2, written in the language of the Gentiles instead of in the Hebrew of the Jews? God used Aramaic to customize this portion of His Word to its recipients. Since these prophecies related directly to Gentile kingdoms, God decided to communicate them through the Gentile language. Dr. McGee comments:

> The significance of this change is quite remarkable: God is now speaking to the world, not just to His nation. Israel has gone into Babylonian captivity. God has taken the scepter out of the line of David, and He has put it in Gentile hands. It will stay there until the day He takes the scepter back. When He does, nail-pierced hands will take the scepter, because it is God's intention for Jesus to reign.[7]

A Directive for Death

As a result of his dreams, Nebuchadnezzar called in the Chaldean astrologers and magicians to help interpret his dreams. This shows that Nebuchadnezzar was deep into the occult. But in spite of all the demonic activities that certainly went on in Babylon, we do not find Daniel being consumed with exorcism or with the works of the devil. His focus, unlike the focus of many who blame everything on Satan and his demons, was on God! By living a consecrated life, Daniel did not have to be consumed with the works of the devil.

Nebuchadnezzar's magicians could not do anything for him. At first they wanted the king to tell them the dream so they could make up an interpretation. But when Nebuchadnezzar demanded that they tell him *both* the dream and the interpretation, the astrologers knew they were caught—there was nothing they could do (2:5-8). The moment they lied about the content of the dream, the king would know it!

Upon receiving a negative response from his magicians and astrologers, Nebuchadnezzar became angry because there was no one who could help him. As a result, a decree went out, commanding all the wise men of Babylon to be destroyed (2:9-12). It is at this point that Daniel's resolution to stand up for God became particularly significant (cf. Daniel 1:8). Though Satan most likely wanted to use the king's anger towards all the magicians to destroy Daniel, God had different plans and publicly exalted His servant before the king himself.

Make sure you do not miss this point: we will always face spiritual warfare when God is using us. Daniel certainly did! But this is a message that the average Christian in North America simply refuses to accept. Many are trained to think that when the church is doing well and Christians are committed to God, there will be no problems. Where did we get this idea? We certainly did not find it in the Bible. Satan tried to destroy Daniel through Nebuchadnezzar, and he also wants to destroy every Christian who is doing God's will and seeking to lift up His standards. How, then, can we face Satan's strong opposition? How can we overcome the discouragement and the fear he wants to flood into our hearts? We can stand strong by going to God, just like Daniel did.

Daniel Seeks "Mercies from God"

The events of Daniel 2 continue with Arioch, the one in charge of enforcing the king's decree, going to Daniel and his companions so that they too could be killed (Daniel 2:13). Make sure to notice Daniel's poise when faced with the reality of the king's anger (2:14-16). Daniel did not run away or despair because his confidence was in God. That is the mark of a mature Christian. If our confidence is in anything but God, our misplaced hope will fail us sooner rather than later. But when we put all our confidence in God, we have assured peace.

Instead of running *away* from the king, Daniel went directly *to* him. With boldness and confidence in God, Daniel interceded for all the wise men and asked for some extra time that he might be able to tell the king the interpretation of his dream. Daniel 2:17-19 is so important that I think it is worth it for us to read this passage one more time. It reads:

> Then Daniel went to his house, and made the decision known to Hananiah, Mishael, and Azariah, his companions, that they might seek mercies from the God of heaven concerning this secret, so that Daniel and his companions might not perish with the rest of the wise men of Babylon. Then the secret was revealed to Daniel in a night vision. So Daniel blessed the God of heaven.

With impending death, Daniel went to his close friends and together they sought mercies from the God in heaven. While we know we deserve punishment for our sins, this passage fills us with hope because it reminds us that we can seek and receive mercies from God. No matter how we have sinned, God does not want to destroy us. On the contrary, He wants to pour out His mercy on us as we seek Him. That is why Daniel turned to God at that time. Dr. Coleman Luck comments: "His [Daniel's] next act was not to go to the library to consult books on the interpretation of dreams. He did not even go to his friends for advice. Instead he called them to a prayer meeting. It is good to have praying friends! Those who walk closest to God still realize their need of much intercession."[8]

One night during the Civil War, a stranger came to the home of the famous pastor Henry Ward Beecher. When he knocked, Mrs. Beecher went to see who was there. Opening the door just a bit, she found a tall stranger covered in wraps up to his eyes against the cold weather. He asked to see Pastor Beecher but refused to give his name. Beecher's life had been threatened more than once during those days, so Mrs. Beecher closed the door and returned to their upstairs room, leaving the visitor standing in the cold. When Beecher learned that someone was at his door, he at once climbed down the stairs and welcomed the man into his home. Some time later, when her husband rejoined her in the bedroom, Mrs. Beecher learned that the muffled stranger was the President of the United States, Abraham Lincoln. He was facing a crisis and went to Beecher for much needed prayer.

Lincoln, much like Daniel, understood the only way he was going to overcome his problems would be through prayer. What about you? Where do you turn when things get rough? Do you seek mercies from heaven?

Daniel's Model in Prayer

When the situation seemed hopeless, Daniel turned to God in prayer. When his prayer was answered and it looked like Daniel's problems would be solved, what did Daniel do? He prayed some more. This time around, his prayer was not a petition but thanksgiving and praise. Take a look at the prophet's beautiful prayer in Daniel 2:20-23:

> Daniel answered and said: "Blessed be the name of God forever and ever, for wisdom and might are His. And He changes the times and the seasons; He removes kings and raises up kings; He gives wisdom to the wise and knowledge to those who have understanding. He reveals deep and secret things; He knows what is in the

59

darkness, and light dwells with Him. I thank You and praise You, O God of my fathers; You have given me wisdom and might, And have now made known to me what we asked of You, for You have made known to us the king's demand.

Daniel's prayer reminds us of God's power to change times, remove kings, and reveal secret things—things we need to understand. Daniel erupted in praise to his God! What about you? Do you regularly bring all your needs before God and praise Him for taking care of them?

Daniel's Interpretation about Future World Governments

The remainder of chapter two contains the outcome of God's intercession on behalf of Daniel and his friends. Arioch, the king's servant, quickly brought Daniel before the king (Daniel 2:24-25) because he knew the other wise men were being put to death due to the king's decree.

Before declaring God's revelation, Daniel humbly gave all the glory to the "God in Heaven" who had enlightened him and revealed the secret (Daniel 2:28-30). Daniel witnessed to the king! He was not afraid to speak up for Jehovah before a polytheistic pagan king.

He then proceeded to share something only God and Nebuchadnezzar himself would have known: the king had dreamed about a statue made out of different metals. What the king did not know was that the statue ultimately symbolized the decline of his own kingdom and God's sovereignty over the affairs of men (Daniel 2:31-33). Dr. John MacArthur writes:

Daniel lived 600 years before Christ, yet he outlined the course of history, even up to our lifetime. We shouldn't be shocked at that.

The Old Testament prophesied the destruction of Babylon (Isaiah 13:19-22), Egypt (Ezekiel 30:13-16), Tyre (Ezekiel 26:1-28:19), and Sidon (Ezekiel 28:21-23); and they were destroyed exactly as foretold. It also prophesied that a man named Cyrus would release Israel from captivity (Isaiah 45:1, 13), and about 200 years later he did (Ezra 1:1-4). One of the greatest proofs of the Bible's divine inspiration is fulfilled prophecy, because the prophecies are externally verified in human history.[9]

In the following verses, Daniel revealed the four future Gentile world governments that would dominate the earth until Christ's second coming. The image from Nebuchadnezzar's dream, with its four different metals, represented four world empires. The identities of three of these Gentile world empires are identified in Daniel. Daniel 2:38 identified Babylon as the head of gold, Daniel 5:28 identified the kingdom of the Medes and the Persians, and Daniel 8:21 referred to the Greece of Alexander the Great. After Alexander's death, Greece was divided into four different kingdoms (as prophesied in Daniel 8:22). The following chart makes the historical unfolding of Nebuchadnezzar's dream even clearer:

All these things were prophesied centuries before they happened. As the metals that constituted the statue progressively got worse, so these four empires progressively degenerated throughout history. But the chief end of this dream was to point to a final kingdom, one that will never deteriorate because Jesus Christ will be its king. May we be ready to join Christ when He returns to rule on earth with His righteousness!

Part	Material	Empire	Time Period
Head	Gold	Babylonian	606 BC – 539 BC
Chest/Arms	Silver	Medo-Persian	539 BC – 331 BC
Belly/Thighs	Bronze	Grecian	331 BC – 146 BC
Legs/Feet	Iron/Clay	Roman	146 BC – 476 AD

Discussion Questions

1. Why is it important to study biblical prophecy?

2. What did Jesus mean by "the times of the Gentiles" in Luke 21:24?

3. Why is it significant that a portion of Daniel 2 was written in Aramaic instead of Hebrew?

4. What was Daniel's response in light of the kings' decree to have all the wise men killed?

5. What does it mean to seek "mercies from God" during difficult times? How can you do that?

6. How do you usually react during crises? How did Daniel respond?

7. Briefly outline the king's dream. What were the four metals interpreted to represent?

That's Not All

You can find sermon outlines in the "Sermonars" section at the back of the book. These pages may be freely reproduced, either from the book or from the accompanying CD-ROM for any devotional or ministry use.

Chapter Five

Daniel's Dream: The Interpretation; The Colossal Results!

As we saw in the previous chapter, Nebuchadnezzar had a dream he could not understand, but God providentially placed a young man named Daniel in Babylon to faithfully serve Him in the midst of that ungodly society. Although the king's pagan wise men were unable to interpret his puzzling dream, Daniel sought the Lord in prayer, received special revelation from Him, and boldly declared the meaning of the dream to Nebuchadnezzar.

As we continue our journey through Daniel and take a closer look at the meaning of the image in Nebuchadnezzar's dream, keep in mind the setting of this passage. It was about 600 BC, and Daniel had been in Babylon for three years. This young man was preparing to tell the greatest monarch of his day what was going to take place in the centuries to come. Daniel declared the succession of armies and nations that would control the world after Babylon was long gone. He would declare to king Nebuchadnezzar the "times of the Gentiles" (Luke 21:24b), an era that began in 586 BC, when Nebuchadnezzar destroyed Jerusalem and the Jewish temple, and will end with the second coming of Jesus Christ, when the Gentile domination over Jerusalem will end.

Therefore, today we are living in the times of the Gentiles. Through Nebuchadnezzar's dream, God was foretelling human history between Nebuchadnezzar's time and the beginning of the Millennium, when

Christ will reign on earth. In other words, the king's dream was history pre-written, which, because of its broad temporal scope, makes Daniel 2 one of the most important prophecies in the Scriptures. Dr. J. Vernon McGee comments on this passage:

> We are in one of the great sections of the Word of God as far as prophecy is concerned. The multimetallic image (chapter 2), the four beasts (chapter. 7), and the seventy weeks of Daniel (chapter 9) form the backbone and ribs of biblical prophecy. You could never have a skeleton of prophecy without these passages of Scripture in the Old Testament.[1]

This is why so many believers are illiterate as far as biblical prophecy is concerned: they do not have a good understanding of these passages (Daniel 2, 7, and 9). Therefore, let us take the time to look carefully at the remaining portion of Daniel 2.

The Dream and the Interpretation

Read carefully Daniel 2:31–38, which contains the description of Nebuchadnezzar's dream and Daniel's initial interpretation (note the "we" in verse 36, indicating that the interpretation came from Daniel and from God Himself):

> You, O king, were watching; and behold, a great image! This great image, whose splendor was excellent, stood before you; and its form was awesome. This image's head was of fine gold, its chest and arms of silver, its belly and thighs of bronze, its legs of iron, its feet partly of iron and partly of clay. You watched while a stone was cut out without hands, which struck the image on its feet of iron and clay, and broke them in pieces. Then the iron, the clay, the bronze, the silver, and the gold were crushed together, and became like chaff from the summer threshing floors; the wind carried them away so that no trace of them was found. And the stone that struck the image became a great mountain and filled the whole earth. This is the dream. Now we will tell the interpretation of it before the king. You, O king, are a king of kings. For the God of heaven has given you a kingdom, power, strength, and glory; and wherever the children of men dwell, or the beasts of the field and the birds of

the heaven, He has given them into your hand, and has made you ruler over them all—you are this head of gold.

With God's help, Daniel was able to do what no one could: enter the king's mind and to discern the content of his dream. Not only that, but Daniel was also given the ability to explain what the image was all about! Dr. Arthur E. Bloomfield comments:

> The great world-empires mentioned by Daniel did not all cover exactly the same territory. The movement of empires was from east to west, each succeeding empire extending its domain farther toward the setting sun. But there was one piece of land which was in all the world empires—the land of Palestine. In fact, if all the land of the empires was put on a map, Palestine would be in the center. By degrees, Palestine fell into the hands of Babylon.[2]

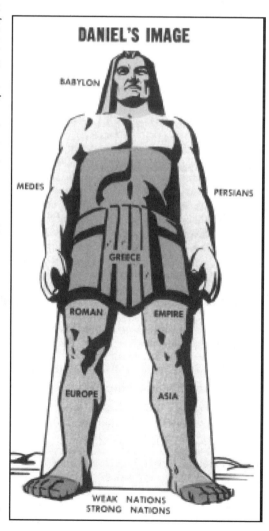

From the very beginning of his interpretation, where he identified the head of the statue as Nebuchadnezzar, Daniel made it clear that the image had to do with different empires that significantly impacted the world because of their power. That explains why in Daniel 2:37-44 the word "kingdom" appears nine times. According to Daniel's interpretation, the image represented Gentile world kingdoms. This is also confirmed by Daniel's use of

Aramaic (a Gentile language) to write this entire passage (as discussed in the previous chapter).

Gentile World Empires Symbolized and Identified

Before we proceed with the interpretation of Nebuchadnezzar's dream, this truth must be firmly planted in your mind (otherwise nothing will make sense): the four Gentile world empires symbolized by the great image fulfill "the Times of the Gentiles" Jesus referred to in Luke 21:24. Three of the four empires are identified in Daniel's prophecy. History accurately corroborates the biblical record and completes the fourth empire. The fourth empire, though not explicitly identified, is undeniably the Roman Empire.

Using the image as a symbol, Daniel proceeded to identify the four world kingdoms that constitute the times of the Gentiles. They are:

- Babylon (Daniel 2:36–38): The city of gold was also represented by a lion in Daniel 7.

- Medo-Persia (Daniel 5:28; 8:20): This dual kingdom was represented by a bear in Daniel 7.

- Greece (Daniel 8:20, 21): The Greeks were represented by a leopard in Daniel 7.

- Rome: suggested in Daniel 9:26 and symbolized as the fourth beast in Daniel 7.

Let us then take a closer look at each one of these four kingdoms and see what we can learn from each one of them:

1. The Babylonian Empire (606-539 BC): The Head of the Image–Gold

According to Daniel 2:32, the image's head was of fine gold. Therefore, the first world empire, without any question, was the Babylonian Empire. Daniel made this clear in Daniel 2:37, where he identified Nebuchadnezzar as the golden head. Nebuchadnezzar reigned in Babylon for forty-four years, between 605 and 561 BC. After his death, Nebuchadnezzar was succeeded by his son, Merodach, who after two years of wickedness was assassinated by his brother-in-law, Neriglissar, who in turn seized the throne, reigned for four years, and was killed in battle in 556 BC. Neriglissar's son, Laborosoarched, was beaten to death after having reigned for nine months.

Nabonidus, another son-in-law of Nebuchadnezzar, who had married the widow of Neriglissar, seized the throne and reigned for seventeen years. During that entire time, the Persians threatened to invade Babylon, a very well-fortified city, but kept waiting for the right opportunity. That happened while Nabonidus went on a military expedition and his son, Belshazzar (Daniel 5), a co-regent or "second ruler," was left in charge of the city of Babylon. Belshazzar conducted a drunken orgy, and the city fell to the Persians. With the death of Belshazzar, the Babylonian Empire ceased to exist. As the prophet Jeremiah predicted in Jeremiah 25:11, Babylonian dominance over Judah lasted for exactly seventy years. After that, all the great empires that followed were increasingly inferior in power and might to Babylon (as represented by the different metals found in the image).

2. The Medo-Persian Empire (539-331 BC): The Chest and the Arms–Silver

Daniel described the empire that would follow Babylon as the chest and the arms of silver (Daniel 2:32) and as a kingdom inferior to Nebuchadnezzar's (Daniel 2:39). He also recorded in advance the fall of Babylon and the transition of the kingdom to the Medo-Persians in Daniel 5:30–31, which reads: "That very night Belshazzar, king of the Chaldeans, was slain. And Darius the Mede received the kingdom, being about sixty-

two years old." Furthermore, the ram from Daniel 8:20 (with its two horns) was identified as the kings of Media and Persia, thus corresponding to the two arms of the statue in Daniel 2. While the Babylonian Empire was single-headed, the Medo-Persian Empire was a dual empire. The left arm of the image represented Media (the weaker kingdom), whereas the right arm represented Persia (the stronger kingdom).

This is how Babylon fell to the Medes and to the Persians: Cyzxares, king of the Medes (called "Darius" in Daniel 5:31) summoned to his aid his nephew Cyrus (of the Persian Empire) to defeat Babylon. By diverting the Euphrates River (which went through the city of Babylon), Cyrus' soldiers were able to have access to the river gates, since they were no longer protected by the waters of the Euphrates. In spite of Babylon's magnificent walls, Cyrus and his army were able to march into Babylon through the dried riverbed of the Euphrates. They slipped into the city on the night of the annual festival and overcame the Babylonians.

Cyrus is significant in the Scriptures for two reasons. First, the prophet Isaiah predicted that Cyrus would conquer Babylon 175 years before that happened! Isaiah 45:1-2 states: "Thus says the LORD to His anointed, to Cyrus, whose right hand I have held—to subdue nations before him and loose the armor of kings, to open before him the double doors, so that the gates will not be shut: 'I will go before you and make the crooked places straight; I will break in pieces the gates of bronze and cut the bars of iron." This is exactly how Cyrus penetrated the city of Babylon—the river gates were left open and the city was inattentive because of their drunken orgy festival. A wild party brought the city of Babylon down.

Second, Isaiah also prophesied 175 years earlier that Cyrus would issue a decree allowing the Jews to return to Jerusalem and give them the opportunity to rebuild the Jewish temple. Isaiah 44:27-28 states, "Who says to the deep, 'Be dry! And I will dry up your rivers'; who says of Cyrus, 'He is my shepherd, and he shall perform all my pleasure, saying to Jerusalem, You shall be built, and to the temple, your foundation shall be laid." This was also confirmed by Ezra in Ezra 6:3-5, which reads:

> In the first year of King Cyrus, King Cyrus issued a decree concerning the house of God at Jerusalem: "Let the house be rebuilt, the place where they offered sacrifices; and let the foundations of it be firmly laid, its height sixty cubits and its width sixty cubits, with three rows of heavy stones and one row of new timber. Let the ex-

penses be paid from the king's treasury. Also let the gold and silver articles of the house of God, which Nebuchadnezzar took from the temple which is in Jerusalem and brought to Babylon, be restored and taken back to the temple which is in Jerusalem, each to its place; and deposit them in the house of God."

After conquering Babylon in 539 BC, Cyrus, as an act of courtesy (since Media was the older of the two kingdoms), and because he had other military campaigns to finish, assigned the government of Babylon to his uncle, Darius, the king of Media, who ruled for two years. The Medo-Persia Empire was inferior to the Babylonian Empire in wealth, luxury, and magnificence, although its territory was larger. It is also interesting to note that when Nebuchadnezzar dreamed the dream of Daniel 2, Persia was only a Babylonian vassal state. Apart from divine revelation, Daniel would have had no political or military reasons to think that Persia would some day rule over Babylon.

Do you see how all these facts are so much more than meaningless historical facts? They bring to life the reliability of the Scriptures. The Bible is not a dusty book. It is God's very Word, inspired by His Holy Spirit and worthy of our reverence and trust! These are the kind of passages we should be sharing with those who are skeptical about the supernatural nature of the Scriptures.

3. The Grecian Empire (331-146 BC): The Belly and the Thighs—Bronze

Daniel identified the third empire in Daniel 2:32 as the belly and the thighs of the statue, which were made of bronze (cf. Daniel 2:39). The angel Gabriel also identified this empire in Daniel 8:21 as the male goat that destroyed the ram (the Medo-Persian Empire). Read closely Daniel 8:20-22, which states: "The ram which you saw, having the two horns—they are the kings of Media and Persia. And the male goat is the kingdom of Greece. The large horn that is between its eyes is the first king. As for the broken horn and the four that stood up in its place, four kingdoms shall arise out of that nation, but not with its power."

After a great battle in 331 BC, Alexander the Great conquered the Medo-Persians and became absolute lord of the Grecian Empire to an extent never attained by any of its previous kings. Alexander conquered cities with his bloodthirsty and lustful soldiers. He often murdered his own friends in drunken frenzies. He encouraged such excessive drinking among his followers that on one occasion twenty of them died as a result of their drunken binge. One day, Alexander drank six quarts of liquor and was seized with a violent fever of which he died eleven days later, on June 13, 323 BC. Alexander the Great conquered Egypt, part of Europe, and most of the land from Asia Minor to India—practically the entire known world—before he died in his early thirties.

Once again, keep in mind that in Nebuchadnezzar's time, the Greeks were a group of warring tribes. But even though Greece was unimportant at the time of Daniel 2, the prophecy was fulfilled and Greece eventually became a world power.

Dr. W. A. Criswell comments on the fact that the part of the statue that referred to Greece was made out of brass:

> It is easy to imagine what an astonishing impression the Greeks must have made on the civilized world. Consider the contrast between their soldiers and the soldiers of the Persian army. Had you seen a soldier of Media or Persia in the days when they controlled the civilized world, he would have looked like this: On his head would have been a soft, turban-like covering. He would have been clothed with a tunic with sleeves and with trousers full and long. That would have been the Medo-Persian soldier. But when you saw a Greek soldier, he would have had on his head a helmet of brass and on his body a breastplate of brass and before him he would be carrying a shield of brass. That is why the classic writers of ancient days referred to the "brazen coated Greeks." Brass became a sign and a symbol of Greek conquest and of the Greek empire.[3]

4. The Roman Empire (146 BC-AD 476): Legs–Iron; Feet–Part Iron, Part Clay

The fourth and final empire is described as the legs of iron, with its feet partly of iron and partly of clay (Daniel 2:33). Daniel 2:40-42 describes it in more detail. It reads:

> And the fourth kingdom shall be as strong as iron, inasmuch as iron breaks in pieces and shatters everything; and like iron that crushes, that kingdom will break in pieces and crush all the others. Whereas you saw the feet and toes, partly of potter's clay and partly of iron, the kingdom shall be divided; yet the strength of the iron

shall be in it, just as you saw the iron mixed with ceramic clay. And as the toes of the feet were partly of iron and partly of clay, so the kingdom shall be partly strong and partly fragile.

Daniel saw in the image a fourth Gentile empire that would be the biggest of all four empires—the Roman Empire, which was ruling over the world at the time of the birth of Christ. History tells us of "the iron legions" of Rome. Regarding Daniel 2:40, Leupold comments: "The Roman legions were noted for their ability to crush all resistance with an iron heel. There is apparently little that is constructive in the program of this empire in spite of Roman law and Roman roads and civilization, because the destructive work outweighed all else, for we have the double verb 'crush and demolish.'"[4]

In Daniel's day, iron was the strongest metal known to man. Likewise, the Roman Empire is without any question the strongest empire the world has ever known. The Babylonian Empire lasted 70 years and the Medo-Persian and Grecian Empires lasted not much longer than 200 years, but the Roman Empire lasted more than 500 years in the west (until AD 476) and more than 1,500 years in the east (until AD 1453). No empire has ever come close to its strength and endurance.

We know the legs of iron (v. 33) refer to the Roman Empire because it subdued what remained of the Greek Empire and was uniquely strong. It established itself as a world power during the first century before Christ and extended its territory even farther than Alexander's conquests.

But how can we know for sure this fourth empire is Rome? First, history clearly tells us that the Roman Empire took over after the fall of the Greeks. That is indisputable in any history book. No other world superpower existed after the Grecian Empire. Second, Daniel 9:26 also indicates that Rome was the fourth empire Daniel referred to. This verse reads: "And after the sixty-two weeks Messiah shall be cut off, but not for Himself; and the people of the prince who is to come shall destroy the city [Jerusalem] and the sanctuary [the Jewish temple]. The end of it shall be with a flood, and till the end of the war desolations are determined." We know that Jerusalem and the Jewish temple were destroyed by the Romans in AD 70. Third, we also know that the Antichrist is to be the last emperor or dictator of the revived Roman Empire (as seen later in the book of Daniel). Furthermore, the fact that the fourth empire is divided into "two legs" implies that it would be divided into two parts. The two legs of the statue indicate the natural division between the eastern and western ends of the empire. It is not surprising that this happened to the Roman Empire, which was divided in 364 AD into its "Eastern Division," with Constantinople as the capital, and its "Western Division," with Rome as the capital.

As was the case with the other empires, it is worth keeping in mind that when Nebuchadnezzar had his dream, Rome was only a village along the Tiber River. Apart from divine revelation, there was no way Daniel's interpretation could have been an "intelligent guess." There were almost 500 years between the day when Daniel interpreted the king's dream and Rome's appearance as a superpower. Thus, humanly speaking, Daniel had no reason whatsoever to predict that Rome would become the final great empire contained in the statue.

Consider the following quotations that describe very well the rise and the fall of the Roman Empire:

> The arms of the Republic, sometimes vanquished in battle, always victorious in war, advanced rapid steps to the Euphrates, the Danube, the Rhine, and the ocean; and the images of gold, or silver, brass, that might serve the nations and their kings, were successively broken by the iron monarchy of Rome.[5]

> No great world power follows Rome. The Roman Empire is the last, and it will be in existence in the latter days. Actually, it exists today. All of these other empires were destroyed by an enemy from the outside, but no enemy destroyed Rome. Attila the Hun came in and sacked the city, but he was so awestruck by what he saw that he realized he could not handle it. He took his barbarians and left town. The Roman Empire fell apart from within—no enemy destroyed it. Rome is living in the great nations of Europe today: Italy, France, Great Britain, Germany, and Spain are all part of the old Roman Empire. The laws of Rome live on, and her language also ... Her warlike spirit lives on also: Europe has been at war since the empire broke up into these kingdoms.[6]

> You see, the Roman Empire fell apart like Humpty Dumpty. There have been many men who tried to put it together again, but they have not succeeded. That was one of the missions of the Roman

Catholic Church at the beginning. Also, Charlemagne attempted to put it back together. Napoleon tried to do so, and also several emperors of Germany. Hitler and Mussolini attempted it, but so far the man has not yet appeared who will accomplish it. God is not quite ready for him to appear.[7]

The Revived Roman Empire–Future/Tribulation

The Scriptures make it clear that God is not through with the Roman Empire. As Dr. McGee pointed out above, a man will come some time in the future to reunite the Roman Empire. This man, the Antichrist himself, will also lead mankind in its final rebellion against God before the end of the world. Concerning the revived Roman Empire, Daniel 2:43 states, "As you saw iron mixed with ceramic clay, they will mingle with the seed of men; but they will not adhere to one another, just as iron does not mix with clay." Let us, then, take a closer look at this final empire that is key to all the end-times prophecies yet to be fulfilled.

Its Division

The final form of the Roman Empire will have a tenfold division, represented by the ten toes of the image. Daniel 2:41 makes this very clear by stating, ""Whereas you saw the feet and toes, partly of potter's clay and partly of iron, the kingdom shall be divided; yet the strength of the iron shall be in it, just as you saw the iron mixed with ceramic clay." Thus, the ten toes of the image and the ten kings indicate that the final form of the Roman Empire will be a ten-nation confederacy. Daniel 7:24 states, "The ten horns are ten kings who shall arise from this kingdom. And another shall rise after them; he shall be different from the first ones, and shall subdue three kings." This is also confirmed by Revelation 17:12: "The ten horns which you saw are ten kings who have received no kingdom as yet, but they receive authority for one hour as kings with the beast."

Its Dictator

The Bible tells us that out of the ten-nation confederacy there will arise one ruler, called the "little horn" in Daniel 7:8. He is also called "that man of sin... the son of perdition" (2 Thessalonians 2:3) and the "anti-christ" (I John 2:18). He will be a great world ruler who will put together the ten-nation coalition, which eventually will provoke the great battle of Armageddon. But once the ten-nation confederacy takes its form and the Antichrist establishes his rule, it will not be long until the prophetic stone smashes all opposition and fills the whole earth. That stone is none other than Jesus Christ.

The Stone Which Smashes the Image: Jesus Christ

Read closely the following verses about the stone that will smash man's wicked empires once and for all:

- Daniel 2:34-35, "You watched while a stone was cut out without hands, which struck the image on its feet of iron and clay, and broke them in pieces. Then the iron, the clay, the bronze, the silver, and the gold were crushed together, and became like chaff from the summer threshing floors; the wind carried them away so that no trace of them was found. And the stone that struck the image became a great mountain and filled the whole earth."

- Daniel 2:44-45, "And in the days of these kings the God of heaven will set up a kingdom which shall never be destroyed; and the kingdom shall not be left to other people; it shall break in pieces and consume all these kingdoms, and it shall stand forever. Inasmuch as you saw that the stone was cut out of the mountain without hands, and that it broke in pieces the iron, the bronze, the clay, the silver, and the gold—the great God has made known to the king what will come to pass after this. The dream is certain, and its interpretation is sure."

- Matthew 21:44, "And whoever falls on this stone will be broken; but on whomever it falls, it will grind him to powder."

The stone represents Jesus Christ, who will vanquish the image in one blow! Notice the sequence: this will not happen until after the formation of the ten toes. Whereas the legs of the image did not appear until AD 364, when the Roman Empire was divided into its Eastern and Western Divisions, the ten toes have not developed yet. But once again, the timetable for destruction is clear according to Daniel 2:44. Christ's coming, repeatedly mentioned in Scripture (see Zech 14:1-3; Joel 3:2, 9-16; Isa

34:1-8; Psalm 2), is going to be climactic, catastrophic, and cataclysmic. When Christ came to earth for the first time, he was lowly like a lamb; in His Second Coming, Jesus will be a lion, ready to take charge and rule over the Earth.

What Should Our Response Be?

So what should our response be in light of these awesome prophecies? First, we should have a response of worship and awe—just like Nebuchadnezzar. Daniel 2:46 beautifully describes that pagan king's worshipful response: "Then King Nebuchadnezzar fell on his face, prostrate before Daniel, and commanded that they should present an offering and incense to him. The king answered Daniel, and said, 'Truly your God is the God of gods, the Lord of kings, and a revealer of secrets, since you could reveal this secret.'" Isn't this truly amazing? The powerful Nebuchadnezzar knelt before his Jewish servant because he realized Daniel represented the only true God who controls all the events of human history. Even Nebuchadnezzar could not help but worship God in light of His sovereignty.

Second, we should have a response of trust and peace. After all, the same God who controls all the nations of this world is also overseeing our lives. There is no need to fear what people can do to us or to let our circumstances steal our peace. Because our loving and merciful God is in charge of everything, we can trust Him! We have the confidence that even if we go through the fire, God will be with us there (cf. Daniel 3:24-25).

Why Daniel Was Promoted in the Babylonian Kingdom

What was the outcome of Daniel's dependence on God? The king promoted him in the Babylonian kingdom. But Daniel was not only faithful to God, he was also faithful to his three friends. He remembered them and sought their promotion. Take a look at Daniel 2:48-49:

> Then the king promoted Daniel and gave him many great gifts; and he made him ruler over the whole province of Babylon, and chief administrator over all the wise men of Babylon. Also Daniel petitioned the king, and he set Shadrach, Meshach, and Abed-Nego over the affairs of the province of Babylon; but Daniel sat in the

gate of the king.

Ultimately, Daniel was promoted because he was a truthful follower of God. It took courage for him to stand before Nebuchadnezzar and tell him that his kingdom was not going to last and that, in fact, others were coming after him. As we continue to learn more about Daniel, may the Lord stir our spirits so that He will develop in our lives those same traits that made Daniel a committed servant of God.

Discussion Questions

1. How was Daniel able to interpret the king's dream? What process did he go through before interpreting it?

2. Has God ever empowered you to do something you could not have done by yourself? What happened?

3. What Gentile empires made up the statue Nebuchadnezzar had dreamed about?

4. How do we know what empire each segment of the statue represented?

5. What do Nebuchadnezzar's dream and Daniel's interpretation teach you about God?

6. Who is the stone that smashed the statue? How will He do that?

7. What should be our response to the prophecy of Daniel 2?

8. What were the results of Daniel's interpretation?

That's Not All

You can find sermon outlines in the "Sermonars" section at the back of the book. These pages may be freely reproduced, either from the book or from the accompanying CD-ROM for any devotional or ministry use.

Chapter 6

Why God Allows Severe Trials

As you read this chapter, you or someone you love may be experiencing some incredible trials. At times, we tend to think that once we become Christians, we will no longer experience difficulties. Yet many times it seems we have more trials after becoming Christians than before we made a commitment to follow Jesus. Sometimes it just does not make sense. Doesn't God want to provide us with a good life? Why do things seem to get harder when we are trying so hard to obey Him? Yet God, for some reason, allows all kinds of problems to come into our lives.

For some, this means family problems. Perhaps you are a godly parent who has worked hard to raise God-fearing children, yet your children seem to have wandered away from God. For some it is financial problems. Why does it seem like money comes so easily to some but others always seem to struggle financially? Others have lost loved ones or close friends to death. Perhaps you have had to stand by and watch as some of the godliest people you have known have had their lives brought to a premature close. The ache of death abides for many months and years after someone dies. We ask, "Why did God let that happen to this person?" or "How could God take this person whom I love so much away from me?" Still others struggle with emotional problems. They cannot sleep at night. Maybe they wrestle with the pain of depression.

In this chapter, we will uncover some truths that have the potential to be life-changing as we seek to answer the question, "Why does God allow such severe trials in our lives?" I have had many trials in my life. As

I look back on them now, I can say that they were some of the greatest things that ever happened to me. However, I must be honest: they were also the toughest and most difficult times I have ever experienced. I can remember several times when I literally thought, "My ministry is over!" This was not because of some crazy thing I did, but the result of internal struggles I was facing. In those times, I remember looking up to heaven and saying, "God, why are you allowing this in my life?"

The Image in the Desert–Daniel 3:1-7

Before we begin our exposition of Daniel 3, let us take a moment to review the background and set the context. It is always dangerous just to pick up the Bible and start reading without first considering the context of the passage. This is, unfortunately, how many cults have been started; their founders took verses out of context and missed the pure, biblical truth.

In chapter two of his book, Daniel interpreted Nebuchadnezzar's dream concerning the giant statue made from different materials. Daniel had been summoned to interpret the dream because none of the other wise men or diviners could determine what it meant. In the previous chapter, we described in detail how the statue and its composition represented four world empires (Babylon, Assyria, Greece, and Rome). Additionally, we saw how history unfolded exactly as Daniel prophesied it would. At the end of chapter two, Nebuchadnezzar praised Daniel's God for allowing Daniel to understand the dream.

However, as we will see later in the book, the king's praise was only temporary. Nebuchadnezzar was still a long way from truly believing in the God of Israel. Many of us live our lives much like Nebuchadnezzar. We call out to God when we are in a foxhole with bombs dropping all around us. However, we forget all about God when things are going our way. We think we can handle it on our own. We will see in this study of Daniel that true faith is much more than "foxhole religion."

This study brings us to the third chapter of the book of Daniel. How much time has passed between the events of chapter two and those of chapter three? The Greek translation of the Old Testament, the Septuagint, adds that this event happened in the 18th year of Nebuchadnezzar. This is fifteen years after Daniel interpreted the dream correctly to the king. Daniel would have been about thirty-five years of age, and Nebuchadnezzar was back to his old polytheistic ways! Interestingly, Daniel is not mentioned even a single time in chapter three. It is likely that during this time he was gone on the king's business. However, who we do see in chapter three are Daniel's three friends: Shadrach, Meshach, and Abed-Nego. These men, who have just been briefly mentioned earlier in the book, are now the central figures in chapter three.

Daniel 3 opens with a description of an image made by Nebuchadnezzar:

> Nebuchadnezzar the king made an image of gold, whose height was sixty cubits and its width six cubits. He set it up in the plain of Dura, in the province of Babylon. And King Nebuchadnezzar sent word to gather together the satraps, the administrators, the governors, the counselors, the treasurers, the judges, the magistrates, and all the officials of the provinces, to come to the dedication of the image which King Nebuchadnezzar had set up. So the satraps, the administrators, the governors, the counselors, the treasurers, the judges, the magistrates, and all the officials of the provinces gathered together for the dedication of the image that King Nebuchadnezzar had set up; and they stood before the image that Nebuchadnezzar had set up. Then a herald cried aloud: "To you it is commanded, O peoples, nations, and languages, that at the time you hear the sound of the horn, flute, harp, lyre, and psaltery, in symphony with all kinds of music, you shall fall down and worship the gold image that King Nebuchadnezzar has set up;" and whoever does not fall down and worship shall be cast immediately into the midst of a burning fiery furnace." So at that time, when all the people heard the sound of the horn, flute, harp, and lyre, in symphony with all kinds of music, all the people, nations, and languages fell down and worshiped the gold image which King Nebuchadnezzar had set up (Daniel 3:1-7).

Exactly how large and impressive was this image that Nebuchadnezzar constructed? Consider these points:

- Since a cubit was 18–22 inches long, 60 cubits high by 6 cubits across translates into 90–110 feet tall (the size of a 10-story building) and only 9–11 feet wide.

- The statue was a gold replica of Nebuchadnezzar himself or possibly a replica of the great image Nebuchadnezzar dreamed about in chapter two, except this statue was all gold.

- Since this huge statue was made of gold; it shone in the sun for miles!

Additionally, Dr. Donald K. Campbell notes, "The image was erected in the 'plain of Dura, in the province of Babylon' (3:1). The word '*dura*' is still common in the Mesopotamian region and simply means 'walled place.' Just six miles south of ancient Babylon is a place called by this name where archeologists have identified a large brick construction, forty-five feet square and twenty feet high, as the base or pedestal for the image."1 To put these figures in perspective, consider the Statue of Liberty: the Statue of Liberty is 111 feet tall, excluding its base. The image that Nebuchadnezzar constructed (over a period of several years) was 90-110 feet tall, excluding the base! Oddly, the ratio of the statue width to height was 1 to 10; most statues are built to a 1 to 5 ratio (like human beings). Therefore, this statue was very tall and very narrow.

However, the most striking feature of the statue was not its height, but its adornment. The image was covered entirely in gold! It is unlikely that it was solid gold. Archeology reveals that most Babylonian architecture had a hardwood base covered with other substances. Whether it was solid gold or not, it shone in the sun for miles. McGee writes, "Babylon was situated on a plain, surrounded by flat country. Although it was a city of skyscrapers for its day, the sheer height of the image made it visible for a great distance. The plain of Dura was like an airport—flat and expansive—allowing a great multitude to assemble for worship of the image, actually the worship of the king."2 Moreover, the image's dimensions are all in 6's, thus representing the Antichrist. Revelation 13:18, "Here is wisdom. Let him who has understanding calculate the number of the beast, for it is the number of a man: his number is 666."

Nebuchadnezzar built the statue of himself most likely as a model of the image he had seen in his dream. Clearly, he was vacillating between religions. He got just enough out of religion to confuse it. If you get just a little bit of faith without a proper foundation, you do not have anything at all.

Disobedience in Allegiance to God—Daniel 3:8-18

As we move onto the next section of chapter three, notice the disobedience of the three Hebrews to the king's command due to their allegiance to God. This is proper civil disobedience illustrated for us in Scripture. Look at verses 8-18:

> Therefore at that time certain Chaldeans came forward and accused the Jews. They spoke and said to King Nebuchadnezzar, "O king, live forever! You, O king, have made a decree that everyone who hears the sound of the horn, flute, harp, lyre, and psaltery, in symphony with all kinds of music, shall fall down and worship the gold image; and whoever does not fall down and worship shall be cast into the midst of a burning fiery furnace. There are certain Jews whom you have set over the affairs of the province of Babylon: Shadrach, Meshach, and Abed-Nego; these men, O king, have not paid due regard to you. They do not serve your gods or worship the gold image which you have set up." Then Nebuchadnezzar, in rage and fury, gave the command to bring Shadrach, Meshach, and Abed-Nego. So they brought these men before the king. Nebuchadnezzar spoke, saying to them, "Is it true, Shadrach, Meshach, and Abed-Nego, that you do not serve my gods or worship the gold image which I have set up? Now if you are ready at the time you hear the sound of the horn, flute, harp, lyre, and psaltery, in symphony with all kinds of music, and you fall down and worship the image which I have made, good! But if you do not worship, you shall be cast immediately into the midst of a burning fiery furnace. And who is the god who will deliver you from my hands?" Shadrach, Meshach, and Abed-Nego answered and said to the king, "O Nebuchadnezzar, we have no need to answer you in this matter. If that is the case, our God whom we serve is able to deliver us from the burning fiery furnace, and He will deliver us from your hand, O king. But if not, let it be known to you, O king, that we do not serve your gods, nor will we worship the gold image which you have set up."

Notice that the passage records at the beginning: "certain Chaldeans came forward and accused the Jews." Anti-Semitism is nothing new. However, God preserves his people. Throughout history, from Pharaoh to

Hitler, world leaders have tried to destroy the Jews, but they have never succeeded! We ought to love every Jewish person on this planet, whether they are believers or not, because they are God's chosen people.

Imagine this for a moment: Nebuchadnezzar has been waiting for years for this image to be complete. Now, the day has finally arrived when everyone will bow down to the statue and worship him—everyone except for three courageous men of God! This is why he was so incensed when they refused to bow; they were spoiling his big day. These three men stood out like a sore thumb among the 300,000 people who bowed before the image. They were the only ones not bowing. The question we must ask ourselves as we look at the end of the passage is, "Are we willing to take a stand for truth and for what we believe the way these men did?" Not only did they stand up, but they stood in front of hundreds of thousands of people who were gathered on the plain of Dura. What are we like at our jobs? When everyone is gathered around laughing at a dirty story, are we the kind of people who politely excuse ourselves? When someone is at a computer terminal with a pornographic website on the screen, do we take a stand for the Lord and politely leave that cubicle? When we discover money that is not ours and have the opportunity to take it without anyone knowing, what do we do? Do we put it in our pockets or do we seek to return it to whom it belongs? Are we honest when we complete our tax returns?

Read carefully what Dr. Geoffrey King writes about this passage:

> This is a great story. It would be three out of about 300,000. Are you loyal enough to Jesus Christ to stand alone or be one of such a pitiful minority as that? And why didn't they bow down? Why not? "When in Rome do as Rome does." When in Babylon do as Babylon does; you must not bring all the Jerusalem prejudices to Babylon. You know, they could have easily said: "Babylon has been very good to us and we have good positions in Babylon, and it won't do any harm to bow down to this image." Why not?[3]

We know that we are really real with Jesus when we are faced with the opportunity to sin but choose righteousness and obedience. However, we must make up our minds beforehand to obey because every moment we are unsure about what we should do, we will very likely fall. This is what is wrong with many of us! We have not made up our minds about whom we will serve (cf. Daniel 1:8).

Why God Allows Trial: The Fiery Furnace–Daniel 3:19-25

What happened to Shadrach, Meshach, and Abed-Nego? Let us read on and find out:

> Then Nebuchadnezzar was full of fury, and the expression on his face changed toward Shadrach, Meshach, and Abed-Nego. He spoke and commanded that they heat the furnace seven times more than it was usually heated. And he commanded certain mighty men of valor who were in his army to bind Shadrach, Meshach, and Abed-Nego, and cast them into the burning fiery furnace. Then these men were bound in their coats, their trousers, their turbans, and their other garments, and were cast into the midst of the burning fiery furnace. Therefore, because the king's command was urgent, and the furnace exceedingly hot, the flame of the fire killed those men who took up Shadrach, Meshach, and Abed-Nego. And these three men, Shadrach, Meshach, and Abed-Nego, fell down bound into the midst of the burning fiery furnace. Then King Nebuchadnezzar was astonished; and he rose in haste and spoke, saying to his counselors, "Did we not cast three men bound into the midst of the fire?" They answered and said to the king, "True, O king." "Look!" he answered, "I see four men loose, walking in the midst of the fire; and they are not hurt, and the form of the fourth is like the Son of God."

One scholar reports that temperatures in these kilns could reach 1,000 C (1,800 F)![4] Another scholar writes, "One could only imagine the fear that engulfed the crowd as flames leap from the top of the furnace and the smoke billowed forth."[5] We see something very important in this passage. If you listen to the "name-it-and-claim-it" crowd, they will tell you that if you just get right with Jesus, God will bless you and make everything wonderful for you. Were Shadrach, Meshach, and Abed-Nego right with God? Yes! Did God make it really wonderful for them? Not exactly how we would expect Him to. God loved them so much that He tested them. Even when they were being thrown into the fiery furnace, Shadrach, Meshach, and Abed-Nego had no idea God was going to protect them. Why does God put us in the furnace? Why does he allow these trials to manifest themselves in our lives?

Reasons God Sends You Trials

Trials and temptations are two different things. Temptations are when we are seeking after sin. Trials are those unique situations in our lives when we are doing what we are supposed to be doing and things do not add up; problems come instead of blessings. There are four reasons why God sends trials into our lives. These are four answers to the question, "Why does God allow severe trials?"

1. *To reveal the genuineness of your faith.* Trials build our faith. Peter writes in his first epistle, "In this you greatly rejoice, though now for a little while, if need be, you have been grieved by various trials, that the genuineness of your faith, being much more precious than gold that perishes, though it is tested by fire, may be found to praise, honor, and glory at the revelation of Jesus Christ" (1 Peter 1:6). When we obey God in good times, we prove little about our faith; however, it is when we continue to obey even when our world seems to be collapsing all around us that the true character of our faith is revealed. The enemies of Shadrach, Meshach, and Abed-Nego were burned up. Daniel 3:22 says, "Therefore, because the king's command was urgent, and the furnace exceedingly hot, the flame of the fire killed those men who took up Shadrach, Meshach, and Abed-Nego." Only the ropes used to bind the three men burned up in the furnace.

2. *To remind us that our eternal home is in heaven, not here.* We can tend to get very comfortable here on earth. As believers, we are not supposed to feel at home apart from heaven. God has us on a mission. We are not supposed to just coast through life! We are to reach the world with the gospel! God has a plan to use us in ministry, but sometimes we get too comfortable to take notice. So sometimes God uses trials to get our attention, to put our focus right again! C.S. Lewis wrote in his wonderful book *The Problem of Pain*, "God whispers to us in our pleasures, speaks in our conscience, but shouts in our pains: it is His megaphone to rouse a deaf world."[6]

3. *Trials are not the consequences of disobedience to God.* Some so called "trials" are the result of a person's own disobedience and sin. But the truth is that these people are not in trial; they are in the consequences of their own sin, and they are misinterpreting these consequences as trials. If you have inherited the consequences of your sin, do not call that a trial. Instead, ask God if there is some area of compromise in your life.

4. *To attract people to Jesus Christ because of His grace,* which is evident in our lives through the supernatural strength and peace we experience while suffering. Why does God let some people suffer with health issues they cannot prevent or cure? He does this so that other people will see His strength and grace in their lives and be brought to a saving knowledge of Jesus Christ.

Trials Demonstrate God's Greatness—Daniel 3:26-30

Observe how Nebuchadnezzar's perspective is completely changed by God's faithfulness to Shadrach, Meshach, and Abed-Nego in Daniel 3:26-30:

Then Nebuchadnezzar went near the mouth of the burning fiery furnace and spoke, saying, "Shadrach, Meshach, and Abed-Nego, servants of the Most High God, come out, and come here." Then Shadrach, Meshach, and Abed-Nego came from the midst of the fire. And the satraps, administrators, governors, and the king's counselors gathered together, and they saw these men on whose bodies the fire had no power; the hair of their head was not singed nor were their garments affected, and the smell of fire was not on them. Nebuchadnezzar spoke, saying, "Blessed be the God of Shadrach, Meshach, and Abed-Nego, who sent His Angel and delivered His servants who trusted in Him, and they have frustrated the king's word, and yielded their bodies, that they should not serve nor worship any god except their own God! Therefore I make a decree that any people, nation, or language which speaks anything amiss against the God of Shadrach, Meshach, and Abed-Nego shall be cut in pieces, and their houses shall be made an ash heap; because there is no other God who can deliver like this." Then the king promoted Shadrach, Meshach, and Abed-Nego in the province of Babylon.

If we respond the way God wants us to when we go through trials, we will grow in Him. The first step in a right response to trial is thanksgiving. When we are facing a trial in our lives, we need to thank God for that trial and what He is going to do in and through us as we remain faithful to Him through it. Second, we must commit the trial to the Lord. How do we know when we have committed it to the Lord? We take our hands off of it!

In spite of what we see in this passage, we will discover in Daniel 4 that Nebuchadnezzar is still not converted, although he sounds like he is after seeing God intervene for these three Jewish young men. There are many of us who have a very shallow interpretation of what it means to be a Christian. We think that if someone shows up at church and says he likes God, then he is a Christian. However, this is simply not the case. You can get close to the truth and feel God working and yet not be converted. There are legions of people like this in the church today.

As we close this chapter, reflect on the words of Dr. M. R. DeHaan:

> But beyond the prophetic lesson, there is also a most comforting lesson for every believer here. To all who will stand firm for their faith in God and the Lord Jesus Christ, there is also the promise of persecution. It has ever been thus. No saint in any age of history has ever been popular with the world. If you and I are going to stand for what we believe to be the truth of God, and refuse to be swayed from it no matter what the cost, we too shall find that the world is no friend to grace. And in the measure that we dare to stand true for God and be on fire for Christ, in that measure we shall suffer persecution.[7]

May we embrace the honor of suffering for our Master's sake (cf. Phil 1:29).

Discussion Questions

1. Why is it foolish to think that when we become believers we will no longer have any problems?

2. Having studied this chapter, how would you answer someone who asked, "Why did God let that happen to this person?"

3. What is "foxhole religion"? Do we as Christians sometimes struggle with this?

4. What are subtle ways that you draw attention to yourself and your accomplishments? What sin is at the root of this behavior? What practical way we can combat it?

5. Give real-life examples of situations where one ought to disobey the government. How does Romans 13:1–5 fit it to your understanding of civil disobedience?

6. What are practical ways/situations where we can graciously and winsomely take a stand for truth at work? At school? In politics? In ethical issues?

7. C. S. Lewis said, "God whispers to us in our pleasures, speaks in our conscience, but shouts in our pains: it is His megaphone to rouse a deaf world." How does God use pain as a megaphone to rouse a deaf world?

8. What is the difference between trials and consequences for sin in our lives? How can we tell the difference when we are in the midst of difficult circumstances?

9. What practical steps should we take if we determine that the difficulty we are facing is the result of disobedience?

That's Not All

You can find sermon outlines in the "Sermonars" section at the back of the book. These pages may be freely reproduced, either from the book or from the accompanying CD-ROM for any devotional or ministry use.

Daniel

Chapter Seven

When and How God Brings a Man Down

One of the saddest and most embarrassing stories in the history of evangelicalism is the fall of Jim and Tammy Bakker and of their PTL (Praise The Lord) Ministry. Supported by 500,000 donors, Jim Bakker raised more than $500 million in the last ten years of PTL. However, all was not well at the ministry. Reporter Charles Shepard received a Pulitzer Prize for his 635-page book titled *Forgiven*, which looked deep into the arrogance and spiritual disarray of Bakker's life, Jim's affair with Jessica Hahn, the hush money, and the ministry's shallow approach to feel-good Christianity.[1]

Ten years before Bakker fell, Christian Broadcaster Pat Robertson rather cryptically wrote Jim Bakker a letter, dated September 15, 1977. It read, "Jim, God does not bless falsehood, and the Bible says he resists the proud... unless you face reality and ask God's forgiveness, He is going to bring you down. God is speaking to you through all the things that are happening. I pray you will get the message." Unfortunately, however, Bakker did not get the message, and the Christian community received irreparable harm from his life of indulgence and compromise. God brought this man down, and pride was a significant factor in the cause of Bakker's demise.

The sad fate of the Bakkers reminds us of what happened to Jimmy Swaggart, first cousin to rock-and-roll pioneer Jerry Lee Lewis, who was born in a sharecropping town in rural Louisiana. By 1987, he was one of the most popular television preachers in the world, with a weekly television audience of 2.1 million in the United States and a worldwide audience of 500 million in 143 countries. Sadly, however, in a sleazy motel west of New Orleans, Jimmy's life and ministry were destroyed. Pride brought Jimmy Swaggart down. We must always remember this truth: Where there is sin, there is always pride. Pride is at the very core of sin; it says, "I will do it my way, and I don't care what God says."

As we examine Daniel chapter four, we see two majestic themes unfold before us. Let us explore them together below.

Two Majestic Themes of Daniel Chapter Four

1. The sovereignty and absolute control of God

The sovereignty and absolute control of God are found on every page of the book of Daniel. Consider these verses:

- Daniel 4:17b, "In order that the living may know that the Most High rules in the kingdom of men, gives it to whomever He will, and sets over it the lowest of men."

- Daniel 4:25b, "...till you know that the Most High rules in the kingdom of men, and gives it to whomever He chooses."

- Daniel 4:32, "...until you know that the Most High rules in the kingdom of men, and gives it to whomever He chooses."

- Daniel 4:35, "All the inhabitants of the earth are reputed as nothing; He does according to His will in the army of heaven and among the inhabitants of the earth. No one can restrain His hand or say to Him, 'What have You done?'"

God is in control! Daniel tells us clearly that God is in control of nations and leaders. God is working in the world! What about terrorism and war? God is in control of it all. Nothing happens by chance or accident.

2. Pride brings any man or woman down

The second majestic theme we find in chapter four is that pride brings any man or woman down! We must remind ourselves of this frequently.

Look at what God has to say about pride in His word:

- Daniel 4:37, "Now I, Nebuchadnezzar, praise and extol and honor the King of heaven, all of whose works are truth, and His ways justice. And those who walk in pride He is able to put down."

- Proverbs 6:16, "These six things the LORD hates, yes, seven are an abomination to Him: A proud look, a lying tongue, hands that shed innocent blood..." Notice what is at the top of the list of things God hates: pride.

- Proverbs 8:13, "The fear of the LORD is to hate evil; pride and arrogance and the evil way and the perverse mouth I hate."

- Proverbs 11:2, "When pride comes, then comes shame; but with the humble is wisdom."

- Proverbs 16:5, "Everyone proud in heart is an abomination to the LORD; though they join forces, none will go unpunished."

- Proverbs 16:18, "Pride goes before destruction, and a haughty spirit before a fall."

- Proverbs 21:4, "A haughty look, a proud heart, and the plowing of the wicked are sin."

- Proverbs 29:23, "A man's pride will bring him low, but the humble in spirit will retain honor."

- Isaiah 48:11b, "I will not give My glory to another."

- James 4:6, "God resists the proud, but gives grace to the humble."

This was Nebuchadnezzar's problem: he was proud! He was an evil man in God's sight. He wanted to be known by men. He was power hungry. Many of Nebuchadnezzar's actions were very similar to those of Saddam Hussein. On January 29, 2003, President George W. Bush declared in his State of the Union address:

> The dictator who is assembling the world's most dangerous weapons has already used them on whole villages, leaving thousands of his own citizens dead, blind or disfigured. Iraqi refugees tell us how forced confessions are obtained: by torturing children while their parents are made to watch. International human rights groups have

catalogued other methods used in the torture chambers of Iraq: electric shock, burning with hot irons, dripping acid on the skin, mutilation with electric drills, cutting out tongues, and rape. If this is not evil, then evil has no meaning.[2]

As we look at Daniel 4, we see a king who was very much like Saddam Hussein. Nebuchadnezzar was known to kill people on the spot and to do whatever came to his mind. But lest we become too self-righteous when talking about such evil men, let us not forget the condition of our own hearts. It is easy to condemn men like Nebuchadnezzar and Saddam Hussein; however, what brought them down, what brought them to a place of despicable evil is the same thing that will bring us down: pride!

We must always be on guard against pride in our lives, lest we fall like so many others have. The height of pride in our lives is when we say to God, either by our word or by our actions, "God, I don't want you to run my life. I'm going to do what I want when I want!"

But change is possible. By God's grace, we do not have to remain enslaved to our destructive pride. That is exactly what happened to Nebuchadnezzar. J. Vernon McGee has insightfully noted:

This is Nebuchadnezzar's marvelous testimony, and it shows de-

Nebuchadnezzar's Pride
With pride, Nebuchadnezzar exclaimed: "Is not this great Babylon, that I have built...by the might of my power, and for the honor of my majesty?" Daniel 4:30.

velopment in the faith of this man. Back in Daniel 3:29 he issued a decree and expressed a conviction. Here he gives a personal testimony. There it was a decree; here it is a decision. There it was conviction, and here it is conversion. Chronologically, this testimony should come at the end of this chapter because it grew out of his experience recorded here.[3]

Dr. Gordan Lindsay helps us put the events of Daniel 4 in perspective. He writes, "The conversion of Nebuchadnezzar is one of the most amazing cases in the Bible. In a way it exceeds that of Saul of Tarsus. Saul had a religious background, but Nebuchadnezzar, the world's most powerful man, was a heathen king. We must regard his conversion largely as the result of Daniel's prayers."[4] Gifted Bible scholar and pastor John MacArthur comments on this passage, writing, "In Daniel 4 we see what I believe is Nebuchadnezzar's conversion to faith in the true God. Some commentators have appropriately titled the chapter 'The Conversion of Nebuchadnezzar.' It relates how God broke his pride by humbling him and then turning his heart toward Him in faith. God did so, in part, through another dream."[5]

Dr. William Keith Hatfield rightly observes:

> According to Jeremiah 29, Nebuchadnezzar roasted two of the Jews with fire. In 2 Kings 24 he imprisoned 18-year-old Jehoiakim for 36 years over some offense. In 2 Kings 25, he killed the sons of King Zedekiah and then put out his eyes so that that would be the last sight he ever saw. He was cruel, proud, mean, vindictive, fierce, and violent... and yet he believed; against all odds, he believed![6]

This is an excellent reminder that if the grace of God can reach Nebuchadnezzar, it can reach anyone.

Now that we have set the stage for the events of Daniel 4, let's turn our attention to the text itself. In this chapter, we will not only see how and when God brings a man down, but how He—in His wonderful grace—can restore him.

Witness of Nebuchadnezzar's Conversion—Daniel 4:1-3

As we look at these first three verses of chapter four, notice their content and where they are placed in the flow of events in the chapter:

Nebuchadnezzar the king, to all peoples, nations, and languages that dwell in all the earth: Peace be multiplied to you. I thought it good to declare the signs and wonders that the Most High God has worked for me. How great are His signs, and how mighty His wonders! His kingdom is an everlasting kingdom, and His dominion is from generation to generation. (Daniel 4:1-3)

These verses are actually separate from the main narrative we are about to explore. In these preliminary verses of chapter four, we see Nebuchadnezzar's total conversion! Nebuchadnezzar proclaimed his faith in an edict, a Babylonian state address! Speaking in a pagan language, this man proclaimed to all the land that Jehovah has changed his life. Therefore, we find that these three verses are actually a conclusion, not an introduction. The conviction behind these words that Nebuchadnezzar spoke grew out of the experience we find recorded in the rest of the chapter.

Many scholars including Wood, Young, Rushdoony, and Walvoord, believe that Nebuchadnezzar had a genuine salvation experience. However, not all scholars agree with this conclusion. For instance, Calvin, Keil, Pussey, and Archer think that the king's faith fell short. I am inclined to agree with those scholars in the former group rather than those in the latter. After the events of this chapter, Nebuchadnezzar is no longer the polytheistic, arrogant person that he was before he was brought to faith. He is a beautiful witness to the power and the grace of the Most High God. What happened in Nebuchadnezzar's life to bring him to a point of faith and truth in Jehovah? We find out as we explore the rest of chapter four.

Wild Nightmare–Daniel 4:4-12

I, Nebuchadnezzar, was at rest in my house, and flourishing in my palace. I saw a dream which made me afraid, and the thoughts on my bed and the visions of my head troubled me. Therefore I issued a decree to bring in all the wise men of Babylon before me, that they might make known to me the interpretation of the dream. Then the magicians, the astrologers, the Chaldeans, and the soothsayers came in, and I told them the dream; but they did not make known to me its interpretation. But at last Daniel came before me (his name is Belteshazzar, according to the name of my god; in him is the Spirit of the Holy God), and I told the dream before him, saying: "Belteshazzar, chief of the magicians, because I know that the Spirit of the Holy God is in you, and no secret troubles you, explain to me the visions of my dream that I have seen, and its interpretation. These were the visions of my head while on my bed: I was looking, and behold, a tree in the midst of the earth, and its height was great. The tree grew and became strong; its height reached to the heavens, and it could be seen to the ends of all the earth. Its leaves were lovely, its fruit abundant, and in it was food for all. The beasts of the field found shade under it, the birds of the heavens dwelt in its branches, and all flesh was fed from it" (Daniel 4:4–12).

In the early portions of this passage, it does not seem like Nebuchadnezzar is converted, because he is not. He is speaking historically, much as we do when we give our testimony. He is speaking of what was, not about what is. The Aramaic word (this portion of Daniel is written in Aramaic, not Hebrew) translated "rest" meant that Nebuchadnezzar was "free" from apprehension and fear. Additionally, the word translated "flourishing" means that his life was literally "growing green." Nebuchadnezzar was prospering, and he was at peace. He was the man at the top, without any worries.

It is important that we understand where these events fall on the timeline of the book of Daniel and in history. Nebuchadnezzar ruled forty-three years (605–562 BC) and following his seven-year period of insanity, he was restored to his throne for at least a few months. If we add two years to the seven years of insanity, it works out to be Nebuchadnezzar's thirty-fourth year as king. It has been thirty-two years since his first dream (2:1), which means that Daniel was now about forty-nine years of age. The great scholar Philip Newell points out:

Again, we must recognize this chapter [Daniel 4] to be prophetic as well as historic. In the seven-year derangement of Nebuchadnezzar which it forecasts and then relates, it is possible to see a foreshadowing of the bestiality and debasement under Antichrist which will at the end of the age characterize the Gentile nations, which are here symbolized by the Babylonian king. Earth's inhabitants (except, of course, those whose names are written in the book of life, see Rev. 13:8) will be spiritually insane and worship the beast and the dragon who gives him his "power, and his throne, and great authority" (Rev. 13:2). We are plainly told in 2 Thes. 2:11 that God Himself will "send them strong a delusion, that they should believe a lie." And this fearful doom engulfs them "because they received not the love of truth that they may be saved."[7]

What Dr. Newell points out so astutely is that there is both an initial application and also a prophetic forecasting to the seven years of the Tribulation period at the end of time.

Watchers–Daniel 4:13-15

> I saw in the visions of my head while on my bed, and there was a watcher, a holy one, coming down from heaven. He cried aloud and said thus: "Chop down the tree and cut off its branches, strip off its leaves and scatter its fruit. Let the beasts get out from under it, and the birds from its branches. Nevertheless leave the stump and roots in the earth, bound with a band of iron and bronze, in the tender grass of the field. Let it be wet with the dew of heaven, and let him graze with the beasts on the grass of the earth." (Daniel 4:13-15)

One of the unique features of Daniel is that we learn a great deal in this book about angels and how God uses them to accomplish His purposes. We see in this passage that the angel (i.e., the "watcher") is the one who issues God's judgment on Nebuchadnezzar. The moment the angel speaks, insanity falls on Nebuchadnezzar. The word translated "watcher" is actually the Hebrew word for "messenger" and is often translated "angel." The word literally means "one who is awake." This word is used in verses 13 and 17 and is employed to describe a class of heavenly beings known as "watchful ones," literally "ones who do not sleep." These angels are awake all the time, and they are constantly watching.

Every Christian has a guardian angel who is watching over him or her every moment. We know this because Hebrews 1:14 says, "Are they not all ministering spirits [angels] sent forth to minister for those who will inherit salvation?" These angels never sleep. When we go to bed, our angels are watching us; when we get up and drive to work, our angels are in the car with us. (I think some of us wear our angels out by the way we drive.) These "watchers" see all and tell all. Many believers today think that they can maintain secret lives away from the gaze of God. However, we do not have any privacy from God and His angels; they are always with us, watching over us. Psalm 139 tells us that we cannot escape from God's presence anywhere. Dr. McGee wrote:

> These watchers see all, hear all, and tell all. Many believers today think they can live in secret that they are not under the eye of God. We talk about wanting to enjoy our privacy, but if you want to know the truth, you and I haven't any privacy. Psalm 139:7-12 tells us that we cannot get away from God, no matter were we go. Secret sin on earth is open scandal up in heaven. His created intelligences know all about you.[8]

Dr. F. Bettex adds:

> How important is this look into the celestial government. Hence on high there are thrones from which watchmen and holy ones with immortal, searching eyes observe all our actions, being constantly concerned with the honor of God, equipped with wisdom to deliberate, gifted with divine power to intervene when the poor child of dust elevates himself too much to his own detriment and to that of others. Also now they watch and work invisibly, as sensed by men in great times, over countries and nations.[9]

We are not to pray to angels; they are servants of God, not gods themselves. However, there are angels that God uses to protect and watch over His people who will inherit salvation. It would be truly amazing if we could look into the spiritual realm and see all the angels that surround believers all over the Earth.

Watchful Eye and Will of God–Daniel 4:16-17

> Let his heart be changed from that of a man, let him be given the heart of a beast, and let seven times pass over him. 'This decision is by the decree of the watchers, and the sentence by the word of the holy ones, in order that the living may know that the Most High

rules in the kingdom of men, gives it to whomever He will, and sets over it the lowest of men' (Daniel 4:16-17).

Verse 17 teaches powerfully about the sovereignty of God. God gives leadership to whomever He pleases, even to the lowest of men. Did you know that God actually gives evil leaders to nations that are disobedient to Him?

In this chapter, we see the supremacy of God. He is over all! That is why I believe true biblical Christianity is not a subjective religion that allows us to do whatever we want! God is not a man; He is holy and separate from all sin; He is incalculably far above us, and He is working His plan in the world. The prophet Isaiah wrote, "Behold, the nations are as a drop in a bucket, and are counted as the small dust on the scales; look, He lifts up the isles as a very little thing. And Lebanon is not sufficient to burn, nor its beasts sufficient for a burnt offering. All nations before Him are as nothing, and they are counted by Him less than nothing and worthless" (Isa 40:15-17). Paul reiterates this same idea in Ephesians 1:11, "In Him also we have obtained an inheritance, being predestined according to the purpose of Him who works all things according to the counsel of His will."

You can always tell a mature Christian from an immature Christian by their view of God. When you have an exalted view of God and trust in Him and His sovereign control, your life reflects Christian maturity. The mature Christian is the one who has stepped into the yoke of Jesus Christ and found peace and rest in Him (Matthew 11:28-30). J. I. Packer says in his book *Knowing God* that when we trust God's sovereignty we can lay down on the couch of God's rest.[10]

Turn your attention again to the last phrase of verse 17, "and sets over it the lowest of men." God appoints evil and inept rulers over nations who have rebelled against Him and His Word. We see evil kings in the Northern Kingdom of Israel (every one of them was evil); in the Southern Kingdom only eight of nineteen could be considered reasonably "good." Why did the Northern Kingdom experience this procession of awful rulers? God placed those rulers over them because the people of Israel were in disobedience to God.

God permits some of the basest of men to reach positions of power. This is surprising to some, but consider Adolf Hitler. Over seventy percent of evangelical Christians in Germany voted for Hitler during his rise to power in the 1930s. Consider also Napoleon, who rose to power after the atheistic French Revolution. Consider Lenin and Stalin, who murdered 20 million Russians in the name of progress and utopia. Look at the United States—many of our elected officials in recent years have been anything but godly leaders. When the level of personal integrity in the leadership of a nation is lowered, the entire nation wanes.

Warning Given by a Grieved Daniel–Daniel 4:18-27

"This dream I, King Nebuchadnezzar, have seen. Now you, Belteshazzar, declare its interpretation, since all the wise men of my kingdom are not able to make known to me the interpretation; but you are able, for the Spirit of the Holy God is in you." Then Daniel, whose name was Belteshazzar, was astonished for a time, and his thoughts troubled him. So the king spoke, and said, "Belteshazzar, do not let the dream or its interpretation trouble you." Belteshazzar answered and said, "My lord, may the dream concern those who hate you, and its interpretation concern your enemies! The tree that you saw, which grew and became strong, whose height reached to the heavens and which could be seen by all the earth, whose leaves were lovely and its fruit abundant, in which was food for all, under which the beasts of the field dwelt, and in whose branches the birds of the heaven had their home—it is you, O king, who have grown and become strong; for your greatness has grown and reaches to the heavens, and your dominion to the end of the earth. And inasmuch as the king saw a watcher, a holy one, coming down from heaven and saying, 'Chop down the tree and destroy it, but leave its stump and roots in the earth, bound with a band of iron and bronze in the tender grass of the field; let it be wet with the dew of heaven, and let him graze with the beasts of the field, till seven times pass over him'; this is the interpretation, O king, and this is the decree of the Most High, which has come upon my lord the king: they shall drive you from men, your dwelling shall be with the beasts of the field, and they shall make you eat grass like oxen. They shall wet you with the dew of heaven, and seven times shall pass over you, till you know that the Most High rules in the kingdom of men, and gives it to whomever He chooses. And inasmuch as they gave the command to leave the stump and roots of the tree, your kingdom shall be assured to you, after you come to know that Heaven rules. Therefore, O king, let my advice be acceptable to you; break off your sins by being righteous, and your iniquities by showing mercy to the poor. Perhaps there may be a lengthening of your prosperity" (Daniel 4:18-27).

We see the character of Daniel in this passage. He did not proclaim God's message to Nebuchadnezzar like the paid preachers who commanded the people to bow down to the statue of Nebuchadnezzar in chapter three, but as a prophet and a man of God. This passage says Daniel was "appalled" (the Aramaic word literally means "astounded") by the horror of what Nebuchadnezzar's dream meant. Why? Because it concerned the king that Daniel had been witnessing to all those years!

Do you think that Daniel cared about Nebuchadnezzar and the state of his soul? I am sure he did. MacArthur notes, "Twenty-five or thirty years had passed since Daniel revealed and interpreted the king's first dream. It seems logical to conclude that Daniel, who was the prime minister of Babylon, told Nebuchadnezzar all he could about God in those intervening years. Daniel cared about him."[11] Daniel was not a prophet who received a vision of such horrible consequences with joy. He did not delight in the judgment that was about to come on Nebuchadnezzar; he was grieved. Is that our attitude when we find out someone we do not particularly care for is suffering? Is that the heart of Jesus? We are never commanded to hate sinners. We are called to show them the love of Jesus Christ. We need to beg God for a heart of compassion for the lost so that their fate grieves us just as Daniel's heart was grieved when he realized Nebuchadnezzar's fate.

In the latter part of chapter four, we see Nebuchadnezzar's fate: a weird insanity. Let us observe how God brought Nebuchadnezzar down.

Weird Insanity–Daniel 4:28-33

All this came upon King Nebuchadnezzar. At the end of the twelve months he was walking about the royal palace of Babylon. The king spoke, saying, "Is not this great Babylon, that I have built for a royal dwelling by my mighty power and for the honor of my majesty?" While the word was still in the king's mouth, a voice fell from heaven: "King Nebuchadnezzar, to you it is spoken: the kingdom has departed from you! And they shall drive you from men, and your dwelling shall be with the beasts of the field. They shall make you eat grass like oxen; and seven times shall pass over you, until you know that the Most High rules in the kingdom of men, and gives it to whomever He chooses." That very hour the word was fulfilled concerning Nebuchadnezzar; he was driven from men and ate grass like oxen; his body was wet with the dew of heaven till his hair had grown like eagles' feathers and his nails like birds' claws (Dan 4:28–33).

What happened to Nebuchadnezzar? What was wrong with him? A malady came over Nebuchadnezzar, perhaps similar to lycanthropy, a form of insanity which makes the patient think and act like he or she is a wolf. A similar disorder, kunanthropy, makes a patient think he is a dog and act like one. Biblical scholar R. K. Harrison recounted this personal experience:

A great many doctors spend an entire, busy professional career without once encountering an instance of the kind of monomania described in the Book of Daniel. The present writer, therefore, considers himself particularly fortunate to have actually observed a clinical case of lycanthropy in a British mental institution in 1946. The patient was in his early 20's who reportedly had been hospitalized for about five years. His symptoms were well developed on admission, and diagnosis was immediate and conclusive. He was of average height and weight with good physique, and was in excellent body health. His mental symptoms included pronounced antisocial tendencies, and because of this he spent the entire day from dawn to dusk outdoors, on the grounds of the institution... His daily routine consisted of wandering around the magnificent lawns which the otherwise dingy hospital situation was graced, and it was his custom to pluck up and eat handfuls of the grass as he went along. On observation he was seen to discriminate carefully between grass and weeds, and on inquiry from the attendant, the writer was told the diet of this patient consisted exclusively of grass from the hospital lawns. He never ate institutional food with other patients, his only drink was water... the writer was able to examine him cursorily, and the only physical abnormality noted consisted of a lengthening of the hair and a coarse, thickened condition of the finger-nails. Without institutional care, the patient would have manifested precisely the same physical conditions as those mentioned in Daniel 4:33 [of Nebuchadnezzar].[12]

The actions of Nebuchadnezzar are not an unknown psychological phenomenon. However, in his case, they were induced by God. Nebuchadnezzar, although warned, waited one year and did not repent! God graciously gave him time to repent, but Nebuchadnezzar wasted that time. The king who felt superior to other men sunk to a subhuman level!

Nebuchadnezzar had become obsessed with his own success and the city he had constructed. One author made these remarks about the city which the king had built:

[Babylon] was a vast city, four-square, 56 miles in circuit, with walls 350 feet high and 87 feet thick—wide enough for six chariots to race abreast. Herodotus, the ancient Greek historian, visited Babylon about 100 years after Nebuchadnezzar's time and was overwhelmed by its grandeur. Over 200 years later, Alexander the Great planned to make the city headquarters for his vast empire but died there at 32... the Ishtar Gate was 40 feet high... Nebu-

Babylon as it Appears Today
The great city of Babylon, once the pride of its rulers, and of the ancient world, now lies humbled in the dust of centuries.

chadnezzar had at least 3 palaces in Babylon. Most of the bricks taken out of Babylon in the archaeological excavations bear the... name and inscription of Nebuchadnezzar stamped on them. Babylon was 60 miles in circumference, and included an area 3 times as large as London, England. It was laid out in 625 squares, formed by the intersection of 25 streets at right angles.

Truly, the city of Babylon was an incredible accomplishment, a testimony to human ingenuity and ability, literally one of the Seven Wonders of the World. But Nebuchadnezzar forgot where all that talent, wealth, and ingenuity came from, and God brought him down. God humbled Nebuchadnezzar so that He might restore him and use him for His purposes.

A Wonderful Conversion - Daniel 4:34-37

Let us read the conclusion of this wonderful account of Nebuchadnezzar's conversion:

> And at the end of the time I, Nebuchadnezzar, lifted my eyes to heaven, and my understanding returned to me; and I blessed the Most High and praised and honored Him who lives forever: for His dominion is an everlasting dominion, and His kingdom is from generation to generation. All the inhabitants of the earth are reputed as nothing; He does according to His will in the army of heaven and among the inhabitants of the earth. No one can restrain His hand or say to Him, "What have You done?" At the same time my reason returned to me, and for the glory of my kingdom, my honor and splendor returned to me. My counselors and nobles resorted to me, I was restored to my kingdom, and excellent majesty was added to me. Now I, Nebuchadnezzar, praise and extol and honor the King of heaven, all of whose works are truth, and His ways justice. And those who walk in pride He is able to put down (Daniel 4:34-37).

Look back at verses 1-3 of chapter four:

> Nebuchadnezzar the king, to all peoples, nations, and languages that dwell in all the earth: Peace be multiplied to you. I thought it

good to declare the signs and wonders that the Most High God has worked for me. How great are His signs, and how mighty His wonders! His kingdom is an everlasting kingdom, and His dominion is from generation to generation.

Never forget that God is able to put down those who walk in pride. Thankfully, He is also able to restore them when they turn to Him in repentance.

Jerry Falwell arranged for his son, Jerry, Jr., to meet Billy Graham. Following the meeting with Dr. Graham, Jerry, Jr. said something very insightful. When asked what it was like to meet with Billy Graham, he responded, "Billy doesn't know who he is." When we realize that the only good thing in us is God, we empty ourselves and become humble. Scholar Adam Clarke commenting on Nebuchadnezzar's proclamation in Daniel 4:1–3, writes: "This is a regular decree, and is one of the most ancient on record, and no doubt was copied from the state-papers of Babylon."[13] Daniel has preserved it in the original language. Dr. Grotius states, 'Daniel gives this wonderful history, not in his own words, but in those of the published edict itself, that there might remain no doubt about its trustworthiness.'"[14] Adam Clarke thinks that is very probable that Nebuchadnezzar was a true convert, and that he died having faith in the God of Israel.

It was December 7, 1941, when Mitsuo Fuchida, a proud and militant Japanese commander, led the attack on Pearl Harbor. His brilliant military career ended with the defeat of Japan and the close of the war. Returning to his home village near Osaka, he took up farming. One day, Fuchida was summoned to Tokyo to testify in the war crimes trials and was handed a pamphlet as he got off the train. He was intrigued by the title, "I was a Prisoner of Japan."

It was the story of Jacob DeShazer, the Doolittle raider who was converted to Christ in a Japanese prison camp while reading the Bible. Fuchida's curiosity was aroused from his reading of the incident, and he went to a bookstore and bought a Bible. When he went home he began reading it. "Every night I read the Bible," he said. "I read while plowing the rice fields. One night I read that Jesus died and that He prayed, 'Father, forgive them, for they know not what they do.' I realized I was one of 'them' for whom Jesus prayed."

At the age of forty-seven, on April 12, 1950, Fuchida received Christ as Savior and began a new life. Though later asked to consider heading Japan's air force as commander-in-chief, Fuchida turned down the invitation and spent the rest of his life traveling in Japan, the United States, and Canada, sharing what God had done in his life. Nebuchadnezzar had a similar dramatic conversion! Praise God that when He brings us to our knees, we can look up, see the cross, and trust Christ. That is precisely what Nebuchadnezzar did. I cannot wait to see him in heaven someday!

Discussion Questions

1. In what sense could pride be said to be the root of all other sin? In what way is pride a part of every sin we commit?

2. What are the two majestic themes we find in Daniel 4? List other passages in Daniel where these themes are developed.

3. Whether or not Nebuchadnezzar was truly converted has been the subject of much debate? Based on this chapter and reading the text of Daniel, do think Nebuchadnezzar's conversion was genuine? Why or why not?

4. How does God bring a man down? What are patterns that we see in the life of someone whom God is about to bring down?

5. What should we do if we find these patterns developing in our own lives?

6. Have you experienced God's rest? Where does Matthew 11:28–30 say that we find God's rest? How is that rest obtained and maintained?

7. What does this account of God bringing Nebuchadnezzar down teach us about His grace?

That's Not All

You can find sermon outlines in the "Sermonars" section at the back of the book. These pages may be freely reproduced, either from the book or from the accompanying CD-ROM for any devotional or ministry use.

Daniel

Chapter Eight

Saddam Hussein, Belshazzar . . . What are the Final Days of a King?

As we look at Daniel 5, we meet Nebuchadnezzar's grandson, Belshazzar (not to be confused with Belteshazzar, the name given to Daniel when he was taken captive to Babylon). Belshazzar was the last king of the Babylonian Empire. As secular historians will confirm, the Babylonian empire lasted for seventy years. The prophet Jeremiah predicted well in advance that God would raise up a kingdom to take His people into captivity for seventy years. Jeremiah predicted that the empire would dissipate as quickly as it rose up.

What we find in Daniel 5 is an account of the last night of Belshazzar's rule of the Babylonian Empire. On that very evening when Babylon was overthrown, Belshazzar, Babylon's young, pagan monarch, decided to get drunk, have a party, and turn it into a big orgy. We can infer from the text that an orgy took place even though this is not explicitly stated. First, the noble's wives were at the party. Typically, wives would never come to such occasions. However, in Daniel 5 all the wives and all the concubines were present. Additionally, everyone at the party was drinking. In fact, at one point Belshazzar became so inebriated that he jumped on a table and drank wine from the gold vessels extracted from the Jewish temple in Jerusalem that used to be set aside solely for use in worshiping Jehovah in the holy of holies.

Belshazzar would have known his grandfather's story well, how God had humbled Nebuchadnezzar, a prideful, terrorist king, through seven years of insanity. Belshazzar could have easily told the story of how after seven years of insanity, Nebuchadnezzar converted to the God of Jehovah and forsook all other gods. Yet there was one thing that Belshazzar forgot. It was the same thing that Saddam Hussein, who was fascinated with Nebuchadnezzar, also forgot. Both Belshazzar and Saddam Hussein forgot what Daniel wrote in Daniel 2:21, "And He changes the times and the seasons; He removes kings, and He raises up kings; He gives wisdom to the wise and knowledge to those who have understanding." They forgot that God is ultimately in control of who holds the power in a country and that He can remove someone from a position of power just as quickly as He placed them there in the first place.

Dr. Charles Dyer, Senior Vice President of Moody Bible Institute, has visited present-day Babylon, fifty miles south of Baghdad. He writes in his book The Rise of Babylon:

> Saddam Hussein had invited us to Iraq for a cultural festival (The International Babylon Festival), to see the beauty of the new Babylon that was rising from the ruins... I looked down at the Babylonian ruins and saw 2,500 year old bricks that were ordered into place by Nebuchadnezzar. Over the centuries thousands of bricks have been taken out of the rubble and used to build nearby villages.

> Today the rebuilders of Babylon are laying additional bricks inscribed, "Rebuilt in the era of our President Saddam Hussein." In 1980, all that existed of the site of ancient Babylon were dusty ruins, or ruins of ruins. But during the next two decades, over 60,000,000 bricks were laid in the reconstruction of Nebuchadnezzar's fabled city.

> On the exact cite of ancient Babylon, he [Saddam Hussein] has reconstructed the southern palace of Nebuchadnezzar, including the processional street, a Greek theater, many temples, what was once Nebuchadnezzar's throne room, and a half-scale model of the Ishtar Gate.

> On the seal of the International Babylonian Festival there is a picture of Nebuchadnezzar and super-imposed on it is a picture of Saddam Hussein.[1]

Again, what both of these men, Belshazzar and Saddam Hussein, forgot was that God, not them, was and is in control of the world and its rulers. God can and does remove kings as we read above in Daniel 2:21. It is a fact that God removed Belshazzar. Daniel 5 cryptically records the end of the Babylonian Empire just as God had revealed it would happen through Nebuchadnezzar's dreams (cf. Daniel 2). Just as predicted, the Medes and the Persians overthrew Babylon almost effortlessly on the night when Belshazzar held a drunken orgy. However, before exploring this chapter in detail we must examine four important points about its context and influence.

1. Timetable

How old was Daniel when the event recorded in chapter 5 took place? Chapter 5 fixes the date of the fall of Babylon at 539 BC. This is thirty-two years after Nebuchadnezzar's second dream and twenty-three years after his death. This means that Daniel was about eighty-one years old.

Additionally, we must also be aware of the challenging chronology presented in the book of Daniel. The chapters are not arranged on a strictly chronological basis. For instance, Daniel 5 records the end of Belshazzar and of the Babylonian kingdom by the conquest of the Medes and Persians (539 BC). However, Daniel 7:1 reads, "In the first year of Belshazzar king of Babylon..." Therefore, the events must have occurred, chronologically, before the events of Daniel 5. Daniel's first vision came when he was sixty-seven years old. Again, Daniel 8:1 reads, "In the third year of the reign of King Belshazzar a vision appeared to me—to me, Daniel—after the one that appeared to me the first time." This is Daniel's second vision (551 BC).

Therefore, it is very important as we study these chapters that we understand the timetable of events. Another section of the book that can potentially cause confusion chronologically is Daniel 9:2. It reads, "In the first year of his [King Darius] reign I, Daniel, understood by the books the number of the years specified by the word of the LORD through Jeremiah the prophet, that He would accomplish seventy years in the desolations of Jerusalem." This was Daniel's third vision, which occurred thirteen years later (538 BC). In Daniel 10-12, we find Daniel's fourth vision, which came to him in 536 BC during the reign of Cyrus, the chief ruler serving under Darius (both rulers began reigning at the same time).

Therefore, while the chronology of the events may seem confusing at first glance, it is not contradictory or abnormal for this particular genre of biblical literature.

2. Context of Daniel 5

Two years after the death of Nebuchadnezzar, war broke out between the Babylonians and the Medes. This war continued for more than twenty years. Finally, Xerxes, king of the Medes (the same person called Darius in Daniel 5:31), called upon his nephew Cyrus, who was a Persian, to come to his aid. In the seventeenth year of Nabonidus (Belshazzar's father) and the third year of Belshazzar, Cyrus laid siege to the city of Babylon. The reason Belshazzar could throw a drunken orgy even though he knew that Cyrus was camped outside the city wall was because of the strength of the Babylonian fortifications. Belshazzar believed the wall of Babylon to be impenetrable.

It is interesting to note that the conflict between Babylon and Persia is still going on today. The Persians are present-day Iranians. In 1980, Saddam Hussein invaded Iran launching the Iran/Iraq war. The hostilities are simple to understand: the two countries, Iraq and Iran, share the Islamic religion, but Iranians are not Arabs. They are Persians who speak a different language and have a distinct social, cultural, and ethnic heritage.

3. Fulfilled Prophecy

Some 175 years before the events of Daniel 5 took place, Isaiah correctly predicted that Cyrus would devastate Babylon: "Who says of Cyrus, 'He is My shepherd, and he shall perform all My pleasure, saying to Jerusalem, "You shall be built," and to the temple, "Your foundation shall be laid"'" (Isaiah 44:28). Additionally, examine Isaiah 45:1, "Thus says the LORD to His anointed, to Cyrus, whose right hand I have held—to subdue nations before him and loose the armor of kings, to open before him the double doors, so that the gates will not be shut." This prophecy refers to the river gates that guarded the Euphrates River as it ran through Babylon. It was these very gates that Cyrus exploited as a point of entry into the unconquerable fortress of Babylon.

4. Critics Silenced

Scholars adhering to higher criticism in liberal seminaries and universities, until the last two or three decades, have been notorious for claiming that the events of the Bible did not really happen and that they are merely metaphorical. They have particularly tried to discount the book of Daniel because there was no previous evidence outside the Bible that Belshazzar ever existed. However, recent archaeological discoveries, such as the Nabonidus Chronicle, have now confirmed that Belshazzar, Nabonidus' oldest son, was made co-regent with his father and did serve as king while his father was away from Babylon during most of his seventeen-year reign.

This confirms the biblical record to the smallest details. Scholar and author Dr. Leon Wood notes, "It may be observed that, for many years, liberal writers declared that Belshazzar was unhistorical and the book of Daniel was in error in speaking of him as Babylonia's last king. It was known that Nabonidus held this position, and the existence of Belshazzar was unknown from ancient records then in hand... the Bible has again been proven accurate and the liberal critics wrong."[2] Therefore, as we turn our attention to the text of Daniel 5, we can have total confidence in its accuracy and ability to reveal God's truth to us.

The Handwriting on the Wall
The fall of Babylon, unexpected by King Belshazzar, came in confirmation of sacred prophesy.

The Party—Daniel 5:1-4

> Belshazzar the king made a great feast for a thousand of his lords, and drank wine in the presence of the thousand. While he tasted the wine, Belshazzar gave the command to bring the gold and silver vessels which his father Nebuchadnezzar had taken from the temple which had been in Jerusalem, that the king and his lords, his wives, and his concubines might drink from them. Then they brought the gold vessels that had been taken from the temple of the house of God which had been in Jerusalem; and the king and his lords, his wives, and his concubines drank from them. They drank wine, and praised the gods of gold and silver, bronze and iron, wood and stone (Dan 5:1-4).

In this passage, we read of a drunken orgy. There are 1,000 partiers gathered with Belshazzar who, in defiant pride, uses the vessels taken from the Jewish temple in Jerusalem (cf. 1 Kings 7:47-51; 10:21) to get drunk. Notice the word "tasting" in verse 2. The underlying Aramaic word carries the idea of not only sensing the flavor of the wine, but feeling its effects or being under its influence. We live in a world today that is very much like Babylon. Many people today live only for the weekend party. Montgomery cites sources which tell of one Persian king who fed 15,000 persons daily and that Alexander the Great entertained 10,000 guests at a marriage festival.[3] According to Esther 1:1-4, Xerxes I held a party lasting 180 days for a large number of people.

Recently, actor Colin Ferrell, who has starred in Hollywood films such as *The Recruit* and *Phone Booth*, said in an interview that he was no longer interested in relationships—only sex. Dr. James Dobson, who recently appeared on Larry King Live, stated that he believes pornography is at the root of every broken home and marriage in America. So, you see, our culture is not all that different, in some respects, from that of ancient Babylon.

Dr. Leon Wood has had the unique opportunity of actually standing in the room where this party took place 2,500 years ago. He writes:

> I have personally stood in this room. It measures 165 feet long by 55 feet wide, and has plastered walls (see Daniel 5:5). Most of the plaster is now gone, but the remains of the walls still stand several

feet high. Especially important is the niche at the middle of one of the longer walls, directly opposite the door of entrance into the room. It is here that the king would have sat, no doubt on a slightly raised platform, so that he could be seen by all present.[4]

It is clear that Belshazzar had not learned from Nebuchadnezzar's prideful folly and gracious restoration to the throne by God Almighty. Quite to the contrary, he was full of pride and lust on the very eve of his city's invasion.

The Prophecy—Daniel 5:5-9

In the same hour the fingers of a man's hand appeared and wrote opposite the lampstand on the plaster of the wall of the king's palace; and the king saw the part of the hand that wrote. Then the king's countenance changed, and his thoughts troubled him, so that the joints of his hips were loosened and his knees knocked against each other. The king cried aloud to bring in the astrologers, the Chaldeans, and the soothsayers. The king spoke, saying to the wise men of Babylon, "Whoever reads this writing, and tells me its interpretation, shall be clothed with purple and have a chain of gold around his neck; and he shall be the third ruler in the kingdom." Now all the king's wise men came, but they could not read the writing, or make known to the king its interpretation. Then King Belshazzar was greatly troubled, his countenance was changed, and his lords were astonished (Dan 5:5-9).

This is an amazing passage that reminds us of Malachi 3:16, which states that God has a "book of remembrance." It reminds us that God is always observing us and writing in His book! God registers everything we do! Notice the impact the disembodied hand had on a drunken man: Belshazzar was on the very verge of a heart attack. It would startle many people if they caught a glimpse of the eternity they are headed to without Jesus Christ.

Early in my ministry I was going to Richmond, Virginia for a crusade. I was staying at a Holiday Inn near a busy intersection. One evening as I was waiting outside the hotel to be picked-up, I saw a motorcycle run into the back of a car and burst into flames in the middle of the intersection. In that moment, a thought flashed through my mind: "I wonder if that kid is a Christian." I immediately ran from the hotel over to the intersection. By that time the police and EMS had arrived; however, I pushed through and said, "I am a minister! Let me through!" I did not expect them to let me through, but they did! I immediately went to the young man who was facedown on the ground moaning, and as odd as it seems, I said to him, "I am a minister; I am a believer. Do you know Christ?" The young man listened to me. This man was all of a sudden faced with eternity. We never know when we will all of a sudden be faced with eternity. Are you ready?

In a similar situation, my wife and I recently found out that one of the ladies in the church was diagnosed with cancer. One day as we were traveling, I got a call from this woman's son, saying that his mother only had one or two days to live; she was faced with eternity. When we arrived at the hospital later that day, the whole atmosphere was focused on eternity. Wouldn't it make you shutter for a moment if all of a sudden you were faced with eternity?

Belshazzar was having a party when, all of a sudden, a hand was writing on the wall. The room was transformed from a party to a prophecy. Let's look at the rest of Daniel 5 and see how Belshazzar is brought from a state of complacent pride to one of compliant fear.

The Prominent Queen Mother—Daniel 5:10-12

> The queen, because of the words of the king and his lords, came to the banquet hall. The queen spoke, saying, "O king, live forever! Do not let your thoughts trouble you, nor let your countenance change. There is a man in your kingdom in whom is the Spirit of the Holy God. And in the days of your father [Aram. grandfather] light and understanding and wisdom, like the wisdom of the gods, were found in him; and King Nebuchadnezzar your father [Aram. grandfather]—your father the king [Aram. grandfather]—made him chief of the magicians, astrologers, Chaldeans, and soothsayers. Inasmuch as an excellent spirit, knowledge, understanding, interpreting dreams, solving riddles, and explaining enigmas were found in this Daniel, whom the king named Belteshazzar, now let Daniel be called, and he will give the interpretation" (Dan 5:10-12).

Notice that the queen was not at the banquet. She came later, perhaps because she was summoned. Josephus said she was the wife of Nebuchadnezzar or Nabonidus, probably the grandmother of Belshazzar, or possibly Nitocris, the daughter of Nebuchadnezzar and Nabonidus' wife and Belshazzar's mother. Also notice that twice in the passage the queen referred to Daniel by his Hebrew name (Daniel), not his Babylonian name (Belteshazzar). It is also clear from what the queen said that even in his elder years, Daniel was still well-known for the Spirit of God who lived within him. Thus, once again, faithful Daniel was brought before the leader of the Babylonian Empire to interpret a sign.

The Prophet—Daniel 5:13-21

Then Daniel was brought in before the king. The king spoke, and said to Daniel, "Are you that Daniel who is one of the captives from Judah, whom my father the king brought from Judah? I have heard of you, that the Spirit of God is in you, and that light and understanding and excellent wisdom are found in you. Now the wise men, the astrologers, have been brought in before me, that they should read this writing and make known to me its interpretation, but they could not give the interpretation of the thing. And I have heard of you, that you can give interpretations and explain enigmas. Now if you can read the writing and make known to me its interpretation, you shall be clothed with purple and have a chain of gold around your neck, and shall be the third ruler in the kingdom." Then Daniel answered, and said before the king, "Let your gifts be for yourself, and give your rewards to another; yet I will read the writing to the king, and make known to him the interpretation. O king, the Most High God gave Nebuchadnezzar your father a kingdom and majesty, glory and honor. And because of the majesty that He gave him, all peoples, nations, and languages trembled and feared before him. Whomever he wished, he executed; whomever he wished, he kept alive; whomever he wished, he set up; and whomever he wished, he put down. But when his heart was lifted up, and his spirit was hardened in pride, he was deposed from his kingly throne, and they took his glory from him. Then he was driven from the sons of men, his heart was made like the beasts, and his dwelling was with the wild donkeys. They fed him with grass like oxen, and his body was wet with the dew of heaven, till he knew that the Most High God rules in the kingdom of men, and appoints over it whomever He chooses" (Dan 5:13-21).

Rather than coming in an attempt to impress the king, Daniel came like a true minister of the gospel. He could not be bought or vainly impressed by this young, pagan king. Daniel came to Belshazzar and told him he had a major problem: Belshazzar had forgotten that God is the one in control. In his pride, Belshazzar had done exactly the same thing Nebuchadnezzar had done.

Dr. Oliver Green comments on Daniel's attitude and character as he once again stood before a pagan ruler:

> Daniel, God's faithful prophet, did not tremble before the king. He had no fear; he had but one duty and responsibility: to be faithful to the Word of God written on the wall, and to tell the king exactly what God had spoken. That is the responsibility of every minister, evangelist, and Bible teacher. We are responsible only to God. A minister called and ordained of God to preach the gospel owes his allegiance to God, regardless of the age or dispensation. He must fear no one...[5]

Montgomery adds, "There is no finer example of the preacher's dictum in the Bible than this stern and inexorable condemnation."[6]

The Pride–Daniel 5:22-24

> But you his son, Belshazzar, have not humbled your heart, although you knew all this. And you have lifted yourself up against the Lord of heaven. They have brought the vessels of His house before you, and you and your lords, your wives and your concubines, have drunk wine from them. And you have praised the gods of silver and gold, bronze and iron, wood and stone, which do not see or hear or know; and the God who holds your breath in His hand and owns all your ways, you have not glorified. Then the fingers of the hand were sent from Him, and this writing was written (Daniel 5:22-24).

Similar to the demise of Nebuchadnezzar, Belshazzar's pride brought him down. As we noted above, Belshazzar failed to learn from the example of his grandfather. He had no doubt seen how God had humbled Nebuchadnezzar; yet he himself fell into the same trap. Let this be a warning to us: we must learn from the failures and success of those who have come before us, lest we prove true the classic dictum, "Those who do not study history are doomed to repeat it."

Personalized Message—Daniel 5:25-31

And this is the inscription that was written: MENE, MENE, TEKEL, UPHARSIN. This is the interpretation of each word. MENE: God has numbered your kingdom, and finished it; TEKEL: You have been weighed in the balances, and found wanting; PERES: Your kingdom has been divided, and given to the Medes and Persians. Then Belshazzar gave the command, and they clothed Daniel with purple and put a chain of gold around his neck, and made a proclamation concerning him that he should be the third ruler in the kingdom. That very night Belshazzar, king of the Chaldeans, was slain. And Darius the Mede received the kingdom, being about sixty-two years old (Dan 5:25-31).

Let us examine what these strange words meant:

- MENE, MENE meant "numbered, numbered," or "counted, counted." God had numbered the days of the Babylonian kingdom and it was coming to an end that fateful night!

- TEKEL meant "weighed." God had weighed Belshazzar's behavior and found it woefully lacking.

- UPHARSIN meant "divided" or "broken in pieces." God acts by careful calculation. He weighs our thoughts, intents, and motives.

Belshazzar (his name literally meant "Bel protects the prince") was executed that very night! We know the date: the 16th day of Tishri, 539 BC, which is October 11th or 12th. The Babylonian Empire, seventy years old, came to an end that night. We know the rest of the story. The Persians diverted the Euphrates River and entered the city through the channel that allowed the river to flow under the city walls.

Agents in Babylon's Fall

Much like the Roman Empire, the Babylonian Empire collapsed much more from internal pressures and corruptions than outside forces. It is interesting to note that many of the agents which led to the demise of the Babylonian Empire are rampant in our present-day American culture. What are they?

• Alcohol

• Lust for pleasure

• Sexual deviance

• Idolatry

• Blasphemy

Bible teacher Dr. John MacArthur notes, "The worship of pagan gods often involved sexual perversion. In digs around Babylon, archaeologists have discovered artifacts engraved with pornographic pictures. But I don't know that their pornography can be any worse than what has appeared in America. Our nation has abandoned itself to vice and lust."[7] Think for a moment: if this is what brought Babylon down, what is God saying to America?

All five of the elements that brought Babylon to her knees are present in our country and growing more rampant all the time. What does this mean for our nation? It means that our nation cannot last forever if it continues down the path it has embarked upon; no nation ever has. It is high time we pray for America. Why not take a moment right now and pray for our country, lest we too be weighed in the balance and found wanting?

Discussion Question

1. What similarities do you see between Belshazzar and Nebuchadnezzar? How are they different? What do these men have in common with more recent dictators like Adolph Hitler or Saddam Hussein? Do see any of these same characteristics in your life?

2. How would you explain the chronology of Daniel to a friend who is not familiar with the book? Where do the events of this chapter fit into that timetable?

3. Review the archeological evidence for the historicity of Daniel discussed in this chapter. How would you use this information to help a skeptical friend trust the Scriptures? Take a few minutes to role-play this conversation with a friend.

4. Have you ever been faced with eternity? How did this affect your relationship with God?

5. What does the inscription "MENE, MENE, TEKEL, UPHARSIN" mean? Explain how it was fulfilled in the book of Daniel.

6. If God were to "weigh" your life, would it be found worthy or wanting? What are some practical steps that lead to a God-honoring life?

7. We listed a number of elements that contributed to the fall of Babylon. How have these elements affected great civilizations throughout history (e.g. the Roman Empire, Europe, America)?

8. What can you and your church do to help redeem a nation and culture that seem to have strayed so far away from the truth?

That's Not All

You can find sermon outlines in the "Sermonars" section at the back of the book. These pages may be freely reproduced, either from the book or from the accompanying CD-ROM for any devotional or ministry use.

Daniel

Chapter Nine

Ninety-Year-Old Daniel in the Lions' Den

An Overview

The story of Daniel in the lions' den (Daniel 6) is probably one of the most popular in the entire Bible. Before we make our way through this amazing story, let us remind ourselves where we are in the book. Daniel has twelve chapters and is usually divided into two main sections. Daniel 1 through 6 is mainly historical, while the remaining chapters (7–12) are mainly prophetic in content.

In Daniel 1, we read about Daniel's deportation to Babylon and his commitment not to be defiled by the pagan influence of that ungodly society. In chapter 2, Nebuchadnezzar had a dream that only Daniel was able to interpret. The king was so impressed with that young Jewish man that he promoted him and his friends. In the following chapter (Daniel 3), Daniel's friends, Shadrach, Meshach, and Abed-Nego, were delivered from the fiery-furnace after refusing to bow down to the king's newly-made statue. In Daniel 4, the prophet interpreted another dream and Nebuchadnezzar, the most powerful monarch in the Old Testament, was brought down. He lived in insanity for seven years until God healed him and, we believe, he was converted to belief in the God of the Jews.

Nebuchadnezzar lived one year of his life as a believer, and then he died. After his death, there was no king who could even begin to accomplish what Nebuchadnezzar had done for Babylon. Consequently, we see the dwindling of the Babylonian kingdom without Nebuchadnezzar's strong leadership. Thus, in Daniel 5, we read about the last king of the Babylonian Empire, Belshazzar. This man, controlled by his appetites, had a drunken orgy as the Persian army encircled the city of Babylon. He thought Babylon was undefeatable, but the Medo-Persian army would prove him wrong. Just as the Lord had predicted through Isaiah 175 years earlier, the Persian army overwhelmed the city with little difficulty.

The last verse of Daniel 5 reads, "And Darius the Mede received the kingdom, being about sixty-two years old." The prophet Jeremiah had predicted that the first big Gentile empire, Babylon, would last seventy years. He wrote that this kingdom would come up, serve its purpose, and then dissipate—that is precisely what happened. The second Gentile kingdom was the Medo-Persian Empire (539–331 BC), illustrated by the chest and the two arms in the king's dream, which showed the duality of this kingdom.

Daniel 6:1–28 actually closes the first main section of the book by narrating what happened to Daniel as a result of his unwavering faithfulness to his God while the Medo-Persians were in power. In the beginning of the book, Daniel was just a teenager; in chapter 6, Daniel was anywhere between 82 and 90 years old. Actually, Daniel 6 records one of the final events in Daniel's life, since the events recorded in Daniel 7–12 fall chronologically under Daniel 6 (cf. Daniel 8:1; 9:1; 10:1, 11:1).

The Medo-Persian Kingdom

Daniel 6:1 describes the government of the new Medo-Persian government: "It pleased Darius to set over the kingdom one hundred and twenty satraps, to be over the whole kingdom." Darius was the new Medo-Persian king who set up satraps to assist him in ruling over the empire. The word "satrap" (translated "prince" in the King James Version) means a "governor" or a "viceroy" who possessed both civil and military powers over a large province of the empire. It literally meant "protector of the realm" and was used to designate those who supervised over this world-wide empire. In our culture, the equivalent position would be that of a "governor." So we should think of the empire as being divided into 120 provinces that were ruled by 120 governors. Between the 120 governors and the king were three key individuals that we would call "secretaries of state" or even "vice presidents." Dr. Joyce Baldwin comments on the transition of the government from the Babylonians to the Medo-Persians, as well as where Daniel fit in the government:

> Despite the change of government, Daniel continued to enjoy favor. This is the point of interest connecting the two chapters. The Persian Empire, which incorporated that of the Medes, a vast area forming an arc to the north of the Babylonian territories, extended eventually to Asia Minor, Libya, and Egypt to the west, and to the Indus river and the Aral Sea to the east. It was the largest empire the world had yet seen, hence the urgent need for an efficient organization from the very beginning. This division of the whole kingdom into satrapies is known from Esther 8:9... strictly the text speaks only of the appointment of satraps and above the satraps were three overseers, of whom Daniel was one.[1]

Daniel's Prominent Position

Thus, Daniel continued to have a position of influence before the new Medo-Persian government. Daniel 6:2 states, "And over these, three governors, of whom Daniel was one, that the satraps might give account to them, so that the king would suffer no loss." The King James Version refers to the three governors as three "presidents," representing the three men who held the highest offices under the king and who ruled over the affairs of the kingdom as his representatives. Albert Barnes comments: "It is not improbable that these three presided over distinct departments, corresponding somewhat to what are now called 'secretaries'—as Secretaries of State, of the Treasury, of Foreign Affairs..."[2]

Among these three key figures, Daniel was the first and the highest. Therefore, the position of influence that Daniel enjoyed in the Babylonian kingdom was carried providentially into the Medo-Persian Empire. Even though Daniel was well advanced in years, he continued to bless the king with all his godly wisdom and insight. The situation around him had changed, and he himself had grown much older, but Daniel continued to be a faithful servant. Dr. Leon J. Wood writes about Daniel's situation in Daniel 6:

> Politically, the situation was quite different from that of the prior chapters. Then, Babylon had been the country in control; now it was Medo-Persia. The exact length of time that had passed since the fall of Babylon cannot be determined, but at least a few months had elapsed, for the new regime was now established and jealousies had been formed. Probably, no less than two years had gone by, meaning that Daniel was about 83.[3]

For a while in the new kingdom, things seemed to be fine. However, shortly after the new government was in place, it was evident that the two other "presidents" were not quite on the same level as Daniel. It was Daniel's distinction and his fellow servants' jealousy that led to the events of Daniel 6:4–28.

Daniel's Distinction

Daniel 6:3 makes it very clear that there was something special about Daniel that set him apart from all the other governors and satraps. This verse states: "Then this Daniel distinguished himself above the governors and satraps, because an excellent spirit was in him; and the king gave thought to setting him over the whole realm."

We learn two main things about Daniel from Daniel 6:3. First, he "distinguished himself." The root idea of the word "distinguish" is the word "shine." Darius had an amazing governmental structure in place with hundreds of officials working under him, but there was one among them all—Daniel—who outshone the others. Second, an "excellent spirit" was in him. This expression refers to that which hangs over or which is abundant or more than enough, that which is great, excellent, preeminent. Daniel was definitely set apart by the Lord and used to make a great difference wherever he was.

How Do I Cultivate an "Excellent Spirit?"

How can we cultivate an "excellent spirit" such as Daniel's? To answer this question, we must be able to answer another one: If Daniel had an excellent spirit, how did he cultivate it? Let me suggest several ways.

First, very early in his life Daniel made up his mind about purity. We see this in Daniel 1:8, which states, "But Daniel purposed in his heart that he would not defile himself..." As a teenager in a foreign land, Daniel was thrown in an ungodly society where he had the freedom to do as he pleased. But Daniel did not let the passing pleasures of sin entice him. As a young man, he decided to live a pure life and not to defile himself with what the king had to offer him. Have you made that decision?

If you want to have an excellent spirit like Daniel's, you must make the continuous decision to stay away from sin. I was watching TV in a hotel room one day when I noticed that there was a channel that offered "adult" movies. I also noticed that there was an option to completely block that channel from being accessed while I was in that hotel room. Do you know what I did? I immediately typed in the code. I did that because I know as a believer who has walked twenty-seven years with the Lord that impurity of any kind can take anybody down. I have noticed that when a Christian becomes involved with impure things, he will lose his spiritual appetite. Some people have no desire for prayer or for God's Word because they are feeding their minds with sin! That was definitely not the case with Daniel.

Second, Daniel had an excellent spirit because he had an insatiable love for learning. Daniel 1:17 states, "As for these four young men, God gave them knowledge and skill in all literature and wisdom; and Daniel had understanding in all visions and dreams." For instance, Daniel and his friends were able to quickly learn the language of the Chaldeans and to become knowledgeable about their way of life and academic discoveries. But nowhere along the way in his quest for learning did Daniel eradicate Jehovah from his thinking. God was always important to Daniel, even as he grew intellectually and learned new things. His worldview was definitely God-centered.

Third, Daniel was in control of his emotions and words. Self-control is an important mark of spiritual maturity. Daniel was not an emotional rollercoaster susceptible to his circumstances. Read closely Daniel's response when Arioch was carrying out Nebuchadnezzar's order to kill all the wise men in Babylon: "So Daniel went in and asked the king to give him time, that he might tell the king the interpretation" (Daniel 2:16). Daniel knew there was a death warrant out for him but with calm and poise he asked the king for more time. He was emotionally stable even under intense pressure. We will also see this later in chapter 6, when Daniel was thrown in the lions' den. What about you? Are you in control of your emotions?

Fourth, Daniel was faithful in his vocational responsibilities. Daniel was such a faithful servant that the kings he served probably wished all their servants were like him. When Daniel's enemies tried to take him down, they first examined the quality of his work, trying to find something they could accuse him of. Take a look at Daniel 6:4, "So the governors and satraps sought to find some charge against Daniel concerning the kingdom; but they could find no charge or fault, because he was faithful; nor was there any error or fault found in him." Daniel's enemies eventually transitioned from finding fault in his work (which they could not do) to finding fault in his faith in Jehovah. Would that be true of you? Are you such an excellent worker that no one can find fault in the quality of your service?

Fifth, Daniel's testimony was impeccable. Daniel 6:5 states, "Then these men said, 'We shall not find any charge against this Daniel unless we find it against him concerning the law of his God.'" But once again, Daniel was above reproach. For seventy years he had been praying to His God at least three times a day.

Sixth, Daniel was fervent in his prayer and devotional life. Consider Daniel 6:10-12:

> Now when Daniel knew that the writing was signed, he went home. And in his upper room, with his windows open toward Jerusalem, he knelt down on his knees three times that day, and prayed and gave thanks before his God, as was his custom since early days. Then these men assembled and found Daniel praying and making supplication before his God. And they went before the king, and spoke concerning the king's decree: "Have you not signed a decree that every man who petitions any god or man within thirty days, except you, O king, shall be cast into the den of lions?" The king answered and said, "The thing is true, according to the law of the Medes and Persians, which does not alter."

David taught in Psalm 55:17 that when we pray, we should do so three times a day: in the morning, afternoon, and evening. This was so important to the Jews that they eventually incorporated three distinct hours of prayer in their synagogues: the third, the sixth, and the ninth hours. As a young man deported to Babylon, Daniel developed the habit of praying three times a day—a habit that remained until the end of his life. Don't you think that meeting with God in prayer three times a day would give you an excellent spirit? It certainly did so in Daniel's life.

Daniel's Death-Defying Dilemma

Because of their antagonism against Daniel, his enemies finally figured out a way to bring charges against him. Take a look at Daniel 6:6-13:

> So these governors and satraps thronged before the king, and said thus to him: "King Darius, live forever! All the governors of the kingdom, the administrators and satraps, the counselors and advisors, have consulted together to establish a royal statute and to make a firm decree, that whoever petitions any god or man for thirty days, except you, O king, shall be cast into the den of lions. Now, O king, establish the decree and sign the writing, so that it cannot be changed, according to the law of the Medes and Persians, which does not alter." Therefore King Darius signed the written decree. Now when Daniel knew that the writing was signed, he went home. And in his upper room, with his windows open toward Jerusalem, he knelt down on his knees three times that day, and prayed and gave thanks before his God, as was his custom since early days. Then these men assembled and found Daniel praying and making supplication before his God. And they went before the king, and spoke concerning the king's decree: "Have you not signed a decree that every man who petitions any god or man within thirty days, except you, O king, shall be cast into the den of lions?" The king answered and said, "The thing is true, according to the law of the Medes and Persians, which does not alter." So they answered and said before the king, "That Daniel, who is one of the captives from Judah, does not show due regard for you, O king, or for the decree that you have signed, but makes his petition three times a day."

Daniel's dilemma was very clear. He only had two options: to follow the decree and cease from praying for thirty days, or to continue his habit of praying to Jehovah three times a day and be sent to the lions' den. For many, the decision would be obvious: take the path of least resistance and save yourself. But not so with Daniel. He was willing to be faithful to his God no matter the cost! Daniel continued to pray just as if there were no decree threatening his life.

Daniel's Dynamic Prayer Habits

Let us take a closer look at Daniel's response to the king's decree.

First, we notice that he prayed with his windows open (Daniel 6:10). This clearly indicates Daniel's boldness as he continued to pray to God. Daniel knew exactly what was going to happen. He knew that there were people after him, watching him very closely. So what did he do? The same thing he had always done: he opened his window and prayed to God. No intimidation could stop Daniel!

Second, we also notice that Daniel prayed towards Jerusalem. This reminds us that he had not forgotten the prophet Jeremiah, the Jewish temple, or the teachings of Jehovah, although seventy years had passed since he was first deported to Babylon. We know from Daniel 9:2 that the book of Jeremiah was in Daniel's possession in that pagan city. How many times do you think Daniel read the following promises (among so many others) written by Jeremiah?

- Jeremiah 29:12-13, "Then you will call upon Me and go and pray to Me, and I will listen to you. And you will seek Me and find Me, when you search for Me with all your heart."

- Jeremiah 33:2, "Call to Me, and I will answer you, and show you great and mighty things, which you do not know."

Daniel took the word of the Lord as written by Jeremiah to heart and lived by it!

Third, Daniel prayed by getting down on his knees. Don't forget that Daniel was around ninety years of age, but he was still kneeling three times a day! At ninety, Daniel was not looking for a cane or wanting to find an easy chair. He was fueled by his walk with God and not at all ready to call it quits. There is nothing that can make us stronger than walking close to Christ.

Fourth, Daniel gave thanks before his God. Thankfulness in a time like that does not seem to fit, does it? Would you give thanks to God if you knew that in few minutes there would be strong retaliation against you? This is another mark of spiritual maturity: giving thanks to God at all times. Paul wrote in 1 Thessalonians 5:18, "In everything give thanks; for this is the will of God in Christ Jesus for you." When we thank God during times of hardship, we are actually expressing our absolute confidence in Him! We are declaring that we believe He is able to see us through whatever is going on in our lives. Do you have such confidence in God?

Fifth, we also notice that Daniel made petitions to God (as indicated by his accusers in Daniel 6:13). The New International Version translates "making petition" as "asking God for help" (Daniel 6:11). That is precisely what a petition is: a cry for help. Do you need God to do something for you? Why don't you do what Daniel did? Why don't you cry out to God and ask Him to deliver you?

Daniel in a Den of Lions

Daniel knew there was a price for disobeying the king's decree, but being faithful to God was more important for him than saving himself. Consider the price Daniel had to pay for doing what was right:

> And the king, when he heard these words, was greatly displeased with himself, and set his heart on Daniel to deliver him; and he labored till the going down of the sun to deliver him. Then these men approached the king, and said to the king, "Know, O king, that it is the law of the Medes and Persians that no decree or statute which the king establishes may be changed." So the king gave the command, and they brought Daniel and cast him into the den of lions. But the king spoke, saying to Daniel, "Your God, whom you serve continually, He will deliver you." Then a stone was brought and laid on the mouth of the den, and the king sealed it with his own signet ring and with the signets of his lords, that the purpose concerning Daniel might not be changed. Now the king went to his palace and spent the night fasting; and no musicians were brought before him. Also his sleep went from him. Then the king arose very early in the morning and went in haste to the den of lions. And when he came to the den, he cried out with a lamenting

voice to Daniel. The king spoke, saying to Daniel, "Daniel, servant of the living God, has your God, whom you serve continually, been able to deliver you from the lions?" Then Daniel said to the king, "O king, live forever! My God sent His angel and shut the lions' mouths, so that they have not hurt me, because I was found innocent before Him; and also, O king, I have done no wrong before you." Then the king was exceedingly glad for him, and commanded that they should take Daniel up out of the den. So Daniel was taken up out of the den, and no injury whatever was found on him, because he believed in his God (Daniel 6:14–23).

The den of lions was actually a pit. The idea is that the den was underground, probably a cave constructed for that purpose. Dr. Harry Bultema comments: "A lions' den consisted of a square hole in the ground, divided by a wall into two parts. In this wall is a door which can be opened and closed from above... from this description, it is evident that these dens looked very much like our present-day bear pits in our zoos."[4] Following the same line of thought, Dr. Wood writes:

The dens of lions they had in mind were apparently an underground cavity, perhaps an adapted natural cave with an opening at the top. Daniel is said to have been drawn up out of it in verse 23.

Later, the conspirators, when cast in, were eaten by the lions before they came to the bottom of the den in verse 24. It may have also been a side entrance through which to let lions in and out, but that may not have been used often. The den must have been large to allow for several lions to move about and also to permit all of the conspirators and their families to be cast in at one time (verse 24). Such a place would have been foreboding to people. The lions would have been kept nicely hungry so that they would quickly devour anyone cast within there as punishment."[5]

Someone once described the amazing events that happened when Daniel was thrown in that treacherous place as follows:

As the guards closed the hole and went their way, Daniel slid gradually to the floor of the den. The big lions had come bounding from their caverns at the inflow of light. All stopped suddenly short, as if reigned up by a powerful hand on the bridle. The initial roars died away as they formed a solid group and looked towards this man who stood in their den in easy reach. Others of the great beasts yawned and then lay down on the floor, but no one made a move to advance toward Daniel. "Thanks be to Jehovah," Daniel breathed, "He stopped the mouths of these lions so that they have done me no harm." Daniel then sat down on the floor and leaned back against the wall to make himself comfortable for the night. Soon, two cub lions moved in his direction, not stealthily or crouching as though to make an attack, but an obvious friendliness, and one lay on each side of Daniel as though to give him warmth and protection in the chilly dungeon. Then, their mother, an old lioness, crept over and lay in front of the prophet. He gently stroked their backs as they each turned their heads and licked his hand. Enclosed by the lioness and her cubs, Daniel's head was pillowed on the back of one of the cubs as the four slept soundly in perfect peace and tranquility.

Should we ever wonder that God cares for us and is capable of delivering us at all times after reading this amazing account from Daniel's life? Most definitely not!

Standing Guard over Daniel

God never abandons us. No matter how desperate or seemingly hopeless our circumstances might be, God always watches over His children according to His sovereign plans. The problem is that many times we think we have the authority to determine how and when God should come to our rescue. When we do that, it is possible we will become disappointed with the way God intervenes.

Daniel did not know what was going to happen when he was thrown into the lions' den, but he knew God would not fail him, even if that meant that he would die and be ushered into His presence. Of course, Daniel did not die. Daniel explained to the king his deliverance as follows: "My God sent His angel and shut the lions' mouths, so that they have not hurt me, because I was found innocent before Him; and also, O king, I have done no wrong before you (Daniel 6:22)."

Daniel's explanation reminds us that every Christian has a guardian angel to protect, guide, and guard him (cf. Hebrews 1:14, "Are they not all ministering spirits sent forth to minister for those who will inherit salvation?"). Dr. Albert Barnes asserts, "Daniel does not say whether the angel was visible or not, but it is rather to be presumed that he was, as in this way it would be more certainly known to him that he owed his deliverance to the intervention of an angel, and this would be to him a manifest token of the favor and protection of God."[6]

Read carefully the precious promise of Psalm 34:7, "The angel of the LORD encamps all around those who fear Him, and delivers them." What a great assurance we have of God's love through the tender care of his holy angels in our lives!

A Dramatic and Unexpected Death and Then a Conversion

Read the conclusion of this amazing chapter from Daniel's life:

And the king gave the command, and they brought those men who had accused Daniel, and they cast them into the den of lions—them, their children, and their wives; and the lions overpowered them, and broke all their bones in pieces before they ever came to the bottom of the den. Then King Darius wrote: to all peoples, nations, and languages that dwell in all the earth: peace be multiplied to you. I make a decree that in every dominion of my kingdom men must tremble and fear before the God of Daniel. For He is the living God, and steadfast forever; His kingdom is the one which shall not be destroyed, and His dominion shall endure to the end. He delivers and rescues, and He works signs and wonders in heaven and on earth, who has delivered Daniel from the power of the lions. So this Daniel prospered in the reign of Darius and in the reign of Cyrus the Persian (Daniel 6:24-28).

As we close this terrific account of Daniel's faithfulness to God and the Lord's amazing deliverance, make sure you notice the following observations:

1. Daniel left his detractors to God. He did not seek revenge or take the matter into his own hands.

2. King Darius, like Nebuchadnezzar, seemed converted to Jehovah God (as indicated in his declaration to the whole empire). Once again, God used Daniel to impact the lives of people around him for all eternity.

3. This chapter does not mention the return of the Jews to Jerusalem by Cyrus' decree; however, Ezra does. Daniel could have easily bragged about the fact that God had used him to impact the king who would eventually allow the Jews to return home. But Daniel was too humble for that!

4. This is the last picture we see of Daniel prior to his death. As far as we know, Daniel remained faithful to his God until his last days!

When God allows us to stumble into a lions' den, He has not forgotten us! Tragically, when we find ourselves in a fiery furnace or in the midst of lions, we question if God still cares for us. Daniel teaches us that problems may come our way even when we do what is right. But even then, God never forsakes us!

God always meets our needs in His time. But sometimes, His time is not ours. When that happens, let your resolution be to remain faithful to God and to wait on Him for his deliverance. May David's words in Psalm 27:1-3 always be true of us:

The LORD is my light and my salvation; whom shall I fear? The

LORD is the strength of my life; of whom shall I be afraid? When the wicked came against me to eat up my flesh, my enemies and foes, they stumbled and fell. Though an army may encamp against me, my heart shall not fear; though war should rise against me, in this I will be confident.

Discussion Questions

1. Daniel 6:3 states that Daniel had an excellent spirit. How did Daniel cultivate such a spirit? How can you do the same? (Make sure to list practical ways)

2. Write down Psalm 55:17. Was this Psalm true of Daniel's life? Is it true of yours?

3. How is your prayer life? How long do you spend in prayer on any given day? Brainstorm some practical ways to improve your prayer life.

4. What does it take to be faithful to God under pressure? What are some circumstances in your own life that might tempt you to deny your relationship with the Lord? What are you willing to do about it?

5. What are five key observations that we can make about Daniel's prayer in Daniel 6:6-13? What do they mean? Why are they important?

6. What are you saying to God when you are thankful to Him even during times of distress?

7. Can you think of a time when God delivered you from a situation that seemed hopeless? What did He do to deliver you? How can that give you comfort to face the difficulties that tomorrow may hold for you?

That's Not All

You can find sermon outlines in the "Sermonars" section at the back of the book. These pages may be freely reproduced, either from the book or from the accompanying CD-ROM for any devotional or ministry use.

Chapter Ten

Profiling the Antichrist

In this chapter, we come to a passage that is one of the most difficult in the entire Bible. So far in the book of Daniel, we have had pretty easy reading. Most of it has consisted of historical narrative which recounts Daniel's days in the pagan city of Babylon. However, as we look at Daniel 7:19-28, we find a different type of literature—prophecy. If we can understand the next six chapters in this book, we will have a very solid grasp on biblical prophecy. These six chapters are composed of four visions, or dreams, given to Daniel by God. We discover in these dreams a number of characters seen by Daniel, including the Son of God, who will reign over an eternal kingdom, and an evil man known as the Antichrist, who will rule over a kingdom that will envelop the Earth.

With this passage, we move from the visions of Nebuchadnezzar to the visions of Daniel. And lest you think I interpret this passage incorrectly, notice what God also gives to Daniel besides the dream. With the dream comes an angelic visitor who gives Daniel the interpretation. With this information, we can be confident of what God is saying through the symbols in these visions.

Just how powerful can a preview of the end times be? Donald Campbell, a faithful minister of the gospel, tells a story about a retired Army colonel who introduced himself to Campbell after this minister had given a message on end times prophecy. Having been retired from the army for only a short time, he told Campbell that the last thing he did in the military was participate in a mock staging of World War III. Joining other officers from the Pentagon, he left Washington, D.C. and went to a remote underground retreat that had been established to carry on the affairs of government in the event of a nuclear attack.

Once they arrived at the retreat, these military men staged the "final conflict" between the nations. They projected that it would begin with a nuclear exchange between Israel and the Arab nations. The great superpowers, the United States and Russia, would then be drawn into the war. Finally, the European nations would join the conflict. The ensuing worldwide nuclear warfare would result in the loss of 55 million lives in the United States alone. This Christian officer was so shaken at the prospect of this war that he resigned his commission and now spends his time trying to reach people with the gospel of Jesus Christ before the end comes.[1]

Only God knows how the world is going to end, and only God knows how He will bring America to its knees. Do you believe that God had a hand in the founding of this nation? I certainly believe He did, but we have become very arrogant. He knows, however, just how to bring this country down! The very prospect of such an act greatly impacted one high-ranking Army officer, just as a preview of the end times has had a profound impact on everyone who has received it. What does the Bible say about the end times? Daniel caught a glimpse of it, and it left him overwhelmed! But through his vision, Daniel became the first biblical writer to tell us about a unique, satanically-inspired individual who will come and lead the nations in the final rebellion against God.

Impact of the Vision

Daniel describes the impact his visions had on him in Daniel 7:28, "This is the end of the account. As for me, Daniel, my thoughts greatly troubled me, and my countenance changed; but I kept the matter in my heart." The display and description of the Antichrist coming to the world in the end times left Daniel absolutely overwhelmed! Let me make this point very clear lest anyone wonder: the Scriptures emphatically teach that just as there is a Christ and a Holy Spirit living inside each Christian, the Antichrist will someday come to this world. It is troubling to me that there are so many pulpits and so many ministers who are silent about this fact. Why would anyone be silent about one of the most horrific things that will ever hit Earth? But you may think, "What are we going to do when the Antichrist arrives?" The answer is: nothing, because believers will not be here when this man is revealed. We will be spared, but we must still send out a warning to anyone who has never placed their faith in Christ.

Other biblical authors have described the Antichrist as well. Notice what John wrote in 1 John 2:18, "Little children, it is the last hour; and as you have heard that the Antichrist is coming, even now many antichrists have come, by which we know that it is the last hour." John wrote those words nearly twenty centuries ago. If John felt that it was the last hour when he was writing, what message does that convey to us?

Paul describes this man and his times in 2 Thessalonians 2:3, "Let no one deceive you by any means; for that Day will not come unless the falling away comes first." What is this "falling away?" It is a reference to a mass apostasy. But this falling away will not be made up of people who hate God. It will consist of people who invent a god, a savior, a church, and a faith that accommodates their lifestyle. What will happen after this falling away occurs? Paul says, "the man of sin is revealed, the son of perdition, who opposes and exalts himself above all that is called God or that is worshiped, so that he sits as God in the temple of God, showing himself that he is God" (2 Thessalonians 2:4). This describes what the Antichrist will do in the middle of the seven-year Tribulation. He will initially come onto the scene as a man of peace, a man who will draw the nations together in the most tumultuous part of the world, the Middle East. In the middle of the Tribulation, however, he will announce that he is God.

Take note also of John's description of this man in Revelation 13:1, "Then I stood on the sand of the sea. And I saw a beast rising up out of the sea, having seven heads and ten horns, and on his horns ten crowns, and on his heads a blasphemous name. Now the beast which I saw was like a leopard, his feet were like the feet of a bear, and his mouth like the mouth of a lion." This vision makes sense in light of other images that we have seen in Daniel.

What do these three animals represent? They represent three different nations. The final world power will be an amalgamation of these European powers. But where will the Antichrist get the power to lead such a group? John says in verse 2 that, "the dragon gave him his power, his throne, and great authority."

As Daniel himself testified, he was overwhelmed by the vision that he saw because it represented this man of sin. I cannot even imagine what it must have been like. Daniel had been through so much, but when he saw the Antichrist and masses of people falling under his sway, he was still overwhelmed.

Timetable of Daniel 7

Daniel 7:1 gives us a timetable for this vision: "In the first year of Belshazzar king of Babylon, Daniel had a dream and visions of his head while on his bed. Then he wrote down the dream, telling the main facts." The chronology of Daniel does not follow the order of the chapters. The events of chapter 7 come before those of chapter 5, in which Belshazzar has a drunken orgy before receiving the handwriting on the wall. That very night, Persian forces conquered the city of Babylon and Belshazzar died. Thus, we see that Daniel's vision in chapter 7 had to come before the events of chapter 5. Chronologically, chapter 7 takes us back in time to a point fourteen years prior to Belshazzar's drunken party in chapter 5. Daniel would have been sixty-eight years old at the time of the vision.

Daniel 7 may be divided into two parts: Daniel's vision in verses 1–14, and the interpretation of the vision in verses 15–28. This chapter also provides us with our introduction to the Antichrist who is to come, since this is the first time he is mentioned in all of Scripture. Here he is pictured symbolically as a boastful little horn with a shrewd intellect. This horn has sprung up from a beast so terrible that it defied description. The other kingdoms were described as animals, but this final kingdom is not even described as an animal because it is so horrific no beast could begin to convey it. Keep this in mind, for this man and this kingdom are coming upon the world! Dr. James Montgomery Boice described the Antichrist, writing, "Antichrist will be a substitute for Christ, as much like Christ as is possible for a tool of Satan. He will talk about justice and love, peace and prosperity. He will be brilliant and eloquent. In short, he will appear as an angel of light, as Satan himself often does, and will be hailed by millions as a superman who will save mankind."[2]

Look for a moment how Daniel introduces his vision of the Antichrist in Daniel 7:7. He writes, "After this I saw in the night visions, and behold, a fourth beast, dreadful and terrible, exceedingly strong. It had huge iron teeth; it was devouring, breaking in pieces, and trampling the residue with its feet. It was different from all the beasts that were before it, and it had ten horns." The fourth beast Daniel sees is not identified with any known animal since nothing in the animal kingdom is fierce and terrible enough to portray this kingdom. Remember: this is the kingdom out of which the Antichrist will rise.

An angel tells Daniel that the four beasts represent four kings which shall arise out of the earth (Daniel 7:17). The fourth beast represents the fourth kingdom, which is the revived Roman Empire (verse 23). The ten horns symbolize ten rulers that will arise out of the region once controlled by Rome (verse 24). The kings will all rule at the same time, a phenomenon not to be found in the past. We expect that the Roman Empire in this form will reappear and that the ten rulers will be in power in the end times (see Rev 13:1, 17:12).

But notice that Daniel writes in 7:24, "another shall rise after them." Another ruler, in addition to the ten and different from them, will rise to power (verse 24). This is the "little horn" of verse 8, the one who is called "Antichrist." When this little horn comes up, he arises in a very nonchalant way. But as he begins to expose himself, his first act is to conquer three other kings. Thus, he will begin his rise to power.

Distinguishing Traits of the Antichrist

The narrative recorded in Daniel 7 gives us six distinguishing traits of the Antichrist:

1. The Antichrist will be an unequaled orator

This trait is described in Daniel 7:8, which says, "I was considering the horns, and there was another horn, a little one, coming up among them, before whom three of the first horns were plucked out by the roots. And there, in this horn, were eyes like the eyes of a man, and a mouth speaking pompous words." The Antichrist will have a fairly inconspicuous beginning. Initially, he will not necessarily appear unique or special, but notice what else Daniel says in 7:8, "...before whom three of the first horns were plucked out by the roots. And there, in this horn, were eyes like the eyes of a man, and a mouth speaking pompous words." The phrase "eyes like the eyes of a man" suggests tremendous personal magnetism and dominance. Darby states:

> This power is clear-sighted and penetrating in its intelligence. It not only possesses strength, but it has thoughts and plans besides those of ambition and government. It is a beast that works morally, that occupies itself with knowledge, and sets itself up with pretension full of pride and daring. It has a character of intelligence, moral and systematic (in evil), and not merely the strength of a conqueror. This horn has the eyes of a man.[3]

Daniel wishes to know more about this little horn, so he inquires about it and what it will do. In 7:19-20 he writes:

> Then I wished to know the truth about the fourth beast, which was different from all the others, exceedingly dreadful, with its teeth of iron and its nails of bronze, which devoured, broke in pieces, and trampled the residue with its feet; and the ten horns that were on its head, and the other horn which came up, before which three fell, namely, that horn which had eyes and a mouth which spoke pompous words, whose appearance was greater than his fellows.

The answer he receives is in 7:25, "He shall speak pompous words against the Most High." When the Antichrist comes onto the scene, he will begin to negotiate and will bring together the troubled countries of the Middle East. As he speaks, he sways the crowds because he has Satan's power on him.

2. The Antichrist will be most unusually attractive

The text says of him that his appearance was greater than his fellows (7:20). The word used here means, "abundant in size or in rank." He has a stature and a charisma about him that sets him apart from those around him.

3. The Antichrist will be a most clever leader

As we saw before, verse 20 says that he has "eyes," which makes reference to his mental ability, his intellect, and his cleverness. He will be able to solve the problems of the world with his cleverness and wisdom.

Not long ago, I read a book about Saddam Hussein, the former dictator of Iraq. As I read sections of it, I was overwhelmed because I realized that during recent years there have been two nations that literally illustrated what conditions will be like when the Antichrist is here: North Korea and Iraq. In Iraq before the fall of Saddam and in North Korea to this day, public spaces abound with pictures of the dictator. In North Korea, their dictator is even revered as a god! But in reality, he is nothing more than a cruel despot. These dictators have spent millions and millions of dollars building armaments while their own people are starving.

It is sad to say, however, that the man who is coming makes these men look like choir boys. His magnetism will attract millions to him. Multitudes will follow him even though he will gain power ruthlessly. Daniel 7:8 informs us that within the ten-nation confederation, he will rise up and subdue three other kings. The text says they will be "plucked out by the roots." This phrase literally means "to squeeze out, to push out by subterfuge, to come in and cleverly replace." Daniel 11:21 teaches the same: "And in his place shall arise a vile person, to whom they will not give the honor of royalty; but he shall come in peaceably, and seize the kingdom by intrigue." The process is very simple: he immediately sets up a covenant in the Middle East that promises that the Jews can live in their homeland, unharrassed by their Arab neighbors. But in the middle of the Tribulation, he interrupts the covenant, walks into the Jewish temple, proclaims himself God, and demands that the entire world worship him.

4. The Antichrist will be a cruel leader

Let me expose a myth at this point. I have met many Christians who believe that after Jesus comes at the Rapture, no one during the Tribulation will be able to become Christians. That is simply not true. They will still have access to the Scriptures. Dr. Henry Morris writes: "Millions upon millions of copies of the Bible and Bible portions have been published in all major languages and distributed throughout the world... Removal of believers from the world at the Rapture will not remove the Scriptures, and multitudes will no doubt be constrained to read the Bible in those days... and give their testimony for the Word of God." J. Vernon McGee has said that one of the greatest revivals in the history of the world may take place during the Tribulation period[5], and I agree. I believe that every one of your friends and neighbors that you witnessed to and shared Christ with, even though they rejected Him, will see the stark reality when Jesus Christ comes back. Do you know what will happen to scores of people? They will say, "It was true! I should have said yes!" They will bow the knee to Jesus Christ, but they will be in a different dispensation. No longer will there be this era of grace. Instead, the Antichrist will come onto the scene and enact his plan, which includes persecution of believers.

Daniel is careful to mention that the Antichrist will attack Tribulation saints! He makes this point in 7:21-25:

> I was watching; and the same horn was making war against the saints, and prevailing against them, until the Ancient of Days came, and a judgment was made in favor of the saints of the Most High, and the time came for the saints to possess the kingdom. Thus he said: "The fourth beast shall be a fourth kingdom on earth, which shall be different from all other kingdoms, and shall devour the whole earth, trample it and break it in pieces. The ten horns are ten kings who shall arise from this kingdom. And another shall rise after them; he shall be different from the first ones, and shall subdue three kings. He shall speak pompous words against the Most High, shall persecute the saints of the Most High...

What these verses say is that the Antichrist will wear them out. This phrase is used elsewhere to refer to wearing out garments. We know that there will be an identification system during the end times, the mark of the beast. Do you think any God-fearing, truly redeemed Christian during the Tribulation will want to be the first in line for this identification system? Absolutely not! When they refuse to receive the mark, the Antichrist will know who they are and will slowly cut them off from society.

We see this movement toward identification in our own time. Recently, an article in *Newsweek* magazine reported that right now the Department of Homeland Security in the United States is planning to assign a national identification number to every single one of us. There are instruments today that can read the retina of your eye. There are even microchips that can store every last bit of information about you. We are living in a different age than our spiritual forefathers. They could not imagine such things!

The Antichrist will harass people who come to Christ during the Tribulation. He will not let them have a moment of rest. Dr. Philip Newell describes it this way:

> The expression "wear out" (persecute) is the English rendition of

a Chaldee word meaning to afflict, exclusively in a mental state. Something of what may be implied here has already been terribly and tragically seen in the trial and "confession" of Cardinal Mindszenty, whose very personality the Russians disrupted, after a hundred hours or intensive and persistent questioning and periodic injections of actedron and mescaline. The first of these is a synthetically manufactured drug which at first enlivens the physical functions, producing a sensation of strength, but which, if persisted in, produces dizziness, headaches and inability to relax. The second of these drugs originates in a certain type of cactus and induces in human being a state of schizophrenia, or "split personality." What fearful disintegration of the human entity may be expected therefore in "him whose coming is after the working of Satan with all power and signs and lying wonders (2 Thess 2:9-10)."[6]

Dr. Newell is saying that if you think the mind-altering drugs we have are something, they are nothing until the man of sin begins to use them. If you are not certain that you are a Christian, I urge you to make sure today, because we still have the opportunity for grace. If you are holding onto something else, today you had better run to Christ and say, "Lord, today I want to be forgiven." You can come to Christ in the Tribulation, but believers during that time will suffer persecution such as has never been experienced.

5. The Antichrist will be a cultic leader

We have already seen that the Antichrist will speak pompous words against the Most High. As he exalts himself, he will very slowly begin to repudiate Jehovah God. He will then begin to initiate changes to bolster his power. Daniel 7:25 says, "[He] shall intend to change times and law. Then the saints will be given into his hand for a time and times and half a time." The last phrase refers to a period of three and a half years. The Antichrist will enter the newly rebuilt temple in Jerusalem and proclaim himself God in the middle of the Tribulation period. So after he sets himself up as God, the people of God will need to get ready. We have seen nothing like the worldwide, systematic move against believers that the Antichrist will initiate at that time.

The Antichrist will attempt to take God's place. He will ask the people to fall down and worship him. Then what will he do to support this demand? He must begin to make changes, because we have a culture that is based on belief, with a calendar that reminds us of the advent of the Savior. Much of our law is based on the Ten Commandments. What must he do, then? He must change the moral law of the universe. He will produce amazing signs, miracles, and wonders to accomplish this feat.

Daniel wrote that the Antichrist will change the "law." He used the word in the singular. This seems to convey the fundamental, basic conditions of human society, which even in our own day are in the obvious process of disintegration. What will he change? If I had to guess five changes, I would guess these.

- First, I think he will change the whole calendar. I think he will eliminate the traditional week, in which we work Monday through Friday and have the weekend off, including Sunday for worship. We are already seeing reference to Christ in our dates removed. Universities no longer say "before Christ," they say "before the common era."

- Second, I think he will change the definition of the family. I think he will do away with the roles of the father, mother, and children.

- Third, I think he will get rid of the permanency of marriage.

- Fourth, I think that he will reject Christians as outlaw extremists. As believers speak out against the other changes, the Antichrist will unleash his wrath on them.

- Fifth, I think that the basic norms of biblical sexuality will be blurred.

The Antichrist will continue on the work that Satan is doing today because he is Satan's man! Notice what Paul writes in 2 Thessalonians 2:8–9, "And then the lawless one will be revealed, whom the Lord will consume with the breath of His mouth and destroy with the brightness of His coming. The coming of the lawless one is according to the working of Satan, with all power, signs, and lying wonders." The Antichrist will possess *dunamis*, which is the same word used for the power of the gospel. Don't be naïve: this is not a person who is just going to say a few curse words and try to freak people out. He is coming with "dynamite," having Satanic power.

144

6. *The destruction of the Antichrist*

Appreciate what Daniel writes in 7:26–27, for it gives us hope: "But the court shall be seated, and they shall take away his dominion, to consume and destroy it forever. Then the kingdom and dominion, and the greatness of the kingdoms under the whole heaven, shall be given to the people, the saints of the Most High. His kingdom is an everlasting kingdom, and all dominions shall serve and obey Him."

What will happen after the Second Coming of Christ? Jesus will usher in the Millennial Kingdom, His 1,000 year earthly reign. And guess who will reign with Him? Every person saved in this period of time known as "grace." The Antichrist will think that his power is great, but it will be taken from him by "the court." The court is God's angelic assembly, which at the appointed hour will take action against the Antichrist. Newell writes:

> The elders, then, appear to be those chief princes of whom Michael himself is one (Daniel 10:13). Together they constitute the grand administrative council of God's universal rule, concerning which Jehovah Himself cried by Jeremiah 23:18, "For who hath stood in the council of Jehovah, that he should perceive and hear His word?" This council seems to have a definitely assigned place of meeting (Isa. 14:13; Ezek. 28:14,16) and a regularly scheduled day on which all angelic beings, including Satan himself, must report before it (Job 1:6; 2:1)... other Scriptures suggest to us the manner in which information is reported before this solemn tribunal.[7]

Daniel wraps up his vision in verse 28, "This is the end of my account. As for me, Daniel, my thoughts greatly troubled me, and my countenance changed, but I kept the matter in my heart."

The Antichrist is coming, but according to John, his spirit is already here! In 1 John 4:3, he writes, "And this is the spirit of the Antichrist, which you have heard was coming, and is now already in the world." The stage is already being set for the coming of the Antichrist. How? Can we not see the moral conditions sliding into decay, preparing for the last days? We can also see the stage being set economically. We need only look at history to see this fact.

The abject conditions of the economy in Germany after World War I helped catapult Adolf Hitler to power. The German treasury was low in gold; the budget was unbalanced. Sound familiar? In 1919 the German mark was worth 25 cents. Within four years, 4 trillion marks were needed to equal one dollar of U.S. currency. The German middle class lost all their savings. The value of every pension was wiped out. All security was gone, and the people were willing to listen to any leader who would help them solve their problems. Enter Adolf Hitler!

It was Nicolai Lenin who said, "The surest way to overthrow an existing social order is to debauch the currency."[8] What do you think would happen in the United States if a charismatic, wonder-working leader were to walk across the American scene and say, "I have the answer to the economic stress of this country?" The stage is being set, and the only way of escape is to believe in Jesus Christ.

Discussion Questions

1. Why do Christians shy away from discussing and proclaiming the truth about the Antichrist?

2. What traits will characterize the falling away of the end times? (See 1 Tim 4:1-3; 2 Tim 3:1-9)

3. How will the Antichrist initially come into power? How will he deceive the world before showing his true colors at the mid-point of the Tribulation?

4. What will the Antichrist's reaction to Christians be? How will he persecute them?

5. What character traits will the Antichrist possess that will draw people to him?

6. Who will give the Antichrist his power? How will this power be manifested?

7. What will the end of the Antichrist be? (See Rev 19:20-21)

8. The Antichrist will seek to take the place of Christ in this world. How do we see this attitude at work in the world already? What people, groups, or ideologies are seeking to remove Christ from the public eye?

Chapter Eleven

Your Invitation to Christ's Eternal Kingdom

The world today is in unrest. Every Sunday I read the *New York Times*, and one week recently I saw picture after picture of millions in Europe marching in protest against our president, George W. Bush, hoping that he would put an end to the war in Iraq. The prospects at the outset of the war were truly frightening. We did not know what sort of weapons Saddam Hussein possessed. Apparently we overestimated his weaponry, but what if we had underestimated it just as badly? What if Iraq had possessed nuclear weapons? Any way you slice it, the situation in the Middle East is a dangerous one.

It seems that the United States was wrong in thinking that we could merely remove Saddam from power and be done with war in the Middle East. In Pakistan alone there are 7,000 extreme Islamic schools, training some 1.5 million students to be loyal to Osama Bin Laden. When we see such devotion to terror, we must wonder where the world is going. What kind of kingdom is coming?

Dr. Linus Pauling, a Nobel Prize-winning scientist, has said that he is afraid that the greatest catastrophe in the history of the world will occur in the next twenty-five to fifty years. He said that he is nonetheless an optimist and believes the human race *might* survive. What optimism—we *might* survive!

What does the future hold? Is there any way for man to know what is ahead? Who is going to rule the world? God alone knows the future, of course, but He has revealed in the Bible everything that man needs to know about coming events. When you have confidence in God's Word, the fear of future events is taken away.

Some people are writing and talking about doomsday, an unexpected world war. Could this happen? Professor Alfred Weber, a great historian and economist, said in his book *Farewell to European History* that to a person who is endowed with historical perspective it must be clear that we are at the end of world history as we know it.[1] H. G. Wells, another well-known historian, in his book *The Mind at the End of Its Tether*, said, "I predict that the generation in which you and I live will be the last generation on earth."[2] These men were not ministers; they were historians. Some were professors. What were they saying? Their message is that the world cannot go on with the turmoil and interracial strife that exists today. The Middle East has reached the boiling point, yet so many of us are absorbed with America that we do not realize it.

Strange things are happening in the world today. Many people in the world are afraid that the situation in Iraq and North Korea could plunge the world into a massive worldwide war. In light of this concern, does it not make sense for us to understand the prophetic plan that God has delineated in His Word? It would give us an incredible amount of peace.

Scholars have said that Daniel 7 is the summit of Scripture. It is certainly the center of gravity for the entire book of Daniel. The scribes who preserved the Old Testament said that Daniel 7 was considered to be the greatest chapter in the Old Testament. From the chart on the next page, we can get a better understanding of Daniel 7 and how it relates to chapter 2.

Think back for just a minute before we move on. If you recall, in Daniel 2 Nebuchadnezzar had a dream which he was unable to decipher. Daniel, providentially, was in Babylon as a deportee. Though he was only 20 years old, he had been blessed by God with wisdom and skill in all types of things because of his obedience to the Lord. Daniel providentially interprets the king's dream. This is the essence of Daniel 2.

In his dream, the great Nebuchadnezzar represented a world Gentile empire, with three others coming after him. He stood aghast as a young Hebrew boy interpreted the dream that is now connected to the vision we see in chapter 7. In Daniel 2, the image Nebuchadnezzar saw was the

GENTILE WORLD EMPIRES	MAN'S VIEW/ DANIEL 2	GOD'S VIEW/ DANIEL 7
Babylon	Head of gold	Lion with eagle's wings
Medo-Persia	Arms/breasts of silver	Bear with 3 ribs in teeth
Greece	Belly and thighs of brass	Beast like a leopard
Rome	Legs of iron	Nameless beast/iron teeth
(A long parenthesis: This church age, which God did not reveal to Daniel.)		
Revived Roman Empire	Feet and Ten Toes	Ten horns of 4th beast and "the little horn," who is the Antichrist
Gentile Dominion will end with the return of Christ	The smiting stone	The coming of the Son of Man in Glory

image of an idol with different sections. In chapter 7, Daniel sees four different beasts that represent the different sections of Nebuchadnezzar's idol. The first three beasts are represented by different specific animals, but the fourth is so terrible that no real animal can describe it. Brace yourself—that fourth beast is the future revived Roman Empire that some European nations are presently moving toward. It is the kingdom that the Antichrist will come from, and it is so vicious and pernicious that no animal can begin to describe it.

In Daniel 2, Babylon was represented by the head of gold; in chapter 7, it is a lion with eagle's wings. The second kingdom, Medo-Persia, is pictured in chapter 2 by the duality of the silver arms and breast. In chapter 7, it is seen as a bear with three ribs in its teeth. Greece, the third kingdom, makes up the belly and thighs of brass in the idol of Daniel 2.

In chapter 7, it is a beast like a leopard with four wings and four heads. After Alexander the Great's death, his kingdom was split among his four generals; thus, this beast had four wings and heads. The fourth kingdom, Rome, is pictured as legs of iron on the idol of chapter 2, while it is a nameless beast with iron teeth in chapter 7.

After this last kingdom, there is what we might call a long parenthesis. This simply refers to a delay in the fulfillment of God's prophetic plan. In this parenthesis we find the church age, the dispensation of grace, which God did not reveal to Daniel. After this delay, we find the revived Roman Empire, which will come to power as we move toward the end of the age. This empire is represented by the feet and toes of the idol. Notice the devaluation in the idol as we move from top to bottom. The head is made of gold, but the feet and toes are made up of clay. These feet and toes are represented by the ten horns of the fourth beast in chapter 7.

Finally, in both chapters we see that the Gentile dominion will end with the return of Christ. His return is represented by the smiting stone in chapter 2. But notice how it is pictured in Daniel 7: Daniel describes the coming of the Son of Man in glory!

Timetable of Daniel 7

Daniel 7:1 gives us the timetable for this chapter: "In the first year of Belshazzar king of Babylon, Daniel had a dream and visions of his head while on his bed. Then he wrote down the dream, telling the main facts." Remember that chapter 7 precedes the events of chapter 5. Daniel says that his vision occurred in the first year of Belshazzar. Belshazzar was a co-regent of Babylon with his father Nabonidus. Belshazzar's first year was approximately 553 BC. If Daniel was fifteen when he was taken to Babylon in captivity at 605 BC, then he would be about sixty-seven years old in chapter 7. This means that the dream which Nebuchadnezzar had would have occurred over fifty years ago. Do you think delay means that God will fail to fulfill His plan? Absolutely not!

Dr. Louis Talbot, the former chancellor of Biola University, the man who taught Dr. J. Vernon McGee, offers a helpful explanation of the relationship between these two chapters in the book of Daniel. He writes:

> Chapters 2 and 7 of the book of Daniel present the same general prophecy, but from different points of view. Both outline the entire

period of "times of the Gentiles," which began with Nebuchadnez-zar and will end with the return of Christ in glory. In chapter two Nebuchadnezzar, "the natural man," saw Gentile world dominion from the standpoint of the godless world; whereas Daniel, "the spiritual man," saw it from God's viewpoint. Consequently, Nebu-chadnezzar's vision presented the image of man, noble, stately, and magnificent; Daniel's vision set forth four powerful, Gentile world empires, represented by four ravenous, monstrous beasts, depicting the moral character of the nations. The image which Babylon's king saw filled him with pride, and later he set up a golden image, demanding worship of himself; the vision which Daniel saw pre-sented Gentile world power in God's unsullied light, revealing the brutality, the fierceness, and greed of these Christ-rejecting king-doms of men.[3]

Here is a helpful summary of chapter 7:

• Verses 2-8 reveal the four beasts (four Gentile world empires)

• Verses 9-12 show the judgment from the Ancient of Days

• Verses 13-14 present the triumphant coming of the Son of Man

• Verses 15-27 give the explanation of the preceding images

Perhaps you are thinking, "How do we really know that those beasts represent empires?" We are told as much in Daniel 7:17, "Those great beasts, which are four, are four kings which arise out of the earth." Not only do we have the record of Daniel's dream, but we also have a record of the explanation given to him by an angel. Dr. J. Vernon McGee has a helpful comment on Daniel's prophecies:

> God gives to Daniel several visions of four beasts which are quite remarkable. Daniel had these visions at three different periods. The vision of chapter 7 was in the first year of King Belshazzar. In chap-ter 8 the vision was seen in the third year of the reign of Belshazzar. In chapter 9 it was in the first year of Darius; in chapter 10 it was in the third year of Cyrus; and in chapters 11 and 12 the vision was seen in the first year of Darius. Daniel did not record these visions in the historical section (chapter 1-6) but gathered these propheti-cal visions together in this second section of his book.[4]

This is amazing to me. We know Daniel has been full of wisdom since he was a young man, and now as an old man he carefully arranges the chronology of his book. On the chronology of Daniel 7 in particular, Dr. Harry Bultema offers this comment:

> So here, too, we have a significant chronological reference. The first year of Belshazzar must have been a sad one for Daniel. With grief he must have come to the conclusion that Belshazzar was a frivolous crown prince. It was a time during which Daniel was ignored. We saw earlier that Belshazzar did not even know him, and not to know a great man like Daniel is a failure to appreciate him.[5]

When Belshazzar was in the drunken orgy of chapter 5, it took the queen mother to come and tell this ignorant little kid that there was one person who could interpret the handwriting on the wall. Notice that she didn't use the pagan name Belteshazzar, which had been given to Daniel by Nebuchadnezzar; rather, she used his Hebrew name, Daniel.

Do you know why I think God gave Daniel this vision? I think he asked God to clarify for him some information concerning the future empires that would come. God heard his prayer, and consented.

This chapter ties together the entire book of Daniel. Dr. Norman W. Porteous writes: "With this chapter we reach the heart of the book of Daniel. It is related so closely to what precedes and also to what follows that, when one makes the obvious division of the book into stories and visions, it is very difficult to determine whether chapter 7 ought to be linked more closely with the former or with the latter."[6] This passage reaches into the previous narrative with its ties to chapter 2. It also reaches futuristically by delineating the world empires.

This vision was given to Daniel about 553 BC. We are going to see Daniel take a telescope and look over centuries with absolute accuracy. With this confidence in the accuracy of God's Word, let us take a closer look at this vision.

The First Beast–The Lion (Babylon)–Daniel 7:2-4

Daniel describes the first beast in verses 2-4 of his vision:

> Daniel spoke, saying, "I saw in my vision by night, and behold, the four winds of heaven were stirring up the Great Sea. And four great

beasts came up from the sea, each different from the other. The first was like a lion, and had eagle's wings. I watched till its wings were plucked off; and it was lifted up from the earth and made to stand on two feet like a man, and a man's heart was given to it."

If you look at some of the ancient maps of the Middle East, you will see that they refer to the Mediterranean Sea as "the Great Sea." Daniel is not talking about the Dead Sea or the Sea of Galilee; he is talking about the Mediterranean Sea. All of the empires that we will look at surround the Mediterranean Sea.

This term is probably also a reference to the "sea of humanity." Out of the sea of humanity, Gentile empires arise. The narrative in this chapter is in Aramaic, not Hebrew. God is speaking the language of pagans, and He is reminding us where these pagans came from. The term "four winds" represents the heavenly powers and forces by which God sets the nations of the world in motion.

Daniel is not the only prophet to use this image for Babylon. The prophet Jeremiah described Nebuchadnezzar as a lion. He writes, "Set up the standard toward Zion. Take refuge! Do not delay! For I will bring disaster from the north, and great destruction. The lion has come up from his thicket, and the destroyer of nations is on his way. He has gone forth from his place to make your land desolate. Your cities will be laid waste, without inhabitant (Jer. 4:6-7)." In 586 BC, these words were fulfilled when Nebuchadnezzar devastated the city of Jerusalem.

This beast clearly describes the Babylonian Empire, which ruled from 605-538 BC. The lion speaks of Babylon's strength, the wings of the rapidity of its development, and the heart reminds us of Nebuchadnezzar's conversion in chapter 4. What happened to the king during those six years of insanity? He got right with God, and when this took place, he stopped conquering lands. He was finally at peace.

Talbot comments on exactly how the lion typifies Babylon:

> From man's point of view, Babylon appeared in its greatness as fine gold, but God permitted Daniel to see its real moral character, which was that of a ravenous lion. As the lion is the king of the forest, so Nebuchadnezzar's monarchy was more absolute than any of those which succeeded it. The lion, a "symbol of strength and courage," typified Babylon, "the head of gold." The eagle's wings speak

to us of the swiftness of conquest and of the wide-spread power of Babylon's great king. In the British Museum today one can see the winged lions, carved in stone, that once symbolically guarded Babylon. Again, the lion is ferocious, as well as majestic; and Nebuchadnezzar had the power of life and death—a power which he evidently exercised; for "whom he would, he slew."[7]

The Second Beast—The Bear (Medo-Persia)—Daniel 7:5

It is interesting to see how God views these empires. In chapter 2, we saw things from the human perspective. In this chapter, we see things from a heavenly point of view. How impressed is God with these empires? He gave three verses to Babylon, but He only gives one to Medo-Persia: "And suddenly another beast, a second, like a bear. It was raised up on one side, and had three ribs in its mouth between its teeth. And they said thus to it: 'Arise, devour much flesh!'" This beast clearly describes the Medo-Persian Empire, which devastated Babylon in 538 BC. Babylon, as it was before that point, was finished; the Medo-Persians ruled the scene until 331 BC. This empire was typified as the breasts and arms of silver in Daniel 2:32, 39, as well as the ram in 8:3-4, 20.

The Persian element of this empire was stronger than that of the Medes. Consequently, the bear in this verse is said to be raised up on one side. The Medo-Persian Empire was as unpredictable and cruel in its attacks as a bear. Isaiah wrote in Isaiah 13:17-22 of Medo-Persia's destruction of Babylon. He tells us that they would not be bribed or turned aside for a price, but they would mutilate the bodies of young soldiers and they would not spare the unborn child or the little children.

The Third Beast—The Leopard (Greece)—Daniel 7:6

Daniel wrote in 7:6, "After this I looked, and there was another, like a leopard, which had on its back four wings of a bird. The beast also had four heads, and dominion was given to it." The leopard symbolizes the Greek Empire, which ruled from 331-146 BC, when it was stopped by the Roman Empire. The Grecians were typified by the belly and thighs of brass in Daniel 2:32, 39 and as the goat in 8:5-14, 21-22. The first ruler of this empire, Alexander the Great, died in 323 BC in Babylon. However, in ten short years he had conquered the entire Medo-Persian Empire.

Alexander the Great, who was heir to Philip of Macedon, conquered Medo-Persia and extended the Grecian Empire into even wider borders. He did it all so quickly that it is said he "wept because there were no more worlds to conquer." Known as one of the world's mightiest conquerors, Alexander overthrew several hundred thousand Persians with thirty thousand soldiers. It has been suggested that the leopard's spots may well represent the many nations and tongues that fell under his command. But Alexander did not spread Grecian influence merely through force. He took Persians into his army, encouraged his soldiers to intermarry, and began a policy to Hellenize Asia by establishing Greek cities in the eastern part of the empire.

After Alexander's death, his vast empire was divided by his generals into four parts, typified by the four heads and four wings of the leopard. These generals were:

1. Antipater, and later Cassander, who gained control of Greece and Macedonia

2. Lysimachus, who ruled Thrace and a large part of Asia Minor

3. Seleucus I Nicator, who governed Syria, Babylon, and much of the Middle East (all of Asia except Asia Minor and Palestine)

4. Ptolemy I Soter, who controlled Egypt and Palestine

Dr. John Walvoord stated: "In view of the transparent fact that Alexander did have four generals who succeeded him and divided his empire into four divisions, neither more nor less, it would seem that the interpretation of the four wings and four heads as referring to the divisions of the Grecian Empire with their rulers is the best interpretation."[8]

The accuracy of this prophecy is so powerful that even Alexander the Great himself was moved by it. Ironside relates the following story:

> There is an interesting story related by Josephus, to the effect that when Alexander was marching through Syria, after the conquest of Tyre, with his armies headed toward Jerusalem, which he intended to destroy, the high priest and his companions robed themselves in their priestly garments and marched in solemn procession out of the city to meet the conqueror. Alexander is said to have recog-

nized the high priest as one whom he had seen in a vision. From his hand he received a copy of the book of Daniel, in which the prophecies concerning himself were pointed out. Because of what was there written, he accepted the submission of the Jews, granted them religious toleration, and left their city unharmed.[9]

Let me quote from Josephus himself:

> And when the book of Daniel was shown him wherein Daniel declared that one of the Greeks should destroy the empire of the Persians, he supposed that he was the person intended; and as he was then glad, he dismissed the multitude for the present, but the next day he called them to him and bade them ask what favors they pleased of him; whereupon the high priest desired that they might enjoy the laws of their forefathers, and might pay no tribute on the seventh year. He granted all they desired; and when they entreated him that he would permit the Jews in Babylon and Media to enjoy their own laws also, *he willingly promised to do hereafter what they desired* [emphasis added].[10]

Do you find it amazing that a Jewish priest could come to Alexander and show him the book of Daniel? Is it not astounding that this great conqueror, instead of decimating the city of Jerusalem, would see himself predicted and thus give the Jews religious freedom? This truly amazing account recorded by Josephus verifies the fulfillment of God's Word. The Jewish leaders knew that the prophecy of Daniel, which had been written when Belshazzar was still reigning in Babylon several hundred years earlier, applied to Alexander the Great in their own day. In exact detail, God fulfills His prophetic Word!

The Fourth Beast—The Nondescript Beast (Rome)— Daniel 7:7-8

Daniel 7:7-8 describes the fourth beast which Daniel saw:

> After this I saw in the night visions, and behold, a fourth beast, dreadful and terrible, exceedingly strong. It had huge iron teeth; it was devouring, breaking in pieces, and trampling the residue with its feet. It was different from all the beasts that were before it,

and it had ten horns. I was considering the horns, and there was another horn, a little one, coming up among them, before whom three of the first horns were plucked out by the roots. And there, in this horn, were eyes like the eyes of a man, and a mouth speaking pompous words.

This beast was so horrible that there was no animal that could convey it! It represented both the historic Roman Empire and the revived Roman Empire, which is yet to come. This future empire will be a confederation of ten kings in a European coalition.

Daniel said this beast was "devouring, breaking in pieces." A good illustration of this was the Roman destruction of the Jewish temple in AD 70, when the Roman general Titus marched into the city and destroyed it. Talbot says of this fourth beast:

> It was this fourth, nameless beast that cast the early Christians to the lions in the amusement arena; yea, it was this beast that crucified our Lord, upon a Roman cross, permitting Israel also to thrust her Messiah out of the world which He had created. It was the fourth beast that extended her borders farther than had any of the first three, literally surrounding the Mediterranean Sea. This beast was known as imperial Rome and conqueror of the world.[11]

The Father Seated in Total Control–Daniel 7:9-11

We have thus seen the four world empires symbolized through these four beasts. Is this not a clear picture of world history? The correspondence is exact. But with these four beasts in our mind and the promise of a revived Roman Empire, how are we to relax? We can only go to bed at night because of the picture of God that is given to us in Daniel 7:9-11. In verse 9, Daniel writes, "I watched till thrones were put in place..." What thrones are those? They do not represent world empires, they represent someone else. We know that God the Father will reign, but who will reign with Him? We will! Do you know whose thrones those are? What a humbling thought–they are our thrones! We will reign with God, sinners justified by Jesus Christ.

Daniel continues, writing:

The Ancient of Days was seated; His garment was white as snow, and the hair of His head was like pure wool. His throne was a fiery flame, its wheels a burning fire; a fiery stream issued and came forth from before Him. A thousand thousands ministered to Him; ten thousand times ten thousand stood before Him. The court was seated, and the books were opened.

What court is Daniel talking about? We learned in the last chapter that he is describing the angelic court. All of the angelic hosts are waiting for the Father's command. There is no fear or worry in heaven; all is under the watchful eye of the Ancient of Days.

Notice that the court is seated and the books are opened. What day is it? It is judgment day! They are looking at the *books*; the word there is plural. Do you know that God has the sins of every lost man written down? Every last one of them!

The Ancient of Days in this passage is none other than God the Father. The Jews hold the opinion that it is they who are represented here because their Scriptures claim they will be the future judges of the kingdom. This claim is obviously inaccurate. When Daniel says that he saw thrones put in place, these thrones are for the believers of all ages who will be seated with the Father. These thrones were surrounded by an incredible angelic company, 100 million standing before the Father alone, with another million ministering directly to Him.

Destruction of the Antichrist

In the midst of such a beautiful scene, we see the destruction of the Antichrist. His end is recording in Daniel 7:11-12, "I watched then because of the sound of the pompous words which the horn was speaking; I watched till the beast was slain, and its body destroyed and given to the burning flame. As for the rest of the beasts, they had their dominion taken away, yet their lives were prolonged for a season and a time."

This passage obviously describes the fulfillment of Revelation 19:19-20, which says:

And I saw the beast, the kings of the earth, and their armies, gathered together to make war against Him who sat on the horse and against His army. Then the beast was captured, and with him the false prophet who worked signs in his presence, by which he deceived those who received the mark of the beast and those who worshiped his image. These two were cast alive into the lake of fire burning with brimstone.

Presentation of the Kingdom to the Worthy Christ– Daniel 7:13-14

There are many passages of Scripture that tell us that the Son of Man shall come with the clouds of heaven, in power and great glory:

- Matthew 24:30, "Then the sign of the Son of Man will appear in heaven, and then all the tribes of the earth will mourn, and they will see the Son of Man coming on the clouds of heaven with power and great glory."

- Matthew 25:31, "When the Son of Man comes in His glory, and all the holy angels with Him, then He will sit on the throne of His glory."

- Revelation 1:7, "Behold, He is coming with clouds, and every eye will see Him, even they who pierced Him. And all the tribes of the earth will mourn because of Him. Even so, Amen."

Daniel paints a beautiful picture in 7:13-14. This is one of the most touching passages in all Scripture. The Father will literally hand all the kingdoms of the world to the Son:

I was watching in the night visions, and behold, One like the Son of Man, coming with the clouds of heaven! He came to the Ancient of Days, and they brought Him near before Him. Then to Him was given dominion and glory and a kingdom, that all peoples, nations, and languages should serve Him. His dominion is an everlasting dominion, which shall not pass away, and His kingdom the one which shall not be destroyed.

Think of this! Though we are reading in the Old Testament, this passage speaks of the Son of Man, a phrase used repeatedly for Jesus in the New Testament. No wonder, then, that 1,500 years ago the early church father Jerome correctly identified this person as Jesus Christ. This passage fulfills Psalm 110:1, which says, "The Lord said to my Lord, 'Sit at My right hand, till I make Your enemies Your footstool.'" At Christ's second coming, the kingdoms of men will come to an end. They will be replaced by Christ's eternal kingdom!

How did Daniel react to all of this information? Daniel 7:15–17 tells us: "I, Daniel, was grieved in my spirit within my body, and the visions of my head troubled me. I came near to one of those who stood by, and asked him the truth of all this. So he told me and made known to me the interpretation of these things: 'Those great beasts, which are four, are four kings which arise out of the earth.'" Talbot makes these perceptive remarks about the progressive decay of the world empires:

> Daniel's vision began with a portrayal of the first Gentile power as a lion, the king of beasts; but it ended, as far as the nations are concerned, with this fourth beast for which no name could be found. What deterioration! The same was noted in Nebuchadnezzar's image vision. The head was of fine gold, but the other metals were of an increasingly inferior character, until at last the ten toes were of iron mixed with potter's clay! From gold to clay! From a lion to non-descript! This is the history of the Gentile world dominion as God sees it. This is the history of the Gentile world dominion as God sees it. Outwardly, it may seem to flourish, to make great advancement in civilization, science, and inventions; but morally the nations have become ever-increasingly beast-like in character.[12]

There is a famous song that goes like this: "He's got the whole world in His hands." The next verse says, "He's got you and me brothers, in his hands." What do you think? Do you think the God that you see in these verses can carry you through your problems this week? Absolutely! The God who can bring Gentile powers to their knees and even humble the Antichrist is more than able to see us through anything we might face. Our temporal problems are swallowed up in the eternal power of the Ancient of Days!

Discussion Questions

1. How is Daniel 7 linked to Daniel 2? Why do you think God chose to reveal this information again through another vision?

2. What is "the Great Sea?" Why is it significant that this chapter was written in Aramaic, not Hebrew?

3. What new information do we learn about the Medo-Persian Empire in this chapter?

4. What new information do we learn about the Grecian Empire in this chapter?

5. How was Alexander the Great's policy toward the people he conquered different from that of the empires before him?

6. "Son of Man" was a title that Jesus used frequently to refer to Himself. In light of Daniel 7, what was Jesus saying by using this title?

7. Since these prophecies were fulfilled literally in great detail, what does that tell us about the fulfillment of prophecies which have not yet been fulfilled?

That's Not All

You can find sermon outlines in the "Sermonars" section at the back of the book. These pages may be freely reproduced, either from the book or from the accompanying CD-ROM for any devotional or ministry use.

Daniel

Chapter Twelve

Why Hanukkah? Antiochus Epiphanes, the Hitler of the Old Testament

As we make our way through Daniel, it is important to keep the big picture of the book in mind. For us to effectively understand the smaller portions of this book, we must be able to determine where they fit within the big picture Daniel is painting. As you may well remember, we mentioned earlier that the first six chapters of Daniel are mainly historical, whereas the remaining portion (Daniel 7-12) is mainly prophetic. Daniel 7 focuses on the vision of the four beasts and its interpretation. Daniel 8—the second chapter of the prophetic portion of Daniel—describes and interprets Daniel's second vision (the ram and the goat).

It is in the context of Daniel's second vision that we learn about the Jewish festival of Hanukkah and the events that led to its institution within the Jewish religious system. In this chapter of Daniel, we also read about Antiochus Epiphanes, a frightening type of the Antichrist that reveals to us what he will be like. Additionally, we are also reminded of the precision of God's prophecy and of His absolute control over the affairs of this world.

With this overview in mind, let us embark on our journey though Daniel 8.

Daniel's Second Vision

Daniel 8 opens with the prophet letting us know the specific time when this vision came to him: "In the third year of the reign of King Belshazzar a vision appeared to me—to me, Daniel—after the one that appeared to me the first time" (Daniel 8:1). This vision appeared to Daniel two years after the first vision of chapter 7, when Daniel was sixty-nine years of age. Much has happened since Daniel was first taken captive to Babylon as a teenager. God preserved Daniel in Babylon and placed him in strategic places throughout his life. When Daniel first arrived in Babylon several decades before the events of Daniel 8, he was placed under the service of the great Babylonian king Nebuchadnezzar. After Nebuchadnezzar died, several kings succeeded him, though none was as powerful as Nebuchadnezzar had been. Through all those changes, Daniel remained in a position of authority, faithfully serving the Lord.

Daniel's narrative, which had been in Aramaic (the common Gentile language of the day) between Daniel 2:4 and 7:28, now changes to Hebrew. Why did Daniel go back to writing in Hebrew in Daniel 8:1? The focus of his prophecies changed from the Gentiles to God's covenant people, the Jews. God was thus speaking through Daniel to His people, in their own language. Dr. Arno Gaebelein comments: "We remind the reader once more of the fact that beginning with the 8th chapter to the end of the book of Daniel, the language employed is Hebrew... From now on we are led in prophecy mostly upon Jewish ground and events are revealed which will take place at the close of the time of the Gentiles."[1] John Walvoord complements this thought: "From here to the end of Daniel, the prophecy, even though it concerns the Gentiles, is occupied with human history as it relates to Israel."[2]

So where does the vision of chapter 8 fit within the chronology of the book? We know that the last Babylonian king was Belshazzar, whose inability to lead Babylon led to its fall before the Medo-Persian Empire. Chronologically, then, the vision of chapter 8 fits between the events of Daniel 4 and 5, before Babylon had fallen. J. Vernon McGee comments about the time of Daniel's second vision:

> The vision recorded by Daniel in this chapter was prophetic when it was given, but it has since been fulfilled. Because it has been so clearly and literally fulfilled, this chapter is the basis for the liberal

critic giving a late date for the writing of the book of Daniel. His argument rests on the fact that prophecy concerning the future is supernatural and he does not believe in the supernatural; therefore, this prophecy could not have been written at the time of Daniel, but must have been written afterward as history.[3]

But those of us who believe in the power of God do not have to try to explain away the supernatural nature of Daniel's prophecy. His vision was not accurate because it was written after the events it described had happened. The vision was accurate because it was revealed to Daniel by the One who controls and determines the events of human history. As God predicted, so it was! That is why we can have the confidence that future prophecy will be fulfilled just as past prophecies have been.

The Incredible Impact of Daniel's Second Vision

Before we consider the content of Daniel's second vision, we must bear in mind how that specific vision affected Daniel himself. The impact of this vision on Daniel was unlike any other vision. As the one receiving and proclaiming God's message, Daniel was not indifferent to what God was communicating through him. The impact of this particular vision was so great that Daniel fainted twice during the vision itself. Daniel 8:27 reads, "And I, Daniel, fainted and was sick for days; afterward I arose and went about the king's business. I was astonished by the vision, but no one understood it."

We can learn several things from Daniel's sincere reaction to God's revelation.

First, we see that Daniel was moved by what God told him. Though Daniel was a godly man who had total confidence in God's absolute control of the future, he was struck powerfully by what was to come. He was emotionally distressed when he saw all the suffering that would fall on God's chosen people because of all their disobedience. What a great reminder for us—that by no means should we be indifferent to the truth God communicates to us. How long has it been since you were moved by God's revelation to you?

Second, Daniel's reaction reminds us to be emotionally moved by God's judgment upon the lost. This is one of the reasons why the modern church is so different from the New Testament church. Whereas the early church carried with it the burden of God's impending judgment on those without Christ, the modern church has become indifferent to this sobering reality. Something that should motivate us into action has turned into a piece of information that may be ignored because it does not pertain to us. Oh, that we would learn from Daniel to grieve for the lost souls who do not know the Savior! Are you burdened for those around you who do not know Jesus Christ? Do you really care that judgment is coming?

Third, we also learn from Daniel that after he recovered from his distress, "He went about the king's business" (Daniel 8:27). Have you ever met Christians who say they really love Jesus but never do anything for Him? They are always making plans about the future but never act on them. Although Daniel was aware of the judgment, he pulled himself together and went back to his responsibilities.

Applicable Time Period of the Prophecy

There are two distinct periods of fulfillment mentioned in chapter 8. The first, confirmed by history, was the relatively near future in the evil reign of Antiochus Epiphanes, the eighth king of the Seleucid dynasty who persecuted the Jews in the days of the Maccabees (168–165 BC). The second is the Antichrist, the man of sin who is to come in the final seven years before the second coming of Jesus Christ. Antiochus Epiphanes was, thus, only a type of the Antichrist that is to come at the end of the times. Though Antiochus Epiphanes has historically fulfilled what Daniel saw, the verses below clearly indicate that the same vision is yet to be fulfilled by the Antichrist in the future:

- Daniel 8:17, "So he came near where I stood, and when he came I was afraid and fell on my face; but he said to me, 'Understand, son of man, that the vision refers to the time of the end.'"

- Daniel 8:19, "And he said, 'Look, I am making known to you what shall happen in the latter time of the indignation; for at the appointed time the end shall be.'"

- Daniel 8:23, "And in the latter time of their kingdom, when the transgressors have reached their fullness, a king shall arise, having fierce features, who understands sinister schemes."

• Daniel 8:26b, "And the vision of the evenings and mornings which was told is true; Therefore seal up the vision, for it refers to many days in the future."

This obviously refutes the critics' claim that Daniel was written a century or so before Christ because it is simply too accurate to be written five centuries in advance. The vision was for the future—short and long term! Even Jesus agreed that the vision did not exhaust itself with Antiochus Epiphanes alone. Why? Nearly 200 years after Antiochus, Jesus said, "Therefore when you see the 'abomination of desolation,' spoken of by Daniel the prophet, standing in the holy place (whoever reads, let him understand)" (Matthew 24:15). Clearly, this is a future event!

The Ram: The Persian Empire (Daniel 8:2-3)

With the double fulfillment of Daniel's vision in mind, let us take a closer look at what Daniel actually saw that caused him to be so distressed. Daniel 8:2–3 states:

> I saw in the vision, and it so happened while I was looking, that I was in Shushan, the citadel, which is in the province of Elam; and I saw in the vision that I was by the River Ulai. Then I lifted my eyes and saw, and there, standing beside the river, was a ram which had two horns, and the two horns were high; but one was higher than the other, and the higher one came up last.

As you may well remember, Babylon was the leading nation in Daniel's time. In his vision, Daniel was transported out of Babylon and into Shushan (called Susa by the Greeks), the city that would become the capital of Medo-Persia, the next world empire after Babylon. Shushan was a city about 230 miles east of Babylon and 120 miles north of the Persian Gulf. At the time of the vision, the city was a little, insignificant town at the fringe area of the Babylonian kingdom, an unknown place with absolutely no political or military significance. However, later on it became the very center of the next kingdom.

The ram Daniel saw represented the dual kingdoms of the Medes and Persians, depicted by the two horns. One horn was larger than the other because the Persian kingdom was larger and more powerful than the Medo Kingdom before they became united. This symbolism is clearly identified in Daniel 8:20, which states, "The ram which you saw, having the two horns—they are the kings of Media and Persia."

The Medo-Persian Expansion

After describing the vision of the ram, Daniel went on to depict the expansion of Medo-Persia. Take a look at Daniel 8:4, "I saw the ram pushing westward, northward, and southward, so that no animal could withstand him; nor was there any that could deliver from his hand, but he did according to his will and became great." As it turned out, the expansion of the Medo-Persian and Grecian (Daniel 8:5-8) Empires would directly affect the nation of Israel. Dr. John Walvoord comments: "Beginning in chapter 8, Daniel's second vision concerns the empires of Persia and Greece as they relate to Israel. Under the Persian government, the Israelites went back to rebuild their land and their city, Jerusalem. But Under Grecian domination, in particular under Antiochus Epiphanes, the city and the temple were again desolated."[4]

The Goat: The Grecian Empire (Daniel 8:5-8)

Read carefully Daniel 8:5-8, which describes the next animal (i.e., kingdom) that would succeed the ram (i.e., Medo-Persia). It reads:

> And as I was considering, suddenly a male goat came from the west, across the surface of the whole earth, without touching the ground; and the goat had a notable horn between his eyes. Then he came to the ram that had two horns, which I had seen standing beside the river, and ran at him with furious power. And I saw him confronting the ram; he was moved with rage against him, attacked the ram, and broke his two horns. There was no power in the ram to withstand him, but he cast him down to the ground and trampled him; and there was no one that could deliver the ram from his hand. Therefore the male goat grew very great; but when he became strong, the large horn was broken, and in place of it four notable ones came up toward the four winds of heaven.

As history confirms to us, the goat Daniel saw was the Empire of Greece. Once again, the symbolism of the goat is made plain later on in the prophecy. When we state that the goat represented Greece, we are not speculating or forcing our personal agenda on the Scriptures! Take a look at Daniel 8:21, "And the male goat is the kingdom of Greece. The large horn that is between its eyes is the first king."

Since the goat symbolized Greece, the notable horn was, unquestionably, Alexander the Great. Alexander was the first king of the Grecian Empire. The four horns that replace the great horn represent the four kingdoms that followed and replaced Alexander's dominion. Any history book will confirm that after Alexander died, his four top generals took over and divided the great Grecian Empire into four different divisions— just as the Word of God had predicted hundreds of years in advance. What a great reminder that we can *always* trust what God says!

The Prophecy Regarding the "Little Horn"

Daniel's vision did not end with the division of the Grecian Empire into four smaller kingdoms. In the following section (Daniel 8:9-14), Daniel focuses on a certain "little horn." Read on:

> And out of one of them came a little horn which grew exceedingly great toward the south, toward the east, and toward the Glorious Land. And it grew up to the host of heaven; and it cast down some of the host and some of the stars to the ground, and trampled them. He even exalted himself as high as the Prince of the host;

and by him the daily sacrifices were taken away, and the place of His sanctuary was cast down. Because of transgression, an army was given over to the horn to oppose the daily sacrifices; and he cast truth down to the ground. He did all this and prospered. Then I heard a holy one speaking; and another holy one said to that certain one who was speaking, "How long will the vision be, concerning the daily sacrifices and the transgression of desolation, the giving of both the sanctuary and the host to be trampled under foot?" And he said to me, "For two thousand three hundred days; then the sanctuary shall be cleansed."

This "little horn" here must not be confused with the "little horn" of Daniel 7:8, which is the Antichrist who comes out of the revived Roman kingdom and is allied to 10 other kings. The "little horn" we read about in Daniel 8 came out of one of the "four notable ones," which in turn came out from the goat, namely, the Grecian kingdom (Daniel 8:8, 9). Therefore, the two "little horns" Daniel referred to are not the same. One, the Antichrist, will come from the Roman kingdom; the other came from the Grecian kingdom! Who, then, was this "little horn" Daniel referred to in the passage above? Dr. Leon J. Wood comments:

> As noted, this horn symbolizes Antiochus Epiphanes, who was the 8th king after Seleucus, the general who received the Syrian division of the [Grecian] empire. Antiochus ascended the throne following the murder of his brother, Seleucus Philopator, the former king. The king's son, Demetrius, was the rightful heir to the throne, but he was held hostage in Rome at the time. As a result, Antiochus Epiphanes, through flattery and bribes, was able to seize the throne for himself.[5]

Daniel wrote that the "little horn" (Antiochus Epiphanes) grew exceedingly great toward the south, toward the east, and toward the Glorious Land (verse 9). The "Glorious Land" was Jerusalem, where the Jewish temple was. Antiochus attacked the "host of heaven" (verse 10), meaning the stars (Jeremiah 33:22), which here represent the people of God in Palestine (cf. Genesis 15:5; 22:17; Exodus 12:41; Daniel 12:3). Once again, Dr. Leon Wood states, "The thought is that Antiochus would begin to oppress God's people, the Jews. Then he was seen to cast the stars to the ground, meaning that he would kill many of them. History records that he did indeed do this, killing about 100,000 Jews."[6]

Since Antiochus Epiphanes is such a key figure in Daniel's second vision (both as a historical figure and as a type of the Antichrist—the other "little horn" from Daniel 7:8), let us take a closer look at him.

How Antiochus Epiphanes "Types" the Antichrist

Antiochus' Reign of Terror

By race, Antiochus Epiphanes (ca. 212-162 BC) was a Macedonian; by culture and education, he was a Greek. Consequently, he was a foreigner in the eyes of the Syrians, as well as the Jews, over whom he reigned. Antiochus was the third son of Antiochus III the Great. He had lived in Rome, where he spent his early years as a hostage. After his father died, his brother, Seleucus IV Philopater, ruled from 187 to 175 BC. When his brother was assassinated, Antiochus had to seize the throne from a usurper, Heliodorus. Victorious, he ended up reigning from 175 BC until his death in 163 BC.

According to history, Antiochus enjoyed persecuting people. In Egypt, when he was on his way to conquer the world, he was stopped by the armies of Rome. In fury and frustration, Antiochus turned his forces away from Egypt and marched up through the maritime border of the Mediterranean. He vented his anger by taking his army to Jerusalem and sacking the city. He took 40,000 of the people and sold them into slavery. During that march, Antiochus killed nearly 100,000 Jews!

He also took the golden altar of incense and stood before the inner veil in the Jewish temple.

After plundering the temple, Antiochus decided to destroy the Jewish religion and replace it with Greek worship and Greek culture, a process we call Hellenization. Instead of the Feast of the Tabernacles, Antiochus Epiphanes celebrated in the Jewish temple the Feast of Bacchanalia, worshiping Bacchus, the Greek god of pleasure and wine. He also forced the Jews to observe the Saturnalia, worshiping Saturn by using prostitutes in the Jewish temple for those feast days. Furthermore, Antiochus restricted the observance of the Sabbath and the reading of the Scriptures, burning every copy of the Torah he could find. Ultimately, Antiochus forced the Jews to observe all of his feast days and forbade the institution of circumcision. In the end, every Jewish practice was forbidden on penalty of death. Thus, Antiochus did everything he could to desecrate and destroy the Jewish religion forever.

History records in the book of Maccabees that there were two mothers, deeply committed to their Jewish culture, who determined to circumcise their boys. When Antiochus heard about it, he took the babies, killed them, hung them around each mother's neck, marched the women through the city streets of Jerusalem up to the highest wall and flung them, babies and all, headlong over the wall. Another woman who had seven sons also defied Antiochus' law. To punish her, Antiochus cut the tongues out of the boys' mouths and then fried the boys to death, one at a time; then, he murdered the mother. These are just two examples of the long Jewish agony under Antiochus Epiphanes.

When the Scripture speaks of the desecration of the temple (Daniel 8:13) it is referring to the time Antiochus walked into the sacred place of the Jews to sacrifice a pig. He slit the throat of the pig and sacrificed it on the altar of the Jewish people. Then he took the blood of the animal and sprayed it all over the inside of the temple. Everything that was holy to the Jews had the pig's blood all over it.

How did Antiochus' reign of terror end? There was living in those days a priest in a place called Modein, just outside Jerusalem. The priest's name was Mattathias. He was a patriarch and grieved over the sorrow of the Jewish people. One day, an emissary from Antiochus came to Modein to make the Jews bow down before the altar of Jupiter, the Greek god. When a Jew came to worship Jupiter, Mattathias killed him, and then he killed the officer who was forcing the Jews to bow down. The Maccabean revolt was on! Before his death, Mattathias passed the torch on to his third son, Judas Maccabeus, who eventually won the victory and independence for the Jews.

It was because of Judas Maccabeus that the festival of Hanukkah began. When Judas went back to Jerusalem to cleanse the temple, he wanted to light the lamps in the temple. The ceremony to re-consecrate the temple required eight days, but he only found enough oil for one day.

Tradition says the one cruse of oil lasted not only for the first day, but throughout all eight days. In celebration of that miraculous re-consecration of the Jewish temple, the Jewish people celebrate Hanukkah to this day.

Antiochus and the Antichrist

In light of so much cruelty and so many atrocities, we should ask ourselves: Why did God allow that to happen? Why did He let Antiochus Epiphanes get away with so much for so long? We can identify at least two main reasons why God allowed that to happen. First, Antiochus Epiphanes validates the prophecy concerning the coming of the Antichrist. Just as Daniel 8:23 predicted the rising of Antiochus Epiphanes (which has already come to pass), the prophecy concerning the Antichrist will also be literally fulfilled.

Second, Antiochus Epiphanes gives us a glimpse at what the Antichrist will be like. Through this type (i.e., representation), God was preparing Daniel (and all those who read his prophecy) for the Antichrist, a much more evil king who is coming in the end of times.

Consider, for instance, the following three ways Antiochus typifies the Antichrist who is to come:

1. The proclamation of himself as God in the Jewish temple, referred to "the abomination of desolation." On the coins printed during Antiochus' reign were the words "Theos Antiochus Theos Epiphanes." That means, "Antiochus the Great, God Manifest." Antiochus said he was God, just like the Antichrist will do when he comes. Consider the following verses concerning Antiochus (Daniel 8:11; 11:31) and the Antichrist (Daniel 8:25; 9:27):

   • Daniel 8:11, "He even exalted himself as high as the Prince of the host; and by him the daily sacrifices were taken away, and the place of His sanctuary was cast down."

   • Daniel 11:31, "And forces shall be mustered by him, and they shall defile the sanctuary fortress; then they shall take away the daily sacrifices, and place there the abomination of desolation."

   • Daniel 8:25 "Through his cunning he shall cause deceit to prosper under his rule; and he shall exalt himself in his heart ... He shall even rise against the Prince of princes ..."

   • Daniel 9:27, "Then he shall confirm a covenant with many for one week; but in the middle of the week He shall bring an end to sacrifice and offering. And on the wing of abominations shall be one who makes desolate, even until the consummation, which is determined, is poured out on the desolate."

2. His persecution of the Jews. Just as Antiochus persecuted and killed many Jews (Daniel 8:12), so will the Antichrist seek to destroy the children of God (Daniel 7:25). Take a look:

- Daniel 8:12, "Because of transgression, an army was given over to the horn to oppose the daily sacrifices; and he cast truth down to the ground. He did all this and prospered."

- Daniel 7:25, "He shall speak pompous words against the Most High, shall persecute the saints of the Most High, and shall intend to change times and law. Then the saints shall be given into his hand for a time and times and half a time."

3. The cessation of sacrifices. Like Antiochus, the Antichrist will cause the Jews to cease offering sacrifices to God. Once again, consider the following verses:

- Daniel 11:31, "...and they shall take away the daily sacrifice..."

- Daniel 9:27, "...He shall bring an end to sacrifice and offering..."

It is thus clear that Antiochus Epiphanes is a picture of what is coming in the future, only magnified much more in evil, bloodshed, and disaster!

Gabriel's Clear Interpretation

Daniel's second vision proceeded with Gabriel's clear interpretation. By the way, this is the first time Gabriel is introduced in the Bible. Daniel 8:15–26 reads:

> Then it happened, when I, Daniel, had seen the vision and was seeking the meaning, that suddenly there stood before me one having the appearance of a man. And I heard a man's voice between the banks of the Ulai, who called, and said, "Gabriel, make this man understand the vision." So he came near where I stood, and when he came I was afraid and fell on my face; but he said to me, "Understand, son of man, that the vision refers to the time of the end. Now, as he was speaking with me, I was in a deep sleep with my face

to the ground; but he touched me, and stood me upright. And he said, "Look, I am making known to you what shall happen in the latter time of the indignation; for at the appointed time the end shall be. The ram which you saw, having the two horns—they are the kings of Media and Persia. And the male goat is the kingdom of Greece. The large horn that is between its eyes is the first king. As for the broken horn and the four that stood up in its place, four kingdoms shall arise out of that nation, but not with its power. And in the latter time of their kingdom, when the transgressors have reached their fullness, a king shall arise, having fierce features, who understands sinister schemes. His power shall be mighty, but not by his own power; he shall destroy fearfully, and shall prosper and thrive; he shall destroy the mighty, and also the holy people. Through his cunning he shall cause deceit to prosper under his rule; and he shall exalt himself in his heart. He shall destroy many in their prosperity. He shall even rise against the Prince of princes; but he shall be broken without human means. And the vision of the evenings and mornings which was told is true; therefore seal up the vision, for it refers to many days in the future."

Most of Gabriel's interpretation had to do with the Antichrist. Let us, then, consider a few more traits of the evil that is to come at the end of times.

Traits of the Antichrist

Besides the three traits we considered above when we compared Antiochus to the Antichrist, Gabriel gives us four more:

1. The Antichrist will have fierce features and understand sinister schemes (verse 23). The Antichrist, much like Antiochus Epiphanes, will introduce an alien belief system and mock the Jewish practices instituted by God.

2. His power shall be mighty, but not by his own power (verse 24). The Antichrist will have immense satanic power. This is confirmed by Revelation 13:3b, which states, "The dragon [Satan] gave him his power, his throne, and great authority."

3. Through his cunning, the Antichrist shall cause deceit to prosper under his rule (verse 25). The Antichrist, like Antiochus, will be a master deceiver and manipulator. This is well-illustrated by the following verses from Revelation:

- Revelation 13:8, "All who dwell on the earth will worship him, whose names have not been written in the Book of Life of the Lamb slain from the foundation of the world."

- Revelation 13:16–17, "He causes all, both small and great, rich and poor, free and slave, to receive a mark on their right hand or on their foreheads, and that no one may buy or sell except one who has the mark or the name of the beast, or the number of his name."

4. God is going to destroy the Antichrist, just as he did Antiochus Epiphanes:

- Daniel 8:25, "...But he shall be broken without human means."

- Revelation 19:19–20, "And I saw the beast, the kings of the earth, and their armies, gathered together to make war against Him who sat on the horse and against His army. Then the beast was captured, and with him the false prophet who worked signs in his presence, by which he deceived those who received the mark of the beast and those who worshiped his image. These two were cast alive into the lake of fire burning with brimstone."

Can I give you a very provoking thought as we close this chapter? We have just read about all these Gentile governments and the culmination of the end of times. One cannot help but ask: Where is America in all of this? Consider the following insightful thoughts that might explain what will happen in the future:

The condition of the world, rendered temporarily chaotic by the rapture, may explain why the United States is not found in biblical prophecy. Even though this nation is Christian in name only, America still has a larger percentage of born-again believers in its population than any other important country. When Jesus comes for his own, thousands of responsible leaders in government, industry, education, religion, the arts, and the professions will be removed. With these leaders taken to meet the Lord in the air, the structure of government, industry, education, the arts, and the professions will be so weakened that it will reduce the United States to an impotent and prostrated nation. This also explains why Russia, with its atheistic communist leadership, is virtually unaffected by the rapture and can offer a substantial threat to Israel during the tribulation period. Though all countries where Christians are in place of leadership will be affected by the rapture, it will affect no other country like it will affect the United States. Apparently, she does not recover from this loss, for the United States plays no ascertainable role during the tribulation period. Therefore, the political center of the world during the reign of the Antichrist will shift back to that area within the boundaries of the old Roman Empire in Europe. The Western Hemisphere will be only an adjunct. The locality where the final act of human history will be played out will be Western and Eastern Europe, along with the Middle East. Again, the center of the world political and imperial power will be Western Europe, where it was located when God's prophetic time clock stopped in the first century. It is in this political arena that the king of fierce countenance will demonstrate his diplomatic genius and enable the countries there to recover from the shock of the rapture.[7]

What a joy it is to know that our Lord controls our future and that of our nation, and that in Him we find perfect safety! As we foresee so much impending chaos and destruction, may the cry of our hearts be: "Maranatha! Come, Lord Jesus!"

Discussion Questions

1. Summarize the content of Daniel's second vision.

2. Why do liberal interpreters assign a late date to Daniel? What counter-argument can we offer?

3. How did this second vision impact Daniel? Why? What does this teach us about Daniel himself?

4. What is the double fulfillment of Daniel's prophecy?

5. Who are the "Little Horns" of Daniel 7:8 and 8:9–14?

6. What is a "type" as we use the term in understanding this passage?

7. How did Antiochus Epiphanes serve as a type of the Antichrist?

That's Not All

You can find sermon outlines in the "Sermonars" section at the back of the book. These pages may be freely reproduced, either from the book or from the accompanying CD-ROM for any devotional or ministry use.

Chapter Thirteen

Discovering Prayer Which Causes God to Act

The Importance of Daniel 9

Without question, Daniel 9 is one of the greatest chapters in the entire Old Testament. After Daniel's heartfelt prayer on behalf of his people (Daniel 9:1-19), God sent His angel Gabriel to answer Daniel's petition (Daniel 9:20-23), and to disclose to him the meaning of his vision concerning the First and Second Comings of the Messiah and the Antichrist (Daniel 9:24-27). Therefore, Daniel 9 opens the final prophetic section of the book of Daniel (chapters 9-12) that provides the framework for many of the prophecies found in other Old Testament prophets and in the book of Revelation. If we fail to understand this chapter or the entire prophetic section found in Daniel 9-12, it will be impossible for us to have a firm grasp on biblical prophecy to the extent God wants us to.

Daniel 9:1-23 gives us a glimpse into Daniel's heart. After several decades of captivity in Babylon, Daniel was still passionate about God's people and zealous for God's glory. Unlike many lukewarm Christians who fill our churches every week, Daniel was so burdened for God's plans that he was not afraid to passionately seek the Lord through prayer.

Leonard Ravenhill once wrote: "We have many organizers, but few agonizers. We have many players and payers, but few prayers. We have many singers, but few clingers. Lots of pastors, but few wrestlers; many fears, but few tears. Much fashion, but little passion. Many interferers, but far too few intercessors. Many writers, but few fighters; failing here, we fail everywhere."¹ Thus, in Daniel 9, we see Daniel as the agonizer, the prayer, the clinger, the tearful wrestler who interceded for God's chosen people.

But Daniel was not only devoted to prayer; he was also a man who was constantly in the Scriptures. As chapter 9 opens, we see Daniel not just as a prophet, but also as a student of prophecy! After seventy years of captivity, Daniel, who is now nearly ninety years old, daily and faithfully read and studied the Word of God. Consider Daniel 9:1-2:

> In the first year of Darius the son of Ahasuerus, of the lineage of the Medes, who was made king over the realm of the Chaldeans—in the first year of his reign I, Daniel, understood by the books the number of the years specified by the word of the LORD through Jeremiah the prophet, that He would accomplish seventy years in the desolations of Jerusalem.

Bible scholar H. A. Ironside comments on the opening verses of Daniel 9:

> And so we see, in the opening verses, this devoted man, in the first year of the reign of Darius, bending over the prophetic word in the Holy Scriptures. He did not have anything like as complete a Bible as we have; but he valued what he had, and searched diligently. In fact, the last book that had been added to the Bible was that of Ezekiel. We do not know for certain that this ever came into his hands, but we do know from this passage that he had, at any rate, the book of Jeremiah. As he studied it carefully, he noticed that twice in that book it was written that God would accomplish seventy years in the desolations of Jerusalem.²

Daniel had seen the Babylonian kingdom at its climax, when the Babylonians came to Jerusalem and took almost the entire nation captive. He had also seen Nebuchadnezzar's death and Babylon's gradual weakening as the Medes and the Persians grew in military and political power. During those seventy years when some kings fell while others rose, Daniel devoted himself to searching the Scriptures of his God. In the midst of political chaos, Daniel pleaded with the Lord to reveal to him what He had in store for His chosen people. In spite of his ungodly environment and hopeless circumstances, Daniel was confident God had not forsaken His people.

Thus, rising above his troubled times, Daniel read and re-read Jeremiah 25:11-12, and 29:10:

- Jeremiah 25:1-12, "'And this whole land shall be a desolation and an astonishment, and these nations shall serve the king of Babylon seventy years. Then it will come to pass, when seventy years are completed, that I will punish the king of Babylon and that nation, the land of the Chaldeans, for their iniquity,' says the LORD; 'and I will make it a perpetual desolation.'"

- Jeremiah 29:10, "For thus says the LORD: After seventy years are completed at Babylon, I will visit you and perform my good word toward you, and cause you to return to this place."

Why was the captivity seventy years? Why not a shorter (or longer) period of time? The answer is found in the following verses:

- Leviticus 25:1-4, "And the LORD spoke to Moses on Mount Sinai, saying, 'Speak to the children of Israel, and say to them: When you come into the land which I give you, then the land shall keep a sabbath to the LORD. Six years you shall sow your field, and six years you shall prune your vineyard, and gather its fruit; but in the seventh year there shall be a sabbath of solemn rest for the land, a sabbath to the LORD. You shall neither sow your field nor prune your vineyard.'"

- Leviticus 26:34-35, "Then the land shall enjoy its sabbaths as long as it lies desolate and you are in your enemies' land; then the land shall rest and enjoy its sabbaths. As long as it lies desolate it shall rest—for the time it did not rest on your sabbaths when you dwelt in it."

- 2 Chronicles 36:21, "To fulfill the word of the LORD by the mouth of Jeremiah, until the land had enjoyed her Sabbaths. As long as she lay desolate she kept Sabbath, to fulfill seventy years."

Therefore, Israel was instructed to let the land rest one in every seven years. But since the Jews disobeyed this command for 490 years, they owed God seventy years of sabbath for the land—the exact amount of time they were taken captive to Babylon! What a reminder that the Lord never forgets or overlooks His command and that sin always has consequences. We always pay a high price for taking what belongs to God. When we put our hands on what belongs to God, we bring God's chastening hand into our lives.

After reading the prophet Jeremiah, Daniel was reminded of the seriousness of Israel's deserved punishment. As the Word of God gave Daniel insight into Israel's pitiful situation, Daniel was prompted to pray. This lesson is simple and yet important: when faced with hopeless situations, we must seek the Lord through the Scriptures and through prayer! If we fail to study the Word or be devoted to prayer, we will most assuredly fail to be all God wants us to be.

Thus, Daniel 9:3 states, "Then I set my face toward the Lord God to make request by prayer and supplications, with fasting, sackcloth, and ashes." Commenting on this passage, scholars Dr. Louis Talbot and Dr. Ronald Wallace wrote:

> Daniel had been but a youth when he was taken captive by Nebuchadnezzar. Sixty-nine long years had passed during his exile from Palestine. How often during those years he must have pondered upon God's prophecy through Jeremiah—first that he would send His people into captivity if they did not turn from their idols; then His promise to restore them to their native land after 70 years of discipline.[3]

> Here we are given our first glimpse of Daniel pouring over what he calls the book (verses 1 and 2). We have seen that three times a day he opened his window toward Jerusalem, but there is not the slightest doubt that as frequently he opened these books—the scrolls that the exiles had been careful to bring with them from their homeland, and to copy out for each other's use.[4]

Spurgeon used to say that he disliked when people shared long prayers in public. He thought that people who prayed long in public very likely did not pray much in private. I don't know if that is true, but I do know that just as much as we need oxygen to breath and water to sustain us, we need constant prayer to walk in fellowship with God. His Holy Spirit who dwells in us cries out to be in constant conversation with the Father. Do you experience that hunger to speak with God through prayer? How often do you get on your knees and approach the throne of grace with confidence? Have you determined to meet with God at the beginning of every day? Like Daniel, do you let God's Word give you insight about your circumstances and prompt you to pray? Before we further examine Daniel's exemplary prayer, take a few seconds to ask the Lord to give you insight through this passage and to teach you how to grow in this important discipline!

Elements of God-Moving, God-Answering Prayer

Daniel's prayer in Daniel 9:3-19 is simply amazing. His intercession was so effective that by the time the prophet was done praying, the angel Gabriel had already descended from heaven and was ready to declare God's answer (Daniel 9:20-23). After pouring out his heart to God, it was Daniel's turn to listen to what God had to reveal to him.

But what made Daniel's prayer so impressive? What was so special about it? Let's examine six key elements of Daniel's prayer that teach us how to pray to God more effectively:

1. Daniel had a specific purpose in prayer—he wanted answers!

How do we know Daniel desired to receive answers from God? Because four times in this passage he repeated the word "supplication," and three times he addressed God through different names. Daniel began his supplications by addressing God as Jehovah in Daniel 9:1-14. In Daniel 9:15-19, the prophet approached God as Adonai. Then, in the following verses, he called God Elohim. These three names for God, though equally translated "God" in English, are three distinct Hebrew names. By calling God Jehovah, Daniel was surrendering to God as the One in control. As he transitioned, Daniel petitioned to God as Adonai, declaring that God was his Master and that Daniel was a mere servant. When he finally called upon God as Elohim, Daniel was seeking God as the One always ready and willing to meet all our needs. Thus, Daniel prayed and asked for an answer because he was confident that God's character would not disappoint him. He knew the victory of his people lay with God.

Andrew Murray once wrote, "God's child can conquer everything by prayer. Is it any wonder that Satan does his utmost to snatch that weapon from the Christian or to hinder him in the use of it?"[5] Do not be deceived by Satan. Follow Daniel's example and be assured that we can conquer everything by prayer! If we ask anything according to God's will, we shall receive it from God (John 15:7)! Often we do not have because we do not ask (Matthew 7:7-9). May that never be the case in our lives.

2. Daniel admitted and confessed his sin to God.

We read Daniel's confession of the people's sins in Daniel 9:4-8:

> And I prayed to the LORD my God, and made confession, and said, "O Lord, great and awesome God, who keeps His covenant and mercy with those who love Him, and with those who keep His commandments, we have sinned and committed iniquity, we have done wickedly and rebelled, even by departing from Your precepts and Your judgments. Neither have we heeded Your servants the prophets, who spoke in Your name to our kings and our princes, to our fathers and all the people of the land. O Lord, righteousness belongs to You, but to us shame of face, as it is this day—to the men of Judah, to the inhabitants of Jerusalem and all Israel, those near and those far off in all the countries to which You have driven them, because of the unfaithfulness which they have committed against You. O Lord, to us belongs shame of face, to our kings, our princes, and our fathers, because we have sinned against You."

Daniel confessed the sins of the people by using the Hebrew word *hatta*, which means "to go the wrong way; a headlong trek away from God." Daniel definitely did not try to minimize the seriousness of their rejection of God. He wrote in verse five that they had "done wickedly." The Hebrew word *awon* in this verse implies perversion, a lifestyle that is not pleasing to God, while the word *sur* means apostasy.

Note also the use of the plural pronoun "we" throughout Daniel's prayer. Even though Daniel was not personally guilty of the sins of the nation, he willingly included himself in the same situation as Israel. Thus, "we" appears thirteen times in Daniel's prayer, while "us" is used nine times. Among other things, this definitely reminds us that sin always affects other people besides those who commit it.

So let me ask you this question: do you really confess your sins to God on a regular basis? Do you keep short accounts of your sins before

God? In 1 John 1:9 the importance of confession is stated clearly: "If we confess our sins, He is faithful and just to forgive us our sins and to cleanse us from all unrighteousness." But if we are not careful, we can easily misunderstand this verse. The Greek word *homologeo* (translated "confess") means "to say the same thing." This means that if we say the same thing God says about our sins, He will forgive and cleanse us. Do you agree with God about the seriousness and wickedness of your sins? Do you call your sin "sin"? Because if you do, his righteousness will prevail against your depravity and you will find freedom and cleansing. Consider also the following verses:

- James 5:16, "Confess your trespasses to one another, and pray for one another, that you may be healed. The effective, fervent prayer of a righteous man avails much."

- 1 John 3:22, "And whatever we ask we receive from Him, because we keep His commandments and do those things that are pleasing in His sight."

- 1 John 5:14, "Now this is the confidence that we have in Him, that if we ask anything according to His will, He hears us. And if we know that He hears us, whatever we ask, we know that we have the petitions that we have asked of Him?"

As God's children, we have His promise that He will answer our prayers when we walk in fellowship with Him. God wants to meet our needs; He wants to answer our prayers! Why, then, do so many of us live defeated lives instead of embracing what God wants to give to us through prayer? This happens because we get tired of struggling and give up too easily, failing to confess our sins to God on a consistent basis. The problem is that when we fail to confess our sins to God through prayer, we also fail to be cleaned and restored by Him.

It took Sir Winston Churchill three years to get through eighth grade. He just could not get good enough grades to pass his eighth grade English class—for three years! But he persisted, moved on with his life, and eventually earned a Nobel Prize for literature. How ironic that years later Oxford University asked Churchill to give a commencement address to its graduating class. Churchill accepted the invitation. That day he arrived with his usual props: a cigar, a cane, and a top hat. As Churchill approached the podium, the crowd rose in appreciative applause. Removing the cigar and carefully placing the top hat on the podium, Churchill gazed at his audience and shouted out, "Never give up!" Several seconds passed before he rose to his toes and repeated: "Never give up!" Then he reached for his top hat and walked off. That was the shortest commencement speech ever!

Oh, that we would take these three precious words to our hearts: "Never give up!" There are so many Christians who used to keep a short account of their sins with God right after their conversion. They were so careful to spend daily time with God through prayer and through His Word. But somewhere along the way, they let sin get the best of them, and they stopped having close fellowship with God. Consequently, they never reach spiritual maturity, since merely attending church will never be enough to properly feed their hungry souls.

If that is you, let me encourage you to turn back to God as many times as you turn your back to God. If you sin ten times within an hour, turn to God all ten times. Confess your sins! Seek the Lord in prayer and find Him there, waiting for you and ready to change your heart! May the words penned by Annie S. Hawks and Robert Lowry truly reflect your heart:

> I need Thee every hour, most gracious Lord;
> No tender voice like thine can peace afford.
> I need Thee every hour; Stay Thou near by;
> Temptations lose their power when Thou art nigh.
> I need Thee every hour, in joy or pain;
> Come quickly and abide or life is vain.
> I need Thee every hour; teach me Thy will;
> And Thy rich promises in me fulfill.
> I need Thee every hour, most Holy One;
> Oh, make me thine indeed, Thou blessed Son.
> I need Thee, oh, I need Thee; Every hour I need Thee;
> Oh, bless me now, my Saviour! I come to Thee.[6]

3. Daniel indicates he knows God's Word and, therefore, the consequences of sin.

This is why Daniel's prayer was effective—he prayed in accordance to God's Word! You can never go wrong when you pray according to the Scriptures. Daniel knew what God's Word said and prayed accordingly. Examine Daniel 9:9-16:

To the Lord our God belong mercy and forgiveness, though we have rebelled against Him. We have not obeyed the voice of the LORD our God, to walk in His laws, which He set before us by His servants the prophets. Yes, all Israel has transgressed Your law, and has departed so as not to obey Your voice; therefore the curse and the oath written in the Law of Moses the servant of God have been poured out on us, because we have sinned against Him. And He has confirmed His words, which He spoke against us and against our judges who judged us, by bringing upon us a great disaster; for under the whole heaven such has never been done as what has been done to Jerusalem. As it is written in the Law of Moses, all this disaster has come upon us; yet we have not made our prayer before the LORD our God, that we might turn from our iniquities and understand Your truth. Therefore the LORD has kept the disaster in mind, and brought it upon us; for the LORD our God is righteous in all the works which He does, though we have not obeyed His voice. And now, O Lord our God, who brought Your people out of the land of Egypt with a mighty hand, and made Yourself a name, as it is this day—we have sinned, we have done wickedly! O Lord, according to all Your righteousness, I pray, let Your anger and Your fury be turned away from Your city Jerusalem, Your holy mountain; because for our sins, and for the iniquities of our fathers, Jerusalem and Your people are a reproach to all those around us.

Daniel knew that the Jews had brought all their troubles upon themselves because of their sins. Their seventy years of captivity in foreign Babylon came because they had not given God one Sabbath year in 490 years! If you add it up, it will be clear that they owed God seventy years, and God was going to see to it that they paid their debt.

This information can aid us in prayer by reminding us that God will never answer prayers that are against His Word. When we pray, we must pray in accordance to His will (1 John 5:14)—that is exactly what Daniel did. And we can know God's will through His Word! Much of God's will is in the Bible—whatever is not there, the Holy Spirit will reveal to us according to God's plans and perfect time.

4. Daniel asked for and believed in the forgiveness of God.
This is so important. Based on the truth of God's promises and char-

acter, Daniel knew there was hope for restoration. He prayed in Daniel 9:17-19:

> Now therefore, our God, hear the prayer of Your servant, and his supplications, and for the Lord's sake cause Your face to shine on Your sanctuary, which is desolate. O my God, incline Your ear and hear; open Your eyes and see our desolations, and the city which is called by Your name; for we do not present our supplications before You because of our righteous deeds, but because of Your great mercies. O Lord, hear! O Lord, forgive! O Lord, listen and act! Do not delay for Your own sake, my God, for Your city and Your people are called by Your name.

In verses 15-19 Daniel addressed God as Adonai and Elohim. He no longer used the term Jehovah as he did in verses 4-14. Daniel surrendered in prayer to God who is Lord of everything! He was declaring: "God, you control everything. Your authority is unmatched. Because of that, you have the power to forgive us. Please do so, because no one else can."

I really believe Satan wants to keep many people from praying because he wants them to feel guilty for what they have done. But God wants the very opposite. There is forgiveness with Him. All we need to do is to ask God for it. Daniel's request is so clear: he implored God to hear, to forgive, to listen, and to act! And guess what God did? He heard, forgave, listened, and acted! The same can be true of us when we seek the Lord in prayer. May we take God at His word and always do so!

5. Daniel had a high view of God. He asked big things from God!

Daniel 9:4 states, "And I prayed to the LORD my God, and made confession, and said, 'O Lord, great and awesome God, who keeps His covenant and mercy with those who love Him, and with those who keep His commandments.'" That is the kind of God we serve. How great and awesome is God? He is great and awesome enough to meet every need we have in our lives! If you pray and things do not change right away, what should you do? Keep on praying and trustfully waiting on God (Psalm 27). Whatever your need, keep praying! Plead with God and in the right time (His time!) He will see to it that your prayers are perfectly answered (according to His definition of "perfectly"!).

The sun is 93 million miles away from the Earth. Much closer and smaller than the sun, the moon is *only* 211,463 miles away. You could walk to it in twenty-seven years at twenty-four miles a day. A ray of light, as you may well know, travels approximately 186,000 miles per second. Therefore, a beam of light can reach the moon from earth in one and a half seconds. Light can reach Mercury (50 million miles away) in four and a half seconds, Venus (26 million miles away) in two minutes and eighteen seconds, and Mars (34 million miles away) in four minutes and twenty-one seconds. But I know something in our lives that can travel infinitely faster than light: our prayers! Though God's throne is beyond the farthest star, our prayers reach God the second they leave our lips! Isn't that incredible? So why don't we pray more? Why don't we get up early every day to talk to Him?

Are we truly convinced that our prayers will get to God faster than light gets to us from the sun? Dr. W. E. Beiderwolf asked:

> Who painted the butterfly's wings with all those gorgeous hues? Who threw around the evening sun a drapery of a thousand colors? Who put the red on the robin's breast? From whose palette were the colors mixed that gave the rose its blushing charm and touched the lily with its dreamy white? Who taught the raindrop to take a ray of light from heaven's shining orb and pencil it on the sky in one huge arch of bewildering elegance? God did it all!

Do you agree that this awesome God can handle your problems? Are you willing to turn them over to Him?

6. Daniel's prayer was answered and authenticated by the mighty angel Gabriel.
God's ability to promptly answer our prayers is clearly displayed in Daniel 9:20-23:

> Now while I was speaking, praying, and confessing my sin and the sin of my people Israel, and presenting my supplication before the LORD my God for the holy mountain of my God, yes, while I was speaking in prayer, the man Gabriel, whom I had seen in the vision at the beginning, being caused to fly swiftly, reached me about the time of the evening offering. And he informed me, and talked with me, and said, "O Daniel, I have now come forth to give you skill to understand. At the beginning of your supplications the command went out, and I have come to tell you, for you are greatly beloved; therefore consider the matter, and understand the vision."

God was so pleased with His beloved Daniel that He answered His prayer and gave to him one of the greatest prophecies of all time (which we will cover in the next chapter). And to think that in Christ we too are among God's beloved. Each believer is greatly loved by God—He wants to answer our prayers as a way of reminding us of His tender love. How different we are as Christians than those who are lost. Take a look at the following sad, but true, examples:

- Edward Gibbon was the author of the literary masterpiece *The Decline and the Fall of the Roman Empire*. When he died in London, Gibbon's last words were, "All is lost, irrevocably lost; all is dark and doubtful." He realized too late that the choices he had made throughout his life were about to seal his eternal doom.

- When the French atheist Voltaire came close to the final moments of his life, he was overcome with remorse. Atheists rushed to his side to prevent him from making a statement that would reflect poorly on his enunciated atheism. Voltaire cursed them to their faces and had them banished from his presence. He exclaimed, "Be gone! It is you that brought me to my present condition. Leave me, I say. Be gone. What a wretched glory that you have produced for me." Finally, Voltaire cried out, "I must die, abandoned of God and man!"

- Likewise, Robert Ley, the Nazi propagandist who was strongly anti-Semitic and anti-Christian, echoed the words of Voltaire by writing "Tonight I die, abandoned of God." Shortly after he wrote that note, he hanged himself in his prison cell.

What a glorious hope, to know that our final moments of life do not have to be like these men's, filled with despair and emptiness. As Christians—that is, as beloved children of God—we can be ready to face whatever difficulties come our way, even death! We can do that because ahead of us is a loving Shepherd who guides us through both joys and sorrows. Are you ready to lavishly surrender yourself to God—much like Daniel did—and meet your Adonai, your Jehovah, and your Elohim through prayer?

Discussion Questions

1. Why was the Jewish captivity in Babylon seventy years long?

2. What three names for God did Daniel employ? What are some of the other names of God you know? What do they reveal about God's nature?

3. How did Daniel confess the sins of the people? What did he say to God? How did he treat their sins?

4. Do you confess your sins to God on a regular basis? Why or why not?

5. What do your prayers to God usually consist of? What do you pray about?

6. How does the way you see God impact the way you pray?

7. What are some prayer requests you currently have in your life that need to be brought to God on a consistent basis?

8. Take some time to spend with your Lord in prayer. Pour out your heart to God the way Daniel did. You will not leave disappointed!

That's Not All

You can find sermon outlines in the "Sermonars" section at the back of the book. These pages may be freely reproduced, either from the book or from the accompanying CD-ROM for any devotional or ministry use.

Daniel

Chapter Fourteen

Understanding Daniel's Seventy Weeks: The Old Testament's Greatest Prophecy

Leopold Kahn, a European Jewish rabbi, came to the conclusion that the Messiah had already come after studying the prophecy of the seventy weeks in Daniel 9. He came to this conclusion because this prophecy said that the Messiah would come before the destruction of Jerusalem, which occurred many years ago in AD 70. After reaching this decision, he approached an older rabbi one day and asked the question that every Jew is asking: "Where is the Messiah?"

The older rabbi thought for a moment, then said he didn't know. But he did say that perhaps Kahn should look in New York City. So Leopold Kahn sold almost everything he owned and went to New York City looking for the Messiah. One night, he walked past the door of a gospel mission. He heard singing coming from inside and he decided to investigate. That night, Leopold Kahn heard the gospel message and received Jesus Christ as His Savior and Messiah.

Soon after his conversion, Kahn started the first outreach of what was to become the American Board of Missions for Jews. This whole process started because one man read the prophecy of the seventy weeks and realized it taught that Jesus was the Messiah and had already come! What if I told you there was one special Old Testament passage, perhaps greater than any other, which clearly spoke to the Jewish people of convincing proof that Jesus was the Messiah? Would you want to know what passage it is? Would you want to learn its dynamic truth?

It is important for us to know how to reach Jews for Christ because if you believe in the Scriptures as I do, then you believe that God has a special covenant with the Jewish people. We take God at His word when He said to Abraham in Genesis 12:3, "And I will bless those who bless you, and the one who curses you I will curse." I hope you will realize that we have a powerful tool at our disposal to bless the Jewish people with. It is found right here in the Bible! We have before us in Daniel a prophecy given nearly 600 years before Christ was born that pinpoints the coming of the Messiah. Believe it or not, this passage even specifies the exact month and year that the Messiah would enter Jerusalem and announce to His covenant people that He was the one they had been awaiting for so many years!

Tragically, the majority of believers, even the majority of evangelicals, do not know this prophecy. We do not use it when we witness to the Jewish people. But how can we ignore one of the greatest Messianic prophecies in the Old Testament? We must understand this vital passage, because through it all other prophecies connect. Think carefully as we study Daniel's words. We will have to take this prophecy almost word by word and sentence by sentence to understand exactly what God is revealing to us. We are only going to study three verses, but I guarantee that if you can understand this passage, I could take you anywhere in the Bible and you could understand it.

Scholars have long recognized the importance of this passage. Dr. M. R. DeHaan wrote the following concerning these verses:

> The ninth chapter of the prophecy of Daniel has been frequently referred to as the *very backbone and skeleton of all bible prophecy*, by which we mean that it contains the framework, the general outline, around which all other prophecy is built [emphasis added]. If we err in our understanding of the seventy weeks, we shall err in all the rest of prophetic truth. If we have the proper interpretation of the 70th week of Daniel, we shall have no difficulty in fitting all the rest of prophetic revelation into the general scheme and pattern which God has laid down throughout the Scriptures.[1]

Sir Isaac Newton said we could stake the truth of Christianity on this prophecy alone, because five centuries before Christ was born, His coming was foretold with absolute accuracy.2 We should not be surprised by this accuracy, because we are told in Deuteronomy 29:29 that, "The secret things belong to the LORD our God, but those things which are revealed belong to us and to our children forever, that we may do all the words of this law." Those who follow God and are obedient to Him should understand prophecy! If a believer fails to understand prophecy, something is wrong. We must press for understanding because we receive tremendous energy for our faith when we understand God's Word.

The Vision of the Seventy Weeks—In Answer to Prayer

Let us not forget the context of this prophecy—it came in answer to prayer! As we open Daniel 9, what is the prophet doing? He is studying the prophecies of Jeremiah that he brought with him as a deportee to Babylon. Daniel had seen the Babylonian Empire explode in power, and for seventy years he had served under the incredible leader, Nebuchadnezzar. But he had also seen rulers arise after Nebuchadnezzar who could not maintain the kingdom, and eventually this powerful empire was decimated. The Medo-Persian Empire had come in and defeated Belshazzar as he was in the middle of a drunken orgy. Daniel, as a mature, spiritual man, watches this seventy-year period with the belief that God was still with His people. Every night he had said his evening prayers and, understanding the prophecies of Jeremiah, asked God about the future because the seventy years had been fulfilled. Why did the Jews have to be in captivity for seventy years? As we learned in previous chapters, the seventy years came about because for 490 years, the people of God living in the Promised Land had neglected the Sabbath year. They were supposed to let the land rest every seventy year, but they had failed to do it. Because of this, God took matters into His own hands to get those years back, so He sent Israel into captivity under a pagan king.

Beginning in Daniel 9:3, the prophet said a short prayer with great fervor and intensity. God's response came through Gabriel in 9:23, when Gabriel greets Daniel by saying, "At the beginning of your supplications the command went out, and I have come to tell you, for you are greatly beloved; therefore consider the matter, and understand the vision." The Old Testament's greatest prophecy was given to Daniel in response to his fervent prayer.

What does it do for you when you spend time prayerfully studying God's Word? It gives you understanding. I learned a long time ago that mature Christians are those who have simply spent a long time saturating their hearts and minds with God's Word. If you spend only fifteen minutes a day reading the Bible, you can read through it all in one year. We are always encouraged to hear about the forefathers of our faith, many of whom had read through the Bible nearly 100 times before they died. Have you taken time every day this week to read God's Word? Are you systematically reading through it and memorizing it?

Daniel read the book of Jeremiah, and it gave him insight and prompted him to pray. While everyone else was confused, Daniel knew that the captivity was coming to an end. He received an answer to his prayer from God through the angel Gabriel, who makes his first appearance in the book of Daniel. Gabriel speaks of the coming Messiah in the first part of the vision, and in the latter half he deals with the Antichrist. Let us take a closer look at what he says about the Messiah.

The First Part of the Seventy-Weeks Prophecy—Messiah

The first three verses (24-26) give us information about the Messiah:

> Seventy weeks are determined for your people and for your holy city, to finish the transgression, to make an end of sins, to make reconciliation for iniquity, to bring in everlasting righteousness, to seal up vision and prophecy, and to anoint the Most Holy. Know therefore and understand, that from the going forth of the command to restore and build Jerusalem until Messiah the Prince, there shall be seven weeks and sixty-two weeks; the street shall be built again, and the wall, even in troublesome times. And after the sixty-two weeks Messiah shall be cut off, but not for Himself; and the people of the prince who is to come shall destroy the city and the sanctuary. The end of it shall be with a flood, and till the end of the war desolations are determined (Dan 9:24-26).

Essential Clues to Understand the Seventy Weeks

1. Word Meaning

There are some essential clues that will help us understand the seventy weeks prophecy. Daniel 9:24 gives us the first when it says, "Seventy weeks are determined for your people and for your holy city." Daniel's people were, of course, the Jews, and the holy city was Jerusalem. Because of his prayer and the uniqueness of his life, God allowed Daniel to see His plan for the Jews through the end of the age.

Now God says that seventy *weeks* are determined for the Jews. What is a week? It is a period of seven days, right? But this translation does not accurately capture the Hebrew text. This word does not mean weeks of seven days; the word "week" is used because we have no word in English that is the exact equivalent to the Hebrew word which signifies "sevens." Since they had to choose something, the translators of the King James Version used the word "weeks" instead of "sevens." This Hebrew word would be like our word "dozen." It can be applied to many different things; we simply use it to refer to a group of something. The thought here could be "sevens" of days or "sevens" of years, but the context clearly indicates that it refers to seventy groups of seven years. Thus, we are looking at a time period of 490 years.

Numerous scholars have written on this verse, and it is helpful to note a few of their comments at length:

- Dr. Leon J. Wood—In fact, the Israelites were quite familiar with the idea of sevens of years as well as sevens of days. Their sabbatical year was built on this basis (one year in seven having to be set aside for resting the land, Lev. 25; Dt. 15). Furthermore, the seventy-year period of captivity was based on the idea that seventy of these sabbatical years had not been kept (see 2 Chron. 36:21; cf. Lev. 26:33-35; Jer. 34:12-22). Knowing this, Daniel would have recognized that the seventy years of captivity represented seventy sevens of years in which these violations had occurred; he would have understood Gabriel to be saying simply that another period, similar in length to that which made the captivity necessary, was coming in the future experience of the people.[3]

- Dr. David Jeremiah—How long is seventy weeks of years? Seventy times seven equals four hundred and ninety years. The prophecy is talking about 490 years that are determined or "cut out" of the calendar. Throughout the whole Book of Daniel we have been talking about how God is going to work through the Gentile rulers. But God has "cut out" 490 years that belong to the Jews. He shows how His program will work in that period of time.[4]

- Dr. Donald K. Campbell—The scope of the prophecy covers not 70 years, as Daniel may have hoped, but 70 sevens of years. When Gabriel stated that seventy weeks were decreed concerning Jerusalem and the Jews, he meant that that would be the length of time in which God would fulfill all of His purposes regarding the nation of Israel. The word "week" is literally "sevens" or hepstads. And, since ancient times, it has been generally agreed that the "weeks" or "sevens" were not weeks of days, but weeks of years. The angel is thus saying to Daniel that 70 weeks of years, or a period of 490 years, is required to fulfill Israel's prophetic program.[5]

- Dr. Stephen R. Miller—Daniel divided the seventy sevens into three groups, seven sevens, sixty-two sevens, and a final seven. The first seven sevens (49 years) commence with a command to rebuild Jerusalem (either the decree to Ezra in 458 BC or the decree to Nehemiah in 445 BC) and terminate with the completion of the work of Ezra and Nehemiah about 49 years later (either 409 BC or 396 BC). The next 62 sevens (434 years) extend from the end of the first group of sevens to Christ's first coming (either his baptism in AD 26 or Christ's presentation of himself to the people as Messiah on Palm Sunday in AD 32/33).[6]

Sixty-nine out of the seventy have already been fulfilled. Only the final "week," the final seven years of this prophecy, await fulfillment.

2. Focus

The second clue revolves around the focus of this prophecy. The seventy weeks prophecy is focused on the Jewish people and their city, Jerusalem. This is notable. Although the Jews had been in the Babylonian Captivity for seventy years, God was not finished with them! Many people have thought that God was finished with the Jews. The Israelites may have felt this during their captivity. The Jerusalem temple had been destroyed by Nebuchadnezzar and no effort at reconstruction had been made. They had been in a pagan city for seventy years, and it must have looked like it was all over, but God gave Daniel this prophecy to tell him that He was not done with what He would do for the Jewish people. God's plan for the Jews was not—nor will it ever be—finished! God made a promise to Abraham, and He is going to keep it! How significant this must have been to Daniel, as for seventy long years he had agonized over what had happened to Israel.

In Daniel 9:24, Gabriel lists six specific things that would be accomplished. The first three deal with the first coming of Christ, while the last three deal with His second coming. These six things are:

- "to finish the transgression"—This meant to restrain sin and the Jews in their long trend of apostasy. Sin would not run rampant for centuries upon centuries; God would judge it at the first advent of Messiah with His death on the cross. The word used here speaks of restraining sin, as when a criminal is "locked up" and the door is sealed. This obviously began with the crucifixion of Christ and will be finished entirely at His second coming.

- "to make an end of sins"—The national sins of Israel will come to an end at the second coming of Christ. Also, the sins of Israel and the whole world were atoned for completely during the first advent of Christ, specifically at His crucifixion.

- "to make reconciliation for iniquity"—This means to furnish the actual basis for covering sin by full atonement. The Levitical priests would sacrifice animals and lay them on the altar, but that blood simply covered their sins for a time; it did not take them away. These sacrifices were in anticipation of the Lamb of God, who would take away our sin, not merely cover it.

- "to bring in everlasting righteousness"—Everlasting righteousness will grip Jerusalem and the people of God only at the second coming of Christ! This phrase refers to the return of Christ at the end of the 490 years to establish the Davidic, Millennial kingdom.

- "to seal up vision and prophecy"—Vision is a synonym for prophecy. Every prophecy in the Bible will have been completed when Christ returns. No more Scripture will be needed when it all has been fulfilled!

• "and to anoint the Most Holy"—Many have thought that this refers to the Messiah. In reality, this phrase is a splendid reference to the anointing of the holy of holies in the millennial temple, which is described in Ezekiel's prophecy (Ezek 41–46).

3. When it began

We are referring to 490 years, but there are three divisions in this time span. First, we have 7 "sevens," a period of forty-nine years. After that, we see 62 "sevens," which is a period of 434 years. Finally, we see one last period of "sevens," the time which we refer to as the Tribulation.

According to Daniel 9:25, the seventy weeks began when a decree was issued for the people of God to return to their land and rebuild the Jewish temple. If you are familiar with Old Testament content and chronology, you know that there were basically four different decrees given toward the end of the Babylonian Captivity. Cyrus, the Medo-Persian king, initially allowed some Jews to return to their homeland. Other decrees were issued as well. However, we see that the prophecy mentions something very specific about the decree which started the seventy weeks. Look at Daniel 9:25, "Know therefore and understand, that from the going forth of the command to restore and build Jerusalem..." Not just any decree could fit this description. Although several decrees were issued relative to the Jewish restoration, only one seems to deal directly with the rebuilding of Jerusalem and the temple. Reputable scholars (John Walvoord, Sir Robert Anderson, John Whitcomb, Harold Hoehner) identify the second decree of Artaxerxes I to Nehemiah (445 BC), which specifically mentions the rebuilding of the Jewish temple in Jerusalem, as the decree that Gabriel was referring to in this prophecy.

Notice that the 490 years didn't begin until almost 100 years after Daniel received this prophecy. Do you know what that tells me? It tells me that we all have a place in God's service, but not all of us get to see the spiritual fireworks. We are merely called to be faithful in whatever way God chooses to use us. Some of us will be planters, and others will be harvesters, but it takes everyone doing their part for God's work to be accomplished. Daniel receives the vision and carefully writes it down, but it does not begin to be fulfilled until nearly 100 years later.

Take another look at the last part of Daniel 9:25, which says, "from the going forth of the command to restore and build Jerusalem until Messiah the Prince, there shall be seven weeks and sixty-two weeks; the street shall be built again, and the wall, even in troublesome times." The word "street" literally means the broad places. It speaks of the gigantic plaza, the open court inside the wall of Jerusalem. Daniel is told by the angel Gabriel that there is going to be a command issued to rebuild the city, including the great open court within the walls, the center of city life. At some point in time, the inside square is going to be rebuilt. The word "wall" in Hebrew means "trench." This word very well could mean the moat that goes outside the actual city wall to protect the city from its enemies.

4. Division of the seventy weeks

Gabriel explained that the seventy weeks of prophetic history for the Jews are divided into three sections:

1. Seven weeks of years (49 years). During this time, the city of Jerusalem would be rebuilt.

2. Sixty-two weeks of years (434 years). This section continues until the Messiah comes. This prophecy specifically pinpoints the Messiah's entry into Jerusalem, when His entrance on a colt announced His deity. The Triumphal Entry occurred exactly 483 years after the decree was given by Artaxerxes!

3. The final week of years (7 years). Between the second and third periods of this prophecy is a notable gap. Prophets in the Old Testament saw the future as one might see a mountain range; we notice the peaks, but we do not always see the valleys. Such was the case with this prophecy. Daniel sees truth concerning both the first and second coming of the Messiah, but the gap in between is not revealed to him. It is not unusual at all to see references to Christ's first and second advents placed side-by-side without any mention of a gap. Yet we have seen these gaps played out through the course of history.

Regarding the first division of seven weeks, Chuck Swindoll reminds us, "The opposition that Nehemiah encountered would certainly qualify as 'times of distress' (see 4:1–23; 6:1–9), but it took Nehemiah only fifty-two days to finish building the wall around Jerusalem. The forty-nine-year period must refer to the time it took to reconstruct the entire city, 'with plaza and moat.'"[7]

Regarding the second division, if we add 49 and 434, we come up with a total of 483 years. By using the Jewish calendar, which is based on a 360-day lunar year, we discover that a 483-year period equals 173,880 days. According to New Testament scholar Harold Hoehner, by counting 173,880 days from the first of Nisan (March 5) 444 BC, the day that Nehemiah received the decree, we arrive at Nisan 10 (March 10), AD 33—the very day that Jesus entered Jerusalem as Messiah the Prince! Swindoll comments on this accuracy, saying:

> Amazing! Five centuries before the event, God drew an X on the exact date Jesus would appear as the long-awaited Son of David. On that momentous day, the people spread their garments on the road and shouted, "Blessed is the King who comes in the name of the Lord (Luke 19:38)." In the bright spotlight of Daniel's prophecy, Jesus could hardly be missed. This was Jerusalem's golden day the 173,880th day of Daniel's prophecy, and Jesus was prepared to fulfill all six objectives mentioned in Daniel 9:24. Incredibly, though, his own people refused him. Approaching Jerusalem, the City of Peace, Jesus wept, "If you had known in this day, even you, the things which make for peace!"[8]

How do we know that the Triumphal Entry fulfills this prophecy? "Messiah the Prince" is a title for Jesus Christ in His Messiahship. Daniel wrote that from the official decree to rebuild the city until the official presentation of Messiah the Prince, there would be a certain number of days. At the Triumphal Entry, Jesus rode into Jerusalem on a donkey and offered Himself as the Prince, the King of Israel. Before that day, Jesus had not publicly presented Himself as the Messiah. Do you remember what he had done after every miracle up to that point? He told people to keep quiet about it because His hour had not yet come. But on that day, He came riding into Jerusalem as the Lord's anointed.

This event is recorded in Luke 19. There are many signs in this chapter that point to how special that day was. First, the Savior sent His disciples to procure a colt. To fulfill prophecy, He told them that there would be a colt ready for them. This act was a fulfillment of Zechariah 9:9, which says, "Rejoice greatly, O daughter of Zion! Shout, O daughter of Jerusalem! Behold, your King is coming to you; He is just and having salvation, lowly and riding on a donkey, a colt, the foal of a donkey."

Second, we are told that the whole multitude of disciples, clearly understanding the meaning of this act, begin to shout those well-known words, "Blessed is the King who comes in the name of the Lord (Luke 19:38)!" Third, until that time, Jesus had refused to allow His disciples to make Him known as the Messiah. However, what do we see on that day? Look at His actions in Luke 19:37–42:

> Then, as He was now drawing near the descent of the Mount of Olives, the whole multitude of the disciples began to rejoice and praise God with a loud voice for all the mighty works they had seen, saying: "Blessed is the King who comes in the name of the LORD! Peace in heaven and glory in the highest!" And some of the Pharisees called to Him from the crowd, "Teacher, rebuke Your disciples." But He answered and said to them, "I tell you that if these should keep silent, the stones would immediately cry out." Now as He drew near, He saw the city and wept over it, saying, "If you had known, even you, especially in this your day, the things that make for your peace! But now they are hidden from your eyes."

Jesus mentioned that this was their day. Was this just any other day? No; it was the prophetic day that had been foretold right here in Daniel 9.

5. The specific timetable

The prophetic clock started right on time, when Artaxerxes gave the decree for the city to be rebuilt. Look at the narrative in Nehemiah's own words (Nehemiah 2:1–8):

> And it came to pass in the month of Nisan, in the twentieth year of King Artaxerxes, when wine was before him, that I took the wine and gave it to the king. Now I had never been sad in his presence before. Therefore the king said to me, "Why is your face sad, since you are not sick? This is nothing but sorrow of heart." So I became dreadfully afraid, and said to the king, "May the king live forever! Why should my face not be sad, when the city, the place of my fathers' tombs, lies waste, and its gates are burned with fire?" Then the king said to me, "What do you request?" So I prayed to the God of heaven. And I said to the king, "If it pleases the king, and if your servant has found favor in your sight, I ask that you send me to

Judah, to the city of my fathers' tombs, that I may rebuild it." Then the king said to me (the queen also sitting beside him), "How long will your journey be? And when will you return?" So it pleased the king to send me; and I set him a time. Furthermore I said to the king, "If it pleases the king, let letters be given to me for the governors of the region beyond the River, that they must permit me to pass through till I come to Judah, and a letter to Asaph the keeper of the king's forest, that he must give me timber to make beams for the gates of the citadel which pertains to the temple, for the city wall, and for the house that I will occupy." And the king granted them to me according to the good hand of my God upon me.

Note what these scholars have to say about the divine timetable in Daniel 9:

• Dr. David Jeremiah—Daniel's prophecy tells us that there will be a period of sixty-nine weeks that will begin on a particular day and end on a particular day. Then there will be a gap in time, and finally there will be the Seventieth Week. We understand that the sixty-nine weeks in Daniel refer to groups of years and that a "week" refers to a group of seven years, so the total is 483 years (sixty-nine times seven). Fortunately, we can document the reign of Artaxerxes, so we are able to provide dates to Daniel's prophecy. Artaxerxes began to reign in 465 BC. Nehemiah tells us that the command to rebuild the wall came in the twentieth year of Artaxerxes' reign—445 BC. Nehemiah further tells us that the commandment was made on the first day of Nisan, which on our calendars would be March 14. Now, if you begin counting on March 14, 445 BC and add the exact number of days Daniel refers to, keeping in mind leap years and the fact that they counted 360 days to the year, you would stop counting on April 6, in the year AD 32. According to most scholars, including Sir Robert Anderson's chronology, it was on that day that Jesus Christ rode in the city (Jerusalem) for His Triumphal Entry.[9]

• Sir Robert Anderson—The Julian date of 1st Nisan 445 was the 14th of March. Sixty-nine weeks of years—i.e., 173,880 days—reckoned from the 14th March 445 BC, ended on the 6th of April, AD 32. That day, on which the sixty-nine weeks ended, was the fateful day on which the Lord Jesus rode into Jerusalem in fulfillment of the prophecy of Zechariah 9:9; when, for the first and only occasion in all His earthly sojourn, He was acclaimed as "Messiah the Prince, the King, the Son of David." And here again we must keep to Scripture... no date in history, sacred or profane, is fixed with greater definiteness than that of the year in which the Lord began His public ministry... we can fix the date of the Passion with absolute certainty as Nisan 32 AD... we can appeal to the labors of secular historians and chronologists for proofs of the divine accuracy of Holy Scripture.[10]

- Dr. J. Vernon McGee—The first seven weeks of forty-nine years brings us to 397 BC and to Malachi and the end of the Old Testament. These were "troublous times," as witnessed by both Nehemiah and Malachi. Sixty-two weeks, or 434 years, brings us to the Messiah. Sir Robert Anderson, in his book *The Coming Prince*, has worked out the time schedule.[11]

- Dr. Louis Talbot—It was forty-nine years between the time when the rebuilding of the walls of Jerusalem was started and the completion of the work. The city was built again "in troublous times." Read the wonderful story of Ezra and Nehemiah to see how the enemy opposed the faithful Jewish remnant at every turn—by ridicule, by craft, and by open opposition. But God was with His people; the temple worship was restored; the walls were finished; and God's prophecy was fulfilled. From the close of this period of seven sevens, i.e., 49 years, "unto Messiah the Prince," another sixty-two sevens of years were to be reckoned. Adding these first two periods, we have sixty-nine sevens, or 483 years, at the close of which time the Messiah was to be "cut off, but not for Himself." That really happened; for Christ was crucified exactly at that time. Able chronologists, such as Sir Robert Anderson, have shown that the crucifixion of the Lord Jesus Christ occurred immediately after the expiration of 483 prophetic years of 360 days each from the time designated in Daniel 9:25-26.[12]

Why Does it Matter?

Maybe you are thinking right now, "50 weeks, 70 weeks, who cares!" Why does all of this matter? When I sit down with a Jewish friend, I don't turn to the New Testament to witness to him. We can turn to prophecies just like this one to prove not only that the Bible is true, but that Jesus Christ is Messiah, Savior, and God.

Let me give you four short reasons why this passage matters. First, it reminds me that the God who is in control of the world can handle all my problems and difficulties. Do you have any problems? Just remember that God is in control of all things! He brings nations up and He puts them down. He works His plan and no one thwarts Him, not even a disobedient person. The rain hits the just and the unjust because God is ruler over all. It may shock you to hear this, but sometimes God performs His will when man is in disobedience. Second, prophecy is a preset plan designed by God that nothing can change or interrupt. Would you please lift up your view of God? Never think that God is weak or inactive. He is doing many things. He is sovereign, powerful, and mighty. Third, we should follow Daniel's example and study prophecy so we will be aware of God's end-time work in the world. We can get out of bed and instead of being depressed, we can say "Maybe today! Maybe God will return today!" Fourth, we see that the Antichrist is not a metaphor. He is a real person coming to this earth. Already the spirit of Antichrist has begun. Consequently, every Christian must be discerning regarding the times in which we live.

I close with a thought from Louis Talbot:

> You will have no difficulty in understanding the great interval between the sixty-ninth and seventieth "weeks" if you will always bear in mind the fact that God never reckons time with the Jews when He is not dealing with them as a nation. When He ceases to deal with them as a nation, then the Jewish clock stops. This happened when Christ was "cut-off," crucified; the Jewish clock stopped, and has not yet begun to tick again.[13]

But the Jewish clock will start again one day. During the Tribulation, we will see something amazing. We will see Jews by the thousands come to faith in Christ at that time. The book of Revelation assures us that there will be 144,000 Jewish Billy Grahams! They will preach to the four corners of the Earth, and bring about one of the greatest revivals ever. What a glorious day that will be for God, when His Son is vindicated in the eyes of His covenant people!

Discussion Questions

1. How do we know that God still has a plan for the nation of Israel? (See Gen 15, 17:1-8)

2. What does the word "weeks" mean in this passage and what information does that give us for interpreting this prophecy?

3. What are the three divisions that make up the seventy weeks?

4. What is the focus of this prophecy? How have some aspects of it been partially fulfilled already?

5. What does this prophecy tell us about the coming Antichrist?

6. What do prophecies such as this tell us about the Bible? What do they tell us about God's sovereignty?

7. Why do you think some Christians are so reluctant to study prophecy? Why does the study of prophecy cause such division? How are we to handle division over doctrinal matters in the body of Christ?

8. The chronology of the seventy weeks prophecy clearly identifies Jesus as the Messiah. How would you witness to a Jew from this passage and others in the Old Testament? Make a list of passages you could discuss, such as Is 53 and Ps 22.

That's Not All

You can find sermon outlines in the "Sermonars" section at the back of the book. These pages may be freely reproduced, either from the book or from the accompanying CD-ROM for any devotional or ministry use.

Chapter Fifteen

Watching the Antichrist in the Seventieth Week

In this chapter, we will be looking at Daniel 9:27, which says: "Then he shall confirm a covenant with many for one week; but in the middle of the week he shall bring an end to sacrifice and offering. And on the wing of abominations shall be one who makes desolate, even until the consummation, which is determined, is poured out on the desolate." A new end-times character is introduced to the passage in Daniel 9:26-27, and we learn more about him in 11:36-45. Daniel 11:36 says, "Then the king will do as he pleases." What king is this? The Antichrist, the one who is predicted in 9:26-27. What exactly will he do? The rest of this passage says:

> He shall regard neither the God of his fathers nor the desire of women, nor regard any god; for he shall exalt himself above them all. But in their place he shall honor a god of fortresses; and a god which his fathers did not know he shall honor with gold and silver, with precious stones and pleasant things. Thus he shall act against the strongest fortresses with a foreign god, which he shall acknowledge, and advance its glory; and he shall cause them to rule over many, and divide the land for gain (Daniel 11:37-39).

He will not be unopposed in his activity, however, as we see in the next verses of Daniel 11:

At the time of the end the king of the South shall attack him; and the king of the North shall come against him like a whirlwind, with chariots, horsemen, and with many ships; and he shall enter the countries, overwhelm them, and pass through. He shall also enter the Glorious Land, and many countries shall be overthrown; but these shall escape from his hand: Edom, Moab, and the prominent people of Ammon. He shall stretch out his hand against the countries, and the land of Egypt shall not escape. He shall have power over the treasures of gold and silver, and over all the precious things of Egypt; also the Libyans and Ethiopians shall follow at his heels. But news from the east and the north shall trouble him; therefore he shall go out with great fury to destroy and annihilate many. And he shall plant the tents of his palace between the seas and the glorious holy mountain; yet he shall come to his end, and no one will help him (Daniel 11:40-45).

Some passages in the Word of God are incredibly difficult to understand. They make us think and ponder. But even more than that, they force us to bring together the entire progressive revelation of God to gain a good understanding of God's overall message. This passage, more than many others, is one of the most difficult passages to understand.

Think back to what we have learned so far in the book of Daniel. We are nearing the end of the book; only a few chapters remain for us to study. We have seen that this is a book that contains historical fact but is predictive in nature. We have seen predictions about Gentile world empires that would arise. In chapters two and seven, Daniel carefully interprets visions concerning four empires that would arise, finishing with the revived Roman Empire. This book also predicted the coming of the Messiah, pinpointing the exact day that Jesus would ride into Jerusalem on a donkey and reveal His identity as the Messiah.

However, what is most intriguing to me about the book of Daniel is that it predicts the Antichrist who is to come. Even more spell-binding, it foretells his specific activity in the seven-year Tribulation in Daniel 9:26-27 and 11:36-45.

Many people have speculated about who the Antichrist is. All kinds of theories and names have been suggested. It seems that about every ten years, some new world figure is said to be the Antichrist. One scientist has said that if you take the number 666 and you are clever enough, you can make that number relate to any name there is! Historically, some have thought that Antiochus Epiphanes was the Antichrist. Luther, Calvin, and others believed it to be the pope! Roman Emperors have been suggested, such as Caligula and Nero. One very popular suggestion in the last century has been Adolf Hitler.

So who is the Antichrist? No one knows! Only God knows his identity, in the same way that only the Father knows when Christ will return. Thus, any time I hear a minister on television or in any other venue say that he has a unique formula that reveals the day in which Christ will return, I immediately know that I am listening to a false teacher. Jesus Himself said in Mark 13:32 that no one knows the time of His return but the Father. He also indicated that it would be at a time when we least expect. How, then, can men think they are able to predict it?

The Activity of the Antichrist

Though we do not know the identity of the Antichrist, we are told about his activity. There are several important questions about the Antichrist that find their answers in the passages that we examined earlier in this chapter. Let us look at a few of these questions.

1. When will the Antichrist be revealed?

First, Daniel was told that the Antichrist would not be revealed until the Messiah had been cut off. We see this in Daniel 9:26, "And after the sixty-two weeks Messiah shall be cut off, but not for Himself; and the people of the prince who is to come shall destroy the city and the sanctuary..." The wording of this verse makes it clear that the coming of the Antichrist would still be a future event when the Messiah was cut off. Interestingly, this verse also predicts the destruction of the city of Jerusalem in AD 70. Notice that the coming of the Antichrist is still future even at that point. Daniel does not say the prince who is to come will destroy the city; he says *the people of* the prince who is to come will destroy it. Based on this verse and on the historical event in AD 70, we can see that the Antichrist will come from a revived Roman Empire.

This verse allows us to dispel some of the theories about the identity of the Antichrist. Could Antiochus Epiphanes, who ruled around 168 BC, fit this description? Of course not! Only after the Messiah was cut off and Jerusalem was destroyed could the Antichrist be revealed.

Second, he could not be revealed until after the time that Paul referred to as the "dispensation of the grace of God" for the Gentiles was complete. Only then could the Antichrist be revealed. This explains the gap between the sixty-ninth and seventieth week of Daniel's prophecy in chapter 9. Why didn't Daniel see this gap? Remember, the information he was given concerned the Jews. This gap, however, is a time for the Gentiles! God had planned that He would bring an innumerable company of Gentiles into His eternal fold along with the covenant people, the Jews.

Where do we find this dispensation mentioned in Scripture? Ephesians 3:1-6 describes it:

> For this reason I, Paul, the prisoner of Christ Jesus for you Gentiles—if indeed you have heard of the dispensation of the grace of God which was given to me for you, how that by revelation He made known to me the mystery (as I have briefly written already, by which, when you read, you may understand my knowledge in the mystery of Christ), which in other ages was not made known to the sons of men, as it has now been revealed by the Spirit to His holy apostles and prophets: that the Gentiles should be fellow heirs, of the same body, and partakers of His promise in Christ through the gospel.

Verse 5 applies to Daniel. This dispensation had not been made known in the past. God gave Daniel a prophecy for the Jews because he was a *Jewish* prophet, but God had a plan for the Gentiles also. Daniel could not see that after Messiah was cut off, the Holy Spirit would descend and an age of grace would open up in which God would start calling from the four corners of the Earth thousands of people from all nations to be a people for His name. It is true today that there are Christians throughout the world, in every continent and country. Anywhere you can think of to go, you can find someone there who loves Jesus.

The identity of the Antichrist will not be revealed until this dispensation is complete. And what event will bring this dispensation to a close? The Rapture! It is awesome to think that one day, we will wake up and start our day, but we will never see the evening because we will be caught up to meet the Lord in the air.

Third, the Antichrist will be revealed after a massive expression of false Christianity has been portrayed before men and women. This is what is referred to as "the apostasy." Apostasy does not mean that people stop going to church; it simply means that they start going to a church of convenience. It means that there will be a new generation of ministers who do not talk about sin or hell. They will make everything sound good and feel good.

In 2 Thessalonians 2:3, Paul describes the relationship between the apostasy and the coming of the Antichrist. He says, "Let no one deceive you by any means; for that Day will not come unless the falling away comes first and the man of sin is revealed." The English phrase "falling away" translates the Greek word for apostasy. People will not leave church altogether; they will simply reinvent a church that is not the genuine church. The falling away must come before "the son of perdition, who opposes and exalts himself above all that is called God or that is worshiped, so that he sits as god in the temple of God, showing himself that he is god" (2 Thessalonians 2:3-4).

Finally, the Antichrist will not be revealed until the total removal of Christians from this world at the next great event in God's prophetic plan, the Rapture. Second Thessalonians 2:7-8 teaches this truth: "For the mystery of lawlessness is already at work; only He who now restrains will do so until He is taken out of the way. And then the lawless one will be revealed..." Who currently restrains the work of Satan and the Antichrist? It is the Holy Spirit, who is present in believers. Because the Holy Spirit works through us, we are the salt and light of the world. If it were not for the work of God through believers, this world would be in a much more perilous situation.

Paul emphasizes the order of events in his letter to the Thessalonians. Look again at what he says in 2 Thessalonians 2:7-10, this time in its entirety:

> For the mystery of lawlessness is already at work; only He who now restrains will do so until He is taken out of the way. And then the lawless one will be revealed, whom the Lord will consume with the breath of His mouth and destroy with the brightness of His coming. The coming of the lawless one is according to the working of Satan, with all power, signs, and lying wonders, and with all unrighteous deception among those who perish, because they did not receive the love of the truth, that they might be saved.

The Antichrist will not be revealed until after the glorious day when Jesus returns for us at the Rapture. Do you remember how Tim LaHaye described this event in his novel, *Left Behind?* Hattie Durham, a stewardess on an airplane, and Rayford Steele, a commercial pilot, are about to start having an affair after having flirted with each other for quite some time. Rayford's wife, who does not know about her husband's unfaithful intentions, is a committed Christian who loves Jesus Christ. She had been trying to convince Rayford to become a believer, so he has been exposed to the gospel and the message about the end times.

As the plane is on its way to the United Kingdom, the stewardess leaves the cockpit to check on the passengers. As she heads down the aisle, she is stunned! On seat after seat, there is nothing but empty clothing! She sees this same thing all over the plane. She gets on the intercom and tells Rayford to come take a look for himself. He jumps out of his seat and races back in the plane, but after he sees the seats, he knows what has happened, because his wife had described it to him before.

Eventually, when Rayford gets back home, he goes to his bedroom and pulls back the covers on the bed to find his wife's empty pajamas. She had gone to bed for the night, but Jesus had come before she ever woke up. And of course, lying on the nightstand by the bed was a Bible.[1]

If you don't believe this event is going to happen, you should reconsider your position. All of God's Word and its integrity hinges on that event, because the Scriptures say that Jesus will come. If He does not return, then we can throw our Bibles away, because they can no longer be trusted. This event is extremely important, and we must believe that it will happen and be ready for it when it does.

2. What will the Antichrist do in the 70th week?

Shortly after the Rapture, the 70th week will launch; the gap is over! The dispensation of the grace of God to the Gentiles is finished. What will be the Antichrist's first act? He will immediately confirm a peace covenant between the Jews and their surrounding neighbors. This covenant will guarantee Israel's security as a nation. Israel will then be protected by the revived Roman Empire. Incidentally, this covenant will give the Jews access to the temple site so that the temple can be rebuilt and their ancient system of worship re-established.

If you have been watching the news at all lately, you probably wonder how in the world all of this will happen. The temple mount, where the first temple of Solomon and the temple of Herod were located, is currently under the control of Muslims. The city itself is a place of hostility, where three different religions believe they are on holy ground. The Antichrist will be able to make peace for this area because he is coming with power, signs, and wonders!

The Antichrist will make this treaty, but halfway through this seven-year period, he will break it. Just when everything is starting to look good for the Jews, things will change. Many Jews will even believe that the Antichrist is the Messiah, because he will make it possible for the temple to be rebuilt. They will be predisposed to worship him, but their hopes will be dashed. Daniel 9:27 says, "He shall bring an end to sacrifice and offering. And on the wing of abominations shall be one who makes desolate, even until the consummation which is determined, is poured out on the desolate."

How will he stop the worship of the Jews? He will enter the temple and proclaim himself to be god. He will do what Antiochus Epiphanes did, when he profaned the temple by sacrificing a pig on the altar. Antiochus was thus a type of the Antichrist who is to come.

Obviously, the Jewish temple will have to be rebuilt; otherwise, the Antichrist could not stop the sacrifices and offerings. The Antichrist will cause an abomination against the Jewish religion. He will commit an act that will desolate or ruin what Jews regard as sacred—the temple and the Holy of Holies. By announcing his own deity in the newly rebuilt Jewish temple at the three-and-one-half-year mark, the Antichrist will begin the final three and a half years of the Tribulation, a time known as the Great Tribulation, when there will be unequalled sorrow and death.

Jesus Himself warned his disciples about this time in Matthew 24:15, saying, "Therefore when you see the 'abomination of desolation,' spoken of by Daniel the prophet, standing in the holy place..." While this verse referred initially to Antiochus Epiphanes' blasphemy in the temple in 168 BC, it nevertheless awaits its complete fulfillment, when the Antichrist will set up his own image in the temple during the Tribulation.

After this event takes place, Jesus says, "then there will be great tribulation, such as has not been since the beginning of the world until this time, no, nor ever shall be (Matthew 24:21)." As bad as things are today, it is absolutely nothing compared to the last three and a half years of the Tribulation. The book of Revelation indicates that one out of every two people will die during this particular time. This is a very sobering thought, and we might feel prone to reject it. But we cannot simply erase verses from the Bible! Scripture speaks of devastation in several places:

- Daniel 12:1b, "And there shall be a time of trouble, such as never was since there was a nation."

- Revelation 13:7-8, "It was granted to him to make war with the saints and to overcome them. And authority was given him over every tribe, tongue, and nation. And all who dwell on the earth will worship him, whose names have not been written in the Book of Life of the Lamb slain from the foundation of the world."

- Jeremiah 30:7, "Alas! For that day is great, so that none is like it; and it is the time of Jacob's trouble, but he shall be saved out of it."

Dr. Louis Talbot provides valuable information and commentary on the Antichrist and his false prophet:

> The more I study prophecy, the more it seems to me that this last dictator may be a Gentile. Certainly he will be the last of the Caesars, whether Jew or Gentile. Now we know that his henchman, "the false prophet," of Revelation 13:11-18; 19:20; 20:10, must of necessity be a Jew. He will come imitating Jesus, "the Lamb of God;" for John saw that he had "two horns like a lamb" (Rev. 13:11); yet "he spoke as a dragon." The Jews would hardly accept as their Messiah—though he will be false—one who is not a Jew. This representative of "the beast" in Palestine will, therefore, in all probability be an apostate Israelite. He will receive his power from Satan and be subject to the world dictator.[2]

3. How savage will the Antichrist's rule be?

Daniel 11:35 transitions to a discussion of the Antichrist with the phrase, "until the time of the end." Jerome, Luther, and a host of other Bible scholars identify the central character in the remaining section of Daniel 11 as the Antichrist. How savage will his rule be? Let us look at a few thoughts from Daniel 11:36-45.

Verse 36 says, "Then the king shall do according to his own will; he shall exalt and magnify himself above every god, shall speak blasphemies against the God of gods, and shall prosper till the wrath has been accomplished; for what has been determined shall be done." We see first that the Antichrist, in the newly rebuilt Jewish temple, will exalt himself as god, above any and all "gods" that may challenge his claim, including the God of the Bible. He will demand that the entire world worship him. This feat will be accomplished through the mark of the beast. Without that mark, people will be unable to buy or sell any goods.

Daniel continues in verse 37 saying, "He shall regard neither the God of his fathers..." From this statement, some have felt that the Antichrist must be a Jew. But there is a problem with that interpretation: the word "Elohim" in this context is not referring to the God of the Bible; it is talking about multiple gods. The Antichrist is coming from a culture of polytheism! He may even have a background in the occult. Louis Talbot has stated concerning this verse: "In times past I have held that Daniel 11:37 teaches that the Antichrist himself will be a Jew; upon further study, it seems to me that he may not be, and that we cannot be dogmatic upon this point."[3]

The rest of verse 37 says that the Antichrist will not regard, "the desire of women, nor regard any god; for he shall exalt himself above them all." Chuck Swindoll says, "It seems to suggest that the Antichrist will be a homosexual. If not, he is certainly celibate."[4] What will the Antichrist put in the place of women and other gods? Verse 38 gives us the answer: "But in their place he shall honor a god of fortresses; and a god which his fathers did not know he shall honor with gold and silver, with precious stones and pleasant things." The "god of fortresses" speaks of military technology. He will possess the finest, most advanced technological military equipment for destruction and will place his sole confidence in military might. The Antichrist will sweep into the Glorious Land and subdue nations that come against him. This warfare may include nuclear activity and chemical agents.

Daniel 11:39 describes his satanic power: "Thus he shall act against the strongest fortresses with a foreign god, which he shall acknowledge, and advance its glory; and he shall cause them to rule over many, and divide the land for gain." The foreign god who assists the Antichrist is none other than Satan. And to Israel's great regret, their land will be sold off by the Antichrist.

217

The Battle of Armageddon and the Antichrist—11:40-45

The remaining part of this chapter describes a historic battle that will take place against the Antichrist:

> At the time of the end the king of the South shall attack him; and the king of the North shall come against him like a whirlwind, with chariots, horsemen, and with many ships; and he shall enter the countries, overwhelm them, and pass through. He shall also enter the Glorious Land, and many countries shall be overthrown; but these shall escape from his hand: Edom, Moab, and the prominent people of Ammon. He shall stretch out his hand against the countries, and the land of Egypt shall not escape. He shall have power over the treasures of gold and silver, and over all the precious things of Egypt; also the Libyans and Ethiopians shall follow at his heels. But news from the east and the north shall trouble him; therefore he shall go out with great fury to destroy and annihilate many. And he shall plant the tents of his palace between the seas and the glorious holy mountain; yet he shall come to his end, and no one will help him.

The timetable is clearly stipulated in v. 40—this battle takes place at the time of the end. The king of the South could be a combined Islamic army representing Egypt, Africa, and beyond. Just think about what the Antichrist has done—he has allowed the Jewish temple to be rebuilt (which means the Dome on the Rock and Al Aqsa Mosque, Islamic holy sites, would be moved) and the sacrifices to be re-established. This would not make Islamic people happy with him.

The king of the North here we confidently believe is Russia, perhaps assisted by other nations. "News from the East" could represent the huge army invading from the East that is mentioned in Revelation 9:13-21. Who could possibly amass such an army? Only China!

How are we to respond to all of this? Dr. Louis Talbot sums it up for us very well: "What we need to do is go into all the world, preaching the gospel to every creature, winning men and women to the Lord Jesus Christ before the 'reign of terror' of the Antichrist comes upon the world."5 May we warn our loved ones of the wrath to come, and introduce them to the one who has taken God's wrath for them—Jesus Christ!

Discussion Questions

1. Why do you think people get so caught up in trying to discern the identity of the Antichrist? Why don't people often devote the same effort to studying other doctrines revealed in Scripture?

2. What events had to take place before the Antichrist could be revealed? Is there anything that still has to happen before this man can begin his work? If so, when will this event take place?

3. From what you know of history and politics, why is there currently such hostility in the Middle East? How would the world view a man who could bring about peace in that area?

4. What facts do we know about the Antichrist? What can we not know?

5. When, where, and how will the Antichrist declare himself to be God? What will he do to try and consolidate his power?

6. What does God say about trusting in military might as one's security? (See Ps 20:7, 33:17; Prov 21:31; Is 31:1; Jer 17:5)

7. Jesus frequently spoke on hell and the judgments which will take place in the end times. Why do people tend to overlook or downplay these aspects of Jesus' teaching?

That's Not All

You can find sermon outlines in the "Sermonars" section at the back of the book. These pages may be freely reproduced, either from the book or from the accompanying CD-ROM for any devotional or ministry use.

Chapter Sixteen

Prayer & Demonic Warfare: Discerning the Work of Good and Bad Angels in Our Lives

Prayer is mentioned numerous times throughout the book of Daniel. In chapter 6, Daniel prayed while in the lion's den, and God came and protected him. In chapter 9, Daniel prayed and God gave him a great vision. By the time Daniel was done praying, God had already sent the angel Gabriel to answer Daniel's prayer. Now, in chapter 10, we are exposed to an aspect of prayer that we see nowhere else in the book of Daniel and, perhaps, only in a few other places throughout the entire Bible: how prayer relates to spiritual warfare!

Daniel 10 introduces Daniel's fourth and final vision in the book. The previous vision, found in chapter 9, gave us information about the first and second comings of the Messiah, the Antichrist, and the millennial reign of Christ on earth. This final vision, on the other hand, covers the entire last three chapters of Daniel (Daniel 10–12). Dr. J. Vernon McGee comments, "These last three chapters should be treated as one vision. This vision relates to the nation of Israel in the immediate future and also the latter days. For example, there is the historical 'little horn' and also the 'little horn' of the latter days."[1] Let us now take a closer look at the opening segment of this final vision (Daniel 10:1–21) and see what it teaches us about prayer and demonic warfare.

When Was It?

Daniel 10:1 states, "In the third year of Cyrus king of Persia a message was revealed to Daniel, whose name was called Belteshazzar. The message was true, but the appointed time was long; and he understood the message, and had understanding of the vision." Thus, it is clear that this final vision, which includes chapters 10–12, was given to Daniel in the third year of the reign of Cyrus. Daniel was well over ninety years of age by then. Isn't this amazing? There is no such thing as retiring from God's work, is there? Daniel was already ninety, but God was not yet finished with him.

Verse 1 also lets us know that Daniel was troubled as he went to God in prayer. King Cyrus, raised up by God, had issued a decree and given the Jewish people permission to leave Babylon and to return to Jerusalem so they could rebuild their temple and their city. But to Daniel's surprise, after seventy years of captivity, not all of the Jews wanted to go back home. In fact, only 42,360 Jews out of the entire group that had been deported decided to return to Jerusalem. Take a look at Ezra's description of the group that went back to Jerusalem:

> The whole assembly together was forty-two thousand three hundred and sixty, besides their male and female servants, of whom there were seven thousand three hundred and thirty-seven; and they had two hundred men and women singers. Their horses were seven hundred and thirty-six, their mules two hundred and forty-five, their camels four hundred and thirty-five, and their donkeys six thousand seven hundred and twenty (Ezra 2:64–65).

Unfortunately, those who refused to go were precisely the ones who should have gone: Israel's religious leaders. They had built their new lives in Babylon and were very well settled in that pagan society. To make matters even worse, the Jews who decided to go back unaccompanied by their spiritual leaders faced great difficulties as they tried to obey God. Once again, read carefully Ezra's description of what happened:

> Now when the adversaries of Judah and Benjamin heard that the descendants of the captivity were building the temple of the LORD God of Israel, they came to Zerubbabel and the heads of the fathers' houses, and said to them, "Let us build with you, for we seek

your God as you do; and we have sacrificed to Him since the days of Esarhaddon king of Assyria, who brought us here." But Zerubbabel and Jeshua and the rest of the heads of the fathers' houses of Israel said to them, "You may do nothing with us to build a house for our God; but we alone will build to the LORD God of Israel, as King Cyrus the king of Persia has commanded us." Then the people of the land tried to discourage the people of Judah. They troubled them in building, and hired counselors against them to frustrate their purpose all the days of Cyrus king of Persia, even until the reign of Darius king of Persia. In the reign of Ahasuerus, in the beginning of his reign, they wrote an accusation against the inhabitants of Judah and Jerusalem (Ezra 4:1-6).

Thus, Daniel was undoubtedly aware of both the indifference of those who stayed behind in Babylon and the hardships facing the few who went back to Jerusalem. This provides the background for Daniel 10. Retired from serving the king, Daniel spent considerable time in prayer. He mourned that the Jewish people preferred the luxury and ease of Babylon to the hardships of serving God in Jerusalem. We can see this very clearly in Daniel 10:2-4, "In those days I, Daniel, was mourning three full weeks. I ate no pleasant food, no meat or wine came into my mouth, nor did I anoint myself at all, till three whole weeks were fulfilled. Now on the twenty-fourth day of the first month, as I was by the side of the great river, that is, the Tigris. . ."

Oliver B. Green comments on these verses:

> It is interesting to observe the time of year when Daniel had this season of prayer. He records that it was "in the twenty-fourth day of the first month." The Passover came on the fourteenth day of the first month, and the following day began the Feast of Unleavened Bread, continuing seven days. Therefore, Daniel's 21 days of prayer and fasting included the days of the Passover, the celebration of deliverance from Egypt.[2]

Daniel decided to have a three-week fasting period on the same days when the Jews celebrated the time when Israel came out of their Egyptian bondage. In other words, Daniel was pleading with God to intervene and to deliver Israel as He had done in the past.

Who Was It? A Theophany?

Having established the time and the background of Daniel's prayer and final prophecy, let us take a closer look at what Daniel saw:

> I lifted my eyes and looked, and behold, a certain man clothed in linen, whose waist was girded with gold of Uphaz! His body was like beryl, his face like the appearance of lightning, his eyes like torches of fire, his arms and feet like burnished bronze in color, and the sound of his words like the voice of a multitude. And I, Daniel, alone saw the vision, for the men who were with me did not see the vision; but a great terror fell upon them, so that they fled to hide themselves. Therefore I was left alone when I saw this great vision, and no strength remained in me; for my vigor was turned to frailty in me, and I retained no strength. Yet I heard the sound of his words; and while I heard the sound of his words I was in a deep sleep on my face, with my face to the ground. Suddenly, a hand touched me, which made me tremble on my knees and on the palms of my hands. And he said to me, "O Daniel, man greatly beloved, understand the words that I speak to you, and stand upright, for I have now been sent to you." While he was speaking this word to me, I stood trembling (Daniel 10:5-11).

Who was this who appeared to Daniel? Some believe that in this final vision Daniel had the privilege of seeing a theophany—a preincarnate appearance of Jesus Christ. Since God had already done amazing things through Daniel's prayers (such as shutting the mouths of the lions and sending an angel to meet with him), it is not surprising that Jesus Christ Himself, the second Person of the Trinity, would appear to the beloved prophet in this last prophecy.

On the other hand, there are others who reject the view that this was a theophany. According to them, Daniel saw Michael the archangel. This is based on verse 13, which states: "But the prince of the kingdom of Persia withstood me twenty-one days; and behold, Michael, one of the chief princes, came to help me, for I had been left alone there with the kings of Persia." Still others argue that Daniel 10:5-11 refers to Gabriel, the same angel who had already appeared to Daniel in the past. For instance, Dr. Clarence Larkin writes, "From this we see that the Lord of Glory was not alone in this vision. He was accompanied by a 'heavenly messenger' who was no other than the angel Gabriel."[3] In my opinion, Daniel saw both: the preincarnate Christ (in verses 5-11) and Michael standing by His side (as stated in verse 13).

Whatever the case might have been, it is clear once again that there was a heavenly being (Jesus, Michael, or Gabriel) extolling Daniel's spiritual character. This reminds us that when we pray God's way, we inevitably invite God to work around and within us.

Why the Demonic Interference?

In the same way that God provides spiritual strength every time we pray, Satan also tries to offer spiritual opposition to the work God is accomplishing in our lives. Take a close look at the intriguing words we find in Daniel 10:12-14:

> Then he said to me, "Do not fear, Daniel, for from the first day that you set your heart to understand, and to humble yourself before your God, your words were heard; and I have come because of your words. But the prince of the kingdom of Persia withstood me twenty-one days; and behold, Michael, one of the chief princes, came to help me, for I had been left alone there with the kings of Persia. Now I have come to make you understand what will happen to your people in the latter days, for the vision refers to many days yet to come."

The "Prince of Persia" mentioned here was not a person but a very powerful demon. He had been sent to torment Daniel the moment Daniel uttered his prayers to God. This demon's ultimate purpose was to detain the archangel and to try to abort God's purpose. This reminds us once again that Satan and his demons know very well that God works through our prayers—hence the demons attempt to oppose Daniel, a mighty prayer warrior!

Consider the following insightful comments about the identity of the "prince of Persia" and the works of the devil:

> From this we see that Satan has his kingdom organized in wonderful manner. It is divided into kingdoms and principalities. These divisions correspond with the kingdom divisions of our earth. If Satan has a "Prince of Persia" and a "Prince of Greece", why not a

Prince for every nation? Satan has his limitations. He is not omni-present, neither is he omnipotent or omniscient. He has to depend upon his agents. And so great and powerful are his "princes" that it takes a supernatural being like Michael the archangel to overcome them.[4]

The one who had hindered God's special messenger can only have been a demon, appointed to do this by the chief of demons, Satan him-self. This follows from the fact that he sought to hinder an order of God from being carried out, and he was certainly more than human to be able to war against such a supernatural messenger, commissioned by God. That he is called "the prince of the kingdom of Persia" must mean that he had been assigned by Satan to effect Satan's program in connection with the Persian government. His assignment to that end was evidently a continuing one, for later (verse 20) Daniel's visitor said that he would personally return to do further battle with him.[5]

Furthermore, what is true of nations is also true of individuals. In the same manner that Satan dispatches his agents (demons) to torment entire nations, he also sends them to harass the saints. Satan is not very con-cerned about those who are already lost in darkness, but he really wants to stop those who are faithfully serving the Lord. Dr. Gordon Lindsay de-scribes very well the schemes of the devil as he opposes God's kingdom:

> The extent of the forces he [Satan] assigns to any particular indi-vidual depends to no little degree on the amount of damage that the person is causing to his kingdom. This explains why some men who have been greatly used of God have had their usefulness cut short. Satan, enraged by the success of their ministry, sent special forces to thwart the work they were doing. Alas! Too often the devil has been successful simply because the minister, absorbed in his work, fails to be consistent in his prayer life, and thus to build suf-ficient bulwarks against the attack of the enemy.[6]

I remember my first days as a Christian when I knew nothing about spiritual warfare. But then God, through a series of events, started to teach me that there is a whole spiritual dimension that is very real and impacts our lives, even though we cannot see it. Through the years, God also impressed on my heart the need to be ready to be victorious in this spiritual war. Just like football players must be in shape and ready to take the blows of their opponents, we too must be ready to withstand the devil.

Lest we place our focus solely on Satan and his demons, let us keep in mind what God is doing to protect us and to enable us to have victory. One of the many encouraging things about this chapter of Daniel is the way God provided support to his beloved servant. Though the "prince of Persia" was a strong demon, and though he was able to delay Daniel's prayer for 21 days, Daniel was not left alone—with him was Michael the archangel himself. What a great reminder that no matter how strong the enemies we face, God is always stronger!

Below are some encouraging ways God uses His angels to minister to us as we face dangerous situations (cf. Hebrews 1:14).

What Encompasses the Ministry of Angels to Us?

Read carefully the last few verses of Daniel 10:

> When he had spoken such words to me, I turned my face toward the ground and became speechless. And suddenly, one having the likeness of the sons of men touched my lips; then I opened my mouth and spoke, saying to him who stood before me, "My lord, because of the vision my sorrows have overwhelmed me, and I have retained no strength. For how can this servant of my lord talk with you, my lord? As for me, no strength remains in me now, nor is any breath left in me." Then again, the one having the likeness of a man touched me and strengthened me. And he said, "O man greatly beloved, fear not! Peace be to you; be strong, yes, be strong!" So when he spoke to me I was strengthened, and said, "Let my lord speak, for you have strengthened me." Then he said, "Do you know why I have come to you? And now I must return to fight with the prince of Persia; and when I have gone forth, indeed the prince of Greece will come. But I will tell you what is noted in the Scripture of Truth. (No one upholds me against these, except Michael your prince.) (Daniel 10:15-21)

What a beautiful picture of God's tender care for His people. We learn from this passage at least five truths about the way demons work and how God's holy angels minister to us:

1. Angels understand and comprehend our discouragement. They readily see our weaknesses! In addition to giving us the Holy Spirit as our Comforter, God also gives us His "watchers" and "holy ones" to minister to us and to watch over us. In Daniel 6, when Daniel was helplessly facing the lions, God sent His angel to assist him in that time of weakness and distress. In Daniel 9, Gabriel was by Daniel's side to comfort and enlighten him the moment the prophet was done praying. Isn't it comforting to know that God sends His angels to encourage us when we are down?

2. In unseen and probably unknown ways (to us, at least), at crucial moments angels touch and strengthen us to continue in the work God has called us to do. However, as a note of caution, keep in mind that we should never pray to angels. They are God's servants and do as they are told. Therefore, we should pray to God Himself to encourage us when we need to be encouraged!

3. Angels are constantly fighting demonic spirits who are intent upon our destruction and seek to thwart God's work through us! God has sent us his angels to fight for us!

4. Clearly, there are territorial demons. This is made clear in this passage through the mention of the "Prince of Persia" and the "Prince of Greece." Dr. Leon Wood once again comments:

> These thoughts lead to the conclusion that Satan is interested in hindering God's work with His people at any time and that he may assign special emissaries to influence governments at the highest level to hinder that work. Certainly, this chapter carries significance regarding the nature of struggles between higher powers in reference to God's program on earth (cf. Eph 6:11–12).[7]

Therefore, we must pray for our governments and our leaders, that God will surround them and keep Satan and his demons away!

5. Satan has a sophisticated demonic communication system that he uses to declare war on those most effective for Christ. This is clearly illustrated in this chapter through Daniel's faithfulness and the opposition he faced because of it. The "prince of Persia" knew

he should attack Daniel at that specific time because Satan, somehow, had found out about Daniel's prayer. Although Satan seems to have his schemes in place, God is immeasurably more powerful than Satan. God knows everything—He does not need anyone to help him find things out! What a comfort it is to know that we serve a "God who sees" (cf. Gen 16:13) and who has sovereignly declared all our days in spite of Satan's attacks (Psalm 139:13-16).

As we close this chapter, take a look at Mark Bubeck's admonitions as we stand together against the wiles of the devil:

> I have been working on the final draft of this book while sitting by the fireplace. I've diligently tried to keep the fire going by using a combination of fireplace coal and some kindling wood. One of the problems I've faced is that the kindling wood tends to burn too rapidly. I've discovered something, however, that has an application to this matter of spiritual warfare. By taking some wire and binding the kindling into a close, tight bundle, I've discovered that it burns much more slowly, almost like a large log would burn. The devouring fire is much more limited as the kindling remains bound tightly together.
>
> Something needs to be said about the vital importance of the unity, the closeness of the body of Christ in this matter of warfare. It has been stressed over and over... that the believer's victory is his union to the Lord Jesus Christ, who has our own victory. It is also important to see that in being united to Christ, we are also united to all other members of Christ's body. It is fascinating to note that the great passages on spiritual warfare were not written just to individuals but to churches, organized bodies of believers. Perhaps the greatest passage in the Bible on spiritual warfare is Ephesians 6:10-18.[8]

The apostle Paul wrote in Ephesians 6:18, "Praying always with all prayer and supplication in the Spirit, being watchful to this end with all perseverance and supplication for all the saints." May we develop a heart of prayer that brings us closer together as we stand against the devil. May together we find victory in God, knowing that He who is in us is greater than he who is in the world (1 John 4:4).

Discussion Questions

1. Why did only some of the Jews decide to return to Jerusalem after the king's decree? What happened to them when they got there?

2. Who did Daniel see in the vision of Daniel 10?

3. Why does Satan offer spiritual opposition to the work God is accomplishing in our lives? What are some ways he does that?

4. Who was the "Prince of Persia?"

5. How did the angel minister to Daniel? In what ways do angels usually minister to us?

6. Why should we not pray to angels?

7. What are some things you have learned about prayer from the book of Daniel so far?

That's Not All

You can find sermon outlines in the "Sermonars" section at the back of the book. These pages may be freely reproduced, either from the book or from the accompanying CD-ROM for any devotional or ministry use.

Chapter Seventeen

What Does God Say About War?

Is war ever right? If it is, when is it right? According to the Canadian Army Journal, since 3600 BC the world has only known 292 years of peace. During this period there have been 14,531 wars, great and small, claiming the lives of 3,640,000,000 people. It goes without saying that when we begin discussing war, we also begin discussing death. Since 650 BC, there have been 1,656 arms races, only sixteen of which have not ended in war. The arms races that did not end in war ended in the economic collapse of the countries involved. Since the time of Christ's death, there has not been a single year of peace in the world. A year has never passed since the times of Christ when there have been no wars fought. Great Britain alone has fought 78 wars in the last 500 years; France has fought in seventy-one wars in the same time period. Even the peaceful nation of the Netherlands has fought twenty-three wars. Over the same period, Spain has fought sixty-four wars, while Australia and Germany have endured fifty-two and twenty-three respectively.

This is just a sampling of the war-like nature of our world. Hundreds of thousands of lives have been lost in these conflicts worldwide. Even America in its short history has engaged in fifteen wars. It is clear, therefore, that war is part of our human experience; however, what does God say about it? How should we respond when our country considers the possibility of going to war? Many times religious leaders, Christian and non-Christians alike, condemn war altogether as never being justified. Is there such a thing as a "just war?" If so, when is war justified? Daniel 11 will help us answer some of these questions.

In Daniel 11, we find history written in advance. This is why the critics despise this book so much. It is accurate even in the smallest details of the world history it predicts will occur. Remember, at this point in the narrative Daniel is about ninety years old, and King Darius, the ruler of the Medo-Persian empire, is on the throne. It is interesting to note that the word "Darius" is more of a title than a specific proper name, much like the term "pharaoh" in the Old Testament or "Czar" or "President" in our present context. In this chapter, we will see world history unfolded for us from Daniel's time all the way to Antiochus Epiphanies in 168 BC; that is 300 years of history! It is so exact that critics of the Bible demand that it must have been written after the events took place. The popular theory taught in liberal seminaries today is that Daniel was written about 150 years before Christ's birth. They demand this because apart from the supernatural intervention of God, which they deny, there is no way this chapter could have been written so far in advance and be so accurate.

In the first 35 verses of Daniel 11, there are 135 prophecies that have already been fulfilled. Dr. Louis Talbot commented:

> Since all of chapter ten is preliminary to the vision recorded in chapters 11 and 12, we need not tarry here to review the circumstances under which this prophecy was given to Daniel. Chapter 11 falls logically into two main divisions, verses 1-35 recording detailed prophecies that have long ago been literally fulfilled; and verses 36-45 presenting to us the graphic portrait of the Antichrist and a foreview of his conflicts, which will end in the battle of Armageddon.[1]

Dr. David Jeremiah adds: "God unfolds to Daniel the detailed revelations of what would befall the nation of Israel during the next 300 years. They are so detailed that many skeptics reject the book, exclaiming that no one could possibly have known in such detail the coming events."[2]

Why is this prophecy so important? It is important because it was an answer to prayer. Daniel, God's righteous prophet in Babylon, had prayed for and was concerned about the Jewish nation and what would happen to them. This prophecy is God's answer to Daniel's prayer.

The Year 539 BC

When we read how the angel strengthened and confirmed King Cyrus in the task God had given him, it is an encouragement to us that God strengthens and confirms us as well. It is also important to note as we prepare to look at this chapter and answer the question "What does God say about war?" that Palestine is the geographical and political center of the earth (see Deuteronomy 32:8). The wars recorded in chapter 11 all involve Israel. For centuries the Holy Land has been a battleground for the nations and will host the final battle to end all wars: Armageddon (cf. Daniel 11:40-45). In the battle of Armageddon, the Holy Land will be a field of carnage such as the world has never seen before. The last war will be fought on the plains of Megiddo in the land of Israel.

Kings of War

Daniel 11:2 states, "And now I will tell you the truth: Behold, three more kings will arise in Persia, and the fourth shall be far richer than them all; by his strength, through his riches, he shall stir up all against the realm of Greece." This first prophecy about Persia is quite interesting. The Medo-Persian Empire of Daniel's day had its beginnings in the present day country of Iran. Who was the fourth king who would stir up all the realm of Greece? His name was Xerxes. He was the king who is the focus of the book of Esther. He was the man who armed a military force of 2.6 million soldiers. In order to understand the book of Esther, you must also understand Daniel.

The prophecy in Daniel 11:2 indicated that the Persian Empire would crumble in the face of the Greek Empire. Now let us close our Bibles for a moment and take a look at secular history books. What do they say happened to the Persian Empire? They say that the Persian Empire came to an end when Xerxes took his army of 2.6 million soldiers and fought against a young king from Greece named Alexander the Great. Alexander the Great, with a relatively small army, defeated a king who had an army of over 2 million soldiers. Secular historians confirm the absolute accuracy of the prophecy recorded in Daniel.

Alexander the Great was the unparalleled Greek conqueror who brought nearly the entire known world under his control in a period of ten years. Read carefully what Daniel 11:3-9 says about him:

> Then a mighty king shall arise, who shall rule with great dominion, and do according to his will. And when he has arisen, his kingdom shall be broken up and divided toward the four winds of heaven, but not among his posterity nor according to his dominion with which he ruled; for his kingdom shall be uprooted, even for others besides these. Also the king of the South shall become strong, as well as one of his princes; and he shall gain power over him and have dominion. His dominion shall be a great dominion. And at the end of some years they shall join forces, for the daughter of the king of the South shall go to the king of the North to make an agreement; but she shall not retain the power of her authority, and neither he nor his authority shall stand; but she shall be given up, with those who brought her, and with him who begot her, and with him who strengthened her in those times. But from a branch of her roots one shall arise in his place, who shall come with an army, enter the fortress of the king of the North, and deal with them and prevail. And he shall also carry their gods captive to Egypt, with their princes and their precious articles of silver and gold; and he shall continue more years than the king of the North. Also the king of the North shall come to the kingdom of the king of the South, but shall return to his own land.

Upon his death at age thirty-two, Alexander's kingdom was divided into four kingdoms. Again the prophecy in Daniel is specific and accurate. Next we see the prophecies concerning Egypt and Syria.

Antiochus Epiphanies came from Syria. Read what Daniel 11:10-19 predicted about this Syrian ruler:

> However his sons shall stir up strife, and assemble a multitude of great forces; and one shall certainly come and overwhelm and pass through; then he shall return to his fortress and stir up strife. And the king of the South shall be moved with rage, and go out and fight with him, with the king of the North, who shall muster a great multitude; but the multitude shall be given into the hand of his enemy. When he has taken away the multitude, his heart will be lifted up; and he will cast down tens of thousands, but he will not prevail. For the king of the North will return and muster a

multitude greater than the former, and shall certainly come at the end of some years with a great army and much equipment. Now in those times many shall rise up against the king of the South. Also, violent men of your people shall exalt themselves in fulfillment of the vision, but they shall fall. So the king of the North shall come and build a siege mound, and take a fortified city; and the forces of the South shall not withstand him. Even his choice troops shall have no strength to resist. But he who comes against him shall do according to his own will, and no one shall stand against him. He shall stand in the Glorious Land with destruction in his power. He shall also set his face to enter with the strength of his whole kingdom, and upright ones with him; thus shall he do. And he shall give him the daughter of women to destroy it; but she shall not stand with him, or be for him. After this he shall turn his face to the coastlands, and shall take many. But a ruler shall bring the reproach against them to an end; and with the reproach removed, he shall turn back on him. Then he shall turn his face toward the fortress of his own land; but he shall stumble and fall, and not be found.

Antiochus Epiphanies from Syria was involved in a series of conflicts with the Egyptian ruler known as the Ptolemy. These two fragments of Alexander the Great's kingdom warred for 120 years. During this extended conflict, both Syria and the Ptolemys fought for control of Israel, particularly Jerusalem. This resulted in the Jews becoming bitter enemies of both nations. Here in Daniel we see this conflict foreshadowed exactly as it would be played out hundreds of years later. In verses 21–35, we find a specific prophecy about Antiochus Epiphanies:

And in his place shall arise a vile person, to whom they will not give the honor of royalty; but he shall come in peaceably, and seize the kingdom by intrigue. With the force of a flood they shall be swept away from before him and be broken, and also the prince of the covenant. And after the league is made with him he shall act deceitfully, for he shall come up and become strong with a small number of people. He shall enter peaceably, even into the richest places of the province; and he shall do what his fathers have not done, nor his forefathers: he shall disperse among them the plunder, spoil, and riches; and he shall devise his plans against the strongholds, but only for a time. He shall stir up his power and his courage against the king of the South with a great army. And the king of the South shall be stirred up to battle with a very great and mighty army; but he shall not stand, for they shall devise plans against him. Yes, those who eat of the portion of his delicacies shall destroy him; his army shall be swept away, and many shall fall down slain. Both these kings' hearts shall be bent on evil, and they shall speak lies at the same table; but it shall not prosper, for the end will still be at the appointed time. While returning to his land with great riches, his heart shall be moved against the holy covenant; so he shall do damage and return to his own land. At the appointed time he shall return and go toward the south; but it shall not be like the former or the latter. For ships from Cyprus shall come against him; therefore he shall be grieved, and return in rage against the holy covenant, and do damage. So he shall return and show regard for those who forsake the holy covenant. And forces shall be mustered by him, and they shall defile the sanctuary fortress; then they shall take away the daily sacrifices, and place there the abomination of desolation. Those who do wickedly against the covenant he shall corrupt with flattery; but the people who know their God shall be strong, and carry out great exploits. And those of the people who understand shall instruct many; yet for many days they shall fall by sword and flame, by captivity and plundering. Now when they fall, they shall be aided with a little help; but many shall join with them by intrigue. And some of those of understanding shall fall, to refine them, purify them, and make them white, until the time of the end; because it is still for the appointed time (Daniel 11:21-35).

Antiochus hated the Jews and was known as Syria's vilest and most blasphemous king. In Daniel 8, he is called "the little horn," suggesting that he foreshadows the Antichrist who is yet to come. He conquered Jerusalem and defiled the Jewish temple. Eventually, he killed 80,000 Jews and sold another 40,000 into slavery.

During the reign of Antiochus Epiphanies, there was a revolt known as the Maccabean Revolt. This group stood against the evils of Antiochus Epiphanies. Antiochus had defiled the temple by slaughtering a pig, placing it in the holy of holies, and flinging the pig's blood all over the temple. A priest killed one of Antiochus' men in the temple court, sparking the revolt. This priest's son, Judas Maccabeus, led the revolt that eventually defeated Antiochus and placed Jerusalem and Palestine under Jewish rule for the first time since Alexander the Great's conquests. Look at Daniel 11:32-35:

> Those who do wickedly against the covenant he shall corrupt with flattery; but the people who know their God shall be strong, and carry out great exploits. And those of the people who understand shall instruct many; yet for many days they shall fall by sword and flame, by captivity and plundering. Now when they fall, they shall be aided with a little help; but many shall join with them by intrigue. And some of those of understanding shall fall, to refine them, purify them, and make them white, until the time of the end; because it is still for the appointed time.

What is described in verse 33 is exactly what took place in Jerusalem in 168 BC. The faithful Jewish remnant that stood up to Antiochus Epiphanies had to go to war for what was right. Many men and women died on both sides of the conflict. Yet, in the end, Antiochus was defeated.

This brings us once again to the question we began the chapter with: "What does God say about war?" In the next section, we take a closer look at this important and timely question.

What Does God Say About War?

Consider the following observations and principles on the Bibles teaching on war:

1. God instructed His people to go to war in certain conditions. If we do not believe this, we will have to tear certain pages out of our Bibles. For instance, Numbers 32:20-22 records:

   > Then Moses said to them: "If you do this thing, if you arm yourselves before the LORD for the war, and all your armed men cross over the Jordan before the LORD until He has driven out His enemies from before Him, and the land is subdued before the LORD, then afterward you may return

and be blameless before the LORD and before Israel; and this land shall be your possession before the LORD."

Therefore, we see that there were specific times when God commanded His chosen people, the Jews, to go to war. Notice that Moses said the people would be blameless because the act of war they were to commit was sanctioned by God Himself. God told His people that when they went to war out of obedience to Him, He would be with them and protect them.

2. When the cause is right for war, God promises His presence and protection. This does not mean that no one will be hurt or killed. It simply means that if the cause is just, God will bless it. Where do we find this concept in Scripture? Look at Psalm 27:3, "Though an army may encamp against me, my heart shall not fear; though war should rise against me, in this I will be confident. One thing I have desired of the LORD, that will I seek: that I may dwell in the house of the LORD all the days of my life, to behold the beauty of the LORD, and to inquire in His temple." Some of the promises of the book of Psalms are in the context of war. God promises the Jewish people that as they go to war He will go with them because their cause is right and they are His people, led by Him.

3. War protects the innocent and prevents further death. But what about those who die in the conflict, we ask. Some people have said we should just leave other nations alone and that they will be fine. We do not need to get involved in the affairs of other nations, they say. However, would Adolf Hitler have been fine if we just let him alone? Would Saddam Hussein have been fine if we had ignored him? These were evil men who were committing unspeakable atrocities against millions of innocent people. There are times when the cause is right for war, and we must always stand up for what is right.

Moreover, God promises that war will protect the innocent in Proverbs 15:3, "Plans are established by counsel; by wise counsel wage war." Therefore, we should use every diplomatic means possible to resolve a conflict; however, there are times when diplomacy is no longer effective, and force, even deadly force, must be employed to protect the innocent and prevent further atrocities.

4. God's people are instructed to respond to evil to ensure peace and safety. Proverbs 15:3 says, "The eyes of the LORD are in every place, keeping watch on the evil and the good."

5. Wars come from the spiritual war at work in people's hearts. Mao Zedong was turned off to the gospel by a missionary who was impatient with him. Mao later joined the Communist party and led the deadly Communist revolution in China. Joseph Stalin attended seminary for several years preparing to be a minister, but was turned off by the deadness and rigidity of the denomination he was associated with. He threw away his dreams of ministry and became the leader of Russia, murdering 20 million of his own people. James 4:12 notes the source of these wars, "You lust and do not have. You murder and covet and cannot obtain. You fight and war. Yet you do not have because you do not ask."

6. In God's plan, the end of the world will occur by a war ushering in the second coming of Jesus Christ. Revelation 19:19 proclaims, "And I saw the beast, the kings of the earth, and their armies, gathered together to make war against Him who sat on the horse and against His army." Scripture tells us that in the final conflict Israel will be the hot button that will set off the conflict. When the Antichrist ascends to his throne, the culmination will be the battle of Armageddon: the most devastating war that will ever occur in history.

We live in a world where if the United States fell under nuclear attack, there would be only fifteen to thirty minutes of warning or perhaps none at all. The U.S. has nuclear submarines in every ocean of the world. Each one carries nuclear weapons that could unleash in minutes more explosive force than all the weapons exploded by all the nations involved in World War II, which lasted six years! One submarine has that capability. So what should we do as believers in Christ? We need peace. We must pray for the peace of the nations, defend the cause of the helpless and, particularly, the cause of Israel, God's chosen people.

Discussion Questions

1. When, if ever, do Christians have a responsibility to go to war?

2. When does a country have a responsibility to go to war?

3. Is there a difference between interpersonal conflicts and conflicts between nations? Why or why not?

4. In light of the previous question, how do Jesus' teachings about turning the other cheek, loving one's neighbor, and loving and praying for one's enemies apply to the question of whether or not a nation ought to go to war?

5. As hostilities have grown in recent years between the Arab and Western worlds, Christians have been forced to answer those who claim that the Crusades of the Middle Ages are partly responsible for the tension between Arabs and Westerners. In light of what we have examined about war in this chapter, do you think the Crusades were justified? Why or why not?

6. How would you answer someone who said that they could never follow a religion like Christianity that sponsored the atrocities that took place during the Crusades?

7. Since World War II the United States has been involved in a number of armed conflicts (e.g. Korea, Vietnam, Operation Desert Storm, Operation Iraqi Freedom, etc.). According to the principles examined in this chapter, do you believe these conflicts were just? Why or why not?

That's Not All

You can find sermon outlines in the "Sermonars" section at the back of the book. These pages may be freely reproduced, either from the book or from the accompanying CD-ROM for any devotional or ministry use.

Chapter Eighteen

Eternal Rewards Available For You

Daniel 12 wraps up the prophetic visions of the prophet Daniel. The prophecy in this chapter is part of a larger prophecy which Daniel has been recording since chapter 10. If you recall, in the first part of chapter 10, Daniel had been mourning and praying to God, but the Prince of Persia withheld the response from getting to Daniel for twenty-one days. Michael the Archangel finally fought through that demonic interference and told Daniel in 10:14, "Now I have come to make you understand what will happen to your people in the latter days, for the vision refers to many days yet to come." This statement gives us the context for the prophecy of chapter 12.

In Daniel 11, we answered the question, "What does God say about war?" We saw in that chapter a chronological list of several kings taking us up to Antiochus Epiphanes. In 11:36–45, we were exposed again to the Antichrist. God allows us to see through Daniel's eyes the reign of the evil one who is to come. It is an amazing glimpse, if you remember, describing for us the amalgamation of nations that will lead the world toward the final battle of Armageddon. If you have ever studied the battles of any war, you have probably been moved by the number of casualties in those conflicts. However, nothing we have ever seen will compare to this final battle and the time leading up to it, in which half of the world's population will die. You can see that the final three and a half years of the Antichrist's reign are appropriately called the "Great Tribulation."

We must not overlook the fact that the narrative from chapter 11 continues directly into chapter 12. Chapter and verse divisions are not inspired; they were added to the text of the Bible many years after it was written. At times, a chapter division will break the narrative in an unfortunate location, and I think that this division is an example of that.

Numerous scholars have commented on this chapter division and the overall importance of Daniel 12 for understanding God's prophetic message in the Scriptures:

- Dr. William Keith Hatfield—This chapter brings us to the highpoint of the book. The fourth vision of Daniel that began in chapter 10 reaches its climax in this chapter as we continue the narrative from the previous chapter. Many feel that the chapter division placed here should have been placed after verse 3 or verse 4. The angel Michael, Israel's angel, is present. The end comes in these verses with God's divinely appointed end described.[1]

- Dr. Clarence Larkin—Here again we see that there should be no chapter division, for there is no break in the subject treated. The twelfth chapter begins with the words, "And at that time." What time? The time of the "willful king," which we have seen is the "time of the end" (Dan 11:40). At that time Michael shall stand up. Stand up for, and take the part of Daniel's people. Who is Michael? He is mentioned three times in Daniel (10:13, 21; 12:1), where he is called a "Prince" who stands for Daniel's people—the Jews. He is called in Jude 9 the archangel. He has angels, and in Rev. 12:7-9 he is seen in command of the "Angelic Army" of Heaven. His work seems to be to deliver God's people, particularly the Jews, from the power of Satan, and finally to oust him and his angels from the Heavenlies, and cast them down to earth.[2]

- Dr. J. Vernon McGee—Chapter 12 now concludes the vision which began back in chapter 10. This is all one vision, and everything about it must fit together like a jigsaw puzzle. The problem is that some people dip into this prophecy here and there, making applications as they see fit. We need to remember that this is all one vision, and we were told concerning it: "Now I am come to make thee understand what shall befall thy people in the latter days: for yet the vision is for many days" (Dan 10:14).[3]

- Dr. John Walvoord—The material described as the fourth vision of Daniel beginning in chapter 10 has its climax in the Great Tribulation and the resurrection which follows, mentioned in the early verses of chapter 12. This is also the high point in the book of Daniel itself and the goal of Daniel's prophecies related to both the Gentiles and to Israel. It is comparable to Revelation 19, the high point of the last book of the Bible.[4]

Walvoord compares Daniel 12 to the chapter in Revelation which records the second coming of Christ (Revelation 19). Revelation 19 pictures Jesus as a commander-in-chief on a white horse leading his men into battle. All of the saints of God are riding behind Him, ready to make war with all the armies of the world that have gathered together. That is a very important chapter, and this chapter in Daniel is comparable in its importance because we are going to see that God's plan for the Jews did not stop with the first coming of Christ. God will deal with the Jews through the Tribulation to the Second Coming and into the Millennial Kingdom. With this in mind, let's take a look at this crucial chapter of Daniel.

The Tribulation of Israel–Daniel 12:1a

Daniel 12:1 begins with the phrase, "At that time..." Since this narrative is simply continued from chapter 11, we know that the time being referred to is when the Antichrist is moving toward the latter half of the Tribulation, which will ultimately culminate in the battle of Armageddon. It is at that time that "Michael shall stand up, the great prince who stands watch over the sons of your people..." (Dan 12:1). Since this text continues the thought of 11:40-45, let's take a moment to look at those verses again:

> At the time of the end the king of the South shall attack him; and the king of the North shall come against him like a whirlwind, with chariots, horsemen, and with many ships; and he shall enter the countries, overwhelm them, and pass through. He shall also enter the Glorious Land, and many countries shall be overthrown; but these shall escape from his hand: Edom, Moab, and the prominent people of Ammon. He shall stretch out his hand against the countries, and the land of Egypt shall not escape. He shall have power over the treasures of gold and silver, and over all the pre-

cious things of Egypt; also the Libyans and Ethiopians shall follow at his heels. But news from the east and the north shall trouble him; therefore he shall go out with great fury to destroy and annihilate many. And he shall plant the tents of his palace between the seas and the glorious holy mountain; yet he shall come to his end, and no one will help him.

Arno Gaebelein describes the connection between these chapters when he writes:

How closely this chapter is connected with the events which we have just left in the closing verses of chapter 11 is seen by the first words with which the final chapter in Daniel starts—"And at that time." What time? The time when the willful King domineers over the Jews and commits his evil deeds in Jerusalem and when the King of the North has entered the glorious land.[5]

What initiates the final three and a half years of the Tribulation that are referenced here? The Antichrist will break his treaty with the nation of Israel. If you remember, the Antichrist will sign a covenant with the Jews at the beginning of the Tribulation that will allow them to live in peace in their homeland. Incredibly, the Antichrist will for a time bring about peace in the Middle East. This Roman will be able to negotiate peace in an area that is sacred to three major religions: Christianity, Islam, and Judaism. However, he will break this treaty in the middle of the seven-year Tribulation and will proclaim himself to be god, demanding worship from all people. This event in known technically in the Scriptures as the "abomination of desolation." This will be the height of blasphemy and a tremendous offense to the Jews.

I know that some believers do not believe that this seven-year Tribulation period will take place. I don't know how they can hold that position, however, because the Bible seems clearly to reveal that it will take place. It is first mentioned in Deuteronomy 4:30, "When you are in distress, and all these things come upon you in the latter days, when you turn to the LORD your God and obey His voice." Jeremiah also describes it in his prophecy: "Alas! For that day is great, so that none is like it; and it is the time of Jacob's trouble, but he shall be saved out of it" (Jeremiah 30:7). Notice the focus on the Jews during this time. They are the target group because they rejected their Messiah! God will use the Tribulation to help them see the error of their ways. Other verses mention this time as well, such as Joel 2:2, "A day of thick darkness and gloominess, a day of clouds and thick darkness, like the morning clouds spread over the mountains."

The Tribulation is coming, and the last three and a half years of this time is in full view in Daniel 12. While the Antichrist is doing his work, someone is going to stand up and protect Israel—Michael the Archangel. At the very end of this period, there will be a mass conversion of the Jews. The events of this period correlate with Revelation 6-19, which describes the Tribulation period in great detail. Remember, John is recording the revelation of *Jesus Christ*, as he wrote in the first verse of that book. Jesus Himself spoke of the Tribulation in Matthew 24:21, "For then there will be great tribulation, such as has not been since the beginning of the world until this time, no, nor ever shall be." Take the world's worst wars, its greatest calamities, and its worst terrorist attacks into consideration--they are but a drop in the bucket compared to the Tribulation. But as dangerous as this period will be, Israel will be protected and preserved during this time, as we see in Daniel 12.

The Deliverance of Israel—Daniel 12:1b

Read Daniel 12:1 again: "At that time Michael shall stand up, the great prince who stands watch over the sons of your people; and there shall be a time of trouble, such as never was since there was a nation, even to that time. And at that time your people shall be delivered, every one who is found written in the book." Why does God allow this horrible seven-year era? The Tribulation is designed to prepare Israel to accept their Messiah. God made a covenant with His people through their patriarch, Abraham, and God is going to fulfill His promise. That covenant established spiritual intimacy and relationship between God and the Jews, and even though most Jews today do not embrace God's own Son, someday they will.

A Jew in a New York synagogue was once heard praying, "Oh that thou wouldst rend the heavens, that thou wouldst come down. Lord, send Messiah, and should Jesus of the Gentiles be the one, grant us a sign that we may be sure it is really so and forgive our guilt toward Him!" In the closing days of the Tribulation, surviving Jews will search the Scriptures and discover that they have rejected Jesus, leading them to come to faith in Him as their Messiah. We believe from Old Testament prophecy that they are going to confess Isaiah 53. Many scholars believe that they will pray Isaiah 64:1, "Oh that You would rend the heavens! That You would come down! That the mountains might shake at Your presence."

In response to Israel's desperate prayer and God's plan, Jesus Christ will return, bringing deliverance to His people. That deliverance will be both physical (Zechariah 14:1-4) and spiritual (Zechariah 12:10-13:1). But even at the Second Coming, not every Jew will believe. Ezekiel 20:33-38 indicates that some will be blinded and stay blinded, even after these cataclysmic judgments. According to Daniel 12:1, the ones who will be delivered in that crucial hour are those whose names are "found written in the book."

The Reverend J. C. Hoover, who was at one time a missionary to Jews in Denver, CO, was once riding in a car with a Jewish rabbi. As they drove up in front of the synagogue, the rabbi said, "Mr. Hoover, you Gentile Christians are looking for the Second Coming of your Savior, Jesus Christ, and we Jews are looking for the first coming of our Messiah. Who knows but what He might be the same person!" The rabbi then paused for a moment before asking, "Mr. Hoover, how do you think we will recognize our Messiah?" Quietly and prayerfully, Mr. Hoover read the words of the prophet Zechariah, "And they shall look upon Me whom they have pierced." The rabbi silently got out of the car and walked slowly into his synagogue. It seems that he slowly began to realize the implications of what Hoover had said—Jews will turn to Jesus during the end times.

The Resurrection of Israel—Daniel 12:2

Notice what will happen to these Jews who call on Messiah at the end of the seven years. These believing Jews will be resurrected. This is a different resurrection than the one that will occur when believers are taken at the Rapture. Daniel 12:2 says, "And many of those who sleep in the dust of the earth shall awake, some to everlasting life, some to shame and everlasting contempt." Deliverance, both physical and spiritual, is promised to those believing Jews still alive at the close of the Tribulation. But this passage also indicates that there will be a resurrection of righteous Israelites who died in this time of trouble. This idea is also seen in Revelation

20:4–6, where martyred Tribulation saints are seen to be raised from the dead and exalted at the beginning of the millennial reign.

The Reward of Israel–Daniel 12:3

Daniel 12:3 speaks of the reward that will be received by the righteous Jews who are resurrected at this time: "Those who are wise shall shine like the brightness of the firmament, and those who turn many to righteousness like the stars forever and ever." I like to think of this as the soul-winner's verse. People who lead others to faith in God will have a tremendous reward awaiting them. Though this principle applies to many different believers, here it applies specifically to the Jews who turn to Christ in the Tribulation. It certainly applies to the 144,000 Jewish evangelists preaching Christ during the Tribulation.

Preserve the Prophetic Word–Daniel 12:4

With the close of this prophecy, Daniel is given a specific charge concerning it: "But you, Daniel, shut up the words, and seal the book until the time of the end; many shall run to and fro, and knowledge shall increase." On the basis of this verse, Sir Isaac Newton, the famous scientist, predicted that the day would come when the volume of knowledge would be so increased that people would be able to travel fifty miles per hour! In response to this prediction, the French atheist Voltaire cast great ridicule on Newton and the Bible, saying that such a prediction could never come true. I guess we know who had the last laugh![6]

Daniel's prophetic words were given by the Holy Spirit and they have been faithfully guarded and protected until now, 2,500 years later, we can read exactly what the angel said to Daniel. Do you see the importance of faithfulness? If God calls us to a task, His expectation is that we will be faithful to do precisely what He asks of us. Would the word "faithfulness" characterize you? If your wife or children were asked to describe you in one word, would they say that you are faithful? This trait was evident in Daniel's life, as we have seen in many ways in this great book.

Did you notice the two signs of the end times in this verse? The first is increased travel. How applicable is that to our present day! We truly live in a global market. We can travel to London in eight hours or Frankfurt in fifteen. In less than a day, you can nearly travel around the world! The second sign was an increase of knowledge. Could there be any greater example of this than the Internet?

Angelic Interaction—Daniel 12:5-7

Here again we find interaction between two angels. Take a look at their conversation:

> Then I, Daniel, looked; and there stood two others, one on this riverbank and the other on that riverbank. And one said to the man clothed in linen, who was above the waters of the river, "How long shall the fulfillment of these wonders be?" Then I heard the man clothed in linen, who was above the waters of the river, when he held up his right hand and his left hand to heaven, and swore by Him who lives forever, that it shall be for a time, times, and half a time; and when the power of the holy people has been completely shattered, all these things shall be finished.

There were three people mentioned in this passage. There is an angel on one riverbank, another angel on the other riverbank, and a very unique person clothed in linen who was actually hovering above the water. I believe this was a theophany—Jesus was there, hovering over the river. Did you know that our resurrected bodies will be just like the Lord's? Time will have no bearing and gravity will have no pull on us. We will even be able to walk through closed doors!

We are given the duration again of the last part of the Tribulation. It will be for "a time, times, and half a time," which is an Aramaic expression that adds up to three and a half years. This time is repeated both in Daniel (7:25; 9:27; 12:11-12) and the book of Revelation (11:2; 12:6, 14; 13:5).

Daniel Wants to Know When

Daniel is not satisfied with his understanding of the vision, so he makes a request in 12:8-13 for more information. Look at this exchange:

Although I heard, I did not understand. Then I said, "My lord, what shall be the end of these things?" And he said, "Go your way, Daniel, for the words are closed up and sealed till the time of the end. Many shall be purified, made white, and refined, but the wicked shall do wickedly; and none of the wicked shall understand, but the wise shall understand. And from the time that the daily sacrifice is taken away, and the abomination of desolation is set up, there shall be one thousand two hundred and ninety days. Blessed is he who waits, and comes to the one thousand three hundred and thirty-five days. But you, go your way till the end; for you shall rest, and will arise to your inheritance at the end of the days.

God responded to Daniel's request with four important pieces of information:

1. The events would be far in the future (verse 9). These things weren't going to take place in Daniel's time, yet Daniel was given the revelation because he was faithful and had an intimate relationship with the Lord.

2. Tribulation sufferings would result in the conversion of some and the hardening of others (verse 10). The gospel will still be preached by the 144,000 Jewish evangelists during the Tribulation (Revelation 7), and people will respond. However, the very message that will convert some will harden others in their unbelief.

3. The duration from the Antichrist's blasphemous announcement to the end of the Tribulation will be 1,290 days. This equals the "time, times, and half a time" that we saw earlier; it is three and a half years.

4. Another time span of 1,335 days is mentioned. This span would extend forty-five days beyond the end of the Tribulation. Scholars believe that the judgment of the nations may take place during this forty-five-day period. Another possibility is that it is simply the time span in which the Lord Jesus will set up His kingdom before the beginning of the Millennium.

Leon Wood offers the following explanation on the last point: "It may be the time necessary for setting up the governmental machinery for carrying on the rule of Christ. The true and full border of Israel (from the river of Egypt to the Euphrates, Genesis 15:18) will have to be established, and appointments made of those aiding in the government. A period of forty-five days would again seem to be reasonable in which to accomplish those matters."[7]

Where will you stand when Jesus comes to judge this world? Jesus once stated that two types of people will be divided from one another when he comes to judge:

> When the Son of Man comes in His glory, and all the holy angels with Him, then He will sit on the throne of His glory. All the nations will be gathered before Him, and He will separate them one from another, as a shepherd divides his sheep from the goats. And He will set the sheep on His right hand, but the goats on the left. Then the King will say to those on His right hand, "Come, you blessed of My Father, inherit the kingdom prepared for you from the foundation of the world: for I was hungry and you gave Me food; I was thirsty and you gave Me drink; I was a stranger and you took Me in; I was naked and you clothed Me; I was sick and you visited Me; I was in prison and you came to Me" (Matthew 25:31-36).

There will be words of commendation for some, but others will hear only the stinging pronouncement of judgment: "Then He will also say to those on the left hand, "Depart from Me, you cursed, into everlasting fire prepared for the devil and his angels" (Matt 25:41). Will you be on the right hand or on the left? Jesus has issued His warning; respond by trusting in Him today!

Discussion Questions

1. Chapter and verse divisions were not part of the original text of Scripture. How does that help us with Bible study in general and with Daniel 12 in particular?

2. What will take place at the midpoint of the Tribulation?

3. What is the purpose of the Tribulation? What will it accomplish for the Jewish nation?

4. What verses in the Bible describe what our bodies will be like after they are resurrected?

5. How should knowing about future events affect our lives today? (See 2 Pet 3:10–14)

6. From what we have learned in our study of Daniel, write out a chronological list of major events that will occur during the Tribulation period.

That's Not All

You can find sermon outlines in the "Sermonars" section at the back of the book. These pages may be freely reproduced, either from the book or from the accompanying CD-ROM for any devotional or ministry use.

Daniel

Chapter Nineteen

Daniel's Twelve Principles of Leadership, Success and Achievement

No one can deny that Daniel personifies leadership, success, and incredible achievement. In this, our final chapter on Daniel, we are going to pull out twelve principles from this book that reveal to us why Daniel was such a great man. These principles can truly be applied in every aspect of our lives. People from all walks of life can apply them with equal effectiveness.

To review, we first read about Daniel in this book when he was still a young man, probably no more than sixteen years old. He was taken from his home in Jerusalem against his will when King Nebuchadnezzar forced him to move to the city of Babylon, the largest city of its day, with a population of 1.2 million people. Babylon was a very evil, decadent city that was steeped in polytheism, sexual deviance, and human sacrifice. All in all, it was a very difficult place for a Hebrew boy who had been raised to believe that there was one God, Jehovah, and that man is to serve Him and Him alone.

Every now and then, I host an event called "Pizza with the Pastor." This is a time for me to have a meal with the kids of our church so that I can get to know them better. Honestly, this is one of the toughest assignments of my life because I have to explain sometimes weighty material in very simple terms. One time, a child asked me a profoundly brilliant question: what happened to Daniel after the events of his book? He apparently was too old to travel back to Jerusalem when Cyrus gave the decree allowing Jews to return to that city. According to tradition, Daniel died and was buried just outside of Babylon. A marker can be seen there to this day, though we cannot be certain if that marker truly stands over Daniel's grave. The reason this question is profound is because after all of Daniel's years of faithfulness, he was still not allowed to return to his homeland. Daniel never knew if he would ever see his homeland again or not, but apparently that was not what drove him as a man. It seems that he was driven by the twelve principles that we will discuss in this chapter. May the Lord imbed these principles in our hearts, so that we might love them just as Daniel did!

Principles for Life

Principle #1—Absolute resolve. I have made up my mind!

This principle is illustrated in Daniel 1:8, "But Daniel purposed in his heart that he would not defile himself with the portion of the king's delicacies, nor with the wine which he drank; therefore he requested of the chief of the eunuchs that he might not defile himself." What is the context of this verse? Daniel and his friends were placed in the king's service as eunuchs and, as such, they were assigned a portion of the food that would be prepared for the king himself. He was supposed to go with the crowd and just fit in, even though this food apparently violated the dietary laws that God had given to the Jews. The indoctrination also involved a name change.

But even as a young man, Daniel had made up his mind to honor God's laws, and he displayed an absolute resolve to do just that. The New American Standard translation says that Daniel "made up his mind." A person will never be a leader if he cannot point to a time in his life when he made up his mind to serve God no matter what. We must decide to follow the Lord at all costs!

I accepted Christ on June 21, 1973, but that was not the night that I had absolute resolve. I made that decision two months later after hearing a sermon at a camp that I was attending. The speaker preached a sermon on total surrender and told us that we had to decide who was going to be the lord of our lives. We had to make that decision, even as Christians. That night, I spoke with a counselor and told him that I wanted to make

Christ the lord of my life. That was probably just as significant as the night two months prior to that, when I had initially accepted Christ as my Savior.

The people who fail spiritually are those who have never made the subsequent decision to completely let Christ be the lord of their lives. When did you make this decision? Is there a time that you can point to? Have you decided to go the full distance in following Christ, refusing to let anything hold you back?

Nate Saint, missionary to the Auca Indians, made that decision at Wheaton College. He wrote in his journal, "Lord, make me a fork in the road, so that when people meet me they have to decide about you."1 He made up his mind as a young man that Christ would be his Lord. Later, he boarded a plane and headed off to reach the Auca Indians for Christ. When he landed with Jim Elliot and others, they were speared to death. He had made up his mind and followed Christ to the end, even when it put his life in danger.

If you are not sure that you want to follow God's will next week, then you have not made this decision. If you do not know how you will react when placed in a tempting situation, you have not made this decision. Get on your knees today and ask Jesus to be the lord of your life!

Principle #2—God is my ultimate source for insight and understanding.

In Daniel 2, Nebuchadnezzar had a dream but did not know the interpretation. After summoning his own wise men and magicians, he finally called upon Daniel to come and interpret his dream. But even before Daniel had received this summons, he had spoken with his friends "that they might seek mercies from the God of heaven concerning the secret, so that Daniel and his companions might not perish with the rest of the wise men of Babylon" (Daniel 2:18).

In every person's life, there will be good days and bad days. We can only rise above our circumstances, going beyond the realm of followers to the realm of leaders, when we determine, like Daniel, that God is our ultimate source for insight and understanding. This means that the first thing we do every day should be to seek the One who will give us understanding for the trials we will face that day. It took me a while in my Christian life to realize that I couldn't just do this every once in a while; it has to be a daily commitment. Every day we make decisions that will influence people around us. If I am not staying in touch with God, I cannot lead other people to get in touch with God.

After Nebuchadnezzar's dream, the Chaldean astrologers turned to one another and to their polytheistic gods, but they came up empty-handed. When asked to intervene, Daniel's immediate response was to seek Jehovah! He knew that only Jehovah had the answer, and he asked for mercies from heaven to interpret the dream.

Principle #3–I will expect opposition and harassment when doing God's will.

Daniel is not mentioned in Daniel 3, but his friends Shadrach, Meshach, and Abed-Nego are front and center in the narrative. Nebuchadnezzar, as many pagan kings and dictators have done, demands that he be worshiped and sets up an idol that he expects his subjects to adore. Daniel's three friends refused to follow the king's order, knowing that to worship a statue would amount to idolatry. In Daniel 3:12, some of the king's advisors tell him, "There are certain Jews whom you have set over the affairs of the province of Babylon: Shadrach, Meshach, and Abed-Nego; these men, O king, have not paid due regard to you. They do not serve your gods or worship the gold image which you have set up."

This incident teaches us that the minute we decide to live our lives according to the will of God, we should expect opposition. Daniel and his friends obviously did. They knew that they were going against the prevailing culture in which they lived. There were probably over 300,000 people who knelt down before Nebuchadnezzar's idol, but Shadrach, Meshach, and Abed-Nego refused to be swayed by cultural pressure. We have seen events just like this in our day. Muslims gather by the thousands to kneel for prayer and to worship the Kaaba. Could you imagine being in such a crowd and being confronted with the choice that these men faced?

You probably know how this story ends. These men are tossed into a fiery furnace, but a fourth man appears in the midst of the fire. Jesus Himself decided to walk with them in the midst of that difficulty. Even though they were faced with opposition, they had no need to worry.

Principle #4–Because of His love for us, God has an angel always watching and protecting us.

Daniel 4:13 says, "I saw in the visions of my head while on my bed, and there was a watcher, a holy one coming down from heaven." The minute we strive to be a leader for God, we are confronted with spiritual warfare. Certainly we can take comfort in the indwelling Holy Spirit, that great Paraclete who comes alongside us to help us. But God has given us other helpers as well because He is a loving God. Daniel shows us that because of God's love for us, He always has an angel watching over us and protecting us.

I love how this angel is described as a "watcher." The Hebrew term here emphasizes that no matter where we are or what we are doing, God always has a guardian angel watching over us. Would I go so far as to say that they wait by our beds as we sleep? I think so; after all, that is their job.

Hebrews 1:14 also expresses this idea when it says, "Are they not all ministering spirits sent forth to minister for those who will inherit salvation?" The Holy Spirit is obviously within us, but God the Father shows His great love for us by dispatching His angels, His watchers, to care for us. There were times in the book of Daniel when angels touched him and strengthened him, allowing him to get back on his feet and to continue his prophetic ministry. God has used angels in many different ways, and they are still an important part of our lives today.

Principle #5—I will refuse addictions and always stay in control.

How can we overlook what happened to Belshazzar when he was overcome by addictions? In the middle of one of the neediest times of his life, Belshazzar gets 1,000 of his generals together and throws a drunken orgy. Rather than staying attentive to the growing threat from the Medo-Persians, he indulges his lusts and gluts himself with sensual pleasure. Do you remember what happened that very night? The Medo-Persian forces entered the city through a river gate, just as Isaiah's prophecy 175 years earlier indicated they would. All of the gates were open because the leaders were drunk at a party.

If we want to be leaders, we must gain control over any addictions. We naturally think of drugs when we discuss addictions, but people can be addicted to many things. Some people are addicted to sex and the perverted message of the world. Other people are addicted to television or video games. We must bring whatever may tempt us or whatever seeks to control our lives under the lordship of Christ. We cannot lead others if they cannot follow our example.

Principle #6—My life work will be marked by integrity.

In Daniel 6, Daniel's opponents in the government were seeking to tear him down. They wanted to dig up some dirt on him, but according to Daniel 6:4, they could find none: "So the governors and satraps sought to find some charge against Daniel concerning the kingdom; but they could find no charge or fault, because he was faithful; nor was there any error or fault found in him." His life work was marked by integrity. How difficult it must have been to keep such integrity during seventy years of service under pagan kings! Nevertheless, his entire life was marked by integrity.

Principle #7–When troubled or overwhelmed, I will go to God first and others later.

In Daniel 7, the prophet received a bombastic revelation of coming kingdoms and the Antichrist. It is so overwhelming that Daniel had a hard time handling it. He wrote in 7:28, "This is the end of the account. As for me, Daniel, my thoughts greatly troubled me, and my countenance changed; but I kept the matter in my heart." We already know that it was his habit to pray three times a day, so Daniel undoubtedly spoke to the Lord about what he had seen.

We all have problems of our own to deal with. What is it in your life that overwhelms you? Is it a health problem or some kind of behavioral problem with your children? Is there difficulty at work or in your friendships? When a person is not strong in the Lord, he immediately turns to other people for help when troubles arise. Make no mistake: God intends to use those around us to help us. There truly is wisdom in a multitude of counselors. But as we mature in the Lord, we find ourselves running straight to God when tough problems come up. This is why it is so important to spend time with God every day. Those times renew us.

Daniel faced some situations that were enough to give a seventy-year-old a heart attack. He was thrown into a den of lions, but he was renewed because he was seeking God. In the midst of that den, God sent His angel to shut the mouths of the lions.

Principle #8–My Christianity/spirituality will never be an excuse not to give my employer/family my very best effort.

In chapter 8, we see a repetition of a vision about the Grecian Empire. As Daniel was receiving all of these visions, we must not forget that he had a job to do for the king. Daniel was one of his chief administrators. Though he still had a job to do, he kept receiving these terrible visions.

In 8:23-26, Daniel is given information regarding the Antichrist who would be at work during the Tribulation. How did Daniel handle all of this stress? In his own words, he wrote, "And I, Daniel, fainted and was sick for days; afterward I arose and went about the king's business. I was astonished by the vision, but no one understood it" (Daniel 8:27).

He was greatly affected, but as soon as he was able, he got back to his job for the king. If we are going to be leaders for God, we can never allow our Christianity to become an excuse for withholding our best effort from our employers or our families. We have a number of bosses and executives in our church, and I have heard many of them say that they have employed Christians who were not the best employees. This is sad, since our work ethic on the job reflects our testimony. It reflects upon our character and thus, by implication, the character of Jesus.

Daniel could have been so captivated by these visions that his job performance would suffer. He could have just taken time off and said, "You guys don't get it! You don't have any idea what I've seen!" But we have this little statement that says he went about the king's business. He kept at his job, and he did it with excellence.

Principle #9–I can change things in Heaven and on Earth by my prayers.

In chapter 9 we read about the prayer that Daniel prayed for his people. It is truly a model prayer, one that should inspire awe when we read it. Though it is so great, the entire prayer can be prayed in three minutes. It may be short, but this prayer is so powerful that by the time Daniel finished, the angel Gabriel was standing next to him. He fell on his face when he saw Gabriel, but Gabriel told him to stand up and Daniel was moved by what he heard. Gabriel said to him "At the beginning of your supplications the command went out, and I have come to tell you, for you are greatly beloved; therefore consider the matter, and understand the vision" (Daniel 9:23).

This verse tells us just how powerful this prayer was. The moment Daniel started praying, Gabriel was dispatched to his side. In response to his prayer, God graciously gave him the prophecy of the seventy weeks, the greatest prophetic passage in the Old Testament. It reveals when the Messiah would arrive in his first coming, the events of the Tribulation, the activity of the Antichrist, the second coming of Christ, and Jesus' Millennial Kingdom. Daniel truly lived to see that we can change things in Heaven and on Earth by our prayers.

We must not miss the fact that God invites us all to pray in this manner. We can see relatives come to Christ when we pray for them. I prayed for fifteen years for my mother to come to Christ. We all need to have a list of unsaved people that we are praying for. When will we truly grasp the power of prayer? What things need to be changed in your world? What is truly plaguing you? Take everything to God and lay it out before Him!

Principle #10–When I meet the qualifications, I know God will unload endless blessings on me.

This principle is on display throughout Daniel's life. Daniel 10:12 is just one example of this principle in action: "Then he said to me, 'Do not fear, Daniel, for from the first day that you set your heart to understand, and to humble yourself before your God, your words were heard; and I have come because of your words.'"

We know, of course, that God is sovereign and can do anything He wants at any time He wants. However, we must also remember that we can move God to action by our prayers. I believe that Daniel was blessed time and time again because he met the qualifications of having a clean heart and constant communication with Jehovah.

Principle #11–Nobody knows my future better or understands my needs more clearly than God.

Chapter 11 was a very difficult chapter in which Daniel received a vision covering 300 years of history, from Daniel's day until the reign of Antiochus Epiphanes. God is reminding us here that He writes history in advance. He puts kings up and sets kings down. But notice the statement that we see in this midst of this prophecy: "And some of those of understanding shall fall, to refine them, purify them, and make them white; until the time of the end; because it is still for the appointed time" (Dan 11:35).

We see that God has a very specific timetable. The seventy-year captivity in Babylon was specified by the prophet Jeremiah. God works in forecasting the future, but He does it with an amazing calculation—he has specific time periods worked out in His plan. This is true of "big" historical events and of the "small" events of our life as well. If you are going through a trial, God has a time appointed for it. He has a specific time in mind, and it will not last any longer than God allows.

Verse 35 emphasizes that nobody knows our future or understands our needs better than God. What is your need today? Perhaps you are discouraged and in need of encouragement. Maybe you are struggling with relational problems in your family. No one knows our needs better than God, and He has promised to meet them in His time and in His way.

God will even be in control during the apparent chaos of the Tribulation. This truth is emphasized in the first 12 verses of Daniel 12:

> At that time Michael shall stand up, the great prince who stands watch over the sons of your people; and there shall be a time of trouble, such as never was since there was a nation, even to that time. And at that time your people shall be delivered, every one who is found written in the book. And many of those who sleep in the dust of the earth shall awake, some to everlasting life, some to shame and everlasting contempt. Those who are wise shall shine like the brightness of the firmament, and those who turn many to righteousness like the stars forever and ever. But you, Daniel, shut up the words, and seal the book until the time of the end; many shall run to and fro, and knowledge shall increase. Then I, Daniel, looked; and there stood two others, one on this riverbank and the other on that riverbank. And one said to the man clothed in linen, who was above the waters of the river, "How long shall the fulfillment of these wonders be?" Then I heard the man clothed in linen, who was above the waters of the river, when he held up his right hand and his left hand to heaven, and swore by Him who lives forever, that it shall be for a time, times, and half a time; and when the power of the holy people has been completely shattered, all these things shall be finished. Although I heard, I did not understand. Then I said, "My lord, what shall be the end of these things?" And he said, "Go your way, Daniel, for the words are closed up and sealed till the time of the end. Many shall be purified, made white, and refined, but the wicked shall do wickedly; and none of the wicked shall understand, but the wise shall understand. And from the time that the daily sacrifice is taken away, and the abomination of desolation is set up, there shall be one thousand two hundred and ninety days. Blessed is he who waits, and comes to the one thousand three hundred and thirty-five days."

Principle #12—God is going to give me a great inheritance some day because of my faithfulness.

This final principle comes through in Daniel 12:13, the very last verse of the book: "But you, go your way till the end; for you shall rest, and will arise to your inheritance at the end of the days." What kind of inheritance will it be? It is described in 2 Corinthians 8:9, which says, "For you know the grace of our Lord Jesus Christ, that though He was rich, yet for your sakes He became poor, that you through His poverty might become rich." There are riches in Heaven that we cannot even begin to comprehend.

I hope that someday God will allow me to have a rich *experience* in Heaven. I hope that God will let me travel back in time. I want to go to the mountainside and take a seat to listen to Jesus preach. I want to be in the room with Jesus to see Him raise Jairus' daughter from the dead. I want to see the bitter tears that Peter cried after He cursed and swore, denying the One he had followed for three years. I also want to see the day when Peter gave the first sermon in the church age on the day of Pentecost. I want to sit in the Metropolitan Tabernacle and watch Spurgeon preach.

I cannot point to any passage that says that God will allow me to do that. But what I do have is the promise of 1 Corinthians 2:9, "But as it is written: 'Eye has not seen, nor ear heard, nor have entered into the heart of man the things which God has prepared for those who love Him.'"

Called to Leadership

I urge you to look over these twelve principles and to ask God to help you in the areas where you are lacking. Maybe you are just so focused on the here and now that you cannot see eternity. If we can focus on eternity, we can handle the bumps of life! Maybe you doubt that God really knows your needs. He does, but He still wants you to bring them before **Him in** prayer. How can you tell when you have truly turned something over to God? A feeling of freedom and release comes over you.

I didn't know anything about leadership until I accepted Jesus Christ. Before I accepted Christ, I was a follower. I followed my friends into drug use and all kinds of terrible things. But you know what happened when I accepted Christ and then turned my life over to Him as my Lord? I changed from being a follower to being a leader. This same transformation can happen in you if you will place yourself under the lordship of Christ and follow the principles exemplified in the book of Daniel. The choice is yours!

Discussion Questions

1. In what areas of your life do you need to resolve to let Christ be your Lord? What practical steps can you take to start following Christ in these areas?

2. What is your first response when you are confronted with a perplexing decision? What does this say about where you are putting your trust?

3. Angels play a prominent role in the book of Daniel. What are some ministries of angels? How should we respond to them? (See Col 2:18; Rev 19:10)

4. How can you be a witness at your workplace simply by the way you work? What obstacles hinder you from doing this and how can you overcome them?

5. Daniel models the importance of consistent prayer. How strong is your prayer life? What obstacles hinder you in this area? How can you grow in your prayer life? List practical steps.

6. Daniel clearly reveals how God is in control of empires. Is He even in control of the day-to-day events of our lives? Is He still in control when things aren't going so well? Discuss.

7. Which of the twelve leadership principles described in this chapter is most challenging for you? What steps might you take to be stronger in that area?

8. Make an outline of the book of Daniel. Determine the overall theme and then show how each section and chapter relate to that theme. Tie in other prophetic passages from the Bible with their corresponding chapter in Daniel.

That's Not All

You can find sermon outlines in the "Sermonars" section at the back of the book. These pages may be freely reproduced, either from the book or from the accompanying CD-ROM for any devotional or ministry use.

The Sermonars

On the pages that follow, you will find a series of pages constituting Sermonars, the interactive sermon outlines that we provide at worship services so that our people can follow along with the sermon and leave with a very thorough overview of the material covered.

Regardless of how you use this book, you are invited to utilize the pages that follow in whatever manner meets your needs. How might you use them? These are a few of our ideas.

- You could duplicate our usage of them, reproducing the relevant pages for a church service so that worshippers can follow along through a sermon.

- You could use them in a small-group setting as a guide to discussion.

- To create a more involved setting, you could assign individuals or groups within the class the responsibility of answering various questions. Similarly, you could assign various scripture verses to individuals.

- In an individual study situation, you might employ the Sermonar as a sort of review and self-test. The ability to fill in the various blanks will measure your understanding of the material.

- You could imagine some usage of these pages that never crossed our minds.

Feel free to reproduce any or all of the following pages. Permission to use them in any setting is hereby granted provided that you do not drastically change the original intent of this volume.

Principles of
Leadership, Success,
and Achievement

Why Daniel? End Times, Soon or Later?
Message #1 in the Daniel series
Bible Text: Matthew 24:14-22; Daniel 1:1-7

Jesus in Matthew 24:15, "Therefore when you see the abomination of desolation, spoken of by Daniel the prophet, standing in the holy place (whoever reads, let him understand)."

- Jesus [1]_____ the prophecy of Daniel - and called him the [2]_____. Critics have always despised the book of Daniel!

BACKGROUND
Babylon rebelled against the Assyrian Empire in 626 B.C. and overthrew the Assyrian capital of Nineveh in 612 B.C. Babylon became the master of the Middle East when it defeated the Egyptian armies in 605 B.C. Daniel was among those taken captive to Babylon that year when Nebuchadnezzar subdued Jerusalem.

Daniel 1:21 "Thus Daniel continued until the first year of King Cyrus."

"With verse 1 and this verse we can learn Daniel's life span. Coming to Babylon at about the age seventeen, he died when he was about ninety years of age. He bridged the entire seventy years of captivity. He did not return to Israel but apparently died before the people left Babylon. We actually have no record about that." – Dr. J. Vernon McGee

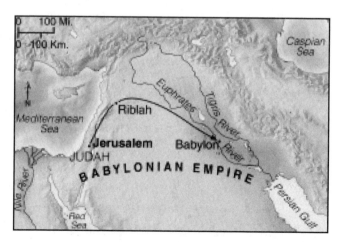

Despite Judah's few good kings and reforms, the people never truly changed.
Their evil continued, and God used Nebuchadnezzar, to conquer Judah, destroy
Jerusalem, and take the people captive to Babylon.

WHY DANIEL?

1. Perfect Plan of God's ³_____ - reminding us God is in control of our lives.

> Daniel 1:1, "In the third year of the reign of Jehoiakim king of Judah, Nebuchadnezzar king of Babylon came to Jerusalem and besieged it. 2) And the Lord gave Jehoiakim king of Judah into his hand."

> Daniel 4:25, "They shall drive you from men, your dwelling shall be with the beasts of the field, and they shall make you eat grass like oxen. They shall wet you with the dew of heaven, and seven times shall pass over you, till you know that the Most High rules in the kingdom of men, and gives it to whomever He wills."

> Daniel 2:37, "You, O king, are king of kings. For the God of heaven has given you a kingdom, power, strength, and glory."

2. Perfect ⁴_____ - reminding us that God has a perfect timetable for us.

> Daniel 9:1, "In the first year of Darius the son of Ahasuerus, of the lineage of the Medes, who was made king over the realm of the Chaldeans - 2) in the first year of his reign I, Daniel understood by the books the number of the years specified by the word of the Lord through Jeremiah the prophet, that He would accomplish seventy years in the desolations of Jerusalem."

- When the people of Israel entered the promised land, God told them every seventh year was to be His - something they ignored for 490 years! The Babylonian captivity last ⁵_____ years - God repaid Israel for cheating Him to the exact year!

3. Peculiar Place and ⁶_____ - reminding us our difficulties are not unique to people pursuing faith.

> Daniel 1:1, "...NEBUCHADNEZZAR king of Babylon came to Jerusalem and besieged it."

> Daniel 1:3, "Then the king instructed ASHPENAZ, the master of his eunuchs, to bring some of the children of Israel and some of the king's descendants and some of the nobles."

> Daniel 1:19, "Then the king interviewed them, and among them all none was found like DANIEL, HANANIAH, MISHAEL, and AZARIAH."

> Daniel 2:14, "Then with counsel and wisdom Daniel answered ARIOCH, the captain of the king's guard, who had gone out to kill the wise men of Babylon."

> Daniel 5:9, "Then King BELSHAZZAR was greatly troubled, his countenance was changed, and his lords were astonished."

> Daniel 6:9, "Therefore King DARIUS signed the written decree."

> Daniel 8:16, "And I heard a man's voice between the banks of the Ulai, who called and said, 'GABRIEL, make this man understand the vision.'"

> Daniel 12:1, "At that time MICHAEL shall stand up, the great prince who stands watch over the sons of your people."

4. Paradigm of Daniel's Life as our [7]_____ - reminding us we can be victorious in living a life of Christian distinction.

> Daniel 1:8, "But Daniel purposed in his heart that he would not defile himself with the portion of the king's delicacies, nor with the wine which he drank; therefore he requested of the chief of the eunuchs that he might not defile himself."

> Daniel 6:4, "So the governors and satraps sought to find some charge against Daniel concerning the kingdom; but they could find NO CHARGE or fault, because he was faithful; nor was there ANY error or fault found in him."

> Daniel 9:22, "And he informed me, and talked with me, and said, 'O Daniel, I have now come forth to give you skill to understand. 23) At the beginning of your supplications the command went out, and I have come to tell you, for you are GREAT BELOVED; therefore consider the matter, and understand the vision."

- Scholars believe Daniel was fourteen to sixteen years old when he came to be trained at the pagan Babylon University for three years. His parents were 900 miles away in Judah. Nebuchnezzar [8]_____ in trying to brainwash Daniel.

5. Prayer's Secrets and [9]_____ - challenging us to receive the riches God wants to give us through prayer.

> Daniel 6:10, "Now when Daniel knew that the writing was signed, he went home. And in his upper room, with his windows open toward Jerusalem, he knelt down on his knees three times that day, and prayed and gave thanks before his God, as was his custom since early days."

> Daniel 9:20, "Now while I was speaking, praying, and confessing my sin and the sin of my people Israel, and presenting my supplications before the Lord my God for the holy mountain of my God."

6. Precision of [10]_____ - reminding us that God is working His preset plan in our world, which will culminate with the return of Christ.

> Daniel 12:8b, "Then I said, 'My Lord, what shall be the end of these things?'"

> Daniel 12:6, "How long shall the fulfillment of these wonders be?"

> Daniel 12:9, "And he said, 'Go your way, Daniel, for the words are closed up and sealed till the time of the end."

> Daniel 2:28, "But there is a God in heaven who reveals secrets, and He has made known to King Nebuchnezzar what will be in the LATTER DAYS."

> Daniel 12:11, "And from the time that the daily sacrifice is taken away, and the abomination of desolation is set up, there shall be one thousand two hundred and ninety days."

- Daniel specifically details the coming Gentile kingdoms that will rule the world - referred to in Scripture and here as the "times of the [11]_____."
- Further, Daniel sets up the timetable of the [12]_____ reign of terror - known as the "abomination of desolation."

DID YOU KNOW?

Out of Daniel's 357 verses, 162 verses are prophetic in nature. Chapter 2 and 7 constitute Scriptures' most sweeping panorama of what was then future world history. His writing exhibits the highest proportion of symbolic prophecy to be found in the Bible.

7. Panic Caused by the [13]_____ - reminding us that the Tribulation will happen, an era we want to avoid.

> Daniel 7:24, "The ten horns are ten kings who shall arise from this kingdom. And another shall rise after them; He shall be different from the first ones, and shall subdue three kings. 25) He shall speak pompous words against the Most High, shall persecute the saints of the Most High, and shall intend to change times and law. Then the saints shall be given into his hand for a time and times and half a time."

> Daniel 9:23, "And in the latter times of their kingdom, when the transgressors have reached their fullness, a king shall arise, having fierce features, who understands sinister schemes. 24) His power shall be mighty, but not by his own power: He shall destroy fearfully, and shall prosper and thrive; He shall destroy the mighty, and also the holy people. 25) Through his cunning He shall cause deceit to prosper under his rule; and he shall exalt himself in his heart. He shall destroy many in their prosperity. He shall even rise against the Prince of Princes; but he shall be broken without human means."

> Daniel 8:27, "And I, Daniel, fainted and was sick for days; afterward I arose and went about the king's business. I was astonished by the vision."

8. Peace and Fulfillment of Covenant by the [14]_____ - reminding us God cannot lie. He will keep His promises to us, too.

> Daniel 9:24, "Seventy weeks are determined for your people and for your holy city, to finish the transgression, to make an end of sins, to make reconciliation for iniquity, to bring in everlasting righteousness, to seal up the vision and prophecy, and to anoint the Most Holy. 25) Know therefore and understand that from the going forth of the command to restore the and build Jerusalem until the Messiah the Prince, there shall be seven weeks and sixty-two weeks; the street shall be built again, and the wall, even in troublesome times.

IT ALMOST TAKES YOUR BREATH AWAY...

Daniel's prophecy of the Seventy Weeks (9:24-27) provides the chronological frame for the coming of Jesus the Messiah from the time of Daniel to the establishment of the His kingdom on earth. The first sixty-nine weeks were fulfilled at Christ's first coming. The vision of the sixty-nine weeks (9:25, 26) pinpoints the coming of the Messiah. The decree (9:25) took place on March 4, 444 B.C. (Neh. 2:1-8). The sixty-nine weeks of the seven years equals 483 years, or 173,880 days (using 360-day prophetic years). This led to March 29, A.D. 33, the date of Christ's Triumphal Entry in Jerusalem. This is checked by noting that 444 B.C. to A. D. 33 is 476 years, and 476 times 365.24219 days per year equals 173,855 days. Adding 25 days for the difference between March 4 and March 29 gives 173,880 days!

ANSWERS

1. affirmed 2. prophet 3. Sovereignty 4. Timetable 5. 70 6. People 7. Example 8. failed 9. Power 10. Prophesy 11. Gentiles 12. Anti-Christ's 13. Anti-Christ 14. Messiah

Principles of Leadership, Success, and Achievement

The Amazing Journey to One of the Wonders of the World
Message #2 in the Daniel series
Daniel 1:1-3

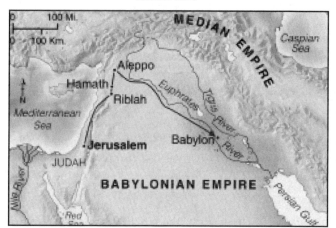

Taken to Babylon
Daniel, as a captive of Babylonian soldiers, faced a long and difficult march to a new land. The 500-mile trek, under harsh conditions, certainly tested his faith in God.

PROPHECY FULFILLED: JERUSALEM'S DESTRUCTION/DEPORTATION

1. Nearly 100 years earlier the prophet [1]_____ (740-681 B.C.) foretold of Judah's destruction and the Jews deportation to Babylon, which was NOT the super-power at the time!

   > Isaiah 39:5-7, "Then Isaiah said to Hezekiah (Judah's king, 715-686 B.C.) 'Hear the word of the Lord of hosts: 6) 'Behold, the days are coming when all that is in your house, and what your fathers have accumulated until this day, shall be carried to Babylon; nothing shall be left,' says the Lord. 7) 'And they shall take away SOME OF YOUR SONS who will descend from you, whom you will beget; and they shall be eunuchs in the palace of the king of Babylon" (cf. 2 Kings 20:16-19).

   - The [2]_____ was clearly foretold. "Nothing shall be left" (v. 6).
   - Most stunning - [3]_____ boys will be taken captive and become eunuchs. "They shall take away some of your son ... they shall be eunuchs" (v.7).

2. God warned [4]_____ (697-642 B.C. Duration: 55 years), Hezekiah's evil son, Judah's subsequent king who rebuilt all the pagan shrines, sacrificed one of his owns sons, practiced sorcery, and set up an idol right in the Temple (2 Kings 21:1-18; 2 Chron. 33:1-20) that he would be deported to Babylon, which at the time was a part of the Assyrian Empire.

2 Kings 21:10, "And the Lord spoke by His servants the prophets, saying, 11) 'Because Manasseh king of Judah has done these abominations (he has acted more wickedly than all the Amorites who were before him, and has also made Judah sin with his idols), 12) therefore thus says the Lord God of Israel: 'Behold, I am bringing such calamity upon Jerusalem and Judah, that whoever hears of it, both his ears will tingle. 13) ...I will wipe Jerusalem as one wipes a dish, wiping it and turning it upside down."

3. God used [5]_____ (627-586 B.C.) to warn the Israelites that Judah was going to fall to Babylon because of their sin. A warning they, again, ignored. God even told them in advance how long the captivity was going to be - 70 years.

    Jeremiah 25:8, "Therefore thus says the Lord of hosts: 'Because you have not heard My words, 9) behold, I will send and take all the families of the north, says the Lord, 'and Nebuchadnezzar the king of Babylon, my servant, and will bring them against this land, against its inhabitants, and against these nations all around, and WILL UTTERLY DESTROY THEM, and make them an astonishment, a hissing, and perpetual desolations.

    "The Book of Daniel opens with a historical statement which recounts the fulfillment of at least one definite prophecy (Jer. 25:8-11), in which God had plainly asserted that He would 'send the king of Babylon, my servant ... against the inhabitants thereof ... and these nations shall serve the king of Babylon seventy years.' As we read of the literal enactment of this prediction, in Daniel 1:1 ... we are struck immediately with a repetition of thought in the prophecy and in its fulfillment. In the prophecy, God plainly speaks of Nebuchadnezzar as 'my servant,' and in Daniel 1:2 we are told that 'the Lord gave Jehoiakim king of Judah into his hand.' This is surely indicative of that sovereign control of earthly matters, otherwise under the domination of Satan himself, exercised by God." –Dr. Philip R. Newell

PROOF OF THE SCRIPTURES' ACCURACY
Researchers are constantly confirming the trustworthiness of the Bible. Dr. Robert Dick Wilson in his book, SCIENTIFIC INVESTIGATION OF THE OLD TESTAMENT, reveals that in 184 cases where the names of kings are translated into Hebrew, it has been done accurately. This means that for 3,900 years the names of these kings have been faithfully transmitted. There are about 40 of those kings living from 2000 B.C. to 400 B.C. Each appears in chronological order "with reference to the kings of the same country and with respect to the kings of other countries ... No stronger evidence for the substantial accuracy of the Old Testament records could possibly be imagined, than this collection of kings." Mathematically, it is 1 chance in 750,000,000,000,000,000,000,000 that this data would be correctly recorded.

THE WORLD'S LARGEST CITY - BABYLON
Babylon is mentioned 250 times in the Bible and is often referred to in the prophecies of Isaiah, Jeremiah, Daniel, and Habakkuk. It is estimated that the ancient city of Babylon was 5 times larger than present-day London and located on both sides of the Euphrates River. A stone bridge connected the two parts of the city. On the banks of the Tigris River 225 miles north of Babylon is the great city of Nineveh, made famous

272

because of Jonah. Sennacherib made Nineveh the capital city of the Assyrian Empire at the end of the 8th century.

4. 6_____ - Herodotus, the 5th century Greek historian, called Babylon the world's most splendid city.
5. 7_____ - Nebuchadnezzar was celebrated as the builder who made Babylon the most famous city in the world.
6. 8_____ - according to Herodotus the city was square - each side was 14 miles long, making a circuit nearly 56 miles, and an area of 196 square miles.
7. ONE OF THE SEVEN 9_____ OF THE WORLD - Nebuchadnezzar built The Hanging Gardens of Babylon in the 6th century B.C. to please his wife.
8. 10_____ to pagan gods were found throughout the city of Babylon, no less than 53 and 180 altars to Isthar!
9. 11_____ is in present day Iraq on the Euphrates River – 54 miles south of modern Baghdad, west of the present riverbed.
10. 12_____ REMAINS - German archaeologists of the Deutsche Orient-Gesellschaft worked at the ancient ruins of Babylon during the years of 1899-1940, and the ruins of the inner city were thoroughly examined.
11. 13_____ - because of its political importance, together with its favorable geographical position, Babylon was the main commercial, educational, and administrative center in all of Babylonia.
12. 14_____ MORALS - Babylon, as the center of a great kingdom, was the seat of boundless luxury, and its people were notorious for their addictions to self-indulgence.

> One historian writes, "Nothing could be more corrupt than its morals, nothing more fitted to excite and allure to immoderate pleasures. The rites of hospitality were polluted by the grossest and most shameful lusts. Money dissolved every tie ... the Babylonians were very greatly given to wine, and enjoyments, which accompany inebriety. Women were present at their convivialities, first with some degree of propriety, but, growing worse and worse by degrees, they ended by throwing off at once their modesty and their clothing."(Bible Encyclopaedia by Dr. Samuel Fallows, C 1913, The Howard-Severance Company, Chicago)

THE DESTRUCTION OF BABYLON FORETOLD

Both 15_____ and 16_____ predicted that Babylon would be brought to absolute ruin - and it has! The prophecy includes never to be 17_____ again - amazingly accurate.

> Isaiah 13:19, "And Babylon, the glory of kingdoms, the beauty of the Chaldeans' pride, will be as when God overthrew Sodom and Gomorrah."

> Isaiah 14:21, "For I will rise up against them, says the Lord of hosts, and cut off from Babylon the name and remnant, and offspring and posterity, says the Lord."

> Jeremiah 51:37, "Babylon shall become a heap, a dwelling place for jackals, an astonishment and a hissing, without an inhabitant."

WHAT BABYLON REPRESENTS IN SCRIPTURE

13. A literal [18]_____ of which the uninhabited remains are viewable in present-day Iraq. 2 Kings, 2 Chronicles, Daniel, and Jeremiah reference a literal city.

14. In the Book of Revelation Babylon represents [19]_____ Christendom or ecclesiastical Babylon, the great harlot, supporting the Anti-christ. Simply stated, the amalgamation of religious groups who will revere the Anti-christ as god of all!

15. Prophetically some believe Babylon of Revelation 18 could typify the [20]_____ _____.

> Revelation 18:10, "Standing at a distance for fear of her torment, saying, 'Alas, alas, that great city Babylon, that mighty city! For in one hour you judgment has come." (cf. Jeremiah chapters 50 & 51, pages 1311-1317 in the Nelson Study Bible)

DANIEL'S FAITHFULNESS

> Daniel 1:8, "But Daniel purposed in his heart that he would not defile himself with the portion of the king's delicacies, nor with the wine which he drank; therefore he requested of the chief of the eunuchs that he might not defile himself."

- If Daniel stayed faithful, [21]_____ can too!

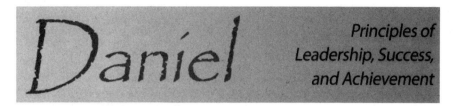

Daniel
Principles of Leadership, Success, and Achievement

P.O.W.s Who Wouldn't Break – Why?
Message #3 in the Daniel series
Bible Text: Daniel 1:8-21

THE DIVISION OF DANIEL
Daniel is principally divided into [1]_____ parts: chapters 1-6 is primarily [2]_____; chapters 7- 12 is [3]_____ and includes [4]_____ of Daniel's visions and a further interpretation of Nebuchadnezzar's dream of chapter 2. (Chapters 1-6 appears in chronological order, while chapter 7 suddenly goes back in time to a date shortly prior to the events of chapter 5. The four visions are then given in their own chronological order.)

JUDAH EXILED
Evil permeated Judah, and God's anger flared against his rebellious people. Babylon conquered Assyria and became the new world power. The Babylonian army marched into Jerusalem, burned the Temple, tore down the city's massive walls, and carried off the people into captivity.

RABID BRAINWASHING OF PRISONERS OF WAR - DANIEL & FRIENDS
1. The Vulnerability of their [5]_____.

> Daniel 1:3, "The king instructed Ashpenaz, the master of his eunuchs, to bring SOME OF THE CHILDREN of Israel ... 4) young men in whom there was no blemish, but good-looking, gifted in all wisdom, possessing knowledge and quick to understand, who had ability to serve in the king's palace."

- Jameison, Fausset & Brown on Daniel's age: [6]_____ years of age
- Dr. Arno C. Gaebelein: [7]_____ years of age
- Sir Robert Anderson: [8]_____ years of age
- Dr. J. Vernon McGee: [9]_____ years of age

The education of Persian youths began at age [10]_____. Note: The Hebrew word used in Daniel 1:3 is yeled - it simply means "borne one" and is used of an infant (Isaac, Genesis 21:8) and young men in 2 Kings 12:8.

2. The Change of their [11]_____.

- Daniel - "[12]_____ is my judge"; Belteshazzar - "whom [13]_____ favors"
- Hananiah - "[14]_____ of the Lord"; Shadrach - "inspired by the [15]_____"
- Mishael - "who is God"; Meshach - "who is like [16]_____"; Azariah - "the Lord is my [17]_____"; Abednego - the servant of the [18]_____-god."

"The purpose in changing their names was to wean them away from their land and religion, and get them to adopt the religion and habits of the heathen nation where their future was to be spent." - Dr. Clarence Larkin

"This change of name, therefore, was designed to denote a consecration to the service of this idol-

Daniel Taken Captive
The youthful Daniel and his companions were taken as captives from their Palestinian home to far-away Babylon.

god, and the change was eminently adapted to make him to who it was given forget the true God, to whom in earlier days, he had been devoted. It was only extraordinary grace which could have kept these youths in the paths of their early training, and in the faithful service of that God to whom they had been early consecrated, amidst the temptations by which they were now surrounded in a foreign land, and the influences which were employed to alienate them from the God of their fathers." - Dr. Albert Barnes

3. The god-less [19]_____ from Babylon University – Change their [20]_____.

4. The Seduction of the city of [21]_____.

5. The Change of their [22]_____.

"Such wine as the king was accustomed to drink. It may be presumed that this was the best kind of wine. From anything that appears, this was furnished to

276

them in abundance; and with the leisure which they had, they could hardly be thrown into stronger temptation to excessive indulgence." – Dr. Albert Barnes

REASONS NEBUCHADNEZZAR FAILED TO BRAINWASH DANIEL

The Hebrew Youth In Prayer
Both in emergencies and in normal times, Daniel sought his God in prayer, and the Lord never failed him.

1. Daniel grew up under a great Spiritual [23]_____ ___.

Daniel grew up, age 1-16, under the godly king [24]___ _____ who led Judah in the greatest spiritual revival during his 31 year reign. (cf. 2 Kings 21:26-23:30; 2 Chronicles 33:25-25:27)

2. Daniel's [25]_____ had a love for God they passed on to him.

3. Daniel, consequently, developed a [26]_____ for God.

Daniel 1:4, "Young men in whom there was no blemish, but good-looking, gifted in all wisdom, possessing knowledge and quick to understand, who had ability to serve in the king's palace, and whom they might teach the language and literature of the Chaldeans."

4. Daniel hid God's [27]_____ in his heart. We make a grave mistake when we seek advice from the ungodly (Psalm 1).

5. Daniel selected committed Christians as his [28]_____.
6. Daniel was experienced and disciplined in [29]_____.
7. Daniel was [30]_____ in his thinking.

Daniel 1:8, "But Daniel purposed in his heart that he would not defile himself with the portion of the king's delicacies, nor with the wine which he drank; therefore he requested of the chief eunuchs that he might not defile himself."

REWARDS OF SPIRITUAL CONSISTENCY

1. God gives special [31]_____.

Daniel 1:17, "As for these four young men, God gave them knowledge and skill in all literature and wisdom; and Daniel had understanding in all visions and dreams."

277

2. God gives / bestows ³²_____ and ³³_____.

>Daniel 1:19, "Then the king interviewed them, and among them all none was found like Daniel, Hananiah, Mishael, Azariah; therefore they served before the king."

3. God alone ³⁴_____ and demotes.

>Daniel 1:20, "And in all matters of wisdom and understanding about which the king examined them, he found them TEN TIMES better than all the magicians and astrologers who were in all his realm. 21) THUS DANIEL CONTINUED UNTIL THE FIRST YEAR OF KING CYRUS."

>God's promotion of Daniel lasted ³⁵_____ years

5. God makes you an ³⁶_____ instead of a follower.

The Glory of Babylon
The greatest of ancient cities was Babylon, with its great wall, hanging gardens, and lofty temples.

WHO WERE THESE PROPHETS?

Who?	When? (B.C.)	Ministered during the reign of these kings	Main message	Significance
Micah	742-687	Jotham, Ahaz, and Hezekiah of Judah (The book of Micah)	Predicted the fall of both the northern and southern kingdoms. This was God's discipline on the people, actually showing how much he cared for them.	Choosing to live a life apart from God is making a commitment to sin. Sin leads to judgment and death. God alone shows us the way to eternal peace. His discipline often keeps us on the right path.
Isaiah	740-681	Azariah (Uzziah), Jotham, Ahaz, Hezekiah, and Manasseh of Judah (the book of Isaiah)	Called the people back to a special relationship with God--although judgment through other nations was inevitable.	Sometimes we must suffer judgment and discipline before we are restored to God.
Nahum	663-654	Manasseh of Judah (the book of Nahum)	The mighty empire of Assyria that oppressed God's people would soon tumble.	Those who do evil and oppress others will one day meet a bitter end.
Zephaniah	640-621	Josiah of Judah (book of Zephaniah)	A day would come when God, as Judge, would severely punish all nations, but afterward he would show mercy to his people.	We will all be judged for our disobedience to God, but if we remain faithful to him, he will show us mercy.
Jeremiah	627-586	Josiah, Jehoahaz, Jehoiakim, Jehoiachin, Zedekiah of Judah (book of Jeremiah)	Repentance would postpone Judah's coming judgment at the hands of Babylon.	Repentance is one of the greatest needs in our world of immorality. God's promises to the faithful shine brightly.
Habakkuk	612-589	Josiah, Jehoahaz, Jehoiakim, Jehoiachin, Zedekiah of Judah (book of Habakkuk)	Couldn't understand why God seemed to do nothing about the wickedness in society. Then realized that faith in God alone would one day supply the answer.	Instead of questioning the ways of God, we should realize that he is completely just, and we should have faith that he is in control and that one day evil will be utterly destroyed.
Daniel	605-536	Prophesied as an exile in Babylon during the reigns of Nebuchadnezzar, Darius the Mede, and Cyrus of Persia. (Book of Daniel)	Described both near and distant future events. Throughout it all, God is sovereign and triumphant.	We should spend less time wondering when future events will happen and more time learning how we should live now so we won't be victims when those events occur.

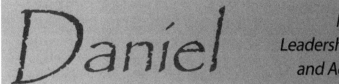

Principles of Leadership, Success, and Achievement

Daniel's Dream About the Future Which Came True!
Message #4 in the Daniel series
Bible Text: Luke 21:24; Daniel 2:1-32

Jesus said in Luke 21:24, "And Jerusalem will be trampled by the Gentiles UNTIL THE TIMES OF THE GENTILES are fulfilled."

"We will see in this section the history of the rule of this world by the Gentiles. Because of the failure of the house of David (Jews), God is now taking the scepter of this universe out from the hands of that line of David, and He is putting it in the hands of the Gentiles. It will be there until Jesus Christ comes again to this earth. Then Christ will take the scepter and rule on this earth as King of kings and Lord of lords. The times of the Gentiles is from the day of Nebuchadnezzar right down through our day until the Lord comes to reign." -Dr. J. Vernon McGee

"Thou Art This Head of Gold"
Fearlessly, Daniel revealed to Nebuchadnezzar that the head of gold is a symbol of great Babylon.

TIMES OF THE GENTILES: This period in history began in [1]_____ B.C. Nebuchadnezzar's destruction of Jerusalem.
TIMES OF THE GENTILES: Concludes - The [2]_____ coming of Jesus Christ, which will initiate the millennial reign of Christ on this earth (Rev. 20:4-6).
TIMES OF THE GENTILES: Why? The Jews' consistent [3]_____ and disobedience to God.

CONTEXT
Daniel 2:1, "Now in the second year of Nebuchadnezzar..." Daniel takes us back to the SECOND year of Nebuchadnezzar's reign, so we know the time frame falls between April 603 and March 602 B.C. The dream occurred during Daniel's three-year education at Babylon University (1:5). He is called upon as a senior in college, age 20, to give an accurate interpretation of the dream of be killed!

DISTURBING DREAM
Daniel 2:1, "Now in the second year of Nebuchadnezzar's reign, Nebuchadnezzar had DREAMS; and his spirit was so troubled that his sleep left him. 2) Then the king gave

281

the command to call the magicians, the astrologers, the sorcerers, and the Chaldeans to tell the king his dreams. 3) And the king said to them, 'I have had a dream, and my spirit is anxious to know the dream.'"

- The Hebrew translated "dreams" is [4]_____. The Hebrew word translated "troubled" refers to a deep disturbance - in our vernacular it would be [5]_____ _____. Sitting at the very top of the world, Nebuchadnezzar wondered about the future - God answered him in a series of tormenting dreams!

In almost every generation people have attached some significance to dreams. In ancient Babylon, however, they were considered to play an important role in the life of people - especially those in positions o f a nation's leadership. Rulers did not disregard them because they believed the dream often conveyed the will of the gods. This is one of the reasons kings surrounded themselves with astrologers and diviners whose chief business was the interpretation of dreams and other omens. –Dr. Fred M. Wood

DIFFERENT LANGUAGE

Daniel 2:4, "Then the Chaldeans spoke to the king in ARAMAIC, 'O king, live forever! Tell your servants the dream, and we will give the interpretation.'"

- Daniel 2:4 - 7:28 are in [6]_____ not Hebrew. Why? The rulers of the world described are [7]_____, not Jews. Aramaic was the language of Gentiles.

"This significance of this change is quite remarkable: God is now speaking to the world, not just to His nation. Israel has gone into Babylonian captivity. God has taken the scepter out of the line of David, and He has put it in gentile hands. It will stay there until the day He takes the scepter back. When He does, nail-pierced hands will take the scepter, because it is God's intention for Jesus to reign." –Dr. J. Vernon McGee

DIRECTIVE FOR DEATH

Daniel 2:5, "The king answered and said to the Chaldeans, 'My decision is firm: if you do not make known the dream to me, and its interpretation, YOU SHALL BE CUT IN PIECES, and your houses shall be made an ash heap. 6) However, if you tell the dream and its interpretation, you shall receive from me GIFTS, REWARDS, and GREAT HONOR. Therefore tell me the dream and its interpretation. 7) They answered again and said, 'Let the king tell his servants the dream, and we will give its interpretation.' 8) The king answered and said, 'I know for certain that you would gain time, because you see that my decision is firm: 9) if you do not make known the dream to me, there is only one decree for you! For you have agreed to speak lying and corrupt words before me till the time has changed. Therefore tell me the dream, and I shall know that you can give me its interpretation.' 10) The Chaldeans answered the king, and said, 'THERE IS NOT A MAN ON EARTH WHO CAN TELL THE KING'S MATTER; therefore no king, lord, or ruler has ever asked such things of any magician, astrologer, or Chaldean. 11) It is a difficult thing that the king requests, and there is no other who can tell it to the king except the gods, whose dwelling is not with flesh. 12) For this reason the king was angry and very furious, and gave the command to destroy all the wise men of Babylon.

13) So the decree went out, and they began killing the wise men; and they sought Daniel and his companions, to kill them."

- Nebuchadnezzar was moved by the enemy in an attempt to destroy [8]_____. We will always face spiritual warfare when God is using us.

DANIEL SEEKING "MERCIES FROM GOD"

Daniel 2:14, "Then with counsel and wisdom Daniel answered Arioch, the captain of the king's guard, who had gone out to kill the wise men of Babylon; 15) he answered and said to Arioch the king's captain, 'Why is the decree from the king so urgent?' Then Arioch made the decision known to Daniel. 16) So Daniel went in and asked the king to give him time, that he might tell the interpretation. 17) Then Daniel went to his house, and made the decision know to Hananiah, Mishael, and Azariah, his companions, 18) that they might SEEK MERCIES FROM THE GOD of heaven concerning this secret, so that Daniel and his companions might not perish with the rest of the wise men of Babylon. 19) Then the secret was revealed to Daniel in a night vision. So Daniel blessed the god of heaven."

- Your most difficult problems are [9]_____ opportunities for God to work on your behalf and reveal His power!

"His (Daniel's) next act was not to go to the library to consult books on the interpretation of dreams. He did not even go to his friends for advice. Instead he called them to a prayer meeting. It is good to have praying friends! Those who walk closest to God still realize their need of much intercession." -Dr. Coleman Luck

DANIEL'S MODEL IN PRAYER

Daniel 2:20, "Daniel answered and said: 'Blessed be the name of God forever and ever, for wisdom and might are His. 21) And He changes the times and the seasons; He removes kings and raises up kings; He gives wisdom to the wise and knowledge to those who have understanding. 22) He reveals deep and secret things; He knows what is in darkness, and light dwells with Him. 23) I thank You and praise You, O God of my fathers; You have given me wisdom and might, and have now made known to me what we asked of You, for You have made known to us the king's demand."

- Daniel's prayer resonates with God's [10]_____ alone to change times; remove kings; give wisdom; reveal secret things - things we need to understand. Daniel erupts in praise to God!

DANIEL'S INTERPRETATION ABOUT FUTURE WORLD GOVERNMENTS

Daniel 2:24, "Therefore Daniel went to Arioch, whom the king had appointed to destroy the wise men of Babylon. He went and said thus to him: 'Do not destroy the wise men of Babylon; take me before the king, and I will tell the king the interpretation.' 25) Then Arioch quickly brought Daniel before the king and said thus to him, 'I have found a man OF THE CAPTIVES of Judah, who will make known to the king the interpretation.' 26) The king answered and said to Daniel, whose name was Belteshazzar, 'Are you able to make known to me the dream which I have seen, and its interpretation?' 27) Daniel answered in the presence of the king, and said, 'The secret which the king has demanded, the wise men, the astrologers, the magicians, and the soothsayers cannot declare to the king. 28) BUT THERE IS A GOD IN HEAVEN who reveals secrets, and He has made known to King Nebuchadnezzar what will be IN THE LATTER DAYS. Your dream, and the visions of your head upon your bed, were these: 29) As for you, O king, thoughts came to your mind while on your bed, about WHAT WILL COME TO PASS AFTER THIS; and He who reveals secrets has made known to you what will be. 30) But as for me, this secret has not been revealed to me because I have more wisdom than anyone living, but for our sakes who make known the interpretation to the king, and that you may know the thoughts of your heart. 31) 'You, O king, were watching; and behold, A GREAT IMAGE! This great IMAGE, whose splendor was excellent, STOOD BEFORE YOU; and its form was awesome. 32) This IMAGE'S HEAD was of fine GOLD, its CHEST and ARMS of silver, its BELLY and THIGHS of BRONZE, 33) its LEGS of IRON, its FEET partly of IRON and partly of CLAY."

"Daniel lived 600 years before Christ, yet he outlined the course of history, even up to our lifetime. We shouldn't be shocked at that. The Old Testament prophesied the destruction of Babylon (Isa. 13:19-22), Egypt (Ezekiel 30:13-16), Tyre (Ezek. 26:1-28:19), and Sidon (Ezek. 28:21-23); and they were destroyed exactly as foretold. It also prophesied that a man named Cyrus would release Israel from captivity (Isa. 45:1, 13), and about 200 years later he did (Ezra 1:1-4). One of the greatest proofs of the Bible's divine inspiration is fulfilled prophecy, because the prophecies are externally verified in human history." -Dr. John MacArthur

- Daniel is soon to reveal the [11]_____ future Gentile World Governments which will control the earth until Christ's second coming!
- The IMAGE represents 4 [12]_____ empires; the different metals represent [13]_____ empires.

"Most Bible students are aware that the great image of the king's dream was intended to portray the whole course of Gentile dominion until its ultimate replacement by the kingdom of God." -Dr. Philip R. Newell

WHAT DO WE SEE:

Part	Material	Empire	Time Period
Head	Gold	Babylonian	606-539 B.C.
Chest/Arms	Silver	Medo-Persian	539-331 B.C.
Belly/Thighs	Bronze	Grecian	331-146 B.C.
Legs/Feet	Iron/Clay	Roman	146 B.C.-A.D. 476

ANSWERS

1. 586 2. second 3. sin 4. plural 5. nightmare 6. Aramaic 7. Gentiles 8. Daniel 9. disguised 10. power 11. four 12. world 13. world 14. Gold 15. Silver 16. Bronze 17. Iron/Clay

Daniel's Image

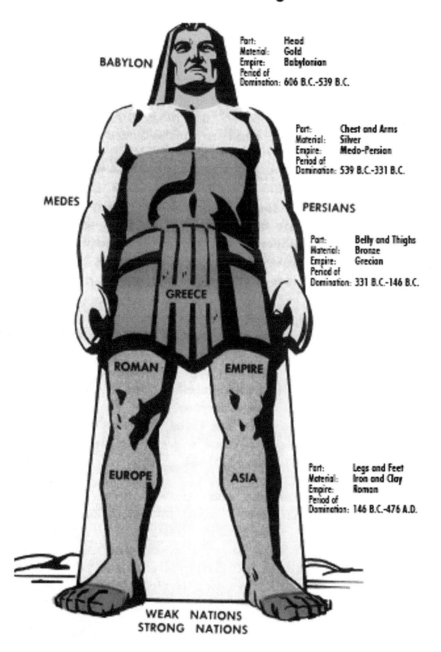

BABYLON

Part: Head
Material: Gold
Empire: Babylonian
Period of
Domination: 606 B.C.-539 B.C.

Part: Chest and Arms
Material: Silver
Empire: Medo-Persian
Period of
Domination: 539 B.C.-331 B.C.

MEDES

PERSIANS

Part: Belly and Thighs
Material: Bronze
Empire: Grecian
Period of
Domination: 331 B.C.-146 B.C.

GREECE

ROMAN · EMPIRE

EUROPE   ASIA

Part: Legs and Feet
Material: Iron and Clay
Empire: Roman
Period of
Domination: 146 B.C.-476 A.D.

WEAK NATIONS
STRONG NATIONS

Daniel

Daniel's Dream! The Interpretation! The Colossal Results!

Message #5 in the Daniel series
Bible Text: Daniel 2:31-49

REVIEW:

The definition for the "Times of the Gentiles" Jesus in Luke 21:24b, "And Jerusalem will be trampled by Gentiles until the times of the Gentiles are fulfilled."

- We are living today in the times of the [1]_____.
- Nebuchadnezzar's dream is history [2]_____.

> We are in one of the great sections of the Word of God as far as prophecy is concerned. The multimetallic image (chp. 2), the four beasts (chp. 7), and the seventy weeks of Daniel (chp. 9) form the backbone and ribs of biblical prophecy. You could never have a skeleton of prophecy without these passages of Scripture in the Old Testament. –Dr. J. Vernon McGee

THE DREAM
Daniel 2:31-35

THE INTERPRETATION
Daniel 2:36-38

> The great world empires mentioned by Daniel did not all cover exactly the same territory. The movement of empires was from east to west, each succeeding empire extending its domain farther toward the setting sun. But there was one piece of land which was in all the world empires – the land of Palestine. In fact, if all the land of the empires was put on a map, Palestine would be in the center. By degrees Palestine fell into the hands of Babylon. –Dr. Arthur E. Bloomfield

From Daniel 2:37-44 the word "kingdom" appears [3]_____ times. Daniel's interpretation makes clear that the image represents world kingdoms.

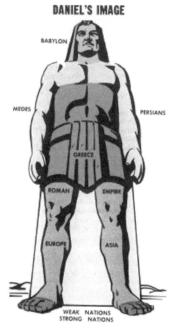

DANIEL'S IMAGE

BABYLON
MEDES
PERSIANS
GREECE
ROMAN EMPIRE
EUROPE
ASIA
WEAK NATIONS
STRONG NATIONS

GENTILE WORLD EMPIRES/GOVERNMENTS/RULERS

Remember, four Gentile World Empires are [4]_____ by the great IMAGE fulfilling The Times of the Gentiles Jesus referred to in Luke 21:24. Three of the four Empires are [5]_____ in Daniel's prophecy. History accurately corroborates the Biblical record and completes the fourth Empire. The fourth Empire, though not identified, is undeniably the [6]_____ Empire.

SYMBOLIZED AND IDENTIFIED

Babylon - Daniel 2:36-38 (Represented by the lion in Daniel chapter 7).
Medo-Persia - Daniel 5:28; 8:20 (Bear in Daniel 7)
Greece - [7]_____ (Leopard in Daniel 7)
Rome - suggested in [8]_____ (Fourth Beast)

> Daniel 2:32, "This image's head was of fine gold ... ."

- The [9]_____ Empire, 606-539 B.C. [10]_____ of the image; [11]_____.

> Daniel 2:37, "You, O king, are a king of kings ... 38) you are this head of gold."

- Nebuchadnezzar began reigning as king of Babylon in 605 B.C. and reigned [12]_____ years. He died in 561 B.C.

> Daniel 2:32, "...its chest and arms of silver ... ."

> Daniel 2:39, "But after you shall arise another kingdom inferior to yours ... ."

- The Medo-[13]_____ Empire 539-331 B.C. [14]_____ and [15]_____; Silver.

> Daniel 2:32, "its belly and thighs of bronze ... "

> Daniel 2:39, "... then, another, a third kingdom of bronze, which shall rule over all the earth."

- The [16]_____ Empire, 331-146 B.C. [17]_____ and [18]_____; Bronze.

> It is easy to imagine what an astonishing impression the Greeks must have made on the civilized world. Consider the contrast between their soldiers and the soldiers of the Persian Army. Had you see a soldier of Media or Persia in the days when they controlled the civilized world, he would have looked like this: On his head would have been a soft, turban-like covering. He would have been clothed with a tunic with sleeves and with trousers full and long. That would have been the Medo-Persian soldier. But when you saw a Greek soldier he would have had on his head a helmet of brass and on his body a breastplate of brass and before him he would be carrying a shield of brass. That is why the classic writers of ancient days will refer to the 'brazen coated Greeks.' Brass became a sign and a symbol of Greek conquest and of the Greek empire.–The late Dr. W.A. Criswell

- Daniel 2:33, "its legs of iron, its feet partly of iron and partly of clay."
- Daniel 2:40-42
- The [19]_____ Empire 146 B.C. - 476 A.D. [20]_____ - Iron; [21]_____ - Part Iron/Clay.

> "The arms of the Republic, sometimes vanquished in battle, always victorious

in war, advanced rapid steps to the Euphrates, the Danube, the Rhine, and the ocean; and the images of gold, or silver, brass, that might serve the nations and their kings, were successively broken by the iron monarchy of Rome." -Edward Gibbons, The Decline and Fall of the Roman Empire, Vol. III

"No great world power follows Rome. The Roman Empire is the last, and it will be in existence in the latter days. Actually, it exists today. All of these other empires were destroyed by an enemy from the outside, but no enemy destroyed Rome. Attilia the Hun came in and sacked the city, but he was so awestruck by what he saw that he realized he could not handle it. He took his barbarians and left town. The Roman Empire fell apart from within – no enemy destroyed it. Rome is living in the great nations of Europe today: Italy, France, Great Britain, Germany, and Spain are all part of the old Roman Empire. The laws of Rome live on, and her language also ... Her warlike spirit lives on also: Europe has been at war since the empire broke up into these kingdoms." -Dr. J. Vernon McGee

"You see, the Roman Empire fell apart like Humpty Dumpty. There have been a lot of men who tried to put it together again, but they have not succeeded. That was one of the missions of the Roman Catholic Church at the beginning. Also, Charlemagne attempted to put it back together. Napoleon tried to do so, and also several emperors of Germany. Hitler and Mussolini attempted it, but so far the man has not yet appeared who will accomplish it. God is not quite ready for him to appear." –Dr. J. Vernon McGee

THE REVIVED ROMAN EMPIRE – FUTURE/TRIBULATION

Daniel 2:43, "As you saw iron mixed with ceramic clay, they will mingle with the seed of men; but they will not adhere to one another, just as iron does not mix with clay."

Its [22]_____: The final form of the Roman Empire will have a ten-fold division, represented by the ten toes of the image (Daniel 2:41).

Daniel 7:24, "The ten horns are ten kings who shall arise from this kingdom. And another shall rise after them; He shall be different from the first ones; and shall subdue three kings."

Revelation 17:12, "The ten horns which you saw are ten kings who have received no kingdom as yet, but they receive authority for one hour as kings with the beast."

Its [23]_____: The Bible tells us that out of the ten-nation confederacy there will arise one [24]_____, called the "little horn" in Daniel 7:8.

Babylon's Crucial Hour
Cyrus the Persian, with his army, entered the golden city through unbarred gates.

289

THE STONE WHICH SMASHES THE IMAGE – JESUS CHRIST

Daniel 2:34, "You watched while a stone was cut out without hands, which struck the image on its feet of iron and clay, and broke them in pieces. 35) Then the iron, the clay, the bronze, the silver, and the gold were crushed together, and became like chaff from the summer threshing floors; the wind carried them away so that no trace of them was found. And the stone that struck the image became a great mountain and filled the whole earth.

Mathew 21:44, "And whoever falls on this stone will be broken; but on whomever it falls, it will grind him to powder."

The Stone represents [25]_____ _____.

WHAT SHOULD OUR RESPONSE BE?

The exact [26]_____ as Nebuchadnezzar's. What does the dream teach us? God has an pre-determined plan; He is in total [27]_____.

Daniel 2:46, "Then King Nebuchadnezzar fell on his face, prostrate before Daniel, and commanded that they should present an offering and incense. The king answered Daniel, and said, 'Truly your God is God of gods, the Lord of kings, and a revealer of secrets, since you could reveal this secret.'"

WHY DANIEL WAS PROMOTED IN THE BABYLONIAN KINGDOM

Daniel 2:48, "Then the king promoted Daniel and gave him many great gifts; and he made him ruler over the whole province of Babylon. 49) Also Daniel petitioned the king, and set Shadrach, Meshach, and Abed-Nego over the affairs of the province of Babylon; but Daniel sat in the gate of the king."

Daniel remembers his three [28]_____ and seeks their promotion!
Daniel was [29]_____: It took courage for him to stand before Nebuchadnezzar and tell him that his kingdom was not going to last, in fact, that others were coming after him.

Daniel
Principles of Leadership, Success, and Achievement

Why God Allows Severe Trials
Message #6 in the Daniel series
Bible Text: Daniel 3:1-30

TIMETABLE: When Did This Happen? The Greek translation of the Old Testament, the Septuagint, adds that this event happened in the 18th year of Nebuchadnezzar. This would mean 15 years after Daniel interpreted the dream correctly to the king. Daniel would be 35-years-of-age, his friends probably near the same age, and, sad to say, Nebuchadnezzar back to his old polytheistic ways!

THE IMAGE IN THE DESERT - DANIEL 3:1-7

A Test of Faith
The Hebrew youth in the fiery furnace were saved by the power of God.

Daniel 3:1, "Nebuchadnezzar the king made an image of gold, whose height was sixty cubits and its width six cubits. He set it up in the PLAIN OF DURA, in the province of Babylon. 2) And King Nebuchadnezzar sent word to gather together the satraps, the administrators, the governors, the counselors, the treasurers, the judges, the magistrates, and all the officials of the provinces, to come to the DEDICATION of the image which King Nebuchadnezzar had set up. 3) So the satraps, the administrators, the governors, the counselors, the treasurers, the judges, the magistrates, and all the officials of the province gathered together for the DEDICATION of the image that King Nebuchadnezzar had set up; and they stood before the image that Nebuchadnezzar had set up. 4) Then a herald cried aloud: 'To you it is commanded, O peoples, nations, and languages, 5) that at the time you hear the sound of the horn, flute, harp, lyre, and psaltery, in symphony with all kings of music, you shall fall down and worship the gold image that King Nebuchadnezzar has set up; 6) and whoever does not fall down and worship shall be cast immediately into the midst of a burning fiery furnace.' 7) So at the time, when all the people heard the sound of the horn, flute, harp, and lyre, in symphony with all kinds of music, all the people, nations, and languages fell down and worshiped the gold image which King Nebuchadnezzar had set up. "

· 60 cubits high by six cubits across - 90-110 feet tall (the size of a 10-story building, the Statue of Liberty is 111 feet high) and only 9 feet wide. Cubit was 18-22 inches long.

- The Statue: A gold replica of [1]_____ himself! Or, possibly a replica of the great image Nebuchadnezzar dreamed about in chapter 2, except this statue is ALL gold.
- Most notable ... this huge statue was made of [2]_____. It shone in the sun for miles!

> "The image was erected in the "plain of Dura, in the province of Babylon: (3:1). The word "DURA" is still common in the Mesopotamian region and simply means "walled place." Just six miles south of ancient Babylon is a place called by this name where archeologists have identified a large brick construction, 45 feet square and 20 feet high, as the base or pedestal for the image." –Dr. Donald K. Campbell

> "Babylon was situated on a plain, surrounded by flat country. Although it was a city of skyscrapers for its day, the sheer height of the image made it visible for a great distance. The plain of Dura was like an airport - flat and expansive - allowing a great multitude to assemble for worship of the image, actually the worship of the king." –Dr. J. Vernon McGee

- The image's dimensions are all in 6's - it represents the [3]_____.

> Revelation 13:18, "Here is wisdom. Let him who has understanding calculate the number of the beast, for it is the number of a man: His number is 666."

DISOBEDIENCE IN ALLEGIANCE TO GOD - DANIEL 3:8-18

> Daniel 3:8, "Therefore at that time certain Chaldeans came forward and accused the Jews. 9) They spoke and said to King Nebuchadnezzar, 'O king, live-forever! 10) You, O king, have made a decree that everyone who hears the sound of the horn, flute, harp, lyre, and psaltery, in symphony with all kinds of music, shall fall down and worship the gold image; 11) and whoever does not fall down and worship shall be cast into the midst of a burning fiery furnace. 12) There are certain Jews whom you have set over the affairs of the province of Babylon: SHADRACH, MESHACH, and ABED-NEGO; these men, O king, have not paid due regard to you. They DO NOT SERVE YOUR gods or worship the gold image which you have set up.' 13) Then Nebuchadnezzar, in rage and fury, gave the command to bring Shadrach, Meshach, and Abed-Nego. SO they brought these men before the king. 14) Nebuchadnezzar spoke, saying to them, IS IT TRUE, Shadrach, Meshach, and Abed-Nego, that you do not serve my gods or worship the gold image which I have set up? 15) Now if you are ready at the time you hear the sound of the flute, harp, lyre, and psaltery, in symphony with all kinds of music, and you fall down and worship the image which I have made, good! But if you do not worship, you SHALL BE CAST IMMEDIATELY into the midst of a BURNING FIERY FURNACE. And WHO IS THE GOD WHO WILL DELIVER YOU FROM MY HANDS? 16) Shadrach, Meshach, and Abed-Nego answered and said to the king, 'O Nebuchadnezzar, we have no need to answer you in this matter. 17) If that is the case, our God whom we serve is able to deliver us from the burning fiery furnace, and HE WILL DELIVER US FROM YOUR HAND, O king. 18) But

if not, let it be known to you, O king, that we do not serve your gods, nor will we worship the gold image which you have set up."

- Three young men who had the courage to stand up for their spiritual conditions - the only 3 among 300,000 people!

This is a great story. It would be three out of about 300,000. Are you loyal enough to Jesus Christ to stand-alone or be one of such a pitiful minority as that? And why didn't they bow down? Why not? 'When in Rome do as Rome does.' When in Babylon do as Babylon does; you must not bring all the Jerusalem prejudices to Babylon. You know, they could have easily said: 'Babylon has been very good to us and we have good positions in Babylon, and it won't do any harm to bow down to this image.' Why not? –Dr. Geoffrey R. King

ANOTHER EXAMPLE OF HATRED FOR THE JEWS - DANIEL 3:12

Daniel 3:12, "There are certain JEWS whom you have set over the affairs of the province of Babylon: Shadrach, Meshach, and Abed-Nego; these men, O king, have NOT PAID THE REGARD TO YOU."

WHY GOD ALLOWS TRIAL: FIERY FURNACE - DANIEL 3:19-25

Daniel 3:19, "Then Nebuchadnezzar was full of fury, and the expression of his face changed toward Shadrach, Meshach, and Abed-Nego. He spoke and commanded that they heat the furnace seven times more than it was usually heated. 20) And he commanded certain mighty men of valor who were in his army to bind Shadrach, Meshach, and Abed-Nego, and cast them into the burning fiery furnace. 21) Then these men were bound in their coats, their trousers, their turbans, and their other garments, and were cast into the midst of the burning fiery furnace. 22) Therefore, because the king's command was urgent, and the furnace exceedingly hot, the flame of the fire filled those men

who took up Shadrach, Meshach, and Abed-Nego. 23) And these three men, Shadrach, Meshach, and Abed-Nego, fell down bound into the midst of the burning fiery furnace. 24) Then King Nebuchadnezzar was astonished; and he rose in haste and spoke, saying to his counselors, 'Did we not cast three men bound into the midst of the fire?' They answered and said to the king, 'True, O king.' 25) 'Look!' he answered, 'I see four men loose, walking in the midst of the fire; and they are not hurt, and the form of the fourth is like the Son of God!'"

- One scholar reports that the temperature in these kilns could reach as high as 1,000 degrees centigrade, i.e., [4]_____ degrees Fahrenheit. "One can only imagine the fear that engulfed the crowd as the flames leaped from the top of the furnace and the smoke billowed forth."

REASONS GOD SENDS YOU TRIALS
1. To reveal the genuineness of your [5]_____ - trials are faith-builders!

2 Peter 1:6, "In this you greatly rejoice, though now for a little while, if need be, you have been grieved by various trials, 7) that the genuineness of your faith,

being much more precious than gold that perishes.. ."

2. To remind us that our eternal home is in [6]_____, not here!

> Hebrews 11:40, "God having provided something better for us, that they should not be made perfect apart from us."

3. Trials are not the [7]_____ of disobedience to God ... sin is!

> James 4:17, "Therefore, to him who knows to do good and does not do it, to him it is sin."

4. To [8]_____ people to Jesus Christ because of His grace so evident in us!

> I Peter 4:12, "Beloved, do not think it strange concerning the fiery trial which is to try you, as though some strange thing happened to you; 13) but rejoice to the extent that you partake of Christ's sufferings, that when His glory IS REVEALED, you may also be glad with exceeding joy."

TRIALS DEMONSTRATE GOD'S GREATNESS - DANIEL 3:26-30

> Daniel 3:26, "The Nebuchadnezzar went near the mouth of the burning fiery furnace and spoke, saying, 'Shadrach, Meshach, and Abed-Nego, servants of the Most High God, come out, and come here.' Then Shadrach, Meshach, and Abed-Nego came from the midst of the fire. 27) And the satraps, administrators, governors, and the king's counselors gathered together, and they saw these men on whose bodies the fire had no power; the hair of their head was not singed nor were their garments affected, and the smell of fire was not on them. 28) Nebuchadnezzar spoke, saying, 'Blessed be the God of Shadrach, Meshach, and Abed-Nego, who sent His Angel and delivered His servants who trusted in Him, and they have frustrated the king's word, and yielded their bodies, that they should not serve nor worship any god except their own God. 29) Therefore I make a decree that any people, nation, or language which speaks anything amiss against the God of Shadrach, Meshach, Abed-Nego shall be cut in pieces, and their houses shall be made an ash heap; because there is NO OTHER GOD WHO CAN DELIVER LIKE THIS.' 30) Then the king promoted Shadrach, Meshach, and Abed-Nego in the province of Babylon."

• As we will see in Daniel chapter 4, still Nebuchadnezzar is not [9]_____, although he seems so after seeing God intervene for the 3 Jewish young men.

IT'S WORTH NOTING ...

> "But beyond the prophetic lesson there is also a most comforting lesson for every believer here. To all who will stand firm for their faith in God and the Lord Jesus Christ, there is also the promise of persecution. It has ever been thus. No saint in any age of history has ever been popular with the world. If you and I are going to stand for what we believe to be the truth of God, and refuse to be swayed from it no matter what the cost, we too shall find that the world is no friend to grace. And in the measure that we dare to stand true for God and be on fire for Christ, in that measure we shall suffer persecution."
> –Dr. M. R. DeHaan

When and How God Brings a Man Down

Message #7 in the Daniel series
Bible Text: Daniel 4:1-37

TWO MAJESTIC THEMES OF DANIEL 4

1. Again, the [1]_____ and absolute control of God!

> Daniel 4:17b, "...in order that the living may know that the Most High rules in the kingdom of men, gives it to whomever He will, and sets over it the lowest of men."

> Daniel 4:25b, "...till you know that the Most High rules in the kingdom of men, and gives it to whomever He chooses."

> Daniel 4:31, "...until you know that the Most High rules in the kingdom of men, and gives it to whomever He chooses."

> Daniel 4:35, "...He does according to His will in the army of heaven and among the inhabitants of the earth. NO ONE can RESTRAIN His hand or say to Him, 'What have You Done?'"

2. [2]_____ brings any man or woman down!

> Daniel 4:37b, "And those who walk in pride He is able to put down."

> Proverbs 6:16, "These six things the Lord hates ... 17) a proud look .. ."

Nebuchadnezzar's Pride
With pride, Nebuchadnezzar exclaimed: "Is not this great Babylon, that I have built...by the might of my power, and for the honor of my majesty?" Daniel 4:30.

Proverbs 8:13, "The fear of the Lord is to hate evil ... pride and arrogance .. I hate."

Proverbs 11:2, "When pride comes, then comes shame."

Proverbs 16:5, "Everyone proud in heart is an abomination to the Lord."

Proverbs 16:18, "Pride goes before destruction, and a haughty spirit before a fall."

Proverbs 21:4, "A haughty look, a proud heart ... are sin."

Proverbs 29:23, "A man's pride will bring him low."

Isaiah 48:11b, "And I will not give my glory to another."

James 4:6, "God resists the proud, but gives grace to the humble."

"This is Nebuchadnezzar's marvelous testimony, and it shows development in the faith of this man. Back in Daniel 3:29 he issued a decree and expressed a conviction. Here he gives a personal testimony. There it was a decree; here it is a decision. There it is a conviction, and here it is conversion. Chronologically, this testimony should come at the end of this chapter because it grew out of his experience recorded here." –Dr. J. Vernon McGee

WITNESS OF NEBUCHADNEZZAR'S CONVERSION - DANIEL 4:1-3

Daniel 4:1, "Nebuchadnezzar the king, To all peoples, nations, and languages that dwell in all the earth: Peace be multiplied to you. 2) I thought it good to declare the signs and wonders that the Most High God has worked for me. 3) How great are His signs, and how mighty His wonders! His kingdom is an everlasting kingdom, and His dominion is from generation to generation."

- The introduction is actually a [3]_____. The conviction of these words grew out of the experience recorded in this chapter. How wonderful: a conversion to Jehovah, by a pagan king, recorded in Aramaic!

- Scholars Wood, Young, Rushdoony and Walvoord believe that Nebuchadnezzar had a genuine salvation experience. Scholars Calvin, Keil, Pusey, and Archer think the king's faith fell short.

WILD NIGHTMARE - DANIEL 4:4-12

- The Aramaic word translated "rest" means that Nebuchadnezzar was "free" from apprehension and [4]_____. He was prospering ... the Aramaic word translated "flourishing" means that his life was literally "growing [5]_____."
- TIMETABLE: Nebuchadnezzar ruled 43 years (605-562 B.C.) and following his 7-year insanity, he was restored to his throne for at least a few months. If we add 2 years to the 7-year of insanity it works out to be Nebuchadnezzar's [6]_____ year ... 32 years since his first dream (2:1). Daniel was now about [7]_____ years of age.

"Again, we must recognize this chapter (4) to be prophetic as well as historic. In the seven-year derangement of Nebuchadnezzar which it forecasts and then relates, it is possible to see a foreshadowing of the bestiality and debasement under Antichrist which will at the end of the age characterize the Gentile nations, which are here symbolized by the Babylonian king. Earth's inhabitants (excepting, of course, those whose names are written in the book of life - see Rev. 13:8) will be spiritually insane and worship the beast and the dragon who gives him his 'power, and his throne, and great authority' (Rev. 13:2). We are plainly told in 2 Thes. 2:11 that God Himself will 'send them strong delusion, that they should believe a lie.' And this fearful doom engulfs them 'because they received not the love of truth that they may be saved.'" -Dr. Philip R. Newell

WATCHERS - DANIEL 4:13-15
- "WATCHER" is an [8]_____, "messenger" is literally "one who is awake." This word is used in v.v. 13 & 17 and is employed for a class of heavenly beings known as "watchful ones" who serve God and intercede on behalf of men. The watcher gave the order to cut down the tree ... and Nebuchadnezzar's mind given over to madness.
- There is more information which teaches us about [9]_____ in the book of Daniel than any other Old Testament book.

   "These watchers see all, hear all, and tell all. Many believers today think they can live in secret, that they are not under the eye of God. We talk about wanting to enjoy our privacy, but if you want to know the truth, you and I haven't any privacy. Psalm 139:7-12 tells us that we cannot get away from God, no matter where we go. SECRET SIN on earth is OPEN SCANDAL up in heaven. His created intelligences know all about you." -Dr. J. Vernon McGee

   Hebrews 1:14, "Are they not ministering spirits sent forth to minister for those who will inherit salvation?"

WATCHFUL EYE AND WILL OF GOD – DANIEL 4:16
- A malady, perhaps similar, lycanthropy is a form of [10]_____ which makes the patient think he/she is a wolf and act like a wolf.
- We see the [11]_____ of God ... His greatness and might!

   Isaiah 40:15, "Behold, the nations are as a drop in a bucket, and are counted as the small dust on the scales. 17) All the nations before Him are as nothing, and they are counted by Him less than nothing and worthless."

   Ephesians 1:11, "...the purpose of Him who works ALL things according to the counsel of His will."

WARNING GIVEN BY A GRIEVED DANIEL - DANIEL 4:18-27
- Here again we see the quality of Daniel ... after hearing the dream he was (*estoman*) "appalled," "[12]_____" by the horror of what the dream meant for the king he had been witnessing to for scores of years!

   "Twenty-five or thirty years had passed since Daniel revealed and interpreted the king's first dream. It seems logical to conclude that Daniel, who was the prime minister of Babylon, told Nebuchadnezzar all he could about God in those intervening years. Daniel cared about him." -Dr. John MacArthur

WEIRD INSANITY - DANIEL 4:28-33

- Nebuchadnezzar, although warned, waited one year and did not [13]_____! God graciously gave him time to repent ... time he wasted. The king who felt superior to other men sunk to a subhuman level!

THE CITY OF BABYLON... was a vast city, four-square, 56 miles in circuit, with walls 350 feet high and 87 feet thick - wide enough for six chariots to race abreast. Herodotus, the ancient Greek historian, visited Babylon about 100 years after Nebuchadnezzar's time and was overwhelmed by its grandeur. Over 200 years later, Alexander the Great planned to make the city headquarters for his vast empire but died there at thirty-two. The height of the walls is not known, but the Ishtar Gate was forty feet high, and the walls would have approximated this size. Nebuchadnezzar had at least three palaces in Babylon. Most of the bricks taken out of Babylon in the archaeological excavations bear the name and inscription of Nebuchadnezzar stamped on them.

- Babylon was [14]_____ miles in circumference, and included an area [15]_____ times as large as London, England. It was laid out in 625 squares, formed by the intersection of twenty-five streets at right angles.

Babylon as it Appears Today
The great city of Babylon, once the pride of its rulers, and of the ancient world, now lies humbled in the dust of centuries.

WONDERFUL CONVERSION - DANIEL 4:34-37

- Never forget: those who walk in pride He is able to put [16]_____!

IT'S WORTH NOTING ...

Scholar Adam Clark says of Daniel 4, "This is a regular decree, and is one of the most ancient on record, and no doubt was copied from the state-papers of Babylon. Daniel has preserved it in the original language." Dr. Grotius states, "Daniel gives this wonderful history, not in his own words, but in those of the published edict itself, that there might remain no doubt about its trustworthiness."

Adam Clark thinks that very probably Nebuchadnezzar was a true convert, that he relapsed no more into idolatry, and that he died in the faith of the God of Israel.

Saddam Hussein, Belshazzar...
What Are The Final Days of a King?

Message #8 in the Daniel series
Bible Text: Daniel 5:1-31

- TIMETABLE: How old was Daniel? Chapter 5 fixes the date of the fall of [1]_____ at 539 B.C., consequently, [2]_____ years had elapsed since Nebuchadnezzar's second dream, and 23 years since his death. Daniel was now about [3]_____ years old.

- CONTEXT OF CHAPTER 5: Two years after the death of Nebuchadnezzar, war broke out between the Babylonians and the Medes. This war, continued, off and on, for more than 20 years. Finally, Cyaxeres king of the [4]_____ (the same person called Darius in Daniel 5:31) called upon his nephew CYRUS, who was a Persian, to come to his aid; and in the 17th year of Nabonidus (Belshazzar's father) and the 3rd year of 36-year-old, Belshazzar, Cyrus laid siege to the city of Babylon.

- PROPHECY [5]_____- 175 years earlier the prophet Isaiah correctly predicted that [6]_____. Isaiah 44:28, "Who says of CYRUS, 'He is My shepherd, and He shall perform all My pleasure, saying to Jerusalem, 'You shall be built,' and to the temple, 'Your foundation shall be laid.'" Isaiah 45:1, "Thus says the

The Handwriting on the Wall
The fall of Babylon, unexpected by King Belshazzar, came in confirmation of sacred prophesy.

Lord to His anointed, to CYRUS, whose right hand I have held - to SUBDUE NA-TIONS before him and loose the armor of kings, to OPEN BEFORE HIM THE DOUBLE DOORS, so that the gates will not be shut."

- CRITICS [7]_____: Archaeological discoveries (The Nabonidus Chronicle) have now confirmed that Belshazzar, Nabonidus' oldest son, was made co-regent with his father and did serve as king while his father was away from Babylon in Tema in Arabia (about 500 miles south) for most of his 17-year reign, apparently for religious reasons. He worshiped the moon god Sin.

> "It may be observed that, for many years, liberal writers declared that Belshazzar was unhistorical and the book of Daniel was in error in speaking of him as Babylonia's last king. It was known that Nabonidus held this position, and the existence of Belshazzar was unknown from ancient records then in hand ... the Bible has again been proven accurate and the liberal critics wrong." -Dr. Leon J. Wood

I. THE PARTY - DANIEL 5:1-4

- We read of a drunken orgy - 1,000 partyers and Belshazzar, in defiant pride, is getting [8]_____ by using the vessels used in the Jewish Temple made by Solomon (see I Kings 7:47-51: 10:21)!
- "TASTING" (v.2) - (te em) carries the idea of not only sensing the flavor of the wine, but feeling it [9]_____, or, being "under the influence."

Did you know?

> Archaeologists have been unearthing the ancient ruins of Babylon for over 100 years, and one scholar, Koldewey, may have discovered the very room where this very event took place! The miraculous encounter obviously transpired in one of the king's palaces in Babylon ... off of the largest of the palace's five courtyards was a huge chamber with three entrances that Koldewey identified as the throne room, and most scholars would agree with this identification. "I have personally stood in this room. It measures 165 feet long by 55 feet wide, and has plastered walls (see Daniel 5:5). Most of the plaster is now gone, but the remains of the walls still stand several feet high. Especially important is the niche at the middle of one of the longer walls, directly opposite the door of entrance into the room. It is here that the king would have sat, no doubt on a slightly raised platform, so that he could be seen by all present." - Dr. Leon J. Wood

II. THE PROPHECY - DANIEL 5:5-9

- Malachi 3:16 reminds us of a "book of [10]_____" before the Lord and He is always observing us and writing in it! God registers everything we do.
- Belshazzar is on the verge of a [11]_____.

III. THE PROMINENT QUEEN MOTHER - DANIEL 5:10-12

- The queen was not a part of the banquet - she came later, perhaps summoned. Josephus said she was the wife of Nebuchadnezzar or Nabonidus, probably the [12]_____ of Belshazzar. Or, possibly Nitocris, the daughter of Nebu-

chadnezzar, and Nabonidus' wife and Belshazzar's mother.
- Notice twice she calls the prophet by his Hebrew name [13]_____, not Belteshazzar, the heathen, pagan name Nebuchadnezzar had given to him.
- Daniel is well known for the [14]_____ of God who lived within him. Are you?

IV. THE PROPHET - DANIEL 5:13-21
- Daniel could not be [15]_____ or vainly impressed by this young, pagan king.
- Daniel reminds this young, inebriated king that only God's supreme [16]_____ dictates every kingdom!

> "Daniel, God's faithful prophet, did not tremble before the king. He had no fear; he had but one duty and responsibility: To be faithful to the Word of God written on the wall, and to tell the king exactly what God had spoken. That is the responsibility of every minister, evangelist, and Bible teacher. We are responsible only to God. A minister called and ordained of God to preach the Gospel, owes his allegiance to God, regardless of the age or dispensation. He must fear no one ... ." - Dr. Oliver B. Green

V. THE PRIDE - DANIEL 5:22-24
- Similar to the demise of Nebuchadnezzar, Belshazzar's [17]_____ brings him down.

VI. PERSONALIZED MESSAGE - DANIEL 5:25-31
- "MENE, MENE" - numbered, numbered, or counted, counted - God had [18]_____the days of the Babylonian kingdom and that fateful night it was coming to an end!
- "TEKEL" - "weighed" - God had weighed Belshazzar's [19]_____ and found it woefully lacking.
- "UPHARSIN" - ("peres," v. 28, where it is used without the conjunction "u" and the plural ending "in") means "[20]_____" or "broken in pieces." God acts by careful calculation, He weighs our thoughts, intents, and motives.
- Belshazzar (his name literally meant 'Bel protect the prince') was [21]_____ that very night! We know the date: the 16th day of Tishri, 539 B.C., which is October 11 or 12. The Babylonian empire, 70 years old, came to an end that night.

AGENTS IN BABYLON'S FALL ...
- [22] _____
- [23] _____ for pleasure
- [24] _____ deviance
- [25] _____
- [26] _____

> "The worship of pagan gods often involved sexual perversion. In digs around Babylon, archaeologists have discovered artifacts engraved with pornographic pictures. But I don't know that their pornography can be any worse than what has appeared in America. Our nation has abandoned itself to vice and lust." - Bible teacher Dr. John MacArthur

SECULAR HISTORY, AGAIN, CONFIRMS THE BIBLICAL RECORD...

The story of the fall of Babylon has been found in four separate sources. They are the historical accounts of Herodotus and Xenophon (of the fifth and fourth centuries B.C. respectively) and the cuneiform records of both Nabonidus and Cyrus of this very occasion (the Nabonidus Chronicle and the Cyrus Cylinder). Both Herodotus and Xenophon tell of the Euphrates River, which flowed under the wall Babylon and through the city, as being diverted so that the riverbed could be used to enter. Neither of the original cuneiform records tells of this aspect of the city's capture, but they do indicate that the fall of the city was remarkably free from bloodshed. Xenophon tells of drunken feasting as being in progress in the city at its fall. - Scholar Dr. Leon J. Wood

ANSWERS

1. Babylon 2. 32 3. 81 4. Medes 5. fulfilled 6 Cyrus 7 Silenced 8. drunk 9. effected 10. remembrance 11. heart attack 12. grandmother 13. Daniel 14. Spirit 15. bought 16. will 17. pride 18. numbered 19. behavior 20. divided 21. executed 22. Alcohol 23. lust 24. sexual 25. idolatry 26. Blasphemy

Daniel

90-Year-Old Daniel in the Lion's Den
Message #9 in the Daniel series
Bible Text: Daniel 6:1-28

- The Gentile World Kingdom: Medo-[1]_____, 539-331 B.C. Represented by silver, in Nebuchadnezzar's image it was the chest and arms - speaking of [2]_____.

- How old was Daniel? [3]_____ years-of-age.

  "Despite the change of government Daniel continued to enjoy favour. This is the point of interest connecting the two chapters. The Persian empire, which incorporated that of the Medes, a vast area forming an arc to the north of the Babylonian territories, extended eventually to Asia Minor, Libya and Egypt to the west, and to the Indus river and the Aral Sea to the east. It was the largest empire the world had yet seen, hence the urgent need for an efficient organization from the very beginning. The division of the whole kingdom into satrapies is known from Esther 8:9 ... strictly the text speaks only of the appointment of satraps and above the satraps were three overseers, of whom Daniel was one." – Dr. Joyce Baldwin

God Honors Fidelity
Daniel was safer in the lion's den with God's protection than he
would have been in the courts of Babylon without it.

303

THE MEDO-PERSIAN KINGDOM

> Daniel 6:1, "It pleased Darius to set over the kingdom one hundred and twenty satraps, to be over the whole kingdom."

- "satraps" - (KJV) "princes" is a word of Persian origin, pronounced ksatrap, it means [4]_____or viceroys in the large provinces of the empire, who possessed both civil and military powers. It means literally "protector of the realm" and was used to designate those who supervised.

DANIEL'S PROMINENT POSITION

> Daniel 6:2, "And over these, three governors, of whom Daniel was one, that the satraps might give account to them, so that the king would suffer no loss."

- "three governors" - (KJV) "three presidents" representing the three men of the highest office who ruled over the affairs of the kingdom under the king.

Daniel was the [5]_____and highest, under the king, in authority!

> Dr. Albert Barnes said, "It is not improbable that these presided over distinct departments, corresponding somewhat to what are now called 'secretaries' - as Secretaries of State, of the Treasury, of Foreign Affairs... ."

> "Politically, the situation was quite different from that of the prior chapters. Then Babylon had been the country in control; now it was Medo-Persia. The exact length of time that had passed since the fall of Babylon cannot be determined, but at least a few months had elapsed, for the new regime was now established and jealousies had been formed. Probably no less than two years had gone by, meaning that Daniel was about 83." – Dr. Leon J. Wood

DANIEL'S DISTINCTION

> Daniel 6:3, "Then this Daniel distinguished himself above the governors and satraps, because an EXCELLENT SPIRIT was in him; and the king gave thought to setting him over the WHOLE REALM."

- "distinguished himself" – the root idea of the word is to [6]_____.
- "an EXCELLENT spirit was in him" - the word means that which hangs over, or which is abundant, or more than enough ... that which is great, excellent, preeminent.

HOW DO I CULTIVATE AN "EXCELLENT SPIRIT"?

1. Early Daniel made up his mind about [7]_____. (1:8)
2. Daniel had an inventive and insatiable love for [8]_____. (1:17)

> "God gave them knowledge and skill in all literature and wisdom; and Daniel had understanding in all visions and dreams."

3. Daniel was in control of his [9]_____and words. (2:16)

> "So Daniel went in and asked the king to give him time, that he might tell the king the interpretation."

4. Daniel was faithful in his [10]_____responsibilities -he was employee of the kingdom! (6:4)

> "So the governors and satraps sought to find some charge against Daniel concerning the kingdom; but they could find no charge or fault, because he

was faithful; nor was there any error or fault found in him."

5. Daniel's Christian [11]_____was impeccable. (6:5)

"Then these men said, 'We shall not find any charge against this Daniel unless we find it against him concerning the law of his God.'"

6. Daniel was fervent in his prayer and devotional life. (6:10)

"Now when Daniel knew that the writing was signed, he went home. And in his upper room, with his windows open toward Jerusalem, he knelt down on his knees three times that day, and prayed and gave thanks before his God, as was his custom since early days."

- Daniel had been faithfully praying, three times a day, for at least [12]_____years. That is a minimum of [13]_____prayers Daniel had asked the Lord!

DANIEL'S DEATH-DEFYING DILEMMA
- Daniel 6:6-13

DANIEL'S DYNAMIC PRAYER HABITS

1. "with his windows open" - speaks of his [14]_____in prayer
2. "toward Jerusalem" - reminds us he had not [15]_____the prophet Jeremiah, the Jewish Temple, or the teachings of Jehovah, although 70 years had passed!

Jeremiah 29:12, "Then you will call upon Me and go and pray to Me, and I will listen to you. 13) And you will seek Me and find Me, when you search for me with all of your heart."

Jeremiah 33:2, "Call to Me, and I will answer you, and show you great and mighty things, which you do not know."

According to Daniel 9:2 the book of [16]_____was in Daniel's hands in Babylon. "I, Daniel, understood...by the word of the Lord through Jeremiah the prophet.. ."

3. "knelt down on his knees" - nearly [17]_____years of age, Daniel is still kneeling
4. "gave thanks before his God" - he knows what is about to happen, the [18]_____ den, and he is thanking God!
5. "but makes his petition" (6:13) - trs. "asking God for [19]_____ "

DANIEL IN A DEN OF LIONS
- Daniel 6:14-23
- "den of lions" - the word means a [20]_____; and the idea is that the den was underground, probably a cave constructed for that purpose.

"A lions' den consists of a square hole in the ground, divided by a wall into two parts. In this wall is a door which can be opened and closed from above ... from this description it is evident that these dens looked very much like our present-day bear pits in our zoos." – Dr. Harry Bultema

STANDING GUARD OVER DANIEL

Daniel 6:22,"My God sent His angel to shut the lions' mouths, so that they have not hurt me."

- Every Christian has a guardian [21]_____to protect, guide, and guard God's children.

  > Hebrews 1:14, "Are they not al ministering sprits sent forth to minister for those who will inherit salvation?"

  > Dr. Albert Barnes, "Daniel does not say whether the angel was visible or not, but it is rather to be presumed that he was, as in this way it would be more certainly known to him that he owed his deliverance to the intervention of an angel, and this would be to him a manifest token of the favor and protection of God."

A DRAMATIC UNEXPECTED DEATH AND THEN A CONVERSION
- Daniel 6:24-28
- Daniel left his detractors to [22]_____.
- King Darius, like Nebuchadnezzar, seems [23]_____to the God, Jehovah!
- Chapter five does not mention the return of the Jews to Jerusalem by Cyrus' decree ... however Ezra does.
- This is the last picture we see of Daniel prior to his [24]_____.

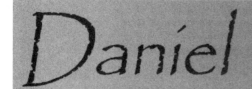

Daniel *Principles of Leadership, Success, and Achievement*

PROFILING THE ANTICHRIST:
Facts You Need To Know
Message #10 in the Daniel series
Bible Text: Daniel 7:19-28

IMPACT OF THE VISION

Daniel 7:28, "This is the end of the account. As for me, Daniel, my thoughts GREAT TROUBLED me, and my COUNTENANCE CHANGED; but I kept the matter in my heart."

* The display and description of the [1]_____ coming to the world at the end times left Daniel overwhelmed!

I John 2:18, "Little children it is the last hour; and as you have heard that the Antichrist is coming, even now MANY antichrists have come, by which we know that it is the last hour."

2 Thessalonians 2:3, "Let no one deceive you by any means; for that Day will not come unless the falling away comes first and THE MAN OF SIN is revealed, the son of perdition, 4) who opposes and exalts himself above all that is called God or that is worshiped, so that he sits as God in the temple of God, showing himself that he is God."

Revelation 13:1, "Then I stood on the sand of the sea. And I saw a beast rising up out of the sea, having seven heads and ten horns, and on his horns ten crowns, and on his heads a blasphemous name. 2) Now the beast which I saw was like a LEOPARD, his feet were like

The Great and Terrible Beast Among the horns of the fourth beast, there came up a horn which blasphemed God.

the feet of BEAR, and his mouth like the mouth of a LION. The dragon gave him his power, his throne, and great authority."

TIMETABLE OF DANIEL CHAPTER 7

Daniel 7:1, "In the FIRST YEAR of Belshazzar king of Babylon, Daniel had a dream a visions of his head while on his bed. Then he wrote down the dream, telling the main facts."

- Chronologically, chapter 7 takes us back in time to a dream Daniel had [2]_____ years prior to Belshazzar's deadly party of chapter [3]_____. Daniel would have been [4]_____ years-of-age. Chapter 7 divides itself in two parts: Daniel's vision in verses 1-14 and the interpretation in verses 15-28.

- Daniel chapter 7 provides our first introduction to the [5]_____who is to come, which is the [6]_____time he is mentioned in all of Scripture. Here he is pictured symbolically as a boastful little horn, with shrewd intellect, having sprung up from a beast so terrible it defied description.

"Antichrist will be a substitute for Christ, as much like Christ as is possible for a tool of Satan. He will talk about justice and love, peace and prosperity. He will be brilliant and eloquent. In short, he will appear as an angel of light, as Satan himself often does, and will be hailed by millions as a superman who will save mankind." – Dr. James Montgomery Boice

DISTINGUISHING TRAITS OF THE ANTICHRIST

1. The Antichrist will be an [7]_____unequalled.

Daniel 7:8, "I was considering the horns, and there was ANOTHER HORN, a little one, coming up among them, before whom THREE of the first horns were plucked out by the roots. And there, in this horn, were eyes like the eyes of a man, and A MOUTH SPEAKING POMPOUS WORDS."

- "eyes like the eyes of a man" - (also in v. 20) suggest tremendous personal magnetism and dominance.

"This power is clear-sighted and penetrating in its intelligence. It not only possesses strength, but it has thoughts and plans besides those of ambition and government. It is a beast that works morally, that occupies itself with knowledge, and sets itself up with pretension full of pride and daring. It has a character of intelligence, moral and systematic (in evil), and not merely the strength of a conqueror. This horn has the eyes of a MAN." – Dr. J. N. Darby

Daniel 7:19, "Then I wished to know the truth about the fourth beast which was different from all the others, exceedingly dreadful, with its teeth of iron and its nails of bronze, which devoured, broke in pieces, and trampled the residue with its feet; 20) and the ten horns that were on its head, and the other horn which came up, before which three fell, namely, that horn which had eyes and A MOUTH WHICH SPOKE POMPOUS WORDS, whose appearance was greater than his fellows."

Daniel 7:25, "He shall speak pompous words against the Most High."

2. The Antichrist will be most unusually [8]_____. It says of him, his "appearance was GREATER than his fellows."

- The word used here means, "abundant in [9]_____, in rank."
3. The Antichrist will be a most clever [10]_____.
  - 7:20 says he has [11]_____- that phrase has reference to his mental ability, his intellect, and his cleverness. He will be able to solve the problems of the world with his cleverness and wisdom.
  - 7:8 in the ten-nation confederation he will rise up and subdue three other kings - "plucked out by the roots," this phrase means literally "to [12]_____ out, to push out by subterfuge, to come in and cleverly replace."

    Daniel 11:21, "And in his place shall arise a vile person, to whom they will not give the honor of royalty; but he shall come in peaceably, and seize the kingdom by intrigue."

4. The Antichrist will be a [13]_____leader.

    Daniel 7:21, "I was watching; and the same horn was making war against the saints, and prevailing against them, 22) until the Ancient of Days came, and a judgment was made in favor of the saints of the Most High, and the time came for the saints to possess the kingdom. Thus he said: 'The fourth beast shall be a fourth kingdom on earth, which shall be different from all other kingdoms, AND SHALL DEVOUR THE WHOLE EARTH, TRAMPLE IT AND BREAK IT IN PIECES. 24) The ten horns are ten kings who shall arise from this kingdom. And ANOTHER SHALL RISE AFTER THEM; He shall be different from the first ones, AND SHALL SUBDUE THREE KINGS. 25) He shall speak pompous words against the Most High, shall PERSECUTE the saints of the MOST HIGH... .'"

  - Literally, he will [14]_____them out. It is a phrase that comes out of the context of wearing out garments. The Antichrist will harass the people who come to Christ during the Tribulation every minute, and he won't let them have a moment's rest.
  - The expression "wear out" (persecute) is the English rendition of a Chaldee word meaning to afflict, exclusively in a mental state. Something of what may be implied here has already been terribly and tragically seen in the trial and 'confession' of Cardinal Mindszenty, whose very personality the Russians disrupted, after a hundred hours of intensive and persistent questioning and periodic injections of actedron and mescaline. The first of these is a synthetically manufactured drug which at first enlivens the physical functions, producing a sensation of strength, but which, if persisted in, produces dizziness, headaches and inability to relax. The second of these drugs originates in a certain type of cactus, and induces in human beings a state of schizophrenia, or 'split personality.' What fearful disintegration of the human entity may be expected therefore in 'him whose coming is after the working of Satan with all power and signs and lying wonders' (2 Thess. 2:9, 10).
    - Dr. Philip R. Newell
5. The Antichrist will be a [15]_____leader.

    Daniel 7:25, "And (He) shall intend to change times and law. Then the saints will be given into his hand for a time and times and half a time."

    The Antichrist will attempt to take God's place. He will ask the people to fall down and worship him. He will change the [16]_____and natural laws of the universe. He will produce amazing signs, miracles, and wonders.

2 Thes. 2:8, "And then the lawless one will be revealed, whom the Lord will consume with the breath of His mouth and destroy with the brightness of His coming. 9) The coming of the lawless one is according to the working of Satan, with all power, signs, and lying wonders."

"Millions upon millions of copies of the Bible and Bible portions have been published in all major languages and distributed throughout the world ... Removal of believers from the world at the Rapture will not remove the Scriptures, and multitudes will no doubt be constrained to read the Bible in those days ... [and] give their testimony for the Word of God." - Dr. Henry Morris

6. The [17]_____of the Antichrist.

Daniel 7:26, "But the court shall be seated, and they shall take away his dominion, to consume and destroy it forever. 27) Then the kingdom and dominion, and the greatness of the kingdoms under the whole heaven, shall be given to the people, the saints of the Most High. His kingdom is an everlasting kingdom, and all dominions shall serve and obey Him."

• How interesting! The court is God's [18]_____assembly which at the appointed hour will take action against the Antichrist!

"The elders, then, appear to be those chief princes of whom Michael himself is one (Daniel 10:13). Together they constitute the grand administrative council of God's universal rule, concerning which Jehovah Himself cried by Jeremiah 23:18, 'For who hath stood in the council of Jehovah, that he should perceive and hear His word?' This council seems to have a definitely assigned place of meeting (Isa. 14:13; Ezek. 28:14, 16), and a regularly scheduled day on which all angelic beings, including Satan himself, must report before it (Job 1:6; 2:1) ... others Scriptures suggest to us the manner in which information is reported before this solemn tribunal." - Scholar Dr. Philip R. Newell

Your Invitation to Christ's Eternal Kingdom
Message #11 in the Daniel series
Bible Text: Daniel 7:1-17

GENTILE WORLD EMPIRES	MAN'S VIEW/DANIEL 2	GOD'S VIEW/DANIEL 7
Babylon	Head of gold	Lion with eagle's wings
Medo-Persia	Arms/breasts of silver	Bear with 3 ribs in teeth
Greece	Belly and thighs of brass	Beast like a leopard
Rome	Legs of iron	Nameless beast/iron teeth
(A long parenthesis: This church age, which God did not reveal to Daniel.)		
Revived Roman Empire	Feet and Ten Toes	Ten horns of 4th beast and "the little horn," who is the Antichrist
Gentile Dominion will end with the return of Christ	The smiting stone	The coming of the Son of Man in Glory

TIMETABLE OF DANIEL 7

Daniel 7:1, "In the FIRST YEAR of Belshazzar king of Babylon, Daniel had a dream and visions of his head while on his bed. Then he wrote down the dream telling the main facts."

- Again, the 7th chapter [1]_____ the 5th chapter of Daniel. Belshazzar was a co-regent of Babylon with his father Nabonidus. Belshazzar's first year was approximately 553 B.C. (This would have been 14 years before the fall of Babylon).

If Daniel was 15 when he was taken to Babylon, in captivity at 605 B.C., then he would be about [2]____ years-old. Nebuchadnezzar had died only 9 years earlier (562 B.C.). Nebuchadnezzar's prophetic dream about future Gentile World Empires (see Daniel 2) would have been over [3]_____ years earlier!

- Verses 2 - 8 reveal the [4]_____beasts (four Gentile World Empires)
- Verses 9 - 12 show the [5]_____from the Ancient of Days
- Verses 13 - 14 presents the triumphant [6]_____of the Son of Man
- Verses 15 - 27 give the [7]_____of it all

Daniel 7:17, "Those great beasts, which are four, are four kings which arise out of the earth."

"God gives to Daniel several visions of four beasts which are quite remarkable. Daniel had these visions at different periods. The vision of chapter 7 was in the first year of King Belshazzar. In chapter 8 the vision was seen in the third year of the reign of Belshazzar. In chapter 9 it was in the first year of Darius; in chapter 10 it was in the third year of Cyrus; and in chapters 11 and 12 the vision was seen in the first year of Darius. Daniel did not record these visions in the historical section (chapters 1 - 6) but gathered these prophetical visions together in this second section of his book." – Dr. J. Vernon McGee

I. THE FIRST BEAST - THE LION (BABYLON) - DANIEL 7:2-4

Daniel 7:2, "Daniel spoke, saying, 'I saw in my vision by night, and behold, the four winds of heaven were stirring up the Great Sea. 3) And four great beasts came up from the sea, EACH DIFFERENT from the other. 4) The first was like a LION and had EAGLE'S WINGS. I watched till its wings were plucked off; and it was lifted up from the earth and made to stand on two feet like a man, and a man's heart was given to it."

- The prophet [8]_____described Nebuchadnezzar as a lion.

Jeremiah 4:6, "Set up the standard toward Zion. Take refuge! Do not delay! For I will bring disaster from the north, and great destruction. 7) The lion has come up from his thicket, and the destroyer of nations is on his way. He has gone forth from his place to make your land desolate. Your cities will be laid waste, without inhabitant."

- This is clearly a prophecy which describes the [9]_____ empire (605 - 538 B.C., described as the head of gold 2:32, 37, 38).
- A lion speaks of Babylon's [10]_____, wings of rapid development, and a heart reminds us of Nebuchadnezzar's [11]_____(chapter 4) - a period which ended the conquering of new lands.

II. THE SECOND BEAST - THE BEAR (MEDO-PERSIA) - DANIEL 7:5

Daniel 7:5, "And suddenly another beast, A SECOND, like a BEAR. It was raised up on one side, and had three ribs in its mouth between its teeth. And they said thus to it: 'Arise, devour much flesh.'"

- This clearly describes the Medo-[12]_____ empire (538-331 B.C., typified as the breasts and arms of silver 2:32, 39 and the Ram 8:3, 4, 20).
- The Persian element was [13]_____than that of the Medes - consequently, the bear is raised up on one side.
- The Medo-Persia Empire was as unpredictable and [14]_____in its attacks as a bear. Isaiah wrote in Isaiah 13:17-22 of Medo-Persia's destruction of Babylon and tells us that they will not be bribed or turned aside for a price, they will mutilate the bodies of young soldiers, and they will not spare the unborn child or the little children.

III. THE THIRD BEAST - THE LEOPARD (GREECE) - DANIEL 7:6

Daniel 7:6, "After this I looked, and there was another, like a LEOPARD, which had on its back four wings of a bird. The beast also had four heads, and dominion was given to it."

- The leopard symbolizes the [15]_____Empire (331-146 B.C., typified by the belly, thighs of brass, 2:32, 39, and the Goat, 8:5-14, 21, 22).
- Alexander the Great died in 323 B.C. in [16]_____. Within 10 shorts years he had conquered the entire Medo-Persian Empire to the borders of India.
- After Alexander's death, his vast Empire was divided by his generals into [17]_____ parts, typified by four [18]_____and [19]_____of the leopard: 1). Antipater, and later Cassander, gained control of Greece and Macedonia; 2). Lysimachus ruled Thrace and a large part of Asia Minor; 3). Seleucus I Nicator governed Syria, Babylon, and much of the Middle East (all of Asia except Asia Minor and Palestine); and 4). Ptolemy I Soter controlled Egypt and Palestine. (See further Daniel 8:8 and 8:21-22).

> "In view of the transparent fact that Alexander did have four generals who succeeded him and divided his empire into four divisions, neither more nor less, it would seem that the interpretation of the four winds and four heads as referring to the divisions of the Grecian Empire with their rulers is the best interpretation." – The late Dr. John Walvoord

IV. THE FOURTH BEAST - THE NONDESCRIPT BEAST (ROME) - DANIEL 7:7, 8

> Daniel 7:7, "After this I saw in the night visions, and behold, a fourth beast, dreadful and terrible, exceedingly strong. It had huge iron teeth; it was devouring, breaking in pieces, and trampling the residue with its feet. It was different from all the beasts that were before it, and it had ten horns. 8) I was considering the horns, and there was another horn, A LITTLE ONE, coming up among them, before whom three of the first horns were plucked out by the roots. And there, in this horn, were eyes like the eyes of a man, and a mouth speaking pompous words."

- This beast was so [20]_____there was not any animal that could convey it! It represents the [21]_____Empire, historically, and the revived Roman Empire, futuristically, out of which the Antichrist will come. (Rome, 146 B.C. - A.D. 476) is typified by legs of iron, feet of iron and clay, 2:33, 40, 41).
- "it was devouring, breaking in pieces" - a good illustration was the Roman destruction of the Jewish Temple in A.D. 70.

THE FATHER SEATED IN TOTAL CONTROL - DANIEL 7:9-11

> Daniel 7:9, "I watched till thrones were put in place, and the Ancient of Days was seated; His garment was white as snow, and the hair of His head was like pure wool. His throne was a fiery flame, its wheels a burning fire; 10) A fiery stream issued and came forth from before Him. A thousand thousands ministered to Him; ten thousand times ten thousand stood before Him. The court was seated, and the books were opened."

- The Ancient of Days is none other than God the [22]_____.
- 'I watched till thrones were put in place" - seated with the Father will be [23]_____from all the ages.
- Talk about an angelic company - there are 100 [24]_____angels standing before

the Father alone - and [25]_____ministering directly to the Father.

DESTRUCTION OF THE ANTICHRIST - DANIEL 7:11, 12

Daniel 7:11, "I watched then because of the sound of the pompous words which the horn was speaking; I watched till the beast was slain, and its body destroyed and given to the burning flame. 12) As for the rest of the beasts, they had their dominion taken away, yet their lives were prolonged for a season and a time."

- This obviously [26]_____Revelation 19:19, 20, "And I saw the beast, the kings of the earth, and their armies, gathered together to MAKE WAR against Him who sat on the horse and against His army. 20) Then the beast was captured, and with him the false prophet who worked signs in his presence, by which he deceived those who received the mark of the beast and those who worshiped his image. These two were cast alive in the lake of fire burning with brimstone."

PRESENTATION OF THE KINGDOM TO THE WORTHY CHRIST - DANIEL 7:13, 14

Daniel 7:13, "I was watching in the night visions, and behold, One like the Son of Man, coming with the clouds of heaven! He came to the Ancient of Days, and they brought Him near before Him. 14) Then to Him was given dominion and glory and a kingdom, that all peoples, nations, and languages should serve Him. His dominion is an everlasting dominion, which shall not pass away, and His kingdom the one which shall not be destroyed."

- Again, we see the [27]_____ of Scripture - Psalm 110:1, "The Lord said to my Lord, 'Sit at My right hand, till I make Your enemies Your footstool.'"
- At Christ's [28]_____ coming, the kingdoms of men come to an end. They will be replaced by Christ's eternal kingdom!

Daniel 7:15, "I, Daniel, was grieved in my spirit within my body, and the visions of my head troubled me. 16) I came near to one of those who stood by and asked him the truth of all this. So he told me and made known to me the interpretation of these things. 17) Those great beasts, which are four, are four kings which arise out of the earth."

WHY HANUKKAH?
Antiochus Epiphanes, Hitler of the Old Testament
Message #12 in the Daniel series
Bible Text: Daniel 8:1-27

DANIEL'S SECOND VISION

Daniel 8:1, "In the THIRD year of the reign of King BELSHAZZAR a vision appeared to me - to me, Daniel - after the one that appeared to me the first time."

- This is two years after Daniel's [1]_____ vision - Daniel was [2]_____years old. The text has been in Aramaic, the common language of the day (2:4 - 7:28), but changes to [3]_____. Why? The focus is on God's covenant people, the [4]_____.
- Chronologically, this vision fits in between Daniel chapters 4 and 5.

"We remind the reader once more of the fact that beginning with the 7th chapter to the end of the Book of Daniel the language employed is Hebrew ... From now on we are led in prophecy mostly upon Jewish ground and events are revealed, which will take place at the close of the times of the Gentiles." – Dr. Arno Gaebelein

"The vision recorded by Daniel in this chapter was prophetic when it was given, but it has SINCE BEEN FULFILLED. Because it has been so clearly and literally fulfilled, this chapter is the basis for the liberal critic giving a late date for the writing of the Book of Daniel. His argument rests on the fact that prophecy concerning the future is supernatural and he does not believe in the supernatural; therefore, this prophecy could not have been written at the time of Daniel, but must have been written afterward as history." –Dr. J. Vernon McGee

The Ram and the He-Goat
The vision revealed in the eighth chapter of Daniel depicts two great world powers in mortal combat.

"From here to the end of Daniel, the prophecy, even though it concerns the Gentiles, is occupied with human history as it relates to Israel."–Dr. John Walvoord

INCREDIBLE IMPACT OF DANIEL'S SECOND VISION

- Daniel was emotionally affected [5]_____by this vision than any of the others. He fainted during the vision, and at the end of the vision.
- After recovery, Daniel went back to [6]_____. 8:27, "And I, Daniel, fainted and was sick for days; afterward I arose and went about the king's business.

    Luke 19:13, "Do business until I come."

    Daniel 8:18, "Now, as he was speaking with me, I was in a deep sleep with my face to the ground; but he touched me, and stood me upright."

APPLICABLE TIME PERIOD OF THE PROPHECY

- [7]_____ distinct periods of fulfillment are referenced in chapter 8:

1. The relatively near future, in the reign of Antiochus Epiphanes, 8th king of the Seleucid dynasty, and his persecution of the Jews in the Maccabean days, 168-165 B.C.

2. The Antichrist, the man of sin, who is to come in the final seven years before the Second Coming of Jesus Christ.

    Daniel 8:17b, "Understand, son of man, that the visions refers to THE TIME OF THE END."

    Daniel 8:19, "And he said, 'Look, I am making known to you what shall happen in the LATTER TIME OF THE INDIGNATION.'"

    Daniel 8:23, "And in the LATTER TIME of their kingdom, when the transgressors have reached their fullness."

    Daniel 8:26b, "For it refers to many days IN THE FUTURE."

- This obviously [8]_____the critics claim that Daniel was written a century or so before Christ because it is simply too accurate to be written in five centuries in advance. The vision was for the future - short and long term!
- Nor does the vision exhaust itself with Antiochus Epiphanes alone. Why? Nearly 200 years after him Jesus said, "Therefore when you see the 'abomination of desolation' spoken of by Daniel the prophet, standing in the holy place (whoever reads, let him understand)" Matthew 24:15. Clearly, this is a future event!

THE RAM - THE PERSIAN EMPIRE (DANIEL 8:2, 3)

    Daniel 8:2, "I saw in the vision, and it so happened while I was looking, that I was in SHUSHAN, the citadel, which is in the province of Elam; and I saw in the vision that I was by the River Ulai. 3) Then I lifted my eyes and saw, and there, standing beside the river was a RAM with two horns, and the two horns were high; but one was higher than the other, and the higher one came up last."

- Shushan (called Susa by the Greeks) was a city about [9]_____miles east of Babylon (where Daniel lived) and 120 miles north of the Persian Gulf. In his vision, Daniel evidently has an out-of-body experience here.

- The RAM represents the dual kingdoms of Medo-[10]_____, indicated by the two horns.
- Clearly, we see in chapter 8 symbolization and [11]_____; there can be no doubt what these symbols mean!

> Daniel 8:20, "The ram which you saw, having the two horns - they are the kings of Media and Persia.

> "The beast of Chapter 7 does not appear except in its final form. The FIRST vision (chap. #2) emphasized Babylon and the Kingdom of Heaven; the SECOND vision (chap. #7) passed over Babylon and Persia and Greece with one verse each, but specialized on the fourth empire - the Roman Empire. The THIRD vision (chap. #8) fills in the details about the Persian and Greek Empires, but, NOTE CAREFULLY, it skips entirely the Roman Empire, except for the little horn. Each symbol is not strained to cover any more than it can do naturally. All the visions culminate with either the establishing of the Kingdom or the destruction of Antichrist (which is actually the same thing). - Dr. Arthur E. Bloomfield

MEDO-PERSIAN EXPANSION

> Daniel 8:4, "I saw the ram pushing westward, northward, and southward, so that no animal could withstand him; nor was there any that could deliver from his hand, but he did according to his will and became great."

> "Beginning in chapter 8, Daniel's second vision concerns the empires of Persia and Greece as they relate to Israel. Under Persian government Israelites went back to rebuild their land and their city, Jerusalem. Under Grecian domination, in particular under Antiochus Epiphanes the city and temple were again desolated." –Dr. John Walvoord

THE GOAT - THE GRECIAN EMPIRE (DANIEL 8:5-8)
- The goat is the Empire of [12]_____; and the notable horn is, unquestionably, [13]_____the Great.

> The 'great horn' symbolizes the first king, namely, Alexander the Great, and the four horns that replace it represent the four kingdoms that follow and replace Alexander's dominion. It was in 334 B.C. that Alexander the Great came 'from the west' (v. 5), nursing a desire to avenge what the Persians had done in Greece some 150 years before. In that year he crossed the Hellespont and defeated the Persian armies under Darius III at the Granicus River. Freeing the Grecian cities of Asia Minor from the Persians, Alexander confronted Darius himself at the Cilician Gates of Syria, winning a second decisive victory at the Battle of Issus near Antioch in 333 B.C. Darius now offered to negotiate, but Alexander swept south to occupy Egypt after taking Tyre and Gaza in prolonged sieges. Retracing his steps through Syria, the conqueror met the Persians and defeated them a third time, even though they amassed much larger and more powerful enemies. This climactic victory took place near the site of old Nineveh ... the year was 331 B.C. when Alexander finally 'cast him (the ram) to the ground and trampled him." -Dr. Donald K. Campbell

- Again, we see symbolization and identification: the goat represents the mighty Grecian Empire.

  Daniel 8:21, "And the male goat is the kingdom of Greece. The large horn that is between its eyes is the first king. 22) As for the broken horn and the four that stood up in its place, four kingdoms shall arise out of that nation, but not with its power."

THE PROPHECY REGARDING THE 'LITTLE HORN'

- This 'little horn' here must not be confused with the 'little horn' of Daniel 7:8, which is the Antichrist, who comes out of the revived [14]_____ kingdom.

- This 'little horn' came out of one of the "four notable ones" which came out from the goat, namely, the [15]_____kingdom (Daniel 8:8, 9).

The Little Horn developed after destroying the Persian ram, the Grecian goat's horn was broken. Out of one of its four divisions arose the powerful "little horn."

  "As noted this horn symbolizes Antiochus Epiphanes, who was the 8th king after Seleucus, the general who received the Syrian division of the empire. Antiochus ascended the throne following the murder of his brother, Seleucus Philopator, the former king. The king's son, Demetrius, was the rightful heir to the throne, but he was held hostage in Rome at the time. As a result, Antiochus Epiphanes, through flattery and bribes was able to seize the throne for himself." –Dr. Leon J. Wood

- The "Glorious Land" is Jerusalem - Antiochus attacked the "host of heaven" meaning the stars (Jer. 33:22), which here represents the people of [16]_____in Palestine (cf. Gen. 15:5; 22:17; Ex. 12:41; Dan. 12:3).

  "The thought is that Antiochus would begin to oppress God's people, the Jews. Then he was seen to cast the stars to ground, meaning that he would kill many of them. History records that he did indeed do this, killing about 100,000 Jews." Dr. Leon J. Wood

HOW ANTIOCHUS EPIPHANES 'TYPES' THE ANTICHRIST

1. The proclamation of himself as God in the Jewish [17]_____, referred to as "the abomination of desolation," which Antiochus did; and Antichrist will do.

  Daniel 8:11, "He even exalted himself as high as the Prince of the host; and by him the daily sacrifices were taken away, and the place of His sanctuary was cast down."

  Daniel 8:25b, "And he shall exalt himself in his heart ... He shall even rise against the Prince of princes ... ."

- [18]_____- Daniel 11:31, "And forces shall be mustered by him, and they shall defile the sanctuary fortress; then they shall take away the daily sacrifices, and place there the ABOMINATION OF DESOLATION." (Antiochus is predicted in detail in Daniel 11:21-45.)

- [19]_____ - Daniel 9:27, "Then he shall confirm a covenant with many for one week; but in the middle of the week he shall bring an end to sacrifice and offering. And on the wing of abominations shall be one who makes desolate, even until the consummation, which is determined, is poured out on the desolate."

    Daniel 12:11, "And from the time that the daily sacrifice is taken away , and the abomination of desolation is set up , there shall be one thousand two hundred and ninety days."

    Matthew 24:15, "Therefore when you see the abomination of desolation spoken of by Daniel the prophet, standing in the holy place (whoever reads, let him understand)."

2. His persecution of the [20]_____.

    Daniel 8:12, "Because of transgression, an army was given over to the horn to OPPOSE the daily sacrifices; and he cast truth down to the ground. He did all this and prospered."

    Daniel 7:25, "He ... shall persecute the saints of the Most High ... Then the saints shall be given into his hand."

3. The cessation of [21]_____.

    Daniel 11:31, "....and they shall take away the daily sacrifice ... ."

    Daniel 9:27, " ... He shall bring an end to sacrifice and offering ... ."

- Antiochus Epiphanes is a picture of what is coming in the [22]_____only magnified much more in evil, bloodshed, and disaster!

GABRIEL'S CLEAR INTERPRETATION

    Daniel 8:15, "Then it happened, when I, Daniel, had seen the vision and was seeking the meaning that suddenly there stood before me one having the appearance of a man. 16) And I heard a man's voice between the banks of the Ulai, who called and said, 'Gabriel, make this man understand the vision.' 17) She came near where I stood, and when he came I was afraid and fell on my face; but he said to me, 'Understand, son of man, that the vision refers to the time of the end.'"

- If we could have only heard this angelic [23]_____. Here is the first introduction to the mighty angel, [24]_____. These angels express a great lesson - there is always a [25]_____, ordained by God, for persecution and judgment (2,300 days).

A FUTURE LOOK AT THE ANTICHRIST: TRAITS OF THE ANTICHRIST

1. "[26]_____ features, understands sinister schemes"(v. 23). - Antichrist, like Antiochus Epiphanes introduces an [27]_____belief system.

2. "his power shall be mighty, but not by his own power" (v. 24). - Antichrist, like Antiochus, will have immense [28]_____power. Rev. 13:3b, "The dragon gave

him his power, his throne, and great authority."

3 "Through his cunning, he shall cause deceit to prosper under his rule" (v. 25).

- Antichrist, like Antiochus, will be a master [29]_____. Revelation 13:8, "All who dwell on the earth will worship him, whose names have not been written in the Book of Life of the Lamb slain from the foundation of the world." 13:16, "He causes all, both small and great, rich and poor, free and slave, to receive a mark on their right hand or on their foreheads, 17) and that no one may buy or sell except one who has the mark or the name of the beast, or the number of his name."

4. God is going to [30]_____the Antichrist, just as did Antiochus Epiphanes. Daniel 8:25b, "But he shall be broken without human means." Revelation 19:19, "And I saw the beast, the kings of the earth, and their armies, gathered together to make war against Him who sat on the horse and against His army. 20) Then the beast was captured ... ."

Think about it .... A truly Scary Thought:

The condition of the world, rendered temporarily chaotic by the rapture, may explain why the United States is NOT found in biblical prophecy. Even though this nation is Christian in name only, America still has a larger percentage of born-again believers in its population than any other important country. When Jesus comes for his own, thousands of responsible leaders in government, industry, education, religion, the arts and the professions will be removed. With these leaders taken to meet the Lord in the air, the STRUCTURE OF GOVERNMENT, industry, education, the arts, and the professions will be WEAKENED that it will reduce the United States to an impotent and prostrated nation. This also explains why Russia, with its atheistic communist leadership, is virtually unaffected by the rapture and can offer a substantial threat to Israel during the tribulation period. Though all countries where Christians are in places of leadership will be affected by the rapture, it will affect no other country like it will affect the United States. Apparently she DOES NOT recover from this loss, for the United States plays no ascertainable role during the tribulation period. Therefore, the political center of the world during the reign of the Antichrist will shift back to that area within the boundaries of the old Roman empire in Europe. The Western Hemisphere will be only an adjunct. The locality where the final act of human history will be played out will be Western and Eastern Europe, along with the Middle East. Again the center of the world political and imperial power will be Western Europe where it was located when God's prophetic time clock stopped in the first century. It is in this political arena that the king of fierce countenance will demonstrate his diplomatic genius and enable the countries there to recover from the shock of the rapture. -Dr. Walter K. Price

Principles of
Leadership, Success,
and Achievement

Discovering Prayer Which Causes God to Act
Message #13 in the Daniel series
Bible Text: Daniel 9:1-23

- As chapter 9 opens we see Daniel not just as a prophet, but also as a student of
  [1]_____! Daniel, for 70 years, now nearly 90, daily and faithfully read
  and studied the [2]_____ of God.

  Daniel 9:1-2, "In the first year of Darius the son of Ahasuerus, of the lineage of
  the Medes, who was made king over the realm of the Chaldeans - 2) in the first
  year of his reign I, Daniel, UNDERSTOOD BY THE BOOKS the NUMBER
  of the YEARS specified by the word of the Lord through Jeremiah the prophet,
  that He would accomplish SEVENTY years in the desolations of Jerusalem."

  "And so we see, in the opening verses, this devoted man, in the first year of the
  reign of Darius, bending over the prophetic word in the Holy Scriptures. He
  did not have anything like as complete a Bible as we have; but he valued what
  he had, and searched diligently. In fact the last book that had been added to
  the Bible was that of Ezekiel. We do not know for certain that this ever came
  into his hands, but we do know from this passage that he had, at any rate, the
  book of Jeremiah. As he studied it carefully, he noticed that twice in that book
  it was written that God would accomplish seventy years in the desolations of
  Jerusalem." - Dr. H. A. Ironside

- Daniel read and re-read Jeremiah 25: 11, 12 and 29:10. From Jeremiah's
  [3]_____ as a youth in the Temple in Jerusalem he was no doubt aware
  of 2 Chronicles 36:21 based on Leviticus 25:4, 5 & 26:34-43.

  Jeremiah 25:11, "And this whole land shall be a desolation and an astonishment,
  and these nations shall serve the king of Babylon SEVENTY years. 12) 'Then it
  will come to pass, when SEVENTY years are completed, that I will punish the
  king of Babylon and that nation, the land of the Chaldeans, for their iniquity,'
  says the Lord; 'and I will make it a perpetual desolation.'"

  Jeremiah 29:10, "For thus says the Lord: After seventy years are completed at
  Babylon, I will visit you and perform My good word toward you, and cause
  you to return to this place."

  Leviticus 26:34, "Then the land shall enjoy its Sabbaths as long as it lies
  desolate and you are in your enemies' land; then the land shall rest and enjoy
  it Sabbaths. 35) As long as it lies desolate it shall rest - for the time it did not
  rest on your Sabbaths when you dwelt in it."

- The Word of God gave Daniel [4]_____and prompted him to [5]_____!

Daniel 9:3, "Then I set my face toward the Lord God to make request by prayer and supplications, with fasting, sackcloth, and ashes."

"Daniel had been but a youth when he was taken captive by Nebuchadnezzar. Sixty-nine long years had passed during his exile from Palestine. How often during those years he must have pondered upon God's prophecy through Jeremiah - first that he would send His people into captivity if they did not turn from their idols; then His promise to restore them to their native land after seventy years of discipline." – Famous Prophecy Teacher Dr. Louis Talbot

"Here we are given our first glimpse of Daniel poring over what he calls the books (vv. 1, 2). We have seen that three times a day he opened his window toward Jerusalem, but there is not the slightest doubt that just as frequently he opened these books - the scrolls that the exiles had been careful to bring with them from their homeland, and to copy out for each other's use." – Scholar Dr. Ronald S. Wallace

ELEMENTS OF GOD-MOVING, GOD-ANSWERING PRAYER
1. Daniel had a specific [6]_____ in prayer - he wanted [7]_____! "I set my face toward ... God to make REQUEST by prayer and supplications" (9:3; see 17, 18, 20, 23).
   - Supplications - telling God your [8]_____ - four times he mentions his "supplications."
2. Daniel admitted and [9]_____ his sin to God. (Hebrew word is *hatta* - means going the [10]_____ way, a headlong trek away from God.)

   Daniel 9:4, "And I prayed to the Lord my God, and made confession, and said, 'O Lord, great and awesome God, who keeps His covenant and mercy with those who love Him, and with those who keep His commandments, 5) we have sinned and committed iniquity, we have done wickedly and rebelled, even by departing from Your precepts and Your judgments. 6) Neither have we heeded Your servants and the prophets, who spoke in Your name to our kings and our princes, to our fathers and all the people of the land. 7) O Lord, righteousness belongs to You, but to us shame of face, as it is this day - to the men of Judah, to the inhabitants of Jerusalem and all Israel, those near and those far off in all the countries to which You have driven them, because of the unfaithfulness which they have committed against You. 8) O Lord, to us belongs shame of face, to our kings, our princes, and our fathers, because we have sinned against You."

   - Verse 5, "we have done wickedly" - (Hebrew awon) implies [11]_____, a lifestyle not pleasing to God. "Departing" - (sur) the word for [12]_____.
   - The word "we" appears [13]_____ times in Daniel's prayer - reminding us that our sin always affects other people. The word "us" appears nine times in the prayer.

     I John 1:9, "If we confess our sins, He is faithful and just to forgive us our sins and to cleanse us from all unrighteousness."

   - "confess" - (Greek homologeo) it means to "say the [14]_____ thing" call your-sin what it is .... Sin!
3. Daniel's indicates he knows God's Word and therefore the [15]_____.

Daniel 9:9, "To the Lord our God belong mercy and forgiveness, though WE have rebelled against Him. 10) WE have not obeyed the voice of the Lord our God, to walk in His laws, and has departed so as not to obey You voice; therefore the curse and the oath written in the Law of Moses the servant of God have been poured out on us, because WE have sinned against Him. 12) And He has confirmed His words, which He spoke against us and against our judges who judged us, by bringing upon us a great disaster; for under the whole heaven such has never been done as what has been done to Jerusalem. 13) As it is WRITTEN in the law of Moses, all this disaster has come upon us; yet we have not made our prayer before the Lord our God, that we might turn from our iniquities and understand Your truth. 14) Therefore the Lord has kept disaster in mind, and brought it upon us; for the Lord our God is righteous in all the works which He does, though we have not obeyed His voice. 15) And now, O Lord our God, who brought Your people out of the land of Egypt with a mighty hand, and made Yourself a name, as it is this day - we have sinned, we have done wickedly! 16) O Lord, according to all Your righteousness, I pray, let Your anger and Your fury be turned away from Your city Jerusalem, Your holy mountain; because for our sins; and for the iniquities of our fathers, Jerusalem and Your people are a reproach to all those around us."

4. Daniel asks and believes in the [16]_____ of God.

> Daniel 9:17, "Now therefore, our God, hear the prayer of Your servant, and his supplications, and for the Lord's sake cause Your face to shine on Your sanctuary which is desolate. 18) O my God, incline Your ear and hear; open Your eyes and see our desolations, and the city which is called by Your name; for we do not present our supplications before You because of our righteous deeds, but because of Your great mercies. 19) O Lord, hear! O Lord, forgive! O Lord, listen and act! Do not delay, for Your own sake, my God, for Your city and Your people are called by Your name."

- In 15-19, Daniel addresses God as Adonai and Elohim and no longer uses the term [17]_____ as he did in 4-14. Daniel surrenders in prayer to God who is [18]_____ of everything!
- Daniel implores God to hear, forgive, listen, [19]_____!

"More things are wrought by prayer than this world dreams of."– Tennyson

5. Daniel has a [20]_____ view of God - He asked big things from God! Daniel 9:4, "And I prayed to the Lord my God, and made confession, and said, 'O Lord, GREAT and AWESOME God."

6. Daniel's prayer is [21]_____ and authenticated by the mighty angel Gabriel.

> Daniel 9:20, "Now while I was speaking, praying, and confessing my sin and the sin of my people Israel, and presenting my supplication before the Lord my God for the holy mountain of my God, 21) yes, while I

was speaking in prayer, the man Gabriel whom I had seen in the vision at the beginning, being caused to fly swiftly, reached me about the time of the evening offering. 22) And he informed me, and talked with me, and said, 'O Daniel, I have now come forth to give you skill to understand. 23) At the beginning of your supplications the command went out, and I have come to tell you, for you are greatly beloved; therefore consider the matter, and understand the vision."

- Each one of us as believers is greatly "beloved" by God - he wants to answer our prayers!

Its worth noting...

"The immediate occasion of this chapter, however, was the discovery by Daniel in the prophecy of Jeremiah that the desolations of Jerusalem would be fulfilled in seventy years. The expression by books may be understood to mean "in books." Jeremiah the prophet, in addition to his oral prophetic announcements, had written his prophecies in the closing days of Jerusalem before its destruction at the hand of the Babylonians. Although the first record of Jeremiah had been destroyed (Jer. 36:23), Jeremiah rewrote it, acting on instructions from the Lord (Jer. 36:28). Jeremiah himself had been taken captive by Jews rebelling against Nebuchadnezzar and had been carried off to Egypt against his will to be buried in a strange land in a nameless grave, but the timeless Scriptures which he wrote found their way across the desert and mountain to far away Babylon and fell into the hands of Daniel." -The late Dr. John Walvoord

ANSWERS

1. prophecy 2. Word 3. teaching 4. insight 5. pray 6. purpose 7. answers 8. needs 9. confessed 10. wrong 11. perversion 12. apostasy 13. 13 14. same 15. consequences 16. forgiveness 17. Jehovah 18. Lord 19. act 20. high 21. answered

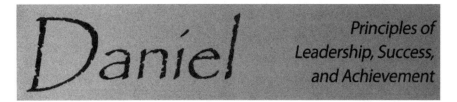

Understanding Daniel's 70 Weeks:
The Old Testament's Greatest Prophesy
Message #14 in the Daniel series
Bible Text: Daniel 9:24,25

Deuteronomy 29:29, "The secret things belong to the Lord our God, but those things which are revealed belong to us and to our children forever, that we may do all the words of this law."

THE VISION OF THE SEVENTY-WEEKS – IN ANSWER TO PRAYER

Daniel 9:23, "At the beginning of your supplication the COMMAND went out, and I have come to tell you, for you are greatly beloved; therefore consider the matter, and UNDERSTAND THE VISION."

- The Old Testament's Greatest Prophecy was received by Daniel in answer to his fervent [1]_____ of 9:3-23.

THE FIRST PART OF THE SEVENTY-WEEKS PROPHECY – MESSIAH

Daniel 9:24, "Seventy weeks are determined for your people and for your holy city, to finish the transgression, to make an end of sins, to make reconciliation for iniquity, to bring in everlasting righteousness, to seal up the vision and prophecy, and to anoint the Most Holy. 25) Know therefore and understand, that from the going forth of the command to restore and build Jerusalem until Messiah the Prince, there shall be seven weeks and sixty-two weeks; the street shall be built again, and the wall, even in troublesome times. 26) And after the sixty-two weeks Messiah shall be cut off, but not for Himself; and the people of the prince who is to come shall destroy the city and the sanctuary. The end of it shall be with a flood, and till the end of the war desolations are determined."

ESSENTIAL CLUES TO UNDERSTAND THE SEVENTY WEEKS

1. WORD MEANING: The Definition of the [2]_____Weeks: It does not mean weeks of seven [3]_____. The word "week" is used because we have no word in the English language that is the exact equivalent of the Hebrew word which signifies seven, and translators of the KJV used "weeks" instead of "sevens." The Hebrew word means simply "[4]_____." The thought could be "sevens" of days or "sevens" of years. The context indicates, indisputably, that it is "[5]_____ sevens = [6]_____ years!

> "In fact, the Israelites were quite familiar with the idea of sevens of years as well as sevens of days. Their sabbatical year was built on this basis (one year in seven having to be set aside for resting the land, Lev. 25; Dt. 15). Furthermore, the seventy-year period of captivity was based on the idea that seventy of these

sabbatical years had not been kept (see 2 Chron. 36:21; cf. Lev. 26:33-35; Jer. 34:12-22). Knowing this, Daniel would have recognized that the seventy years of captivity represented seventy sevens of years in which these violations had occurred; he would have understood Gabriel to be saying simply that another period, similar in length to that which made the captivity necessary, was coming in the future experience of the people." - Dr. Leon J. Wood

"How long is seventy weeks of years? Seventy times seven equals four hundred and ninety years. The prophecy is talking about 490 years that are determined or "cut out" of the calendar. Throughout the whole Book of Daniel we have been talking about how God is going to work through the Gentile rulers. But God has "cut out" 490 years that belong to the Jews. He shows how His program will work in that period of time." - Dr. David Jeremiah

"The scope of the prophecy covers not 70 years, as Daniel may have hoped, but 70 sevens of years. When Gabriel stated that seventy weeks were decreed concerning Jerusalem and the Jews, he meant that that would be the length of time in which God would fulfill all of His purposes regarding the nation Israel. The word "week" is literally "sevens" or hepstads. And, since ancient times, it has been generally agreed that the "weeks" or "sevens" were not weeks of days, but weeks of years. The angel is thus saying to Daniel that 70 weeks of years, or a period of 490 years, is required to fulfill Israel's prophetic program." - Dr. Donald K. Campbell

"Daniel divided the seventy sevens into three groups, seven sevens, sixty-two sevens, and a final seven. The first seven sevens (49 years) commence with a command to rebuild Jerusalem (either the decree to Ezra in 458 B.C. or the decree to Nehemiah in 445 B.C.) and terminate with the completion of the work of Ezra and Nehemiah about 49 years later (either 409 B.C. or 396 B.C.). The next 62 sevens (434 years) extend from the end of the first group of sevens to Christ's first coming (either his baptism in A.D. 26 or Christ's presentation of himself to the people as Messiah on Palm Sunday in A.D. 32/33." - Dr. Stephen R. Miller

2. FOCUS: The Seventy Weeks Prophecy concerns the [7]_____people and their city, Jerusalem. In fact, [8]_____specific things will be accomplished:
   - "to finish the [9]_____"(v.24) - to restrain sin and the Jews in its long trend of [10]_____.
   - "to make an end of [11]_____" (v.24) - the national sins of Israel will come to an end at the [12]_____ coming of Christ.
   - "to make reconciliation for [13]_____" (v.24) - this signifies to furnish the actual basis of covering sin by full atonement, the blood of the crucified [14]_____ _____ who is "cut-off" (v.26).
   - "to bring in everlasting righteousness" (v.24) - refers to the [15]_____ of Christ at the end of the 490 years to establish the kingdom.
   - "to seal up [16]_____and prophecy" (v.24) - no more Scripture will be needed when it all has been [17]_____!
   - "And to anoint the Most [18]_____" (v. 24) - a splendid reference to the anointing of the holy of holies in the [19]_____ temple regarding Ezekiel's proph-

ecy (see Ezek. 41-46).

3. WHEN IT BEGAN: The Seventy Weeks (490 years) began when the [20]_____ is issued, Daniel 9:25, "Know therefore and understand, that FROM THE GOING FORTH OF THE COMMAND TO RESTORE AND BUILD JERUSALEM..." Although several decrees were issued relative to the Jewish restoration, only ONE seems to deal directly with the rebuilding of Jerusalem and the Temple. Reputable scholars (Walvoord, Sir Robert Anderson, Whitcomb, Hoehner) identify the [21]_____ decree of Artaxerxes I to Nehemiah (445 B.C.) which specifically mentions the rebuilding of the Jewish Temple in Jerusalem. This was almost 100 years after Daniel received this climactic vision in 538 B.C.!

4. DIVISION OF THE SEVENTY WEEKS: Gabriel explained that the Seventy Weeks of prophetic history of the Jews are divided into [22]_____ sections or periods: (1) seven weeks of years (49 years) when the city of Jerusalem would be rebuilt. Daniel 9:25, "Know therefore and understand, that from the going forth of the command to restore and rebuild Jerusalem until Messiah the Prince THERE SHALL BE SEVEN WEEKS and SIXTY-TWO WEEKS; the street shall be built again, and the wall, even in troublesome times." (2) The [23]_____ period (62 weeks) of 434 years moves on to "Messiah the Prince." This prophecy specifically [24]_____ the Messiah's entry in Jerusalem on a colt announcing his deity! That occurred exactly 483 years after the decree was given by Artaxerxes! (3) The final 7 years or [25]_____ Week will be after the Messiah has been crucified, the city of Jerusalem destroyed, and there is a notable [26]_____. Daniel 9:26, "AND AFTER THE SIXTY-TWO WEEKS MESSIAH SHALL BE CUT OFF, but not for Himself; and the people of the prince who is to come shall destroy the city and the sanctuary ... ."

Artaxerxes Signed the Decree
Artaxerxes, king of Persia, granted to Nehemiah and his people permission to return and rebuild Jerusalem.

5. THE SPECIFIC TIMETABLE: The prophetic clock [27]_____ as indicated by Nehemiah 2:1, "And it came to pass in the month of Nisan, in the twentieth year of King Artaxerxes." Verse 5, "And I said to the king, 'If it pleases the king, and if your servant has found favor in your sight, I ask that you send me to Judah, to the city of my fathers' tombs, that I may REBUILD IT.' 6) Then the king said to me (the queen also sitting beside him), 'How long will your journey be? And when will you return?' So it pleased the king to send me; and I set him a time. 7) Further-

more I said to the king, 'If it pleases the king, let letters be given to me for the governors of the region beyond the River, that they must permit me to pass through till I come to Judah, 8) and a letter to Asaph the keeper of the king's forest, that he must give me timber to make beams for the gates of the citadel which pertains to the temple, for the city wall, and for the house that I will occupy.' And the king GRANTED THEM TO ME according to the good hand of my God upon me."

"Daniel's prophecy tells us that there will be a period of sixty-nine weeks that will begin on a particular day and end on a particular day. Then there will be a gap in time, and finally there will be the Seventieth Week. We understand that the sixty-nine weeks in Daniel refer to groups of years and that a "week" refers to a group of seven years, so the total is 483 years (sixty-nine times seven). Fortunately, we can document the reign of Artaxerxes, so we are able to provide dates to Daniel's prophecy. Artaxerxes began to reign in 465 B.C. Nehemiah tells us that the command to rebuild the walls came in the twentieth year of Artaxerxes' reign - 445 B.C. Nehemiah further tells us that the commandment was made on the first day of Artaxerxes Signed the Decree. Artaxerxes, king of Persia, granted to Nehemiah and his people permission to return and rebuild Jerusalem. Nisan, which on our calendars would be March 14. Now, if you begin counting on March 14, 445 B.C., and add the exact number of days Daniel refers to, keeping in mind leap years and the fact that they counted 360 days to the year, you would stop counting on April 6, in the year 32 A.D. According to most scholars, including Sir Robert Anderson's chronology, it was on that day that Jesus Christ rode in the city (Jerusalem) for His Triumphal Entry. – Dr. David Jeremiah

"The Julian date of 1st Nisan 445 was the 14th March. Sixty-nine weeks of years — i.e., 173,880 days — reckoned from the 14th March B.C. 445, ended on the 6th April A.D. 32. That day, on which the sixty-nine weeks ended, was the fateful day on which the Lord Jesus rode into Jerusalem in fulfillment of the prophecy of Zechariah 9:9; when, for the first and only occasion in all His earthly sojourn, He was acclaimed as "Messiah the Prince, the King, the Son of David." And here again we must keep to Scripture ... no date in history, sacred or profane, is fixed with greater definiteness than that of the year in which the Lord began His public ministry ... we can fix the date of the Passion with absolute certainty as Nisan A.D. 32 ... we can appeal to the labours of secular historians and chronologists for proofs of the divine accuracy of Holy Scripture." – Sir Robert Anderson

"The first seven weeks of forty-nine years brings us to 397 B.C. and to Malachi and the end of the Old Testament. These were 'troublous times,' as witnessed by both Nehemiah and Malachi. Sixty-two weeks, or 434 years, brings us to the Messiah. Sir Robert Anderson in his book, The Coming Prince, has worked out the time schedule. From the first month of Nisan to the tenth of Nisan (April 6) A.D. 32 are 173,880 days. Dividing them according to the Jewish year of 360 days, he arrives at 483 years (69 sevens). On this day Jesus rode into Jerusalem, offering Himself for the first time, publicly and officially, as the Messiah. After the 69 weeks, or 483 years, there is a time break. Between the sixty-ninth and Seventieth Week two events of utmost importance are to take place: 1. Messiah will be cut off. This is the crucifixion of Christ ... 2. Destruction of Jerusalem, which took place in A.D. 70, when Titus the Roman was the instrument. The final "week" (the seventieth), a period of seven years, is projected into the future and does not follow chronologically the other sixty-nine. The time gap between the sixty-ninth and seventieth weeks is the age of grace - unknown to the prophets (Eph. 3:1-12; I Peter 1:10-12). The Seventieth Week us eschatological; it is the final period and is YET UNFULFILLED." – Dr. J. Vernon McGee

"It was forty-nine years between the time when the rebuilding of the walls of Jerusalem was started and the completion of the work. The city was built again "in troublous times." Read the wonderful story of Ezra and Nehemiah to see how the enemy opposed the faithful Jewish remnant at every turn - by ridicule, by craft, and by open opposition. But God was with His people; the temple worship was restored; the walls were finished; and God's prophecy was fulfilled. From the close of this period of seven sevens, i.e., 49 years, "unto Messiah the Prince," another sixty-two sevens of years were to be reckoned. Adding these first two periods, we have sixty-nine sevens, or 483 years, at the close of which time the Messiah was to be "cut of, but not for Himself." That really happened; for Christ was crucified exactly at that time. Able chronologists, such as Sir Robert Anderson, have shown that the crucifixion of the Lord Jesus Christ occurred immediately after the expiration of 483 prophetic years of 360 days each from the time designated in Daniel 9:25, 26. - Scholar Dr. Louis Talbot

WHY DOES IT MATTER?
- It reminds me that the God, who is in control of the world, can handle all my [28]_____ and difficulties.
- Prophecy is a [29]_____ plan designed by God that nothing can change or interrupt.
- Following Daniel's example (9:1, 2), I should study prophecy in Scripture so I will be aware of God's end-time work in the world.
- The Antichrist is not a metaphor; he is a real person coming to this earth. Already the spirit of Antichrist has begun. Consequently, every Christian must be [30]_____ regarding the times in which we live!

  "You will have no difficulty in understanding the great interval between the sixty-ninth and seventieth "weeks" if you will always bear in mind the fact that God never reckons time with the Jews when He is not dealing with them as a nation. When He ceases to deal with them as a nation, then the Jewish clock stops. This happened when Christ was "cut-off," crucified; the Jewish clock stopped, and has not yet begun to tick again." – Dr. Louis Talbot

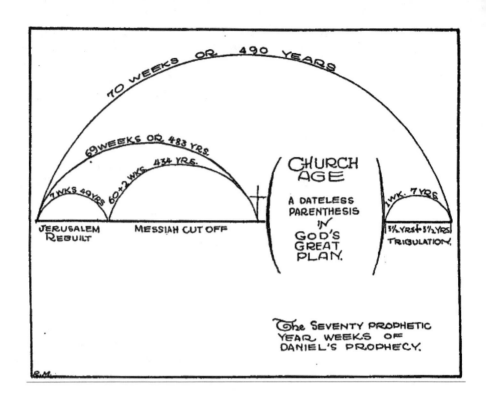

The Seventy Weeks

Daniel 9:24–"Seventy weeks [or 'sevens'] are determined upon Daniel's people and ... holy city" [70x7 equals 490 years].

9:25–"Seven weeks" [7x7 equals 49 years] "from the going forth of the commandment to restore and to build Jerusalem ..."

9:26–"And after threescore and two weeks" [62x7 equals 434 years] "shall Messiah be cut off ..."

Christ was "cut off" [i.e., crucified] at the end of the 69th "week." Between the 69th and 70th "weeks" this church age intervenes–a long parenthesis not seen by Daniel.

9:27–The Antichrist will "confirm the covenant" for one "week" [7 years]. "In the midst of the week, he shall cause the sacrifice and the oblation to cease" [i.e., after 3½ years]. Then the "great tribulation" will follow.

Watching the Antichrist in the 70th Week
Message #15 in the Daniel series
Bible Text: Daniel 9:26, 27; 11:36-45

Daniel 9:27, "Then he shall confirm a covenant with many for one week; but in the middle of the week he shall bring an end to sacrifice and offering. And on the wing of abominations shall be one who makes desolate, even until the consummation, which is determined, is poured out on the desolate."

I. WHEN WILL THE ANTICHRIST BE REVEALED?
A. After [1]_____ shall be cut off (crucified, v. 26).
B. After the "dispensation" of the grace of God for the [2]_____ is complete.

> Ephesians 3:1-6, "For this reason I, Paul, the prisoner of Christ Jesus for you Gentiles - if indeed you have heard of the dispensation of the grace of God which was given to me for you, which in other ages was not made known to the sons of men, as it has now been revealed by the Spirit to His holy apostles and prophets: that the Gentiles should be fellow heirs, of the same body, and partakers of His promise in Christ through the gospel."

C. This explains the [3]_____ between the 69th and 70th Weeks in Daniel prophecy.
D. Massive expression of [4]_____ Christianity (apostasy).

> 2 Thes. 2:3, "Let no one deceive you by any means; for that Day will not come unless the falling away comes first and THE MAN OF SIN is revealed, the son of perdition. 4) who opposes and exalts himself above all that is called God or that is worshiped, so that he SITS AS GOD IN THE TEMPLE OF GOD, SHOWING HIMSELF THAT HE IS GOD."

E. The total removal of Christians at the [5]_____.

> 2 Thessalonians 2:7, "For the mystery of lawlessness is already at work; only He who now restrains will do so until He is taken OUT OF THE WAY. 8) And then the LAWLESS ONE WILL BE REVEALED, whom the Lord will consume with the breath of His mouth and destroy with the brightness of His coming. 9) The coming of the LAWLESS ONE is according to the working of Satan, with all power, signs, and lying wonders, 10) and with all unrighteous deception among those who perish, because they did not receive the love of the truth, that they might be saved."

II. WHAT WILL THE ANTICHRIST DO IN THE 70TH WEEK?
A. He will confirm a "[6]_____" covenant with the Jews and their surrounding neighbors in the final week (7 years).
B. Daniel divides the final week (7 years) in two halves, 3 ½ years each! "in the middle

of the week" (3½ years) the Antichrist will [7]_____the covenant with the Jews. V. 27, "He shall bring an end to SACRIFICE and OFFERING. And on the wing of abominations shall be one who makes desolate, even until the consummation which is determined, is poured out on the desolate."

- This will occur at the [8]_____ point (3½) of the 70 Week of years, i.e., 7 years leading to the Second Coming of Christ.
- Obviously, the Jewish Temple will have been [9]_____ - or the Antichrist could not stop the sacrifices and offerings.
- The Antichrist will cause ABOMINATION against the Jewish religion - this act will desolate or [10]_____ what Jews regard as sacred, the Temple, and the Holy of Holies.
- By announcing his own [11]_____ in the newly rebuilt Jewish Temple at the 3½ year mark, Antichrist will begin the final 3½ years known as the GREAT TRIBU-LATION - a time of unequalled sorrow and death!

> Matthew 24:15, "Therefore when you see the 'abomination of desolation,' spoken of by Daniel the prophet, standing in the holy place (whoever reads, let him understand)."

- The verse refers to Antiochus Epiphanes' blasphemy in the Temple in 168 B.C. (made an altar to Zeus and sacrificed pigs on it), Titus' invasion of Jerusalem in A.D. 70, but, ultimately refers the Antichrist setting us his image in the Temple during the Tribulation.

> Matthew 24:21, "For then there will be great tribulation, such as has not been since the beginning of the world until this time, no, nor, ever shall be."

> Daniel 12:1b, "And there shall be a time of trouble, such as never was since there was a nation."

> Rev. 13:7, "It was granted to him to make war with the saints and to overcome them. And authority was given him over every tribe, tongue, and nation. 8) And all who dwell on the earth will worship him, whose names have not been written in the Book of Life of the Lamb slain from the foundation of the world."

> Jeremiah 30:7, "Alas! For that day is great, so that NONE IS LIKE IT; and it is the time of Jacob's trouble, but he shall be saved out of it."

> "The more I study prophecy, the more it seems to me that this last dictator may be a Gentile. Certainly he will be the last of the Caesars, whether Jew or Gentile. Now we know that his henchman, "the false prophet," of Revelation 13.11 10, 19.20, 20.10, must of necessity be a Jew. He will come imitating Jesus "the Lamb of God"; for John saw that he had "two horns like a lamb" (Rev. 13:11); yet "he spoke as a dragon." The Jews would hardly accept as their Messiah - though he will be false - one is not a Jew. This representative of "the beast" in Palestine will, therefore, in all probability be an apostate Israelite. He will receive his power from Satan, and be subject to the world dictator."
> –Famous Prophecy Scholar Dr. Louis Talbot

III. HOW SAVAGE WILL THE ANTICHRIST'S RULE BE?

Daniel 11:35 transitions to the Antichrist with the phrase, "until the TIME OF THE END... ."

- JEROME, LUTHER, and a host of other Bible scholars identify the central character in the remaining section of Daniel 11, vv. 36-45 as the ANTICHRIST!

Daniel 11:36, "Then the king shall do according to his OWN will; he shall exalt and magnify himself above every god, shall speak blasphemies against the God of gods, and shall proper till the wrath has been accomplished; for what has been determined shall be done."

A. The Antichrist, in the newly rebuilt Jewish Temple, will exalt himself as
   [12]_____ , and above God!

Daniel 11:37, "He shall regard neither the God of his fathers nor the DESIRE OF WOMEN, nor regard any god; for he shall EXALT HIMSELF above them all."

B. Seems to suggest, the Antichrist will be a [13]_____. If not, he is certainly celibate.

C. The word for "God" is "Elohim," a word that is plural, in this context probably refers to "[14]_____."

"In times past I have held that Daniel 11:37 teaches that the Antichrist himself will be a Jew; upon further study, it seems to me that he may not be, and that we cannot be dogmatic upon this point - though, to repeat for emphasis, the false prophet doubtless will be a Jew." –Dr. Louis Talbot

Daniel 11:38, "But in their place (DESIRE FOR WOMEN) he shall honor a god of fortresses; and a god which his fathers did not know he shall honor with gold and silver, with precious stones and pleasant things."

D. The Antichrist sole confidence is in his [15]_____ might! The finest, most advanced technological military equipment for destruction.

Daniel 11:39, "Thus he shall act against the strongest fortresses with a foreign god, which he shall acknowledge, and advance its glory; and he shall cause them to rule over many, and divide the land for gain."

E. This "foreign god" (v. 39) who assists the Antichrist is none other than
   [16]_____. NOTE: To Israel's great regret, their land will be sold-off - Antichrist, v. 39, will "divide the land for gain."

IV. THE BATTLE OF ARMAGEDDON AND THE ANTICHRIST

Daniel 11:40, "At the time of the end the king of the South shall attack him; and the king of the North shall come against him like a whirlwind, chariots, horsemen, and with many ships; and he shall enter the countries, overwhelm them, and pass through. 41) He shall also enter the Glorious Land, and many countries shall be overthrown; but these shall escape from his hand: Edom, Moab, and the prominent people of Ammon. 42) He shall stretch out his hand against the countries, and the land of Egypt shall not escape. 43) He shall have power over the treasures of gold and silver, and over all the precious things of Egypt; and the Libyans and Ethiopians shall follow at his heels. 44) But news

333

from the east and the north shall trouble him; therefore he shall go out with great fury to destroy and annihilate many. 45) And he shall plant the tents of his palace between the seas and the glorious holy mountain; yet he shall come to HIS END, and NO ONE WILL HELP HIM."

A. The timetable is clearly stipulated in v. 40, "at the time of the [17]_____." This is the final battle ... a war of all wars!

B. The king of the South could be a combined [18]_____ army representing Egypt, Africa, and beyond.

C. "The King of the North" - we feel confident is [19]_____, perhaps assisted by other nations.

D. "News from the east" - may be an invading huge army of [20]_____ (see Revelation 9:13-21; and 16:12). Rev. 9:16 stipulates an army of 200 million - only China can meet this qualification!

> "What we need to do is go into all the world, preaching the gospel to every creature, winning men and women to the Lord Jesus Christ before the "reign of terror" of the Antichrist comes upon the world." – Dr. Louis Talbot

ANSWERS

1. Messiah 2. Gentiles 3. gap 4. false 5. rapture 6. peace 7. break 8. halfway 9. rebuilt 10. ruin 11. deity 12. God 13. homosexual 14. gods 15. military 16. Satan 17. end 18. Islamic 19. Russia 20. China

334

Prayer & Demonic Warfare: Discerning the Work of Good and Bad Angels In Our Lives

Message #16 in the Daniel series
Bible Text: Daniel 10:1-21

"These last three chapters should be treated as one vision. The version relates to the nation Israel in the immediate future and also the latter days. For example, there is the historical "little horn" and also the 'little horn' of the latter days." – Dr. J. Vernon McGee

I. WHEN WAS IT?

Daniel 10:1, "In the third year of Cyrus king of Persia a message was revealed to Daniel, whose name was called Belteshazzar. The message was true, but the appointed time was long; and he understood the message, and had understanding of the vision."

A. The final vision, which includes chapters 10-12 was given to Daniel in the third year of the reign of Cyrus. Daniel was well over [1]_____ years of age.

B. What troubled Daniel? King Cyrus had given the Jewish people permission to leave–yet only [2]_____ in number did–only 42,360 Jews.

Ezra 2:64, "The whole assembly was forty-two thousand three hundred and sixty, 65) besides their male and female servants, of whom there were seven thousand three hundred and thirty-seven; and they had two hundred men and women singers. 66) Their horses were seven hundred and thirty-six, their mules two hundred and fortyfive, 67) their camels four hundred and thirty-five, and their donkeys six thousand seven hundred and twenty."

• In Ezra 4:1-6 we learn that the adversaries of God hindered the work severely. Daniel was not doubt aware of all this!

C. Retired ... Daniel spent considerable time in [3]_____! He mourned that the Jewish people preferred the luxury and ease of Babylon to the hardships of Jerusalem.

Daniel 10:2, "In those days I, Daniel, was mourning three full weeks. 3) I ate no pleasant food, no meat or wine came into my mouth, nor did I anoint myself at all, till three whole weeks were fulfilled."

"It is interesting to observe the time of year when Daniel had this season of prayer. He records that it was "in the four and twentieth day of the first month." The Passover came on the fourteenth day of the first month, and the following day began the Feast of the Unleavened Bread, continuing seven days. Therefore Daniel's 21 days of prayer and fasting included the days of the Passover, the celebration of the deliverance from Egypt." - Dr. Oliver B. Green

II. WHO WAS IT? A THEOPHANY?

Daniel 10:4, "Now on the twenty-fourth day of the first month, as I was by the side of the great river, that it, the Tigris, 5) I lifted my eyes and looked, and behold, a certain man clothed in linen, whose waist was girded with gold of Uphaz! 6) His body was like beryl, his face like the appearance of lightning, his eyes like torches of fire, his arms and feet like burnished bronze in color, and the sound of his words like the voice of a multitude. 7) And I, Daniel, alone saw the vision, for the men who were with me did not see the vision; but a great terror fell upon them, so that they fled to hide themselves. 8) Therefore I was left alone when I saw the great vision, and no strength remained in me; for my vigor was turned to frailty in me, and I retained no strength. 9) Yet I heard the sound of his words; and while I heard the sound of his words I was in a deep sleep on my face, with my face, with my face to the ground. 10) Suddenly, a hand touched me, which made me tremble on my knees and on the palms of my hands. 11) And he said to me, 'O Daniel, man greatly beloved, understand the words that I speak to you, and stand upright, for I have now been sent to you.' While he was speaking this word to me I stood trembling."

A. Who was this? Many say a preincarnate appearance of [4]_____. Others object because of v. 13, and say it was the angel [5]_____ or Gabriel (who had appeared to Daniel after his prayer in chapter 9). Or, perhaps better, both of them together!

From this we see that the Lord of Glory was not alone in this Vision. He was accompanied by a "Heavenly Messenger," who was no other than the Angel Gabriel. - Dr. Clarence Larkin

B. Again, we see the heavenly being extolling Daniel's spiritual [6]_____.

III. WHY THE DEMONIC INTERFERENCE?

Daniel 10:12, "Then he said to me, 'Do not fear, Daniel, for from the first DAY YOU SET YOUR HEART TO UNDERSTAND, and to humble yourself before your God, your words were heard; and I have come because of your words. 13) But the prince of PERSIA withstood me twenty-one days; and behold, Michael, one of the chief princes, came to help me, for I had been left alone there with the kings of Persia. 14) Now I have come to MAKE YOU UNDERSTAND what will happen to your people in the latter days, for the vision refers to MANY DAYS YET TO COME."

A. The "prince of Persia" is a strong [7]_____ who was detaining the archangel trying to [8]_____ God's purpose.

"From this we see that Satan has his Kingdom organized in a wonderful manner. It is divided into Kingdoms and Principalities. These divisions correspond with the Kingdom divisions of our earth. If Satan has a "Prince of Persia" and a "Prince of Grecia," why not a Prince for every nation? Satan has his limitations. He is not omnipresent, neither is he omnipotent or omniscient.

He has TO DEPEND UPON HIS AGENTS. And so great and powerful are his "Princes" that it takes a supernatural being, like Michael the Archangel to overcome them." - Dr. Clarence Larkin

B. What is true of nations is true of [9]_____. Satan dispatches his agents (demons) to harass the saints.

"The extent of the forces he assigns to any particular individual depends to no little degree on the amount of damage that the person is causing to his kingdom. This explains why some men who have been greatly used of God have had their usefulness cut short. Satan, enraged by the success of their ministry, sent special forces to thwart the work they were doing. Alas! Too often the devil has been successful, simply because the minister absorbed in his work fails to be consistent in his prayer life, and thus to build sufficient bulwarks against the attacks of the enemy." - Dr. Gordon Lindsay

IV. WHAT ENCOMPASSES THE MINISTRY OF ANGELS TO US?

Daniel 7:15, "When he had spoken such words to me, I turned my face toward the ground and became speechless. 16) And suddenly, one having the likeness of the sons of men touched my lips; then I opened my mouth and spoke, saying to him who stood before me, 'My lord, because of the visions my sorrows have overwhelmed me, and I have retained no strength. 17) For how can this servant of my lord talk with you, my lord? As for me, no strength remains in me now, nor is any breath left in me.' 18) Then again, the one having the likeness of a man TOUCHED ME and STRENGTHENED ME. 19) And he said, 'O man greatly beloved, fear not! Peace be to you; be strong, yes, be strong!' 20) Then he said, 'Do you know why I have come to you? And now I must return to fight with the prince of Persia; and when I have gone forth, indeed the prince of Greece will come. 21) But I will tell you what is noted in the Scripture of Truth. (No one upholds me against these, except Michael your prince."

"The one who had hindered God's special messenger can only have been a demon, appointed to do this by the chief of demons, Satan himself. This follows from the fact that he sought to hinder an order of God from being carried out, and he was certainly more than human to be able to war against such a supernatural messenger, commissioned by God. That he is called "the prince of the kingdom of Persia" must mean that he had been assigned by Satan to effect Satan's program in connection with the Persian government. His assignment to that end was evidently a continuing one, for later (v. 20) Daniel's visitor said he would personally return to do further battle with him." - Dr. Leon J. Wood

A. Angels understand and comprehend our [10]_____. They readily see our weakness!

B. In an unseen, maybe unknown way to us, at crucial moments angels [11]_____ and [12]_____ us to continue.

C. Angels are constantly fighting [13]_____ spirits who are intent upon our destruction and to thwart God's work through us!

D. Territorial demons? Very clear here: prince of [14]_____; and the prince of
[15]_____.

>"These thoughts lead to the conclusion that Satan is interested in hindering God's work with His people at any time and that he may assign special emissaries to influence governments at the highest level to hinder that work. Certainly this chapter carries significance regarding the nature of struggles between higher powers in reference to God's program on earth (cf. Eph. 6:11, 12)." – Dr. Leon J. Wood

E. Satan has a high-tech demonic [16]_____ system which has declared war on those most effective for Christ illustrated to us through Daniel.

ANSWERS

1. 90 2. few 3. prayer 4. Jesus Christ 5. Michael 6. character 7. demon 8. abort 9. individuals 10. discouragement 11. touch 12. strengthen 13. demonic 14. Persia 15. Greece 16. communication

338

What Does God Say About War? Is it Ever Right? If so, When?

Message #17 in the Daniel series
Bible Text: Daniel 11:1-35

"Since all of chapter ten is preliminary to the vision recorded in chapters 11 and 12, we need not tarry long here to review the circumstances under which this prophecy was given to Daniel. Chapter 11 falls logically into two main divisions, verses 1-35 recording detailed prophecies that have long ago been literally fulfilled; and verses 36-45 presenting to us the graphic portrait of the Antichrist and a foreview of his conflicts, which will end in the battle of Armageddon." - Dr. Louis Talbot

"God unfolds to Daniel the detailed revelations of what would befall the nation of Israel during the next 300 years. They are so detailed that many skeptics reject the book, exclaiming that no one could possibly have known in such detail the coming events." - Dr. David Jeremiah

THE YEAR - 539 B.C.

Daniel 11:1, "Also in the first year of Darius the Mede, I, even I, stood up to confirm and strengthen him). [Michael speaking]"

PALESTINE - A BATTLE GROUND OF THE NATIONS

- Palestine is the geographical and political center of the earth (Dt. 32:8). The record of wars recorded here in chapter 11 is because Israel was involved in each of these conflicts. For centuries the Holy Land has been a battle ground of the nations and will host the in final battle to end all wars - [1]_____ (11:40-45).
- In the battle of Armageddon, the Holy Land will be the field of carnage such as the world has never seen, the last war will be fought on the plains of [2]_____ in the land of Israel.

KINGS OF WAR

1. [3]_____ (11:2) - Daniel living under Persian rule is told there will be three kings who will rise in that government, but the fourth would exceed all others. The fourth king, Xerxes, mentioned in Esther as Ahasuerus commanded an army of 2.6 million! Attempting to conquer Greece he was defeated.

Daniel 11:2, "And now I will tell you the truth: Behold, three more kings will arise in Persia, and the fourth shall be far richer than them all; by his strength, through his riches, he shall stir up all against the realm of Greece."

2. [4]_____ (11:3-9) - comes on the scene 150 years later, the mighty conqueror

339

of Greece who defeated the Persians. Upon his death, Alexander's kingdom was divided into ⁵_____ kingdoms.

> Daniel 11:3 "Then a mighty king shall arise, who shall rule with great dominion, and do according to his will. 4) And when he has arisen, his kingdom shall be broken up and divided toward the four winds of heaven, but not among his posterity nor according to his dominion with which he ruled; for his kingdom shall be uprooted even for others besides these."

3. ANTIOCHUS THE ⁶_____ (11:10-19) - in verses 5-35 we have an account of what is known in history as the wars of the Ptolemies, kings of Egypt, against the kings of Syria, a long series of conflicts which covered a period of 120 years. Syria on the north and Egypt on the south (two fragments of Alexander's empire) of Israel became bitter enemies.
   • Verses 5-21 ⁷_____ these wars, now recorded in history!
4. ANTIOCHUS ⁸_____ (11:21-35) - describes Syria's most evil, blasphemous king, who we read about in chapter 8 (the 'little horn'). He was a "type" of the Antichrist to come. He conquered Jerusalem and defiled the Jewish Temple. Eventually, he killed 80,000 Jews and took 40,000 prisoners.
5. ⁹_____ (11:32-35) - the faithful Jewish remnant who stood up to Antiochus Epiphanes, battled with him, and defeated him.

> Daniel 11:32, "Those who do wickedly against the covenant he shall corrupt with flattery; but the PEOPLE WHO KNOW THEIR GOD shall be strong, and carry out great exploits. 33) And those of the people who understand shall instruct many; yet for many days they shall fall by sword and flame, by captivity and plundering. 34) Now when they fall, they shall be aided with a little help; but many shall join with the be intrigue. 35) And some of those of understanding shall fall, to refine them, purify them, and make them white, until the time of the; because it is still for the appointed time."

WHAT DOES GOD SAY ABOUT WAR?

1. In certain conditions God instructed His people to go to ¹⁰_____.

> Numbers 32:20-22, "Then Moses said to them: 'If you do this thing, if you arm yourselves before the LORD for the war, 21) and all your armed men cross over the Jordan before the LORD until He has driven out His enemies from before Him, 22) and the land is subdued before the LORD, then afterward you may return and be blameless before the LORD and before Israel; and this land shall be your possession before the LORD.'"

2. When the cause is ¹¹_____ God promises His presence and protection.

> Psalm 27:3, "Though an army may encamp against me, my heart shall not fear; though war may rise against me, in this I will be confident. 4) One thing I have desired of the Lord, that will I seek: that I may dwell in the house of the Lord all the days of my life, to behold the beauty of the Lord, and to inquire in His temple."

3. War ¹²_____ the innocent and prevents further death.

> Proverbs 20:18, "Plans are established by counsel; by wise counsel wage war."

4. God's people are instructed to respond to ¹³_____ to ensure peace and

safety.

> Proverbs 15:3, "The eyes of the Lord are in every place, keeping watch on the evil and good."

5. Wars come from the [14]_____ war at work in people's hearts.

> James 4:2, "You lust and do not have. You murder and covet and cannot obtain. You fight and war. Yet you do not have because you do not ask."

6. In God's plan the end of the world will occur by a [15]_____ ushering in the Second Coming of Christ.

> Rev. 19:19, "And I saw the beast, the kings of the earth, and their armies, gathered together to make war against Him who sat on the horse and against his army."

Principles of
Leadership, Success,
and Achievement

Eternal Rewards Available For You
Message #18 in the Daniel series
Bible Text: Daniel 12:1-13

This chapter brings us the highpoint of the book. The fourth vision of Daniel that began in chapter 10 reaches it climax in this chapter as we continue the narrative from the previous chapter. Many feel that the chapter division placed here should have been placed after verse 3, or verse 4. The angel Michael, Israel's angel is present. The end comes in these verses with God's divinely appointed end described. – Dr. William Keith Hatfield

Here again we see that there should be no chapter division, for there is no break in the subject treated. The twelfth chapter begins with the words, 'And at THAT TIME.' What TIME? The time of the 'Wilful King,' which we have seen is the 'TIME OF THE END.' Daniel 11:40. At that time Michael shall stand up. Stand up for, and take the part of Daniel's People. Who is Michael? He is mentioned three times in Daniel (10:13, 21; 12:1), where he is called a 'Prince' who stands for Daniel's People - the Jews. He is called in Jude 9 the Archangel. He has angels, and in Rev. 12:7-9 he is seen in command of the 'Angelic Army' of Heaven. His work seems to be to deliver God's people, particularly the Jews, from the power of Satan, and finally to oust him and his angels from the Heavenlies, and cast them down to the earth. –Dr. Clarence Larkin

Chapter 12 now concludes the vision which began back in chapter 10. This is all one vision, and everything about it must fit together like a jigsaw puzzle. The problem is that some people dip into this prophecy here and there, making applications as they see fit. We need to remember that this is all one vision, and we were told concerning it: 'Now I am come to make thee understand what shall befall thy people in the latter days: for yet the visions is for many days' (Daniel 10:14). – Dr. J. Vernon McGee

The material described as the fourth vision of Daniel beginning in chapter 10 has its climax in the great tribulation and the resurrection which follows, mentioned in the early verses of chapter 12. This is also the high point in the book of Daniel itself and the goal of Daniel's prophecies relating to both to the Gentiles and to Israel. It is comparable to Revelation 19, the high point of the last book of the Bible. –The late Dr. John Walvoord

THE TRIBULATION OF ISRAEL - DANIEL 12:1A

Daniel 12:1, "AT THAT TIME Michael shall stand up, the great prince who stands watch over the sons of your people ... ."

- "AT THAT TIME" - refers to the Tribulation, in particular, the final 3½ years ... the worst part of the 7-year period.

   Deuteronomy 4:30, "When you are in distress, and all these things come upon you in the LATTER DAYS, when you turn to the Lord you God and obey His voice."

   Jeremiah 30:7, "Alas! For that day is great, so that none is like it, and it is the time of Jacob's trouble, BUT HE SHALL BE SAVED OUT OF IT."

   Joel 2:2, "A day of darkness and gloominess, a day of clouds and thick darkness, like the morning clouds spread over the mountains."

- Revelation 6 - [1]_____ describes the Tribulation period in great detail.

   Matthew 24:21, "For then there will be great tribulation, such as has not been since the beginning of the world until this time, no, nor ever shall be."

- [2]_____ the archangel has the special position of protecting the nation Israel during the Tribulation.

THE DELIVERANCE OF ISRAEL - 12:1B

   Daniel 12: 1, "At that time Michael shall stand up, the great prince who stands watch over the sons of your people; and there shall be a time of trouble, such as never was since there was a nation, even to that time. And AT THAT TIME your people shall be delivered, every one who is found written in the book."

- The Tribulation, Israel's time of trouble, is designed to [3]_____ her for the coming of Messiah. In the closing days of the Tribulation, surviving Jews will search the scriptures ... they will discover they rejected [4]_____ and will turn in faith and belief in Him as their Messiah.
- Numbers of Jews, at that time, will [5]_____ Isaiah 53 in this critical hour and, many scholars believe they will pray Isaiah 64:1, "Oh, that You would rend the heavens! That You would come down! That the mountains might shake at Your presence."
- In response to Israel's desperate prayer and God's plan, Jesus Christ will return, bringing deliverance to His people. That deliverance will be both [6]_____ (Zechariah 14:1-4) and [7]_____ (12:10-13:1).
- Even at the Second Coming of Jesus not every Jew will believe (Ezekiel 20:33-38). The ones [8]_____ in the crucial hour are those whose names are "found written in the book" (12:1).

THE RESURRECTION OF ISRAEL - 12:2

   Daniel 12:2, "And many of those who sleep in the dust of the earth shall awake, some to everlasting life, some to shame and everlasting contempt."

- Deliverance, both physical and spiritual, is promised to those believing Jews still alive at the [9]_____ of the Tribulation.
- Our passage also indicates there will be a resurrection of righteous Israelites who died in this "previous time of trouble." This is enforced by Revelation 20:4-6, where martyred Tribulation saints are seen to be raised from the [10]_____ and exalted at the beginning of the millennial reign. (Righteous Gentiles also martyred during the Tribulation will be raised as well.) Believers, in the age of grace,

are raised at the Rapture, prior to the Tribulation.

THE REWARD OF ISRAEL - 12:3

Daniel 12:3, "Those who are wise shall shine like the brightness of the firmament, and those who turn many to righteousness like the stars forever and ever."

- Following this resurrection, righteous Jews will be [11]_____ . This would certainly apply to the 144,000 Jewish evangelists preaching Christ during the Tribulation.
- Then angel's long message concerning Israel in the latter days (10:14) comes to an [12]_____ with 12:3.

PRESERVE THE PROPHETIC WORD - 12:4

Daniel 12:4, "But you, Daniel, shut up the words, and seal the book until THE TIME OF THE END; many shall run to and fro, and knowledge shall increase."

- Daniel's prophetic words has been faithfully handed down to us - [13]_____ years later.
- END TIME SIGNS: increased [14]_____ ; increase of [15]_____ , i.e., the internet.

ANGELIC INTERACTION - 12:5-7

Daniel 12:5, "Then I, Daniel, looked; and there stood two others, one on this riverbank and the other on that riverbank. 6) And one said to the man clothed in linen, who was ABOVE THE WATERS of the river, 'How long shall the fulfillment of these wonders be?' 7)Then I heard the man clothed in linen, who was ABOVE THE WATERS of the river, when he held up his right hand and his left hand to heaven, and swore by Him who lives forever, that it shall be for a TIME, TIMES, AND HALF A TIME; and when the power of the holy people has been completely shattered, all these things shall be finished."

- The river is the [16]_____ ... we see two angels and the [17]_____ Himself.
- "TIME, TIMES, HALF A TIME" - [18]_____ years (cf. 7:25; 9:27; 12:11-12; Rev. 11:2; 12:6, 14; 13:5).

DANIEL'S WANTS TO KNOW WHEN - 12:8-13

Daniel 12:8, "Although I heard, I did not understand. Then I said, 'MY LORD, WHAT SHALL BE THE END OF THESE THINGS?' 9) And he said, 'Go your way, Daniel, for the words are closed up and sealed till THE TIME OF THE END.' 10) Many shall be purified, made white and refined, but the wicked shall do wickedly; and none of the wicked shall understand, but the wise shall understand. 11) And from the time that the daily sacrifice is taken away, and the abomination of desolation set up, there shall be one thousand two hundred and ninety days. 12) Blessed is he who waits, and comes to the one thousand three hundred and thirty-five days. 13) But you, go your way till THE END; for you shall rest, and will arise to your inheritance at the end of the days."

GOD'S ANSWER TO DANIEL

1. The events were far in the [19]_____ - "sealed till the time of the end" (v.9).
2. Tribulation [20]_____ would result in some converted and others hardened in unbelief (v. 10).
3. From the Antichrist's blasphemous announcement to the end of the Tribulation: [21]_____ days, 3½ years.
4. Why the extra 30 days? Perhaps the duration of the judgment of the [22]_____ .

> Matthew 25:31, "When the Son of Man comes in His glory, and all the holy angels with Him, then He will sit on the throne of His glory. 32) And the nations will be gathered before Him, and He will separate them one from another, as a shepherd divides His sheep from the goats. 33) And He will set the sheep on His right hand, but the goats on His left. 34) Then the King will say to those on His right hand, 'Come, you blessed on My Father, inherit the kingdom prepared for you from the foundation of the world: 35) for I was hungry and you gave Me food; I was thirsty and you gave Me drink; I was a stranger and you took Me in, 36) I was naked and you clothed Me; I was sick and you visited Me; I was in prison and you came to Me."

> Verse 41, "Then He will also say to those on the left hand, 'Depart from Me, you cursed, into everlasting fire prepared for the devil and his angels.'"

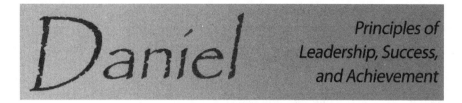

Principles of
Leadership, Success,
and Achievement

Daniel's 12 Principles of
Leadership, Success and Achievement
Message #19 in the Daniel series
Bible Text: The book of Daniel

Principle #1 - Absolute [1]_____. I have made up my mind.

> Daniel 1:8, "But Daniel purposed in his heart that he would not defile himself with the portion of the king's delicacies, nor with the wine which he drank; therefore he requested of the chief of the eunuchs that he might not defile himself."

Principle #2 - God as my ultimate [2]_____ for insight and understanding.

> Daniel 2:18, "that they might seek mercies from the God of heaven concerning this secret, so that Daniel and his companions might not perish with the rest of the wise men of Babylon."

Principle #3 - I will expect [3]_____ and harassment when doing God's will.

> Daniel 3:12, "There are certain Jews whom you have set over the affairs of the province of Babylon: Shadrach, Meshach, and Abed-Nego; these men, O king, have not paid due regard to you. They do not serve your gods or worship the gold image which you have set up."

Principle #4 - Because of His love for us God has an [4]_____ always watching and protecting us.

> Daniel 4:13, ""I saw in the visions of my head while on my bed, and there was a watcher, a holy one, coming down from heaven."

Principle #5 - I will refuse [5]_____ and always stay in control.

> Daniel 5:4, "They drank wine, and praised the gods of gold and silver, bronze and iron, wood and stone."

Principle #6 - My life and work will be marked by [6]_____.

> Daniel 6:4, "So the governors and satraps sought to find some charge against Daniel concerning the kingdom; but they could find no charge or fault, because he was faithful; nor was there any error or fault found in him."

Principle #7 - When troubled or overwhelmed, I will go to God [7]_____ and others later.

> Daniel 7:28, ""This is the end of the account.[1] As for me, Daniel, my thoughts greatly troubled me, and my countenance changed; but I kept the matter in my heart."

Principle #8 - My Christianity/Spirituality will never be an [8]_____ not to give my employer/family my very best effort.

> Daniel 8:27, "And I, Daniel, fainted and was sick for days; afterward I arose and went about the king's business. I was astonished by the vision, but no one understood it."

Principle #9 - I can change things in heaven and earth by my [9]_____.

> Daniel 9:23, "At the beginning of your supplications the command went out, and I have come to tell you, for you are greatly beloved; therefore consider the matter, and understand the vision."

Principle #10 - When I meet the qualifications I know God will unload endless [10]_____ on me.

> Daniel 10:12, "Then he said to me, 'Do not fear, Daniel, for from the first day that you set your heart to understand, and to humble yourself before your God, your words were heard; and I have come because of your words.'"

Principle #11 - Nobody knows my [11]_____ better or understands any needs more clearly than God.

> Daniel 11:35, "And some of those of understanding shall fall, to refine them, purify them, and make them white, until the time of the end; because it is still for the appointed time."

Principle #12 - God is going to give me a great [12]_____ some day because of my faithfulness.

> Daniel chapters 12 & 13

ANSWERS

1. Resolve 2. source 3. opposition 4. angel 5. addictions 6. integrity 7. first 8. excuse 9. prayers 10. blessings 11. future 12. inheritance

348

Notes

Chapter 1

1. J. Vernon McGee, *Thru the Bible with J. Vernon McGee Volume III* (Nashville; Thomas Nelson Publishers, 1983) 532.

2. McGee, *Thru the Bible with J. Vernon McGee*, 528.

3. Clarence Larkin, *The Book of Daniel* (Philadelphia; Rev. Clarence Larkin Est., 1929) 22.

4. Billy Graham, *Angels* (Nashville: W Publishing Group, 1995).

Chapter 2

1. Philip R. Newell, *Daniel* (Chicago; Moody Press, 1975) 19.

2. Robert Dick Wilson, *A Scientific Investigation of the Old Testament* (Chicago; Moody Press, 1959).

3. Samuel Fallows, *Bible Encyclopedia* (Chicago; The Howard-Severance Company, 1913).

4. Dr. S. Franklin Logsdon, *Profiles of Prophecy* (Bowdon Publications, 1964). 157-158.

Chapter 3

1. Ben Barber, "India-Pakistan Reconciliation School," The Washington Times; available from http://chowk.com/show_user_replies.cgi?memb ername=mohajir&start=290&end=299&page=30&chapter=3; Internet; accessed 1 August, 2005. Ben Barber is a State Department Correspondent for the Washington Times.

2. Adolf Hitler, *Mein Kampf* (Amsterdam; Fredonia Books, 2003).

3. Larkin, *The Book of Daniel*, 22

4. Albert Barnes, *Notes on the Old Testament Daniel* Vol. I (Grand Rapids; Baker Books, 1996) 104

5. James Dobson Focus on the Family broadcast.

6. John Leo, *US News and World Report*, 8 October, 2001, available from http://www.usnews.com/usnews/opinion/articles/011008/archive_ 008687.htm; Internet; accessed on 8 August, 2005.

7. Barnes, *Notes on the Old Testament Daniel*, 104

8. Josh Tyrangiel, "Shania Reigns," *Time*, available from http://www. time.com/time/magazine/article/subscriber/0,10987,1101021209- 395355,00.html; Internet; accessed on 8 August, 2005.

Chapter 4

1. Nancy Gibbs, "Apocalypse Now: The biggest book of the summer is about the end of the world. It's also a sign of our troubled times," *Time* 160.1 (2002).

2. J. Vernon McGee, *Thru the Bible Commentary Series: The Prophets Daniel* (Nashville; Thomas Nelson Publishers, 1991), 39.

3. A.C. Gaebelein, *The Prophet Daniel* (Grand Rapids; Kregel Publications, 1963), 18.

4. Gaebelein, *The Prophet Daniel*, 17.

5. H.A. Ironside, *Lectures on Daniel the Prophet* (New York; L.B. Printing

Company, 1920), 25.

6. Fred M. Wood, *The Dilemma of Daniel* (Nashville; Broadman Press, 1985), 43.

7. McGee, *Thru the Bible with J. Vernon McGee*, 534.

8. G. Coleman Luck, *Daniel* (Chicago; Moody Press, 1958) 37.

9. John MacArthur, *The Rise and Fall of World Powers* (Chicago: Moody Press, 1989),

Chapter 5

1. McGee, *Thru the Bible with J. Vernon McGee*, 532

2. Dr. Arthur E. Bloomfield, *The End of The Days: A Study of Daniel's Visions* (Bethany Fellowship, Inc., 1961), 77.

3. Dr. W.A. Criswell. *Expository Sermons on the Book of Daniel* (Grand Rapids: Zondervan, 1976), 64.

4. H.C. Leupold. *Exposition of Daniel* (Grand Rapids: Baker, 1969), 119.

5. Edward Gibbons, *The Decline and Fall of the Roman Empire* Vol. III

6. McGee, *Thru the Bible with J. Vernon McGee*, 541

7. McGee, *Thru the Bible with J. Vernon McGee*, 541

Chapter 6

1. Donald K. Campbell, *Daniel: God's Man in a Secular Society* (Grand Rapids; Discovery House Publishers, 1988), 41.

2. McGee, *Thru the Bible with J. Vernon McGee*, 543.

3. Geoffrey R. King, *Daniel* (Grand Rapids; Wm. B Eerdmans Publishing Co., 1966), 83.

4. C.S. Lewis, *Problem of Pain* (New York; HarperSanFrancisco, 2001).

5. M.R. DeHaan, *Daniel the Prophet* (Grand Rapids; Zondervan Publish-

ing House, 1947) 73-74.

Chapter 7

1. Charles Shepard. *Forgiven* (New York: Random House Value Publishing, 1990).

2. President George W. Bush, "President Delivers: State of the Union," U.S. Capitol, available from http://www.whitehouse.gov/news/releases/2003/01/20030128-19.html; Internet; accessed 1 August, 2005.

3. McGee, *Thru the Bible with J. Vernon McGee,* 550

4. Gordon Lindsay, *The Prophecies of Daniel* (Dallas: Christ for the Nations, 1977), 27.

5. John MacArthur, *The Rise and Fall of World Powers* (Chicago: Moody Press, 1989), 73.

6. William Keith Hatfield, *Dynamics for Living: Commentary on the Book of Daniel* (Columbus: Brentwood Christian Press, 1992), 54.

7. Philip R. Newell, *Daniel,* 52.

8. McGee, *Thru the Bible with J. Vernon McGee,* 552.

9. Dr. F. Bettex. *The Bible and Modern Criticism.* Trans. David Heagle.

10. J.I. Packer, Knowing God (Downers Grove: Intervarsity Press, 1993).

11. MacArthur, *The Rise and Fall of World Powers,* 76.

12. R.K. Harrison. *Introduction to the Old Testament* (Grand Rapids: Eerdmans, 1969), 1116-17.

13. Adam Clarke, *Clarke's Commentary Job-Malachi* (Abingdon Press, 1824) 580.

14. Dr. Hugo Grotius. Cited in Robert Jamieson, A. R. Fausset and David Brown *Commentary Critical and Explanatory on the Whole Bible* (1871)

Chapter 8

1. Charles Dyer, *The Rise of Babylon* (Chicago: Moody Publishers, 2003).

2. Leon J. Wood, *The Prophets of Israel* (Baker Book House, 1979), 354.

3. James A. Montgomery, *The Book of Daniel* (Edinburgh: T&T Clark, 1950).

4. Leon J. Wood, *The Prophets of Israel* (Baker Book House, 1979),

5. Oliver B. Greene, *Daniel Verse by Verse Study*, (Greeneville: The Gospel Hour Inc., 1964), 197.

6. Montgomery, *The Book of Daniel*.

7. MacArthur, *The Rise and Fall of World Powers*, 104.

Chapter 9

1. Joyce Baldwin, Daniel, *Introduction & Commentary* (Downers Grove, Intervarsity Press, 1978), 126.

2. Albert Barnes, *Barnes Notes: Daniel Volume 2* (Grand Rapids: Baker Books,1996), 12.

3. Leon J. Wood, *The Prophets of Israel* (Baker Book House, 1979), 348

4. Harry Bultema, *Commentary on Daniel*, (Grand Rapids: Kregel Publications, 1992), 118.

5. Fred M. Wood, *The Dilemma of Daniel* (Nashville; Broadman Press, 1985), 124-127

6. Barnes, *Barnes Notes: Daniel* Volume 2, 27.

Chapter 10

1. Campbell, *Daniel: God's Man in a Secular Society*.

2. Montgomery, *The Book of Daniel*.

3. J.N. Darby. *Synopsis to the Books of the Bible.* available from http://www.votbg.org/jnd/jnd-dan.htm; accessed 6 August 2005.

5. McGee, *Thru the Bible with J. Vernon McGee.*

6. Newell, *Daniel*, 95.

7. Newell, *Daniel*, 105.

8. Nicolai Lenin, "Notable Quotes," BTP Holdings; available from http://www.btpholdings.com/nquotes.html; Internet; accessed 6 August 2005.

Chapter 11

1. Alfred Weber, *Farewell to European History* (London:Yale University Press, 1948).

2. H.G. Wells, *Mind at the end of its Tether* (Millet Books, 1974).

3. Louis Talbot, *The Prophecies of Daniel* (Wheaton: Van Kampen Press, 1954), 119.

4. McGee, *Thru the Bible with J. Vernon McGee*, 567.

5. Bultema, *Commentary on Daniel*, 198.

6. Norman W. Porteous, *Daniel* (Philadelphia: The Westminster Press, 1965), 95.

7. Talbot, *The Prophecies of Daniel*, 125.

8. John Walvoord, *Daniel: The Key to Prophetic Revelation* (Chicago: Moody Press, 1973), 158.

9. Ironside, *Lectures on Daniel the Prophet*, 127.

10. Paul F. Maier, *Josephus: The Essential Works* (Kregel Publications, 1994), 202

11. Talbot, *The Prophecies of Daniel*, 128-9.

12. Talbot, *The Prophecies of Daniel*, 128.

Chapter 12

1. Gaebelein, *The Prophet Daniel*, 92.

2. Walvoord, *Daniel*, 178.

3. McGee, *Thru the Bible with J. Vernon McGee*, 577.

4. Walvoord, *Daniel*, 178.

5. Leon J. Wood, *The Prophets of Israel* (Baker Book House, 1979), 353.

6. Leon J. Wood, *The Prophets of Israel* (Baker Book House, 1979), 353.

7. Walter K. Price. *The Coming Antichrist* (Moody: Chicago, 1976).

Chapter 13

1. Leonard Ravenhill, *A Treasury of Prayer* (Bethany House Publishers, 1981),

2. Ironside, *Lectures on Daniel the Prophet*, 156.

3. Talbot, *The Prophecies of Daniel*, 162.

4. Ronald S. Wallace, *The Message of Daniel* (Downers Grove: Inter-Varsity Press, 1973), 147.

5. Andrew Murray, *The Prayer Life* (Whitaker House, 1981), 26.

6. Annie S. Hawks and Robert Lowry, "I Need Thee Every Hour," Hymnscript: The Art of Hymns; available from http://www.hymnscript.com/free-art/int01.pdf; Internet; accessed on 7 August, 2005.

Chapter 14

1. DeHaan, *Daniel the Prophet*, 243.

2. Isaac Newton, *The Prophecies of Daniel and the Apocalypse* (Hyderabad: Printland Publishers, 1998).

3. Leon J. Wood, *The Prophets of Israel* (Baker Book House, 1979), 353.

4. David Jeremiah, *The Handwriting on the Wall* Volume III

5. Campbell, *God's Man,* 140.

6. Stephen R. Miller, *The New American Commentary: Daniel* (Nashville: Broadman and Holman Publishers, 1998), 253.

7. Charles R. Swindoll, *Daniel: God's Pattern for the Future* (Plano: Insight for Living, 1996), 117.

8. Swindoll, *Daniel,* 117

9. David Jeremiah, *The Handwriting on the Wall* Volume III

10. Robert Anderson, *The Coming Prince* (Grand Rapids: Kregel Publications, 1975), 127.

11. McGee, *Thru the Bible with J. Vernon McGee,* 588.

12. Talbot, *The Prophecies of Daniel,* 169-70.

13. Talbot, *The Prophecies of Daniel,* 170.

Chapter 15

1. Tim LaHaye and Jerry B. Jenkins, *Left Behind* (Wheaton: Tyndale House Publishing, Inc., 1995).

2. Talbot, *The Prophecies of Daniel,* 203.

3. Talbot, *The Prophecies of Daniel,* 203-4.

4. Swindoll, *Daniel,* 134.

5. Talbot, *The Prophecies of Daniel,* 210.

Chapter 16

1. McGee, *Thru the Bible with J. Vernon McGee,* 589.

2. Greene, *Daniel,* 395.

3. Larkin, *The Book of Daniel,* 222.

4. Larkin, *The Book of Daniel*, 224.

5. Leon J. Wood, *The Prophets of Israel* (Baker Book House, 1979), 353.

6. Lindsay, *The Prophecies of Daniel*, 60-1.

7. Leon J. Wood, *The Prophets of Israel* (Baker Book House, 1979), 353.

8. Mark Bubeck, *Overcoming the Adversary* (Chicago: Moody Publishers, 1984), 154.

Chapter 17

1. Louis Talbot, *The Prophecies of Daniel* (Wheaton: Van Kampen Press, 1954), 191.

2. David Jeremiah, *The Handwriting on the Wall* Volume III

Chapter 18

1. Hatfield, *Dynamics for Living*, 176.

2. Larkin, *The Book of Daniel*, 250-1.

3. McGee, *Thru the Bible with J. Vernon McGee*, 603.

4. Walvoord, *Daniel*, 281.

5. Gaebelein, *The Prophet Daniel*, 196.

6. Newton, *The Prophecies of Daniel*.

7. Leon J. Wood, *The Prophets of Israel* (Baker Book House, 1979), 354.

Chapter 19

1. Russell T. Hitt, *Jungle Pilot: The Gripping Story of the Life and Witness of Nate Saint, Martyred Missionary to Ecuador* (Grand Rapids; Discovery House Publishers, 1997).

Daniel

Daniel Bibliography

The following resources have proven invaluable in the preparation of the preceding chapters and are therefore commended to anyone seeking a deeper understanding of Daniel. However, the reader should be cautioned that not all of the texts listed here share the author's theological positions. As in all things, the reader is encouraged to exercise discernment and discretion when studying God's Word.

Anders, Max. *Holman Old Testament Commentary: Daniel.* Nashville, TN: Broadman and Holman Publishing, 2001.

Anderson, Sir Robert. *Daniel in the Critics Den: A Defense of the Historicity of the Book of Daniel.* Grand Rapids, MI: Kregel Publications, 1990.

Anderson, Sir Robert. *The Coming Prince.* Grand Rapids, MI: Kregel Publications, 1975.

Barnes, Albert. *Notes on the Old Testament: Daniel. Vol 1.* Grand Rapids, MI: Baker Books, 1996.

Boutflower, Charles. *In and Around the Book of Daniel.* Grand Rapids, MI: Zondervan Publishing House, 1963.

Bultema, Harry. *Commentary on Daniel.* Grand Rapids, MI: Kregel Publications, 1988.

Calvin, John. *Calvin's Commentaries. Vol 7-8.* Grand Rapids, MI: Baker Books, 2003.

Campbell, Donald K. *Daniel: God's Man in a Secular Society.* Grand Rapids, MI: Discovery House Publishers, 1988.

Culver, Robert D. *Daniel and the Latter Days.* Chicago, IL: Moody Press, 1954.

De Hann, M. R. *Daniel The Prophet.* Grand Rapids, MI: Zondervan Publishing House, 1957.

Driver, S.R. *The Book of Daniel.* London: Cambridge University Press, 1912.

Feinberg, Charles Lee. *A Commentary on Daniel: The Kingdom of the Lord.* Winona Lake, Indiana: BMH Books, 1981.

Fewell, Danna Nolan. *Circle of Sovereignty: Plotting Politics In The Book of Daniel.* Nashville, TN: Abingdon Press, 1991.

Fisher, Harriet. *The Story of Daniel.* Springfield, MO: The Gospel Publishing House, 1936.

Fyall, Robert. *Focus on the Bible: Daniel.* Ross-shire, Great Britain: Christian Focus Publications, 1998.

Gaebelein, Arno C. *The Prophet Daniel: A Key to the Visions and Prophecies of the Book of Daniel.* Grand Rapids, MI: Kregel Publications, 1955.

Gortner, J. Narver. *Studies in Daniel.* Springfield, MO: Gospel Publishing House, 1948.

Gowan, Donald E. *Abingdon Old Testament Commentaries: Daniel.* Nashville, TN: Abingdon Press, 2001.

Greene, Oliver B. *Daniel: Verse By Verse Study.* Greenville, SC: The Gospel Hour Inc., 1964.

Greig, Doris W. *Courage To Conquer.* Glendale, CA: Joy of Living Bible Studies.

Hall, John G. *Prophecy Marches On. Vol 2.* Newcastle OK: John G. Hall, 1963.

Hatfield, William Keith. *Dynamics For Living: Commentary on the Book of Daniel.* Columbus, GA: Brentwood Christian Press, 1992.

Hewitt, Clarence H.. *The Seer of Babylon*. Boston, MA: Advent Christian Publication Society, 1948.

Howie, Carl G. *The Layman's Bible Commentary*. *Vol 13*. Richmond, VA: John Knox Press, 1961.

Ironside, H. A. *Lectures on Daniel the Prophet*. New York: Loizeaux Brothers Bible Truth Depot, 1942.

Keil, C. F. *Biblical Commentary on the Book of Daniel*. Grand Rapids, MI: Erdman's Publishing Co, 1971.

King, Geoffrey R. *Daniel: A Detailed Explanation of the Book*. Grand Rapids, MI: Erdman's Publishing, 1966.

Lacocque, Andre. *The Book of Daniel*. Atlanta, GA: John Knox Press, 1979.

Lang, G.H. *The Histories and Prophecies of Daniel*. Miami Springs, FL: Conley & Schoettle Publishing Co., Inc, 1985.

Larkin, Clarence. *The Book of Daniel*. Philadelphia, PA: Erwin W. Moyer Co., Printers, 1929.

Lindsay, Gordon. *The Prophecies of Daniel*. Dallas, TX: Christ For The Nations, 1977.

Lucas, Ernest C. *Apollos Old Testament Commentary: Daniel*. Downers Grove, IL: Intervarsity press, 2002.

Luck, G. Coleman. *Everyman's Bible Commentary: Daniel*. Chicago, IL: Moody Press, 1958.

Longman, Tremper. *The NIV Application Commentary: Daniel*. Grand Rapids, MI: Zondervan Publishing House, 1999.

MacArthur, John. *The Rise and Fall of Wold Powers*. Chicago, IL: Moody Press, 1989.

McClain, Alva J. *Daniel's Prophecy of the Seventy Weeks.* Grand Rapids, MI: Zondervan Publishing House, 1940.

McDowell, Josh. *Daniel In The Critics' Den.* San Bernardino, CA: Here's Life Publishers, 1979.

McGee, J. Vernon. *Thru The Bible Commentary: Daniel. Vol 26.* Nashville, TN: Thomas Nelson Publishing, 1991.

Miller, Stephen R. *The New American Commentary. Vol. 18.* Nashville,TN: Broadman and Holman Publishers, 1994.

Montgomery, James A. *A Critical and Exegetical Commentary on The Book of Daniel.* Edinburgh: T.&T. Clark, 1950.

Moore, Carey A. *The Anchor Bible. Vol 44.* Garden City, NY: Doubleday & Company, Inc., 1979.

Newton, Isaac. *The Prophecies of Daniel and the Apocalypse.* Hyderabad, India: Printland Publishers, 1988.

Porteous, Norman W. *Old Testament Library: Daniel.* Philadelphia, PA: Westminster Press, 1965.

Robinson, Thomas. *The Preacher's Complete Homiletic Commentary on The Book of Daniel. Vol 19.* New York: Funk & Wagnalls Company

Russell, D.S. *Daniel.* Philadelphia, PA: Westminster Press, 1981.

Sevener, Harold A. *Daniel: God's Man in Babylon.* Charlotte, NC: Chosen People Ministries Inc., 1994.

Smith, R. Payne. D*aniel: An Exposition of the Historical Portion of the Writings of the Prophet Daniel.* Cincinnati: Cranston & Curts, 1933.

Stahr, James A. *The Book of Daniel.* Dubuque, IA: Emmaus Bible College, 1973.

Stevens, W.C. *The Book of Daniel: A Composite Revelation of the Last Days of Israel's Subjugation To Gentile Powers.* Los Angeles, CA: Bible House of Los Angeles, 1943.

Swindoll, Charles R. *Daniel: God's Pattern For the Future.* Plano, TX: Charles R. Swindoll, Inc., 1996.

Taylor, William M. *Daniel The Beloved.* New York: Harper & Brothers Publishers, 1906.

Towner, Sibley W. *Daniel: A Bible Commentary for Teaching and Preaching.* Atlanta, GA: John Knox Press, 1984.

Walvoord, John F. *Daniel: The Key to Prophetic Revelation.* Chicago, IL: Moody Press, 1971.

Wilson, Robert Dick. *Daniel: A Classic Defense of the Historicity and Integrity of Daniel's Prophecies. Vol 1-2.* Eugene, OR: Wipf and Stock Publishers, 2002.

Wood, Fred M. *Bible Book Study Commentary. Vol 6.* Nashville, TN: Convention Press, 1985.

Young, Edward J. *The Prophecy of Daniel.* Grand Rapids, MI: Erdman's Publishing Co.,1949.

Index

Scripture Index

Ephesians 6:18	229
1 Thessalonians 5:18	128
2 Thessalonians 2:3	73, 137
2 Thessalonians 2:7-10	213
Hebrews 1:14	96, 132, 227, 255, 293, 301
1 Peter 1:6	84
1 John 2:18	137
Revelation 13:7-8	216
Revelation 17-18	17
Revelation 20:4-6	54

A

Abed-Nego	2, 33, 44, 75, 81, 83, 84, 85, 121, 254, 286, 288, 289, 290, 343
Alexander the Great	11, 26, 61, 69, 70, 102, 112, 150, 155, 156, 161, 169, 233, 235, 237, 293, 309, 313
Anderson, Robert	204
Antichrist	11, 12, 14, 16, 29, 71, 73, 74, 80, 135, 136, 137, 138, 139, 140, 141, 142, 143, 144, 145, 146, 149, 158, 160, 163, 166, 170, 171, 173, 174, 175, 176, 177, 178, 179, 95, 206, 196, 207, 209, 210, 211, 212, 213, 214, 215, 216, 217, 218, 219, 221, 232, 236, 239, 241, 243, 244, 245, 249, 256, 257, 292, 303, 304, 305, 306, 307, 309, 312, 313, 314, 315, 316, 325, 326, 327, 328, 329, 330, 335, 336, 342
Antiochus Epiphanes	163, 166, 167, 168, 170, 171, 172, 173, 174, vii, 173, 175, 176, 178, 211, 215, 241, 258, 311, 312, 313, 314, 315, 316, 328, 336
Antipater	155
Aramaic	11, 49, 56, 62, 65, 95, 100, 112, 153, 161, 164, 248, 278, 280, 292, 311
Armageddon	14, 73, 218, 232, 233, 239, 241, 243, 335, 337
Assyria	4, 19, 78, 223, 271, 275
Azariah	2, 8

B

| Babylon | 2, 4, 5, 7, 8, 9, 11, 13, 15, 17, 18, 19, 20, 21, 22, 23, 24, 25, 26, 27, 28, 29, 30, 31, 33, 34, 36, 37, 38, 39, 40, 41, 43, 44, 48, 50, 53, 55, 56, 57, 58, 60, 61, 63, 65, 66, 67, 68, 69, 75, 78, 79, 80, 81, 82, 85, 92, 94, 100, 102, 104, 107, 108, 109, 110, 111, 112, 113, 117, 118, 119, 121, 122, 124, 125, 126, 128, 135, 138, 148, 149, 150, 151, 152, 153, 154, 155, 156, 164, 167, 179, 180, 181, 187, 190, 195, 222, 223, 232, 251, 252, 253, 254, 258, 263, 264, 265, 267, 268, 269, 270, 271, 272, 274, 275, 277, 278, 279, 280, 283, 284, 285, 286, 287, 288, 289, 290, 291, 293, 294, 295, 296, 297, 298, 299, 300, 301, 304, 307, 308, 309, 312, 313, 317, 320, 331, 343, 349 |
| Bacchanalia | 171 |

I

Ironside, H. A.	180

J

Jehoiakim	2, 5, 6
Jeremiah	7, 19, 20, 21, 23, 28, 29, 44, 67, 93, 107, 109, 122, 128, 145, 153, 170, 180, 181, 182, 195, 196, 197, 204, 216, 232, 244, 258, 264, 268, 269, 270, 275, 301, 302, 306, 308, 310, 317, 318, 320, 322, 324, 328, 335, 340, 352, 353
Jeremiah, David	197, 204, 232
Jeroboam	22
Jerusalem	2, 5, 7, 9, 10, 11, 13, 15, 18, 19, 20, 21, 22, 26, 28, 33, 52, 53, 54, 55, 63, 68, 69, 71, 82, 107, 109, 110, 112, 126, 127, 128, 133, 143, 153, 155, 156, 168, 170, 171, 172, 180, 182, 184, 187, 193, 194, 196, 197, 198, 199, 200, 201, 202, 204, 205, 210, 211, 222, 223, 230, 235, 236, 237, 244, 251, 252, 263, 264, 265, 266, 268, 271, 275, 277, 283, 289, 295, 301, 302, 313, 314, 317, 318, 319, 320, 321, 322, 323, 324, 325, 326, 328, 331, 336
Josephus	114, 155, 156, 296, 350
Judea	2

K

King, Geoffrey	82

L

Larkin, Clarence	8, 242
liberal theologians	4
Lindsay, Gordan	93
Lindsay, Gordon	226
Little horn	73, 138, 139, 140, 149, 169, 170, 171, 221, 236, 285, 304, 307, 313, 314, 316, 331, 336
Lowry, Robert	186
Lysimachus	155

M

MacArthur, John	60, 93, 118
Maccabees	166, 172, 337
Manasseh	19, 20, 42, 268, 270, 275
McGee, J. Vernon	5, 8
Medo-Persia	66, 69, 124, 149, 154, 155, 167, 168, 284, 300, 307, 308
Meshach	2, 33, 39, 44, 75, 79, 81, 83, 84, 85, 121, 254, 272, 286, 288, 289, 290, 343
Michael	9
Miller, Stephen R.	198
Mishael	2, 8

N

P

R

S

T

W

Walvoord, John	243
Weber, Alfred	148
Wells, H. G.	148
Wood, Leon	112, 228
Wood, Leon J.	123, 197

X

Xerxes	110, 112, 233, 335

Z

Zechariah	9:9 202
Zedekiah	22, 93, 275